New Directions in Political Science

D0988259

New Directions in Political Science

Responding to the Challenges of an Interdependent World

Edited by

Colin Hay

in association with the
Political Studies Association

Selection, editorial matter and Introduction © Colin Hay 2010

Individual chapters (in order) © Michael Moran, Gerry Stoker, Helen Margetts, Johanna Kantola and Judith Squires, Tariq Modood, Helen Thompson, John Ravenhill, Charlie Jeffery and Daniel Wincott, Stuart Croft, David Held, Kimberly Hutchings 2010

All rights reserved. No reproduction, copy or transmission of this publication may be made without written permission.

No portion of this publication may be reproduced, copied or transmitted save with written permission or in accordance with the provisions of the Copyright, Designs and Patents Act 1988, or under the terms of any licence permitting limited copying issued by the Copyright Licensing Agency, Saffron House, 6–10 Kirby Street, London EC1N 8TS.

Any person who does any unauthorized act in relation to this publication may be liable to criminal prosecution and civil claims for damages.

The authors have asserted their rights to be identified as the authors of this work in accordance with the Copyright, Designs and Patents Act 1988.

First published 2010 by
PALGRAVE MACMILLAN

Palgrave Macmillan in the UK is an imprint of Macmillan Publishers Limited, registered in England, company number 785998, of Houndmills, Basingstoke, Hampshire RG21 6XS.

Palgrave Macmillan in the US is a division of St Martin's Press LLC, 175 Fifth Avenue, New York, NY 10010.

Palgrave Macmillan is the global academic imprint of the above companies and has companies and representatives throughout the world.

Palgrave® and Macmillan® are registered trademarks in the United States, the United Kingdom, Europe and other countries

ISBN 978–0–230–22848–1 hardback
ISBN 978–0–230–22849–8 paperback

This book is printed on paper suitable for recycling and made from fully managed and sustained forest sources. Logging, pulping and manufacturing processes are expected to conform to the environmental regulations of the country of origin.

A catalogue record for this book is available from the British Library.

A catalog record for this book is available from the Library of Congress.

10   9   8   7   6   5   4   3   2   1
19   18   17   16   15   14   13   12   11   10

Printed and bound in China

Contents

List of Tables and Figures   ix

Acknowledgements   x

Notes on the Contributors   xi

**Introduction: Political Science in an Age of Acknowledged
Interdependence**   1
Colin Hay

Acknowledging interdependence   6
Interdependence and inter-disciplinarity   8
Spatial interdependence and the problem of sub-disciplinary
    specialism   11
Conclusion   22

1 Policy-Making in an Interdependent World   25
Michael Moran

Introduction: interdependence old and new   25
Spatial interdependence: discursive construction and
    democratic statecraft   27
Institutional interdependence: government, governance
    and complexity   31
Policy interdependence: specialization, tacit knowledge
    and catastrophic risk   35
Interdependence, statecraft and rhetoric   39

2 The Rise of Political Disenchantment   43
Gerry Stoker

Reflecting on the rise of anti-politics   44
The decline in Britain's civic culture   47
Explaining the rise of disenchantment   56
A new political science of design   60
Conclusion   62

3 The Internet in Political Science   **64**
Helen Margetts

The challenge	65
The current state of our understanding in political science	66
Recent developments and current trends	68
How will – or should – political science develop?	
Challenges and opportunities	72
Political knowledge: what is it rational to 'know'?	72
Voting: reversing turnout decline?	73
Reconfiguring 'The Logic of Collective Action' and the	
ecology of interest groups	74
Leadership: the end of charisma and co-ordination?	76
Political parties: the end of membership?	77
Government–citizen interactions: bringing citizens closer	
to government?	78
Public management reform: from Weber to new public	
management to digital-era governance	80
Political equality	82
Illusions of interdependence	83
Methodological challenges for political science	84
Conclusion	86

4 The New Politics of Equality   **88**
Johanna Kantola and Judith Squires

Introduction	88
'Old' politics of equality	90
The 'new' politics of equality	97
Conclusion	106

5 Civic Multiculturalism and National Identity   **109**
Tariq Modood

Multiculturalism	109
Difference and equality	112
Some implications for liberal citizenship	114
Multicultural citizenship	117
Muslims and identity	119
Navigating groupness	121
National identity and minority cultures	124

6 The Character of the State **130**
Helen Thompson

Globalization and the economic discretion of the state 132
Globalization and the state in the international sphere 134
Globalization and the state as an agent of political
    identity 135
The financial crisis and the state: economic discretion 136
Transnational governance 142
The state as the agent of political identity and
    expectations 144
Conclusions: future intellectual agendas on the state 146

**7 Economic Interdependence and the Global Economic
Crisis** **148**
John Ravenhill

Introduction: The great recession and global economic
    interdependence 148
Something old, something new ... 150
Globalization: how new, how constraining? 152
Regulating the global economy 156
Global economic interdependence and the study of IPE 163
Conclusion 165

**8 The Challenge of Territorial Politics: Beyond
Methodological Nationalism** **167**
Charlie Jeffery and Daniel Wincott

Introduction: why a new direction? The challenge of
    territorial politics 167
Beyond 'methodological nationalism' 173
The territorial politics of elections 178
Rescaling welfare 182
Conclusion 186

9 New Security Challenges in an Interdependent World **189**
Stuart Croft

Contemporary security concerns 190
The evolution of Anglophone international security studies 196
Different meanings of security 200
Conclusion 209

10 Global Challenges: Accountability and Effectiveness   **211**
David Held

The limits of current global governance arrangements   212
Key political challenges   216
Global economic governance: problems and opportunities   218
The politics of global governance change   225
Rethinking politics in a global age   229

11 Global Justice   **231**
Kimberly Hutchings

Introduction   231
Theorizing global justice: between statism and globalism   233
Theorizing global justice: beyond statism and globalism   240
Conclusion: the future of theorizing global justice   246

References   250
Index   289

List of Tables and Figures

Tables

2.1 Postwar UK elections and the proportion of non-voters   53
2.2 Organizational membership, 1959 and 2001   53
2.3 Gendered differences in political activism, 2007   54
2.4 Class differences in political activism, 2007   55
10.1 Comparisons of annual expenditure on luxury items
      compared to estimated funding needed to meet selected
      basic needs   226

Figures

10.1 UN core budget, 1996–97 to 2006–07   223
10.2 International aid as a percentage of Gross National
      Income (world)   223
10.3 Amount that world ODA as a percentage of GNI would
      have to be multiplied by to equal world military
      expenditure as a percentage of GDP, 1989–2004   224
10.4 Ratio of military expenditure to ODA, selected
      countries, 2004   224
10.5 Global consumption priorities (US$ billion)   225

Acknowledgements

This book marks the 60th anniversary of the Political Studies Association (PSA) and it would simply not have been written without its initiative to publish. I was, as I remain remain, deeply honoured, flattered and, indeed, somewhat daunted by the invitation to edit this collection but delighted by how quickly we were able to agree on an appropriately prospective and forward-looking format for this book. I am immensely grateful to the PSA for its support throughout the process and for the opportunity to summon such a distinctive and distinguished cast of authors in exploring *New Directions in Political Science*. It is rare, perhaps even unprecedented these days, to secure an 100 per cent response rate to a set of invitations to contribute to an edited collection – and that this was possible is testament, of course, to the significance of the occasion this volume marks and, in turn, to the central role in the development of the discipline that the PSA has played. Scarcely less remarkable is how easy this volume has proved to edit. That this is so is a consequence of two factors – the immense dedication, commitment and perseverance of the authors in meeting a succession of ever more exacting deadlines, and the energy, enthusiasm and dogged persistence of Steven Kennedy, who (characteristically) has served almost as a second editor to this volume. I am supremely grateful to the contributors and to Steven for seeing this book through to completion on time – and in time for publication at the 2010 Political Studies Association annual conference as planned. I would also like to record my thanks to Palgrave Macmillan's anonymous reader for an extremely helpful and well-informed set of comments on an earlier iteration of the entire manuscript and to Keith Povey and his team for overseeing the text-editing, setting, proofing and indexing of this volume so diligently and efficiently.

COLIN HAY

Chapter 5 draws on the author's *Multiculturalism: A Civic Idea* (Cambridge: Polity Press, 2007) and reproduces material with slight revisions from portions of the original text by kind permission of Polity Press.

Notes on the Contributors

Stuart Croft is Professor of International Security at Warwick University. He is the author of *Culture, Crisis and America's War on Terror* (2006); and was guest editor of both the December 2006 special issue of the journal *International Relations*, and the summer 2007 special issue of *Government and Opposition*, which focused on security and terrorism. He has been Director of the Economic and Science Research Council's New Security Challenges Programme, now also supported by the Arts and Humanities Research Council and Foreign Commonwealth Office, since 2003. He is also Chair of the British International Studies Association 2009–10.

Colin Hay is Professor of Political Analysis at the University of Sheffield, where he is co-Director of the Political Economy Research Centre. He is founding co-editor of the journals *Comparative European Politics* and *British Politics* and a co-editor of *New Political Economy*. He is the author or editor of a number of books, including most recently *The Oxford Handbook of British Politics* (co-edited with Matthew Flinders, Andrew Gamble and Michael Kenny, 2009) and *Why We Hate Politics* (2007, winner of the W. J. M. Mackenzie Prize).

David Held is the Graham Wallas Chair in Political Science, and co-Director of the Centre for the Study of Global Governance, at the London School of Economics and Political Science. Among his most recent publications are *Globalisation/Anti-Globalisation* (2007), *Models of Democracy* (2006), *Global Covenant* (2004), *Global Transformations: Politics, Economics and Culture* (1999), and *Democracy and the Global Order: From the Modern State to Cosmopolitan Governance* (1995). His main research interests include the study of globalization, changing forms of democracy and the prospects of regional and global governance. He is a Director of Polity Press, which he co-founded in 1984.

Kimberly Hutchings is Professor of International Relations at the London School of Economics and Political Science. She is the author of: *Kant, Critique and Politics* (1996); *International Political Theory: Rethinking Ethics in a Global Era* (1999); *Hegel and Feminist*

Philosophy (2003); *Time and World Politics: Thinking the Present* (2008); and *Introduction to Global Ethics* (2010). Her research interests include international political theory, global ethics, feminist theory, Hegel and Kant.

Charlie Jeffery is Professor of Politics and Head of the School of Social and Political Science at the University of Edinburgh. He is managing editor of *Regional and Federal Studies* and recently published, with James Mitchell, *The Scottish Parliament 1999–2000. The First Decade* (2009).

Johanna Kantola is Adjunct Professor at the Department of Political Science, University of Helsinki. She is the author of *Feminists Theorize the State* (2006), *Gender and the European Union* (2010) and editor of *Changing State Feminism* (with Joyce Outshoorn, 2007). She has published articles about gender and politics in various journals and edited volumes. She is the book series editor of Palgrave Macmillan's new *Gender and Politics Series* (with Judith Squires).

Helen Margetts is Professor of Society and the Internet at the Oxford Internet Institute (OII) and Fellow of Mansfield College, University of Oxford. She is author or co-author of a wide range of books and articles as well as a series of policy reports for the National Audit Office, including (with Patrick Dunleavy and others) *Digital-Era Governance* (2006); (with Christopher Hood) *Tools of Government in the Digital Age* (2007); *Government on the Internet* (a joint LSE-OII study for the National Accounts Office 2007); and (with Christopher Hood and Perri 6, editors) *Paradoxes of Modernization: Unintended Consequences of Public Policy Reform* (2010). She is editor of the new journal *Policy and Internet*.

Tariq Modood is Director of the Centre for the Study of Ethnicity and Citizenship at the University of Bristol. He is a regular contributor to the media and policy debates in Britain, was awarded a MBE for services to social sciences and ethnic relations in 2001 and elected a member of the Academy of Social Sciences in 2004. His most recent books are *Multiculturalism: A Civic Idea* (2007) and, as co-editor, *Secularism, Religion and Multicultural Citizenship* (2009)

Michael Moran is W.J.M. Mackenzie Professor of Government at the University of Manchester. His most recent books are *The British*

Regulatory State (2nd edition, 2007) and *Business, Politics and Society: An Anglo-American Comparison* (2010).

John Ravenhill is Professor in the Department of International Relations, Research School of Asian and Pacific Studies, Australian National University. He is the editor of the *Global Political Economy*, the third edition of which is in preparation. His most recent book is *Crisis as Catalyst: Asia's Dynamic Political Economy* (2008).

Judith Squires is Professor of Political Theory and Dean of the Faculty of Social Sciences and Law at the University of Bristol. Her recent publications include *The New Politics of Gender Equality* (2007) and *Contesting Citizenship*, co-edited with Birte Siim (2008). She is reviews editor for *Government and Opposition* and co-editor, with Johanna Kantola, of the Palgrave Macmillan *Gender and Politics* book series.

Gerry Stoker is Professor of Politics and Governance at the University of Southampton, where he is the director of the Centre for Citizenship and Democracy. He has authored or edited over 20 books and published over 70 refereed articles or chapters in books. His most recent book *Why Politics Matters* won the 2006 political book of the year award from the Political Studies Association.

Helen Thompson is Senior Lecturer in the Department of Politics and International Studies at Cambridge University. Her most recent book is *Might, Right, Prosperity and Consent: Representative Democracy and the International Economy 1919–2001*.

Daniel Wincott holds the Blackwell Law and Society Chair at Cardiff Law School. With Charlie Jeffery he has recently completed the first ever systematic comparative survey of public attitudes towards politics at the level of stateless nations and regions in Europe. His other research interests are in European integration and comparative public policy. He has published more than fifty papers, including articles in such journals as the *International Political Science Review*, *Journal of Common Market Studies*, *Journal of European Public Policy*, *Political Studies*, and *Public Administration*.

Introduction: Political Science in an Age of Acknowledged Interdependence

COLIN HAY

The aim of this volume is to address a range of key challenges for political science in the twenty-first century and to identify ways in which the discipline – broadly construed to include the study of both domestic and global politics – might respond to these. Such questions about the relationship between what we study, how we study it and the conclusions we draw seem, on the face of it, both crucially important and yet disarmingly simple. But, in practice, they are rarely discussed – not least because they turn out to rather more difficult to answer than they are to pose. How have politics and political science evolved, and what limits do the former place upon the latter? To what extent are 'real world' developments drivers of the substantive content and the analytical and theoretical preoccupations of contemporary political science? Or, to put this in a slightly different way, how – and, indeed, how *well* – has political science, as a discipline, responded to the challenges posed by 'real world' developments?

Though there is arguably never a bad time to pose such questions, it is perhaps difficult to imagine a better one. Politics, which has of course never commanded universal respect, is – in a manner almost certainly unprecedented since the advent of democracy itself   held today in near universal contempt. As Gerry Stoker shows, if public opinion is anything to go by, politics is failing us – with politicians trusted so little by the public they claim to represent that the very legitimacy of modern democratic institutions in increasingly called into question. What makes this worrying condition worse is that it coincides with an accumulation of economic pathologies – in conventional parlance, an economic crisis – as pronounced in its severity and as global in its scope as anything that has befallen us in living memory. And all of this takes place in a context characterized by the growing awareness of the long-term, cumulative and almost certainly irreversible damage we have collectively wreaked on our environment and, arising in part from this, an increasing recognition

1

of the mismatch between the global character of the problems we face and the rather more parochially national character of the institutions we tend to charge with dealing with them.

This provides the backdrop for the current volume, which seeks to set contemporary political science and its developments within the context of a set of substantive real world political challenges – such as democratic disaffection, economic instability, contemporary security threats and the proliferation of issues necessitating global governance. It seeks to examine the resources that we have at our disposal collectively, as analysts of political processes, for responding to those challenges; and it seeks to map out an agenda and suggest potential new directions for political science. Each contributor has been asked to describe the challenge posed to conventional political science by the real world dilemma their chapter considers, to set out the current state of our understanding of that challenge, to take stock of the extent to which the challenge identified has already led to developments and new directions within the discipline, and to gauge how such recent developments and current trends are likely to shape future trajectories. Each chapter considers how political science is likely to evolve in and through its engagement with the challenge identified. As is perhaps already clear, political science is, here, construed broadly so as explicitly to include international relations – indeed, a key feature of the volume is its desire to transcend, or at least to promote enhanced dialogue between, sub-disciplinary specialisms.

The volume opens with Michael Moran's sustained reflection on the concept and character of interdependence – perhaps the central unifying theme of this volume. In it, he discusses in particular its implications for policy-making and policy-makers. He cautions against a view of contemporary developments as unprecedented historically, suggesting that interdependence can, in fact, be seen to characterize the human condition. He explores the implications of this by differentiating between spatial, policy and institutional interdependence, considering the extent of the challenge posed to both policy-makers and to students of policy-making by each.

Gerry Stoker's concerns are more substantive and specific. He maps and details the contemporary condition of political disenchantment with, disengagement from, and distrust of formal politics and politicians that now engulfs the advanced liberal democracies, considering the very practical challenges it poses to the effective functioning of representative democracy itself. Whilst he cautions against a nostalgia for a mythical past in which citizens were deferential and engaged participants in formal and informal politics alike, he suggests that decisive intervention is now required if our democratic institutions are not to lose their legitimacy. He shows how an empirically focused political science, yet one sensitive to the intensely normative character of any programme of political reform, can help us both diagnose the condition afflicting our polities and, in so doing, come to play an increasingly key role in devising appropriate responses.

In the subsequent chapter, Helen Margetts turns her attention to a potentially more encouraging set of developments – sadly underexplored in the existing literature. Her concern is with the rise of new modes of political association, identification and engagement facilitated by access to and growing use of digital technologies. These, she shows, challenge many of the traditional assumptions we make as political analysts about the sources of political action and, indeed, the limits to collective political action, taking us – if appropriately acknowledged – into analytical pastures new. She maps out that territory for us – in the process, establishing the considerable significance of digital technologies in enabling real-time political association and interaction across previously impenetrable spatial boundaries.

In their chapter, Johanna Kantola and Judith Squires identify and explore the parameters of the new politics of equality and inequality, as they put it, charting in some detail the combination of long-standing and more contemporary policy challenges to which it responds. In particular, they show how reference to equality has remained a perennial theme of the discourse of social policy-making in the advanced liberal democracies, yet how the content of the term has shifted decisively in recent years. They also show, in a manner that chimes with the volume's emphasis on spatial interdependence, how the character of the new politics of equality they discern has been shaped not only domestically, but also increasingly by the interaction of domestic and transnational political processes. In so doing, a series of new actors, operating above the national level, have come to play a decisive role. They explore the implications of this for the content and character of this new politics, establishing an agenda for future research in this area.

Tariq Modood's chapter explores a set of issues no less crucial to the character of the contemporary political landscape – both domestic and international – charting the rise of traditions of civic multiculturalism in a number of liberal democracies in the 1960s and 1970s, and assessing the challenges posed to them in recent years. In particular, he explores the rise of faith-based forms of political identification and association, and the resulting re-politicization of religion – and the right to freedom of religious expression – in a context in which public discourse increasingly constructs faith as an axis of domestic conflict and geopolitical tension.

He shows how, despite many influential voices to the contrary, it is by deepening and reinforcing our civic multiculturalism, rather than by abandoning, that we can best respond to such challenges.

In her chapter, Helen Thompson looks at the changing character of the state in an era marked certainly by the growing awareness of political and economic interdependence. She reflects on the capacity, authority and legitimacy of the state in and through a sustained reflection on the current global financial crisis, showing how this might lead us to challenge and, indeed, reject many of the overstated assumptions about the powerlessness of the state with which claims about globalization have tended to be associated. The global financial crisis, she suggests, demonstrates not only the continued centrality of the state, but also, crucially, the core role it must increasingly come to play in the regulation of markets if stable (let alone environmentally sustainable) growth is to be restored to the world economy.

John Ravenhill explores similar issues and themes from a rather different perspective, gauging the implications of the global financial crisis for our understanding of economic interdependence, the political processes that have sustained and nurtured that interdependence, and the consequences for both of contemporary political and economic dynamics. He sets out an agenda for (international) political economy in the light of the crisis, emphasising particularly the importance of comparative and historical work on the performance of different regimes of financial regulation, and the need for more thorough integration of discussions of global governance and political economy.

Charlie Jeffery and Daniel Wincott pick up a number of themes of the previous two chapters in challenging the tendency in both political science and international relations to methodological (and, indeed, ontological) nationalism. Though their argument is developed principally with respect to the new territorial politics they associate with ongoing processes of devolution and decentralization, its implications are considerably wider. They show how devolution exposes the limits of a methodological nationalism that precludes an adequate consideration of spatial interdependence. But, just as significantly, they argue that the limits of such a methodological nationalism are by no means new. Mapping out an important agenda for future research in this area, they show how we can benefit from revisiting the past in the light of such newly acknowledged interdependence, hinting intriguingly at the new lines of analysis this might open up.

Stuart Croft's chapter deals with one of the prime issues of contemporary concern and controversy in both international and domestic politics today – security. He shows how the breadth and scope of the term has changed and broadened in recent years as an ever-growing set of issues and associated policy domains have become 'securitized', and he relates this broadening of the contemporary security agenda to the changing academic literature on the subject. In the process, he exposes tellingly the limits of an approach to security that focuses too much attention on interdependence and not enough on more traditional relations of hierarchy and dependence.

In his chapter, David Held considers the disparity between our need for effective, legitimate and accountable institutions of global governance, on the one hand, and our capacity to develop such institutions, on the other. He shows that although the case for effective and accountable institutions of global governance is now widely accepted, we have made alarmingly little progress in recent years in building such institutions. In so doing, he reveals much about the nature of the challenge this presents and the impediments we must negotiate, if we are to shift our principal point of response to pressures and problems that are indisputably global from the national to the global level.

Kimberly Hutchings draws our attention to the question of global justice. She shows how a growing recognition by citizens of both the global implications of our collective choices and the planetary character of the resulting politics generates a growing interest in, and politics of, global justice – as citizens, particularly western citizens, increasingly come to appreciate that domestic justice does not necessarily deliver global justice. She examines the philosophical and theoretical challenge posed by the concept of global justice itself, considering the extent to which traditional treatments of justice in political theory might be adapted and modified as we move from the domestic to the genuinely global. In the process, she alerts us to the dangers of an approach to global justice framed almost entirely from the perspective of beneficiaries of existing patterns of global inequality.

As the preceding paragraphs already suggest, the chapters in this volume cover a considerable amount of ground – much of it new or only relatively recently the focus of political scientists' attentions. In this framing chapter, my task is to draw out the core themes that connect these chapters, despite their disparate substantive concerns, and to examine how each of the substantive challenges they address might be seen to pose difficulties to both traditional demarcations of sub-field boundaries and to well-established ways of conducting political analysis. Key themes that emerge are interdependence, the need for inter-disciplinarity and for the transcendence of sub-disciplinary divides.

Acknowledging interdependence

Central to claims as to the distinctiveness of the political context in which we find ourselves today – as it is to the notion of an epochal break with the past that needs to be reflected in new approaches to political science – is the concept of *interdependence*. Indeed, if there is a single concept that captures the challenge that contemporary political developments are seen to pose to conventional approaches to political science it is surely this. That having been said, interdependence is not a simple concept and has, in fact, become synonymous with a range of rather different claims. In what follows, I distinguish between, on the one hand, the interdependence of the political, the economic and the cultural as domains of the social (domain interdependence) and, on the other, the interdependence of spatial scales and levels of analysis (spatial interdependence). But before exploring these in greater detail and the path to inter-disciplinarity and the dissolution of the sub-disciplinary divide between political science and international relations that leads from each respectively, it is first important to establish what we mean by 'interdependence'.

In the most basic and general terms, interdependence might be understood as a relationship between two or (invariably) more factors, processes or variables characterized by reciprocal causation or, perhaps better, mutual conditioning. Thus, if A, B and C are interdependent, then any change in B will result in a change in A and C, any change in A will result in a change in B and C, and any change in C will result in a change in A and B. In short, any change in one will result in a change in all of the others. Yet, this is a necessary – but not in itself sufficient – condition of interdependence. For the relationship between A, B and C to be seen as genuinely interdependent, a further condition must also hold – neither A, B nor C must be the clear driver (or determinant) of changes in the others. An example might serve to clarify the point. We might well have good evidence for suggesting that unemployment, inequality and levels of crime are related (for, generally, they are). But if our understanding of that relationship is that the direction of causation runs consistently from unemployment via inequality to crime, then this is better seen as a relationship of dependence rather than interdependence. A more likely candidate for a genuinely interdependent set of relationships is that between levels of distrust in politicians (A), the projection of self-interested motives onto political actors (the tendency to see politicians as 'in it for themselves') (B), and evidence that we might take as consistent with the self-interested behaviour of political actors (C). Here, it is at least credible to think, a change in any one of these variables is likely to be reflected in a change in the other two. Thus, if, for instance, we become more inclined to view our politicians as motivated by self-interest, we are less likely to trust them and more likely to read their behaviour in such instrumental terms (thereby confirming our initial hunch). By the same token, if we become more convinced of the probity of those we have elected (perhaps following an election in which we have unseated many previous incumbents), we are likely to be less inclined to project narrowly self-interested motives on to them and less likely to read their behaviour in such terms. The point is that there is no consistent direction of causation between these variables – it is equally as likely that a change in A will result in a change in B and C as it is that a change in C will give rise to a change in A and B. And, as long as this remains the case, this is a relationship characterized by interdependence.

Defined in this way, interdependence is a neutral and descriptive concept – neither innately good nor innately bad. Yet, interdependence is hardly likely to prove politically neutral – in the sense that relations that are interdependent (or acknowledged to be interdependent) are likely to be far less tractable and amenable to political intervention than those that are more clearly characterized (or seen to be characterized) by dependence. An age of interdependence is, then, likely to be one in which it is both rather more difficult to govern and, as Gerry Stoker shows, rather more difficult for citizens to hold those that would claim to govern to account. These are themes to which we return.

The crucial point for now is that, understood in such terms, interdependence is widely held to characterize the contemporary political condition. Yet, it is important to proceed carefully here. For one does not need to buy into the notion of an epistemological break necessitated by real world developments (a step-change in levels of interdependence) in order to see interdependence as crucial to our understanding of politics and to the development of the field of political science and international relations. Indeed, as we shall see presently, and as a number of the chapters here assembled show well, it is quite possible to claim that there has neither been a qualitative break with the past, nor even a dramatic increase in levels of interdependence and, yet, still to argue that political analysis needs to adapt itself better to exhibited political interdependence. This, in essence, is the argument of Michael Moran in his chapter on policy-making in an interdependent world.

But it is not only political interdependence (the interdependence and inter-connectedness of political processes in different jurisdictions) that is at issue here. No less significant is the interconnectedness of different realms or arenas of social interaction – the interdependence of the political, the economic and the cultural, for instance (or 'domain interdependence', as I have termed it). It is to this issue and its relationship to inter-disciplinarity that we turn first.

Interdependence and inter-disciplinarity

The interdependence of the political, the cultural and the economic as realms or domains of social interaction is a key theme of the volume, as it is of contemporary political science – and it has potentially great significance for the discipline. For, if it is accepted that the distinction between, say, the political and the economic is an artificial one, then it is but a small (and quite logical) step to acknowledging that the disciplinary boundaries that often circumscribe our analytical endeavours are no less artificial. It is not much more of a step (though a step, nonetheless) to the idea of *inter-disciplinarity* – a recognition of the potential value to be gained from the trading of insights across disciplinary boundaries; and no great leap from there to the idea of *post-disciplinarity* – the dissolution of disciplinary boundaries altogether in pursuit of an integrated social science. Yet, if only for fear of stretching our analytical resources too thinly, none of the authors in this volume would, I think, go quite so far in working through the implications of acknowledged disciplinary interdependence. As this suggests, the limits to an integrated social science might well be more practical than they are theoretical. Put slightly differently, in gaining an analytical purchase on social and political realities there is still value in parsimony, even in an era of acknowledged interdependence – a theme to which we will return presently. If this is accepted, a firm grounding in a disciplinary tradition supplemented by a good eye for the inter-disciplinary transfer of relevant insights might well be a better way to cope with domain interdependence than the embrace of a fully integrated (and post-disciplinary) social science.

Of course, there are different paths from acknowledged interdependence to this kind of inter-disciplinarity. Consider again the relationship between the political and the economic. One might argue for the potential value of an inter-disciplinary political economy by pointing to the increasingly porous nature of the boundary between these two realms (such as might necessitate a transcendence of previously unproblematic disciplinary specialisms). Such a justification takes the form of a working through of the implications of real world developments. Ontological change (a change in nature of social, political and economic reality) needs to be acknowledged epistemologically and methodologically.

Thus, it might be argued, the growing interdependence of the political and the economic, and the growing interpenetration of political and economic dynamics, has rendered anachronistic a previously valid disciplinary distinction. In other words, the world has changed and so must our understanding of it (and, indeed, the way in which we go about organizing ourselves so as best to furnish ourselves with that understanding).

But this is not the only path to an avowedly inter-disciplinary political economy. Certainly no less credible (indeed, from my own perspective, rather more so) is the claim that the distinction between the political and the economic was *always* an artificial or analytical one, rather than a real one. In effect, dissolving the social into separate realms of economic and political behaviour was an analytical strategy, rather than being inherent in the nature of social and political reality itself. In other words, the distinction was not *ontological* but *analytical*. Indeed, it was a distortion of the ontological interdependence of the political and the economic. From such a perspective, the analytical distinction might well continue to be valid and useful insofar as it helps clarify our thinking to refer to political and economic dynamics separately. But it is important that such a distinction does not become an impediment to the analysis of the (ontologically real) social processes it was intended to aid – by giving rise to a rigid disciplinary division of labour such as might preclude an analysis of the interdependence of the political and the economic.

This, I think, is precisely the position adopted by John Ravenhill and Helen Thompson in their chapters for this volume. The distinction between the political and the economic is, for each author, a valid and a useful one – but it is analytical, rather than ontological. At best, it draws attention to different aspects or dimensions of an integrated social, political and economic reality. The danger is that we forget this and, in the process, ontologize – and thereby reify – this analytical distinction, with the effect that we establish and entrench an overly rigid disciplinary fault-line between economics and political science (and, by extension, between other cognate disciplines and political science). The unfortunate effect of this is that the inter-relationship between the economic and the political is lost to us – falling between the tectonic plates of political science and economics to the detriment of each. The consequence is that we fail to consider the political conditions of economic dynamics and the economic conditions of political dynamics. It is these interactions, these interdependencies that constitute the terrain of an avowedly inter-disciplinary political economy, whose value is clearly evidenced in Ravenhill and Thompson's accounts of the current global financial crisis and its likely implications, both economic and political.

In fact, there is a more general point here: almost all of the chapters that follow ride roughshod over what would, until quite recently, have been much more clearly drawn and vigorously defended disciplinary fault-lines. Each draws insight from a range of cognate disciplines (most notably, sociology, psychology, history, philosophy and cultural studies) in a manner still regarded as heretical in some corners of the discipline. Yet, in each case, the approach is much more inter-disciplinary than it is post-disciplinary. For each chapter is quite consciously and explicitly engaged in the analysis of the political (however that is understood), with inter-disciplinarily drawn insights incorporated into, and reassessed in the light of, what are still disciplinarily developed research agendas and concerns. If these chapters are, indeed, representative of new directions in political science, then the research questions we increasingly pose will undoubtedly lead us to engage our colleagues in other disciplines, but they will still lead us back to more familiar terrain to assess the implications of the inter-disciplinary insights thereby generated.

Thus far we have considered two paths from acknowledged interdependence to inter-disciplinarity. But there is a third. Though similar to the second, it is subtly different. It leads from a reflection not on the *analytical* character of the distinction between, say, the political and the economic, but from its *socially constructed* character. The implications are not dissimilar, in that both reflections point to the arbitrary demarcation of the conceptual boundary between the political and cognate realms such as the economic and to the dangers of ontologizing such boundaries. But this third approach also serves to remind us that the categories we deploy are not our own but, rather, are themselves an integral part of the social world we analyze. This, too, is a key theme of the volume as a whole, as it is an increasing focus of attention in contemporary political science and international relations. The point is simply put, though its implications are rather more involved. The categories we deploy and the distinctions we invoke as political analysts have a political and cultural significance beyond the analysis in which we engage. For they are part of the language of politics itself – and, as such, they are a part of the political landscape we seek to understand. Thus, to take a now familiar example, whether we label something as 'political' or 'economic' might have a profound and practical political significance in itself. If we describe an accumulation of economic pathologies as a banking crisis, we are rather more likely to attribute responsibility and culpability to financial market actors than if we refer to this as the product of a regulatory failure. Similarly, whether we view our environmental responsibilities as individual consumer choices or as collective political decisions is likely to have a major bearing on societal responses to environmental degradation – and, indeed, our capacity to overcome the problem of coordination that so often prevents collective solutions to collective problems.

As these examples – and countless others like it – suggest, the boundary between the political and the economic is not merely an issue of academic interest; it is itself the product of ongoing political and social struggles to define and delineate the appropriate reach of public (or state) responsibility. As such, it is not fixed but fluid. Consequently, if we are to hope to capture any of that dynamism in our analysis of the political, we cannot afford to see the current boundaries of public (or state) responsibility as circumscribing the realm of politics. In effect, we need to acknowledge the highly political character of the processes in and through which the shifting boundaries of public and private authority are negotiated and renegotiated. As, in their different ways, the chapters of Helen Thompson, Tariq Modood and Stuart Croft show very well, such boundaries are, if anything, even more intensely contested in times of perceived economic crisis and in a climate characterized by internal security threats (real or imagined). In such times as now, it is even more important that we are able to chart and analyze the shifting boundaries of public and private responsibility, the politicization and depoliticization of potentially contentious issues and, indeed, the changing content of the discourse of politics itself. As this suggests, as well as acknowledging the interdependence of political, cultural and economic dynamics within the academic understandings of politics that we advance, it is no less important that we consider the rather more immediate and practical negotiation of such interdependencies by policymakers and political actors themselves – whether in debating the merits of a more interventionist form of regulation of global financial markets, or in subcontracting decision-making duties to unelected officials, or in making the case for seeing our relationship to the environment as one of collective public rather than individual consumer choice. Each of these issues is about the renegotiation of the boundaries of public and private responsibility and authority; each is about managing political, economic and environmental interdependence.

Spatial interdependence and the problem of sub-disciplinary specialism

Thus far we have concentrated almost exclusively on the interdependence of the political, the economic and the cultural considered as domains of the social; and we have tended to assume that, when we are talking about such interdependence, we are talking about webs of inter-connected processes linking the political with cognate social realms *at the same spatial scale* (whether that be the local, the domestic, the inter-national, or the global). And this is undoubtedly a core concern of contemporary political science, especially in Europe – with the seem-ingly ever greater emphasis placed, not least by funding councils, on inter-disciplinarity. Yet, this sense of interdependence is far from being the principal way in which the term is used in contemporary political science and international relations. Far from it. For the term 'interdepen-dence' has, in fact, become almost interchangeable and synonymous with a rather different sense of the term – with what might be termed 'spatial interdependence'. By this, we refer to the interconnectedness (for some, the *growing* interconnectedness) of social and political processes at different spatial scales – and, typically, to the idea that domestic dynam-ics are shaped (again, for many, *increasingly*) by transnational or global factors, and that transnational or global dynamics are shaped (increas-ingly) by domestic dynamics. It is this sense of the interdependence of outcomes at different levels of analysis or different spatial scales that is generally seen as the most profound challenge that real world develop-ments pose to conventional understandings of both political science and international relations and, above all, to the division of labour between the two. These themes suffuse the volume as a whole, as they do increas-ingly the discipline on which the volume reflects. In this overview chap-ter, then, it is perhaps appropriate to examine in a more general way claims as to the greater extent and salience of interdependence, and the challenge this might be seen to pose to political science and international relations.

In order to do so, however, it is first important to establish the range of contending claims associated with arguments about spatial interde-pendence. But, before even doing that, it is necessary to take a further step backwards and to establish what, specifically, we mean by 'spatial interdependence'. Here again, we are talking about reciprocal causation or mutual conditioning. But, when it comes to spatial interdependence, these relationships are stretched across geographical or territorial boundaries, or between previously discrete spatial scales or levels of analysis. In other words, spatial interdependence is about global–local and local–global connections – situations in which, for instance, actions conceived within one jurisdiction have consequences (typically, unin-tended consequences) within another jurisdiction, or in which transna-tional processes, practices and dynamics condition or circumscribe domestic or local strategies. Contemporary examples are rife, but certainly include the manifestly global consequences of the decisions of mortgage lenders in sub-prime markets in the United States for borrowers, investors and consumers around the world, and the cumulatively consequential character of individual consumer choices for our collective environmental security. As such examples perhaps already serve to indicate, spatial interdependence might well increase the scope and scale of the consequences of one's actions but, typically, is far from empowering.

Such spatial interdependence is increasingly held to characterize the contemporary political condition. But, once again, we need to proceed with caution. For, as a moment's reflection shows, a series of mutually incompatible claims can be – and invariably are – made by authors seeking to establish the need to acknowledge and deal with such interdependence. Different authors undoubtedly do base their argument for the greater attention we must devote to issues of spatial interdependence on different premises. But part of the problem here is that they are very rarely clear and explicit in declaring such assumptions. To guide us through this potential minefield, it is useful to think about the array of potential positions available to us. Though the following list is by no means completely exhaustive, we might start by differentiating between those arguing that:

(i)   spatial interdependence is a novel condition necessitating a new approach to political analysis;
(ii)   spatial interdependence might not be new, *per se*, but we might be exposed to it to a significantly greater extent again, requiring a new approach to political analysis;
(iii)   spatial interdependence might be neither new nor more prevalent, but it might acquire, or have come to acquire, a greater salience – which contemporary political analysts need, as a consequence, to acknowledge;
(iv)   spatial interdependence might not be novel, but its contemporary manifestations are different in character and kind to those with which we are accustomed to dealing, requiring new modes and strategies of political analysis;
(v)   spatial interdependence (and the form it now takes) might be neither new, nor more prevalent, nor more salient – in fact, it might be something of an illusion, and an unhealthy distraction from dependence and the more traditional preoccupations of political analysts; and

(vi)   whether novel, more prevalent, more salient, or none of these, the very *idea* of spatial interdependence and the sensitivity of political actors to it needs to be acknowledged by contemporary political analysts.

Interestingly, the first four of these positions – each of which suggests (albeit for rather different reasons) that spatial interdependence needs to be acknowledged by political analysts far more than it has been to date – might be taken to imply the need to dissolve the traditional sub-disciplinary division of labour between political science and international relations. For, if the parameters of domestic political choice are circumscribed to any significant extent by transnational trends and processes and, conversely, transnational trends and processes are themselves conditioned to any significant degree by domestic political dynamics, then a sub-disciplinary division of labour that leads us to specialize on, and thereby privilege, either one spatial scale to the exclusion of the other can only blind us to key drivers of social and political change. If, in other words, there are domestic conditions of existence of inter- and transnational political dynamics, and vice versa, then what value is there in approaches that close off our capacity to explore them?

Yet here, more than ever, we need to proceed carefully, so as not to risk throwing out the proverbial baby with the bathwater. For, as in the discussion of the choice between inter-disciplinarity and post-disciplinarity, there is a danger that, in our rush to embrace a newly acknowledged form of interdependence (in this case spatial interdependence) that problematizes long-established sub-disciplinary divisions (here between political science and international relations), we dismiss too readily much of what we already do that is valuable. Indeed, to put this in the right sense of proportion, it is perhaps important to remind ourselves that very little traditionally conceived political science explicitly denies the influence of inter- and transnational dynamics – and much of it acknowledges such influences quite openly (whether it follows up on such a concession or not). The converse is no less true of international relations theory – arguably more so. As this suggests, whilst the prospects of a more thoroughgoing dialogue between political science and international relations exist (and there is plenty of evidence in this collection and beyond that such a dialogue is already well established), it would seem somewhat premature to call time on existing sub-disciplinary specialisms. But what most definitely *is* required is the sub-disciplinary equivalent of inter-disciplinarity – inter-sub-disciplinarity, I suppose. In other words, we need to be both more sensitive to, and more eager to correct, the biases and blind-spots that often accompany sub-disciplinary parochialism. But this is just as much about improving the answers we are able to offer to the research questions we *already* pose as it is about recasting research agendas – though one might also hope that a greater dialogue between sub-disciplinary specialists will, in time, generate new research agendas and approaches that privilege no single level of analysis in favour of a more thorough exploration of the relationships between them. This, I suggest, we might think of as a genuinely post-sub-disciplinary venture, an early manifestation of which can be seen in the developing literature on multi-level governance. But the point is that we do not need to choose between inter-sub-disciplinary and post-sub-disciplinary research agendas – for they are not mutually incompatible. Indeed, we are likely to learn a great deal from the dialogue between them.

None of the authors in this volume would, I suspect, have a problem with any of the above, for their chapters exhibit precisely the kind of inter-sub-disciplinarity to which I am pointing. Indeed, even those chapters that focus on traditionally domestic concerns do so in a way that is highly sensitive to the interdependence of levels of analysis. Thus, Charlie Jeffery and Dan Wincott develop, in a manner almost parallel to the above analysis, an account of the spatial interdependence of the regional and the domestic. Yet, despite its ostensible focus on the complex and dynamic relationship between the national and the subnational, their account is also acutely sensitive to the significant role played by transnational processes in the development of the new territorial politics, especially within the EU. Johanna Kantola and Judith Squires are similarly sensitive to the role played by transnational political dynamics in the development of domestic political agendas, seeing this interaction and interdependence as crucial to the emerging character of what they term the 'new politics of equality'. And Tariq Modood's chapter – again, despite its ostensible concerns with the challenge posed to civil multiculturalisms domestically by the rise of faith-based forms of political identification – is no less sensitive to the role of international politics in the contemporary politicization of religion and the rise of faith-based identification in the period since 9/11 and the Iraq War. Helen Thompson's chapter is, quite simply, a case study in spatial interdependence – demonstrating, as it does, through an analysis of the current global financial crisis, just how profoundly mistaken we were to associate globalization with the demise of the state.

The same spirit of inter-sub-disciplinarity characterizes those chapters with more traditionally international or transnational concerns. Thus, Kimberley Hutchings shows how contemporary discussions of global justice must build from an acknowledgement of local–global connections, and the asymmetric distributional and environmental consequences that arise from, say, the routine consumption choices of western citizens. Similarly, David Held shows how domestic dynamics have contributed to the generation of a series of pressing global challenges to which effective and accountable institutions of global governance, such as we have thus far manifestly failed to build, are the only credible solution. Finally, Stuart Croft's chapter shows how profoundly domestic and international security concerns have been interwoven in recent years as domestic politics has been 'securitized' in response to what is perceived to be a global terrorist threat.

Yet, if the authors in this volume are united in embracing spatial interdependence and, with it, a certain inter-sub-disciplinarity, as I have termed it, this should not lead us to hide their often rather different reasons for so doing. Put simply, some see the need to acknowledge interdependence as arising from real world developments that dissolve previously quite legitimate sub-disciplinary divisions of labour. Yet others point to the inherent limitations, as they would see it, of separately demarcated sub-disciplines to deal with the long-standing condition of interdependence. Indeed, if we return to the range of potential positions on the question of spatial interdependence, we find that it is really only the two extremes – the first and the fifth position – that find little or no support in this volume. And, indeed, in the idea that a growing preoccupation with spatial and other forms of interdependence might distract us from issues of enduring significance, even elements of the fifth find some limited backing. In particular, as Chapter 4 by Johanna Kantola and Judith Squires and Chapter 9 by Stuart Croft in their different ways imply, there is a danger that, in our hurry to embrace interdependence, we fail to give adequate consideration to enduring relations of hierarchy, power and dependence.

For some, such as David Held, though the sheer fact of interdependence might not be unprecedented, its scale and scope undoubtedly are. John Ravenhill, writing about the global economy, draws a similar conclusion. Yet, for others – Helen Margetts, most explicitly – it is less the prevalence of interdependence that is at issue (a proposition which, from her perspective, would be very difficult to gauge anyway) than the form and character of that interdependence. Focusing on citizens' use of new digital technologies, she shows, compellingly, how new modes of interdependence are emerging, highlighting their potential, in time, to shape decisively political dynamics at a variety of spatial scales. Such new modes of political association and engagement, she suggests, challenge many of the long-cherished assumptions of political science, necessitating the development of new modes and techniques of political analysis. Others – perhaps appropriately, given their different substantive concerns – are more sceptical of claims as to the unprecedented extent of interdependence, as they are to claims that it has come to acquire a qualitatively new character in recent years. Michael Moran, for instance, in a powerful statement on the nature of policy-making in an interdependent world, argues that there is nothing new about interdependence, *per se*, nor really about any of the forms it currently takes. The implications of his account are clear. Rather than seeing interdependence as a qualitatively new challenge to which today's policy-makers must respond in qualitatively new ways, we need to acknowledge the interdependence of earlier times and examine the way in which it was managed then. From his perspective, in a manner that chimes with many other chapters in this volume, it is the acknowledgement of interdependence (by both academics and policy-makers alike) that is new, not the extent or character of the interdependence we have belatedly come to recognize. The implications of this are intriguing and we come to them presently.

These differences in position are undoubtedly highly significant, and it would be wrong to trivialize them. But there is a danger that, in drawing attention to such differences, we both accentuate them and fail to see the considerable common ground that exists between the authors in this volume. For, although both the extent to which and the manner in which issues of interdependence are dealt with varies significantly between the various chapters that follow (appropriately, given their rather different foci), a number of common – and sometimes surprising – general themes emerge. Taken together they have, I believe, major implications for how we think about interdependence and how political science (broadly conceived) might best respond to the various challenges it poses.

There are three of these common themes, and it is to them that I turn in conclusion.

Interdependence, complexity and the possibility of political science

The first of these common themes is ontological – but, as with many ontological issues, it has potentially major epistemological and methodological implications (and it is perhaps these that should concern us most). Whether we see interdependence as new or not, it is difficult not to see it as newly acknowledged – and that acknowledgement has ontological implications. For an interdependent social and political world is different in kind to one characterized exclusively (or even principally) by relations of dependence. Thus, the nature of the social and political landscape we acknowledge ourselves to inhabit changes quite significantly the moment we come to see the contemporary political condition as one of interdependence.

This matters to us, as analysts of politics, because another synonym of interdependence is *complexity*. An interdependent social and political world is more complex than one characterized principally by relations of dependence – if for no other reason than that situations of reciprocal causation and mutual conditioning do not exhibit highly conserved (and, in principle, generalizable) causal regularities. As a consequence, they do not avail themselves so readily of strategies that presume the existence of precisely such regularities and precisely such generalizability. In short, acknowledging interdependence (whether we regard that interdependence to be novel, more prevalent, more salient, or none of these) is acknowledging (greater) complexity; and acknowledging (greater) complexity might lead us to question anew prior epistemological convictions.

Yet, not for the first time, we need to tread very carefully here. For there are very different ways of responding to acknowledged complexity – and, as I hope to show, there is no particular reason for taking acknowledged complexity as the death-knell of a political science worthy of the name. A couple of points might usefully be made. First, whether we see interdependence as a source of the complexity with which we must contend or not, political analysts have always had to deal with complexity. As such, whilst the concept of interdependence affixes a label to – and, indeed, describes – an element of that complexity, its acknowledgement does not profoundly alter the challenge the political scientist faces. That challenge, as I see it, has always been to achieve some degree of analytical purchase on a complex social and political reality – and that inevitably entails a simplification of the complexity we hold to characterize that social and political reality. In short, political analysis has always been – and is likely to remain – a search for parsimony.

Put in such terms, acknowledged interdependence is perhaps best seen less as a challenge in itself than as a chastening reminder of the difficulty of the task with which our subject matter has always presented us. In our search for an analytical purchase on political realities (and, in the process, for parsimony), we inevitably simplify the complexity of the political world our ontological assumptions admit. And it is good to be reminded of that. But such a reminder need not become a manifesto of despair. Instead, it might be taken as an invitation to recognize and declare more openly the inherent limitations in the approaches that we devise to political analysis. In particular, it encourages us not to abandon the attempt to develop a science of politics but, perhaps, to be more honest about the difficulties inherent in such an enterprise and more clear about our strategies for managing the inevitable parsimony–complexity trade-off.

It has implications, too, for the kind of debate in which we engage with one another. In particular, it suggests that it simply will not do to chide and chastise our peers (as we have often tended to do) for failing to produce models of political reality that are as complex as that reality itself, for no model is capable of reflecting that complexity fully, and it is to misunderstand the value (and, indeed, the nature) of political analysis to suggest that this is a legitimate expectation. Yet, by the same token, it suggests that there should perhaps be more of an onus upon us as political analysts to acknowledge rather more explicitly the almost inevitable biases associated with our preferred strategy for achieving parsimony (whether that parsimony be achieved by ignoring spatial interdependence, turning a blind eye to the role of extra-political variables, presupposing equilibrium conditions, or in the simplifying assumptions we make about human nature). This might well lead us to a more modest political science – but, as a number of the chapters suggest, as long as we retain a capacity for methodological innovation, it need not come at the expense of our capacity to claim a scientific licence for the analyses in which we engage.

New – or newly-acknowledged – interdependence?

A second and, on the face of it, perhaps rather more surprising theme of this volume – especially given its concern with new challenges and new directions – has already been touched upon. It is that claims as to the qualitative novelty of the challenges that contemporary political developments pose, both to policy-makers and to the discipline as a whole, are overblown. Put simply, the argument of a surprising number of the chapters that follow is that the challenges with which they deal are not so much *new* as *newly-acknowledged* – as is the more general condition of interdependence with which they are typically associated.

This is a crucial point, but it is important that we get it right. Contemporary politics does, undoubtedly, present us with a great variety of new practical political problems – and this volume is concerned with a great number of them. Politics (as Gerry Stoker shows) is seen to be failing us in a manner that we have not experienced since the advent of democracy itself; the contemporary economic crisis (as John Ravenhill demonstrates) is as profound and as global in its reach as anything we have experienced in a century; and the rise of new faith-based forms of political identification, association and mobilization (as Tariq Modood shows) challenges profoundly, if not irretrievably, the civic multicultural traditions that developed in many advanced liberal democracies from the 1960s and 1970s. But the point is that we do not need to devise new modes of political analysis and inquiry to deal with such developments. Moreover, in the first two examples, it is important that we do not overemphasize the extent to which these developments are wholly unprecedented – after all, politics has never been universally admired and, when contextualized historically, today's is just the latest in a series of global economic crises. And, if the rise of faith-based political identi-fication challenges civic multiculturalism, then it does so because it exposes a frailty and a set of internal tensions that predate this develop-ment. The frailty exposed is less new than newly-acknowledged.

What is particularly interesting is that the idea of contemporary chal-lenges being not so much new as newly-acknowledged seems to apply with, if anything, even more effect to the concept of interdependence itself. For although, as I have sought to show, interdependence might be seen to capture the essence of the challenge that contemporary political developments pose to political science and to our political systems, a strong theme in a number of the chapters that follow is that there is noth-ing new about it. Michael Moran is perhaps the most explicit on this point, suggesting that interdependence might be seen to characterize the human condition itself. But he would seem, in the process, to be giving voice to a rather wider consensus, the implications of which are very interesting and which he spells out in some detail. If we see interdepen-dence as a timeless feature of social and, by extension, political interac-tion, then this has implications not only for how we look at the present, but also for how we look at the past. As he suggests, it is wrong to see contemporary policy-makers as responding to the new challenges posed by interdependence – for they have always had to deal with interdepen-dence. And, as this implies, a potentially fresh perspective is opened up by looking at, say, the Westphalian order as a means of managing such interdependence.

Charlie Jeffery and Daniel Wincott make a very similar point. Their chapter highlights the dangers of a methodological (and, indeed, an onto-logical) nationalism, which has typically led us to view nation-states as hermetic and self-contained. On the face of it, their argument is that the limitations of such methodological nationalism are cruelly exposed by the rise of a newly-devolved multi-level territorial politics. But what is particularly interesting about their chapter is that they do not argue that the spatial interdependence which characterizes this 'new territorial politics' is itself new; rather, it is simply that we have been made more aware of it by recent developments (devolution, in particular). As does Moran, they explore, in an intriguing and suggestive way, the need to reconsider the past in the light of this newly-acknowledged, but not in itself new, spatial interdependence. In so doing, they point to the much larger and more significant role for sub-national political processes in shaping state-level dynamics that is likely to emerge from such a reassessment.

The politics of (newly-)acknowledged interdependence

If interdependence is perhaps best seen not as new in itself but, rather, as newly-acknowledged, then it is important that we note that it is not only political analysts who have increasingly come to acknowledge this. Interdependence is, just as significantly, newly-acknowledged by those we study – policy-makers and citizens. This, too, is a key theme of the volume as a whole – and the last to which I wish to draw explicit attention in this introductory essay.

If we take policy-makers first, the idea of interdependence has become increasingly central to the way in which politics is practised, as it has to the language of politics itself (and, hence, to the way in which political decisions are communicated and legitimated). Typically, this takes one of two forms: the appeal to globalization and, hence, to spatial interdependence, often as a means of dampening domestic political expectations; and, perhaps increasingly, in what Michael Moran terms 'policy interdependence' – in which policy imperatives in one domain (such as security or competitiveness) come to circumscribe the parameters of policy choice in another (as immigration policy becomes 'securitized' perhaps, or welfare policy recalibrated in the light of attempts to make the labour market more competitive). Here, as in the academic literature, acknowledged interdependence has become synonymous with complexity and, arguably, it has contributed to a diminished sense of the capacity to hold policy-makers to account democratically. For, typically – and, quite possibly, entirely honestly – policy-makers tend increasingly to appeal to global dynamics beyond their control to which they must adapt themselves (by, for instance, internalizing the imperative to secure and maintain competitiveness). But this, almost inevitably, has the effect of weakening the tie between domestic political decision-making and the electorate. In effect, policy-makers must discount the wishes of those who elected them in favour of the policy choices dictated by effective economic management under conditions of global economic interdependence and so forth. In the process, policy-making also tends to be become more technical in content and character and, with this, comes the temptation to subcontract decision-making to unelected experts (central bankers and the like). Arguably, and as Gerry Stoker's chapter shows, such dynamics have contributed significantly to the growing disaffection and disengagement of citizens from formal politics.

Yet, it is not only policy-makers who have come to acknowledge and to embrace interdependence. Citizens, too, have become far more conscious of living in an interdependent world – not least because they are constantly reminded of the fact by political elites invoking globalization! But, as Kimberly Hutchings and David Held demonstrate, albeit in rather different ways, this acknowledgement of greater global interdependence has led to new forms of political subjectivity and to demands for new institutions of global governance. In particular, as Kimberly Hutchings shows, a much greater awareness of the potentially global consequences of consumer choices and environmental resource usage have led to the development of a discourse and an associated politics of global justice. This, as David Held shows, is generating growing demand for a set of effective institutions of global governance that might be held to account in terms of their capacity to see that global justice is delivered. Yet, as he also shows, we are a very long way from such hopes being realized. Acknowledged global interdependence is one thing; effective and accountable institutions of global governance such as might answer to considerations of global justice is, as yet, quite another.

Conclusion

We began with the disarmingly simple question of the relationship between political science broadly conceived and its subject matter – and it is to this that we return in conclusion. Whilst the question itself is, indeed, disarmingly simple, the answer is devilishly difficult. What is clear is that the agenda of political analysis has changed quite decisively in recent years, that it will continue to change and that it should continue to change – as new practical political problems present themselves. Had this volume been commissioned, with broadly the same remit, to mark the fiftieth anniversary of the Political Studies Association, it would almost certainly have looked very different. And I suspect that a volume to mark the seventy-fifth anniversary of the association will look very different again. We can perhaps only hope that this is because, in the next fifteen years, some of the challenges with which this book is concerned will have been resolved. Perhaps more likely is that new and even more pressing concerns will have taken their place.

Yet, although our subject matter has changed, if there is a single lesson to be drawn from the chapters that follow it is surely this: we do not need, and can probably do without, a new political science for new times – and we can certainly do without a new integrated and post-disciplinary social science for new times. The contemporary political challenges to which this volume draws our attention do, indeed, expose some of the limitations of our discipline – in particular, its tendency to disciplinary and sub-disciplinary parochialism, and its difficulty in dealing with relationships that are genuinely interdependent. But two qualifiers are immediately called for: first, these are not only the limitations of our discipline, but of all disciplines. And, second, in what is a now familiar theme, these are not so much new limitations as limitations newly-acknowledged.

The process of facing up to our limitations is, of course, an important one – and, again, a key part of the rationale for this volume. As much as anything, it is about heightening our sensitivity as analysts of politics to what we do badly – in the hope that such a process might lead us to do things a little better the next time. In such a context, acknowledging one's limitations is at least half the battle. But there is a clear danger here. For, if we were to agree that interdependence characterizes the challenge that contemporary political developments pose to us as political scientists, and that disciplinary and sub-disciplinary specialisms prevent us from capturing such interdependence, then it might be tempting to seek to dissolve each and every disciplinary and sub-disciplinary boundary. Yet that, I think, would be a mistake – for two reasons at least.

First, as I have been at pains to suggest, all political science seeks an analytical purchase on its subject matter. It is, as such, about achieving parsimony – and it might well be that, amongst other strategies, turning a temporary blind eye to extra-political variables or to spatial interdependence is not a bad means to that end. The point is that, to make sense of the world, we need to simplify it; and, to simplify it, we need to start somewhere. It is not credible to think that our conceptual apparatus for exploring political realities should – or, indeed, could – bear a one-to-one correspondence to those realities. Our task is not to hold up a mirror to reality – and, hence, to reflect its ontological complexity – but to build and trace narrative paths through it. In other words, the ontological assumptions from which the accounts of politics that we offer as political analysts build cannot, and should not, be chosen on the basis of their philosophical adequacy, for they are means to the end of achieving an analytical purchase on our subject matter.

Second – and, as I have also sought to suggest, even if we accept (as I think we should) that there are insights to be gained by according a greater role to extra-political variables and the interaction of political processes at a variety of spatial scales – this need not entail a dissolution of disciplinary and sub-disciplinary divisions in pursuit of a genuinely post-disciplinary integrated social science. Political science (broadly conceived) and political science and international relations (narrowly conceived) have distinctive, valid, appropriate, and dynamic research agendas – and it is imperative that we have answers to many (if not, perhaps, all) of the research questions they pose. What we need is not different questions but better answers. We are, I suspect, most likely to achieve those answers by acknowledging the limitations of what we already do, by being more sensitive than we are at present to our disciplinary and sub-disciplinary parochialisms, and by actively seeking dialogue with those in other disciplinary and sub-disciplinary fields from whose insights we might learn. But that is a path that leads *from the discipline* and, ultimately, *back to the discipline*; it is the path of inter-disciplinarity and inter-sub-disciplinarity, not post-disciplinarity. On the sixtieth anniversary of the Political Studies Association, that seems to be a highly appropriate note on which to conclude.

Chapter 1

Policy-Making in an Interdependent World

MICHAEL MORAN

Introduction: interdependence old and new

'Interdependence' poses a serious and novel challenge to policy-makers, and to our understanding of the policy process. This chapter is about understanding the nature of that challenge. We are looking at something new here. But in what does the novelty consist? I will argue in the following pages that novelty lies only partly in the changing objective character of the policy-making world, though there is indeed evidence that we are encountering new kinds of interdependence. For their effective management, these new forms of interdependence do certainly require novel institutional creations; the tools of nineteenth-century bureaucracy are no more appropriate to the twenty-first century than is nineteenth-century technology. But there is another form of novelty involved here: it is not simply that the world has changed; the way the world is discursively constructed has also altered. And at least some of the novelty of interdependence lies in the *perception* of its novelty. Thus, making sense of policy-making in an interdependent world has to attempt the difficult task of disentangling what is new about interdependence from what policy advocates *say* is new about it.

Any argument about the significance of 'interdependence' in policy-making has immediately to confront two considerations. First, interdependence is hardly new – indeed, it virtually defines the human condition. As a social science, political science should be uniquely sensitive to this fact. Indeed, the history of the study of politics can be conceived as a history of the study of interdependencies for, at root, it is the study of how we govern ourselves as social animals. The issue is, therefore, whether we are encountering new and more daunting forms of interdependence. Second, interdependence is a complex concept. Even casual reflection soon demonstrates that there is no single kind or source of interdependence.

These two elementary considerations shape this chapter. Since this is a volume about where political science is going – about new problems and new directions – we have to identify what, if anything, is novel about the connection between interdependence, the practice of policy-making, and the study of policy-making. 'If anything', here, is more than a ritual qualifier. Interdependence has always been with us; but whether there exist new kinds of interdependence, and new problems created by inter-dependence, has to be an open question – one that can only be settled by appeal to evidence. It is here that our second opening consideration – the complexity of the concept – becomes relevant. If interdependence takes more than one form, we cannot assume that all its forms change – or remain constant – together. To say something about whether we live in a world of novel interdependence, we have to distinguish, if only schemat-ically, different dimensions of interdependence, and have to say how they are changing or remaining constant.

That is part of the task attempted in this chapter. I work with three concepts of interdependence. *Spatial interdependence* is a fact of policy life, because policy is made in territorial domains – of which the most closely studied is the territorially delimited state. Since policy is made and implemented in territorial space, it has always has had to contend with the facts of interdependence both within and between territorial domains. The key questions now, therefore, relate to whether any new forms of spatial inderdependence have developed, and what these new forms have done to the practice and the academic understanding of policy-making?

Institutional interdependence has, similarly, always been a fact of policy life. We conventionally use images such as the 'machinery' of policy-making to recognize the fact that policy is rarely made by a single institutional component but is, rather, the result of some kind of coordi-nated division of institutional labour; and the *implementation* of policy is virtually a study in institutional interdependencies. So, the critical ques-tion is not: Does institutional interdependence exist and does it shape the policy process? Rather, it is: Are we witnessing new kinds of institutional interdependence and new kinds of consequential problems?

Policy interdependence takes us to the heart of policy – its substance. That policy domains are interdependent is, once again, a truism: at the simplest level, we need only think of the opportunity costs involved in committing to one public spending programme over another. Once again, the critical question therefore is not: 'Do policies interact in this fashion?'

Rather, it is: 'Are there new forms of interdependence within the substance of policies?'

These distinctions are necessarily schematic. It will be plain, for example, that spatial interdependence can spill over into institutional interdependence. Nevertheless, the distinctions give us a vocabulary with which to examine the problems and opportunities of policy-making in an interdependent world.

Spatial interdependence: discursive construction and democratic statecraft

There is nothing novel about spatial interdependence. Indeed, the very invention and endurance of the Westphalian system may be interpreted as an attempt to solve two kinds of interdependence arising from the fact that policy is made in a world of territorial space. The image of a unitary sovereign state was designed to address the problems of internal coordination and hierarchy inside the territorial boundaries of that creation. In the academic literature, the single most influential definition of the character of the state succinctly addresses the link between territory and interdependence: 'a state is a human community that [successfully] claims *the monopoly of legitimate use of physical force* within a given territory' (Weber 1948 [1918]: 78 – emphasis in original). Moreover, the Westphalian system also functioned to delineate the rules governing what was to happen when states knocked up against each – and, in particular, against each other's sovereign borders – in a physically interdependent world.

What then, if anything, is novel about spatial interdependence and about the problems it creates for the practice and the study of policy-making? There are three credible claims to novelty: the growth of spatial interdependence in economic life; the growth of spatial interdependence in a core sphere of state responsibility, the management of human security; and the growth of a *discursive* sense of interdependence.

The first of these is usually gathered under the umbrella of economic globalization. True, there is contention surrounding this subject: about the very meaning of globalization; about how far the changes that have undoubtedly occurred since the early 1970s are, indeed, historically novel, or only amounted to the recreation of an older pattern disrupted by the great wars of the twentieth century; and about just how truly 'global' have been the processes creating an economically interdependent world (see, for instance, Thompson *et al.* 2009). But one comprehensive survey of what we know about the phenomenon concludes that 'accelerated globalization of recent decades has left almost no one and no locale on earth completely untouched, and the pace has on the whole progressively quickened with time' (Scholte 2005: 119). In particular, Scholte argues, the critical domain of finance 'has shifted very substantially out of the territorialist framework that defined most banking, securities, derivatives and insurance business before the middle of the twentieth century' (Scholte 2005: 113). The contributions to this volume by Thompson, Held and Ravenhill develop this argument further.

The *realization* of the extent of spatial interdependence in the entirely traditional state domain of human security might be said to have crystallized on the morning of 11 September 2001, the notorious date of the attack on the World Trade Centre in New York. As with arguments about the spatial interdependence of national economies, a case can also be made against novelty here: that the sense of shock created by the attack obscured the extent to which, over the course of the preceding century, the technologies of warfare had eroded the capacity of any single state to ensure the physical security of its population. But the world after '9/11' is permeated by a very different sense of the impact of spatial interdependence on the state. In particular, a combination of population migrations, cultural change and technological innovation has contributed to the international securitization of policy: to the sense that spatial interdependence is so pervasive that no single state can any longer independently achieve the traditional state missions of ensuring internal or external security for its citizens.

As the terms of this description suggest, the *sense* of spatial interdependence is as important for the practice and understanding of policy-making as is any 'objective' evidence. Indeed, the interdependence of territorial units is so many-sided and complex that we are unlikely to be able to reduce it to a set of metrics that will allow us simply to measure change over time in an intellectually coercive way. That is why the third identified meaning – the growth of a discursive sense of spatial interdependence – is so important. The notion that concepts such as economic globalization are subject to a process of discursive construction has proved particularly influential as the study of policy-making itself has been influenced by the 'cultural turn' in the social sciences (Hay and Rosamond 2002; Forestor 2006; Susskind 2006).

To describe the sense of growing spatial interdependence as a discursively constructed concept is not to suggest that it is a fiction: there are limits to the extent to which ideological mystification can transcend the experiences, and the data, of social reality. On the contrary, rhetorically to construct general accounts of the changing policy environment is the heart of the policy-maker's art, especially when the policy-maker is a democratically elected politician. Indeed, it is the discursively constructed character of spatial interdependence that helps explain why its effects on our understanding of the policy process are so ambiguous: *how* it is discursively constructed determines whether it is a constraining or an enabling factor in policy-making. The early interpretations of the significance of the spatial interdependence of national economies, in particular, pictured its effects largely in the language of constraints – at the most immediate level, sometimes echoing the claims of some of the cheerleaders of globalization that the era of the territorially delimited sovereign state was at an end. But a later generation of scholarship has produced accounts that allow for a significant amount of policy creativity in the face of interdependence. The sources of this creativity are three-fold. First, the exercise of the traditional powers of the Westphalian state – for instance, of physical coercion and fiscal expropriation – though complicated by spatial interdependence, is not extinguished in a spatially interdependent world (Weiss 1998). Second, spatial interdependence, precisely, strengthens relations of dependency. At an economic level, globalization involves the elaboration of a global division of labour, allowing the occupation of specialist 'niches' by national economies and, more importantly, allowing the elaboration of national policy strategies that, in turn, enable nations to occupy those niches (Garrett 1998). Finally, the very act of discursive construction arises because it endows policy-makers with a powerful resource in formulating and implementing policy. The most striking example is provided by the history of economic policy-making in the Anglo-American world during the second 'long boom', lasting from 1992 to 2007. In this era, policy elites were able to invoke images of globalization to legitimize policy strategies that involved the extensive deregulation of labour, product and financial markets. As we shall see later, the catastrophic end of the new 'long boom' also led to the depletion of the intellectual capital that helped legitimize this particular discursive construction.

But the impact of spatial interdependence is not only felt at the level of policy formulation and legitimation. It has also affected the way national policy-making systems are organized. The most sustained and convincing account of this set of effects is provided by Slaughter's notion of the way the unitary (Westphalian) state is being 'disaggregated' (Slaughter 2004). Disaggregation at the national level is, Slaughter argues, visible in the way national policy agencies are, in effect, obliged to formulate their own distinctive 'foreign policies'. In particular, in the most globalized parts of the economy – such as financial services – the interdependent relations between national regulatory agencies joined in international regulatory bodies, in fields such as central banking and securities markets, are at least as important as the 'internal' relations between parts of the national state machine. Spatial interdependence is thus disaggregating national policy-making systems into global networks of agents along lines of specialized policy responsibilities. The general character of Slaughter's argument is well illustrated in specific institutional terms in Braithwaite and Drahos's classic study of global business regulation. Indeed, what they show is that it is not only national policy-making systems that are being disaggregated; the same is true of 'private' institutions in this interdependent world. In *Global Business Regulation* there is a revealing tabular summary of all this (Braithwaite and Drahos 2000: 476–7). It shows, to use a metaphor of which Braithwaite and Drahos are fond, a global *web* of organizations, individuals and social groups. The regulation of contract and property rights, for instance, encompasses major American national trade associations (such as the Motion Picture Association of America) and individual corporate giants (such as IBM). It is a web that joins individual corporate giants with national governments: the regulation of telecommunications includes the governments of both the United States and the United Kingdom and corporate actors such as Time-Warner. Some regulatory spheres are made up of segments of national governments, individual agencies often operating in highly technical spheres: for instance, the International Organization of (national) Securities Commissions for the regulation of securities markets. The web is also marked by an elaborate division of labour, even between corporate giants: they include not only producers of goods and services, but also commercial standard establishing bodies – for instance, credit and bond rating agencies such as Moody's. Mention of Moody's highlights the contingent character of all this interdependence for, in the wake of the global crisis after 2007, their role has been challenged, and attempts are being made to subject them to public regulation, notably by the European Union.

Slaughter's insight concerning the impact of spatial interdependence on the institutional structure of national policy-making systems reminds us of a point with which we began: that, whilst the distinction between different forms of interdependence gives us a handy vocabulary with which to discuss this world, there can be no hard and fast distinction between spatial and institutional interdependence. But it is to the closer examination of the latter that we now turn.

Institutional interdependence: government, governance and complexity

Just as spatial interdependence lies at the traditional heart of the state and of the Westphalian state system, so institutional interdependence lies at the heart of our traditional ideas of the modern state. Weber's notion of the state as involving a monopoly of coercion in a territorially delimited space, and his theory of bureaucracy as a hierarchy of command based on a highly elaborated division of labour, both expressed the perennial character of institutional interdependence in political life: the monopoly of coercion was supposed to be a solution to the problem of interdependence across space; the theory of bureaucracy both described complex institutional interdependencies and offered a hierarchical solution to the problems that they posed.

The most convincing argument about the contemporary significance of institutional interdependence consists, therefore, not in the claim that it is a novel condition facing the policy-maker, but that new kinds of interdependence have made obsolete or ineffective our traditional formal and hierarchical means of coping with interdependence. Much of this sort of literature is now commonly gathered under the heading of a 'governance' school of thought. It is striking that the rise of governance images has been influential in the formally separated sub-disciplines of international relations and the study of domestic state systems. In the former, Rosenau (1990, 1992, 2000) offered an eloquent account of the transformation of the Westphalian system: from one where sovereign states were kingpin, to a system where states were one set of actors in decentralized networks that also involved non-state actors ranging from private corporations to a multitude of NGOs. This is a world of governance that has abandoned the hierarchies of 'government' in place of 'a set of regulatory mechanisms … which function effectively even though they are not endowed with formal authority' (Rosenau 1992: 5). It is a world of 'fragmegration' – a neologism coined by Rosenau – where fragmentation and integration are simultaneously at work in the international state system (Rosenau 2000: 177.)

In the study of domestic politics, an even more emphatic version of the rise of a new kind of interdependence has been offered. The classic account is provided by Rhodes:

> The shift from government to governance in the differentiated polity is my preferred narrative … It focuses on interdependence, disaggregation, a segmented executive, policy networks, governance and

hollowing out. Interdependence in intergovernmental relations and policy networks contradicts the authority of parliamentary sovereignty and a strong executive. Institutional differentiation and disaggregation contradict command and control by bureaucracy. Thriving functional representation contradicts territorial representation through local governments. (Rhodes 1997: 87)

One of the most attractive features of this image of a new kind of institutional interdependence is that it leads, especially in the work of Rhodes, to a confrontation with the real world of policy – especially with the real world of policy fiascos. Policy failure, in this view of the world, is due to the attempt to employ the old hierarchical solutions to problems of institutional interdependence. Relying on Weberian state and bureaucratic theory is akin to relying on the technology of steam in the age of the combustion engine and the computer. (And, indeed, much of the imagery of line bureaucracy derived from one of the first great systems of coordination in industrial society, that created by nineteenth-century railway organizations.) The solution to the new institutional interdependencies was precisely to recognize the constraints it put on hierarchical government, and to recognize that it demanded a reflexive approach to the solution of policy problems: an approach premised on an engagement with all actors, whether nominally 'private' or 'public'; and an institutional arrangement designed to steer, not command, the networks that clustered around different policy areas.

The 'governance' version of the significance of institutional interdependence is barely two decades old, but the fundamental intellectual assumptions that guide it are not, in fact, particularly novel. The single-most influential analytical framework in political science from the 1950s to the 1970s was promoted in the work of David Easton, now a largely forgotten figure. Easton's 'systems framework for the analysis of political life' was based on the premise that the territorial, bureaucratic state was an unusable fiction, and needed to be replaced by a systems framework in which societal institutions were joined to processes of authoritative decision-making in a continuous cycle of mutually adjusting steering (Easton 1957, 1965). Easton, in turn, was inspired by an older literature on cybernetics that anticipated much of the language of self-steering systems. At the more immediate level of policy analysis, the fiascos of the 1960s and 1970s produced a large literature emphasizing precisely the importance of managing complex interdependency, and the catastrophic consequences of failing to do so intelligently. Pressman and Wildavsky's influential study of *Implementation* stressed the problems of multiple clearances in the long lines of institutional relations involved in 'the complexity of joint action' (Pressman and Wildavsky 1973: 93). That was an early herald of a large literature on 'overloaded government' that argued that modern societies were characterized by 'organised social complexity', La Porte's influential notion (1975). Doing anything significant involved managing a huge range of public and private actors – such a range that it threatened to make advanced industrial societies extremely difficult, or even impossible, to govern (for an application of organized social complexity in this way, see King 1976).

In sketching these antecedents of governance theory, I do not mean to diminish its worth, or to imply that it is just recycling older ideas. It would be amazing, after all, if it had no intellectual antecedents. Indeed, the most attractive feature of governance theory, especially in the hands of someone as creative and as interested in the problems of real-world policy-making as Rhodes, is that it has moved beyond the pessimism of the previous generation of analysts of complex institutional interdependence to try to think out how policy could be made intelligently and implemented effectively in these conditions of institutional interdependence. That is what lies behind the whole examination of strategies of managing self-steering networks. It is worth recalling the older tradition of writings about institutional interdependence – not for antiquarian reasons, but precisely because the process highlights what is novel and creative in contemporary accounts.

Nevertheless, there remains doubt as to whether we really do live in a new world of institutional interdependence, still less in the kind of segmented world without hierarchy that lies at the heart of much of the governance imagery. The most convincing case is probably that made by theorists of governance in the international system, such as Rosenau. It is convincing because it seems to link to two historical changes that can be verified by fairly robust evidence. The first is the kind of globalization – whatever the subtleties of debate about its meaning – that really did seem to be creating new sorts of spatial interdependence; and this new spatial interdependence really does seem to spill over into institutional interdependence. The second is that there also seems to be robust evidence that what it is conventional to call 'global civil society' has become much more densely populated and active in the last generation – and the institutions of global civil society have therefore joined states as significant actors in policy processes (Glasius *et al.* 2002).

But applying the imagery beyond the international system is more problematic, for two reasons. First, there do not seem to be any comparably convincing measures to those that paint change in the international system that would allow us to demonstrate that we are, indeed, living in a new world of domestically disaggregated state authority. That striking examples of networked governance exist is plainly true. But there are other trends that are hard to assimilate to the thesis that we are seeing a new kind of social order of mutual interdependence being created. A considerable body of evidence demonstrates the growing juridification of numerous social spheres, involving the invasion of hitherto autonomous worlds of self-regulation by command law (Moran 2007). States similarly continue, for the purposes of regulation, to colonize new social worlds, such as the regulation of human reproduction, or they tighten their command grip over worlds hitherto lightly regulated (health and safety, financial regulation).

The reference to financial regulation brings us to the second ground for scepticism. In the work of the most eloquent and creative governance theorists, such as Rhodes, governance is a solution to pathologies of command: it offers a more intelligent mode of steering than was possible in the old hierarchical world of government, and is therefore more attuned to a new world of institutional interdependence. Policy-making based on command has provided, and continues to provide, numerous examples of policy fiascos. But the exemplification of policy-making by light-touch steering in the last two decades, across the advanced industrial world, has been the light touch regulation of financial markets, in which the state stepped back from direct command. That system delivered us, after 2007, the greatest banking crisis for a century and the most severe global depression since at least the close of the Second World War. State command has often produced stupid policy outcomes; but the evidence is that theories of light-touch steering that claim to respond to new worlds of high institutional interdependence can be just as stupid. The rhetoric of light-touch control, at least in the Anglo-American world, was not, it is now plain, the product of some functional response to the complexities of control but, rather, of the way power in financial markets lay with interests within the markets. The financiers captured the regulatory system and dignified it with the label of 'light-touch steering' (see also Thompson and Ravenhill, in this volume).

What this suggests is that there might be more to policy-making in an interdependent world than spatial and institutional interdependence. There might be something going on in the very substance of policy; and this brings us naturally to the third aspect of interdependence that informs this chapter.

Policy interdependence: specialization, tacit knowledge and catastrophic risk

Our discussion of spatial and institutional interdependence has established that interdependence is, in itself, nothing new, and this now familiar theme can be repeated in introducing policy interdependence. The idea that policy choices in conventionally defined different domains are interdependent is a truism – and therefore true. Think again of the example given at the start of this chapter: the way the conventional language of budgetary choices pictures decisions to spend on one programme as imposing opportunity costs that restrict freedom to spend on other programmes. If the idea of the interdependence of policy domains is to have purchase, therefore, we have to demonstrate – as we sought to do in the spatial and institutional spheres – that there is something novel at work.

There are, indeed, three credible possibilities – and they are a mix of opportunities and threats. First, new technologies of policy formulation, hard and soft, might allow the imposition of common patterns of control on the policy process. The 'interdependence' here is created by common traits in different domains and our novel understanding of those common traits. Second, it might be that some policies are now so uniquely complex that they cannot be dealt with by action within their own domains, but require the coordinated mobilization of actors and resources across a range of conventionally separated policy spheres. The 'interdependence' here lies partly in a growing perception of the existence of what it has become fashionable among some policy elites to call 'wicked' problems, and partly in the assertion that there does, indeed, exist in the policy world a new category of these problems (for the classic formulation of wickedness dilemmas, see Rittel and Webber 1973; see also Rein 2006). A third credible possibility is that there now exist cases of what might be called 'catastrophic interdependence': a category of policy problems that have consequences so vast and disastrous that they spill over into all areas of human life, and therefore demand comprehensive, coordinated solutions from the state.

One of the striking features of these three senses of interdependence, we shall discover, is that they suggest very different practical solutions.

The notion that interdependence consists in the capacity to subject different policy domains to similar technologies of control is itself not novel: it lies at the root of policy science as a generic sub-discipline linked to the managerial sciences more widely. Indeed, as the 'governmentality' school reminds us, it has even deeper roots – in strategies of measurement and control that were inscribed in the Enlightenment project (Rose 1990, 1999). It is hardly contentious that a variety of well established soft technologies – the most obvious being those developed in management accounting – do, indeed, provide techniques that are patently transferable across different national jurisdictions and different policy domains.

But all this has been given a powerful impetus by two developments, one ideological and the other technological. Scott (1998) shows how an ideology of high modernism now pictures government, irrespective of policy domain, as an opportunity to employ hard and soft technologies of measurement, legibility to the centre, and control in the pursuit of common goals, such as organizational efficiency measured by some common indicators. The power of this ideology lies partly in the way it has its roots in cultural settings wider than those of government itself: in the belief in measurement, classification and standardization in the wider society. The high modernist project encompasses domains of culture (such as architecture and town planning) as well as policy. In Scott's account, the variant examined is authoritarian in character, but high modernism describes exactly the ambitions and technologies associated with the New Public Management (NPM) that spread widely across the advanced capitalist world in the closing two decades of the twentieth century. The core of the new NPM lies in the conviction that there exist technologies of measurement and control that can be used to override the tacit, specialized knowledge of experts and specialists in particular domains (such as education or health) in the pursuit of centrally prescribed standards and goals, whose attainment can, in turn, be gauged by centrally prescribed, standardized performance indicators. This ideological innovation has been supported by innovations in hard technology, notably by the development of unprecedented computing power, which has seemed to overcome historically important restrictions on the ability of policy elites to engage in comprehensive surveillance and analysis of data.

That these high modernist ambitions exist, and that they have been powerfully reinforced in recent decades, can hardly be denied. We might note in passing that they push the policy process in a very different direction from the 'post-modernist' implications of much of the governance school discussed in the previous section. Not only are we looking here at an ideological novelty; we are also, as Dunleavy and his colleagues remind us, looking at the rise of important economic interests in the IT sector that lobby powerfully for this vision of comprehensive control across policy domains using the most advanced technology (Dunleavy *et al.* 2007).

Whether these generic technologies of control can be made to work successfully is, to put it mildly, a contentious matter. Scott's classic is an extended argument for the supremacy of tacit knowledge: for the superiority of 'local', idiosyncratic knowledge of particular cultural domains and particular policy domains. In the effort to gather all policy under a single head, he traces some of the greatest recent policy disasters. But even beyond the special circumstances of authoritarian high modernism, the attempt to gather separate domains under a single technology of control has had, at best, mixed results. The technologies of the NPM are subject to well-known pathologies: evasion, circumvention, perversity, and unintended consequences. And the work of Dunleavy and of Margetts demonstrates that one of the commonest results of attempts to mobilize high technology in the pursuit of modernist control ambitions is, often, expensive policy fiasco (Dunleavy 1995; Margetts 1999).

This reference to fiasco links us to the second sense of policy interdependence: that some policy problems are problems precisely because they spill across conventionally separated domains, and that the solution to these problems requires the recognition of this fact. If we do not recognize this kind of interdependence, then we face disaster. In numerous reports of policy catastrophes there is a common trope: that disaster was foreseeable and avoidable, but was not avoided because different institutional components failed to cooperate and was not foreseen because the evidence of impending catastrophe was not shared and assembled between different parts of the policy machine. Famously, United States military authorities 'knew' that a Japanese attack on Pearl Harbor was imminent, but could not assemble this knowledge into a single institutional location capable of organizing defensive action.

As the reference to Pearl Harbor suggests, the failure to acknowledge this kind of interdependence is hardly new: it is part of what Seidman calls a traditional search for the 'philosopher's stone' of coordination (Seidman 1979: 190). But as the proliferation of task forces, policy problem 'czars' and specialized regulatory agencies suggests, there is indeed a novel sensitivity to the problem. And this sensitivity has good grounds. The growth both of big government and of the policy specialisms that studied big government was accompanied by the organization of state machines into bureaucratically organized empires that ruled policy domains; academic policy specialisms 'shadowed' these empires, developing cadres of policy 'wonks' who, in part, lived off the research commissioned by them. The perception that many policy problems exist because of the interdependence of different social spheres – that, for example, penal policy or health policy cannot be addressed in the vocabulary of these domains alone – is what lies behind the growing sensitivity to the existence of 'wicked' problems. But this sensitivity is best conceived not as a response to the novelty of the problems but, rather, as an enforced rediscovery of an older tradition in policy action and policy analysis. The case of health illustrates this. In the nineteenth century, the policy field of 'public health' produced huge improvements in the health conditions of populations by a cross-disciplinary and cross-agency mix of innovations in hard and soft technologies: discoveries in the epidemiology of some infectious diseases, education of populations in elementary rules of hygiene, engineering advances in the purification of water supply, and the application of the latest construction technologies to gather and store clean water in reservoirs and to pipe it to households. That complex cross-disciplinary mix was submerged in health policy in the twentieth century by a culture that, impressed by advances in curative medicine, elevated a scientific, laboratory based model of medical care over this older tradition (Moran 1999). The realization that modern pandemics such as AIDS require more than laboratory medicine to combat them successfully involves precisely a rediscovery of the nineteenth-century lessons from the theory and practice of public health policy.

Reference to the AIDS pandemic brings us naturally to the third possible sense of policy interdependence: to the claim that there is a category of policy problem the outcomes of which are so comprehensively catastrophic that they spill across all policy domains. The problem creates interdependence because it menaces the whole of human life. The theoretical identification of this class of problem is best associated with a variety of risk society theorists; in the world of policy practice the two commonest candidates are the threat from safety failures in nuclear power generation and the threat of global climate change. Risk theory is poised uncertainly between perception and real threat. In some accounts, such as that offered by Giddens, the emphasis is on the way a sceptical, reflexive culture of modernity produces a heightened sensitivity to the possibility of catastrophic risk, and the way this creates demands on policy elites to recognize the interdependent character of these risks (Giddens 1990, 1999). In other accounts, of which the most popular has been produced by Beck, practical problems – most obviously the safety risks of nuclear power generation – are invoked as evidence that we do, indeed, live in a society where advanced technologies menace the whole of human life as never before (Beck 1992). Risk is objectively collective – and therefore interdependent.

That such catastrophic threats exist cannot be denied; that is the lesson of the long struggle to establish the reality of the threat of global climate change. That particular threat is of special relevance to this chapter, because it is obvious that it poses supremely difficult problems of collection action and, therefore, also involves the issues of spatial and institutional interdependence discussed earlier. But the solutions on offer demonstrate something that will be examined more closely in the next section: that the solution to this kind of catastrophic problem has implications for the ways in which we can think of the practical implications of interdependence. The point is illustrated by reflecting on two very different sets of solutions. Some 'deep green' solutions involve the rejection of the social apparatus and technologies of advanced industrialism, and the creation (or recreation) of small-scale economic organization in which tacit knowledge once again triumphs. At the other end of the spectrum, some official solutions show a confidence in the capacity of high modernism to solve the problem: they involve the creation of institutions – such as those designed for carbon trading – that can function at a global level; and they involve the mobilization of the highest hard technology – for instance, in ambitious barrage schemes and wind farms – to supplant the old carbon-creating technologies.

Interdependence, statecraft and rhetoric

Some of the conclusions to be drawn from this discussion of policy-making in an interdependent world are obvious, some less so. It is plainly the case that one proposition with which we began – that there are many faces of interdependence – is true, even if it is also the case that they interact with each other. It is also plainly true that the social fact of interdependence is not at all new. The act of governing – and the making of policy that governing entails – arises from the very existence of an interdependent world. It is also striking that invocations of the novelty of interdependence are nothing new, and one of the fascinating features of these invocations is that they illustrate how, in the practice of statecraft, such invocations have, at different periods, led to very different policy conclusions. A couple of examples from the preceding discussion will make the point. In the great governing crises of the 1970s that succeeded the end of the long boom, both the academic study of policy-making and practical debate about policy options came to be dominated by a language that had its origins in the recognition of the interdependence created by organized social complexity. That led academically to theories of 'overloaded government', and practically to a rhetoric that pictured some tasks

– such as macroeconomic management in the pursuit of full employment – as too difficult for democratic governments to attempt. Thus, the language of an interdependent world was used to legitimize a statecraft that withdrew government from a range of hitherto accepted social and economic responsibilities. Now consider the very different implications of interdependence conveyed by what we described as the high modernist image of policy-making – an image that has embedded itself in the wider culture, in the ambitions of policy-makers and in parts of the academic literature. This version of interdependence has two key features: it pictures the responsibilities of government as involving the addressing of 'wicked' problems that can only be solved by the coordinated use of the most advanced hard and soft technologies available to the state; and it pictures the policy process itself as interdependent – hence, the same technologies of control can be applied to, and can override the tacit knowledge present in, different substantive policy domains. This language of interdependence has created a statecraft very different from the statecraft of withdrawal: it has drawn policy-makers into hugely ambitious schemes aimed at the wholesale transformation of the social and the natural world.

These examples show how the rhetoric of interdependence can suggest policy strategies that are virtually polar opposites. But some invocations of interdependence are much more ambiguous – or, perhaps more accurately, contradictory. The best example is provided by the most commonly invoked aspect of contemporary spatial interdependence: that allegedly created by new waves of economic globalization. I have tried to argue that part of the novel power of this aspect of interdependence is that, whatever the debates that still divide students of the global economy, it really does connect to economic and social changes that have occurred in the last half century, and that the scale of these changes has been convincingly demonstrated by scholars such as Scholte. It has been possible to create globalization as a powerful discursive construct – as a resource of statecraft – precisely because, when policy-makers invoke the importance of interconnectedness in a globalizing economy, they are not constructing fictions. The rhetoric they use is powerful because it links to observable developments in social reality. But precisely because it is rhetoric – the form of discursive construction wherein lies the art of the democratic politician – it can lead in very different directions. For instance, it can be invoked to try to persuade labour market actors to submit to the dictates of spatially unrestricted markets in labour. After the great financial crisis of 2007–09 it was, by contrast, used by some democratic politicians to try to persuade financial market actors that they needed to submit to new regimes of regulation and control. And, even in the specific field of labour market policies, it could simultaneously legitimize state withdrawal from market regulation, or Scandinavian-style active labour market policies designed to equip a national economy with a labour force suitably skilled and flexible to allow the economy to occupy a lucrative niche in the global division of labour.

It is this serpentine, ambiguous quality that gives to the idea of interdependence its great power – and its weakness. For at least a generation, the idea that we live in an interdependent world has been second nature to those responsible for the making and implementation of policy. As a kind of thought experiment, try imagining a policy-maker who denied outright the 'fact' of interdependence. But it is the very fact that it is second nature that is also a source of weakness. Policy-makers 'know' they live in an interdependent world. But this is merely the background music to the everyday world of policy, which consists in a series of immediate problems – some minor, some catastrophic – that have to be addressed. It is here that the limits of interdependence as an analytic concept become relevant. Indeed, in the academic literature it is striking how easy it is to accommodate the language of interdependence to very different analytical views of the nature of the policy process. Interdependence is meat and drink to the post-modernist governance theorists, with their view of a fragmented, disaggregated world linked by complex networks of interdependence that have to be managed by techniques that disavow the old hierarchical, coercive world of the traditional state. But interdependence is also meat and drink to those who inhabit the world of high modernism: who see a world of huge policy problems, and potential disasters that can only be solved by the universal application of similar control technologies across different policy spheres, and which demand, above all, the discovery of the philosopher's stone of institutional coordination. A language that so comfortably accommodates very different academic orthodoxies, and very different policy preferences, is manifestly useful: it helps provide the vocabulary for both academic debate and arguments about the strategies of statecraft. But it is also manifestly of limited use, at present, in telling us something about the choices we need to make in solving real-world policy problems.

How might it be made more useful? There are surely three things we should do. First, we should recognize that interdependence has different functions in policy advocacy and policy analysis. For the policy-maker, the term is primarily useful as a rhetorical device. It is an undifferentiated concept that can be used promiscuously in the arts of persuasion. It is pointless to complain about this; digesting complex concepts and turning them into something simpler, with rhetorical power, is part of the art of the policy advocate, especially of the democratic politician as policy advocate. Second, we should recognize that, when we use the term in policy analysis, we are commonly talking about very different things – or, at least, as I tried to show in these pages, about a single concept with a number of different dimensions. Once we do that, then there is no option but to struggle with messy empirical complexity: interdependence manifests itself in different ways and to different degrees, whether we are speaking of space, institutions or policy content. The great temptation to which many policy-makers and some policy scholars succumb is that of epochalism: the temptation to believe that the existence of new patterns and new problems has landed us in a completely novel world – of globalism, or of network governance, for example. To do that, as I have tried to show, is simultaneously to inflate and to diminish the understandings of our present problems that we can derive from the existing literature. It is to inflate it precisely because it exaggerates novelty; but it diminishes it because – as is well illustrated by the governance literature – it neglects the degree to which scholars have taken some traditional problems of interdependence and analyzed them in newly creative ways.

The third task is the most difficult of all. Having distanced ourselves from the necessarily simplistic rhetoric of interdependence used in the world of policy advocacy, we need to reconnect to that world, and to feed it into it our heightened sense of complexity and contingency. But that is only to restate the traditional job of the policy analyst: to speak truth to power, especially when the truth cannot be communicated in a few sound bites. The problem of such communication, with decision-makers and the wider public, is one of the themes of Stoker's chapter, which follows.

Chapter 2

The Rise of Political Disenchantment

GERRY STOKER

It is interesting that the study of politics has, at its heart, a subject matter that many of our fellow citizens assert they despise. Sociologists do not face large numbers of people claiming to hate society. Economists might find substantial numbers objecting to global capitalism, but are unlikely to find many who say they dislike the basic mechanisms of economics: 'I wouldn't touch supply and demand with a barge pole' is not a common refrain. Yet, political scientists quite regularly come across citizens who tell them they do not like the practice of politics and are very keen to steer clear of it. The big question in political science, as far as I am concerned, is why so many of our fellow citizens appear to be intensely disenchanted with political practice today. The related question is how the nature of our subject matter should influence the way we study it. Politics is, to a substantial degree, an intentional human creation of rules, institutions and symbols – and that dynamic is one in which we, as a profession, shape whether we recognize it or not. Politics is a human construction – an activity created for a purpose – which might, in part, explain its vulnerability to unease about its operation, given the common human experience of failings and unintended consequences from such activities. Its investigation requires a greater appreciation of the 'science of the artificial', the design of human activities, than is generally afforded by political scientists.

The leading role in understanding politics is taken by the profession of political science. But my argument is that our profession is failing in its attempts to grapple with the emergence of political disenchantment. Political scientists have established and addressed the problem of disenchantment – albeit, in the latter case, at a high level of generality. The profession is also adept at offering trenchant critiques of the various efforts of the political establishment to tackle the problem of political disenchantment. What it is not good at is offering solutions. It is for these reasons that I hold that disenchantment with politics is the defining problem facing political science since it goes to the heart not only of the subject matter of our discipline, but also captures the limitations in the way the discipline has developed.

The argument is developed, first, by reflecting on and exploring the significance of anti-politics and its connection to our growing interdependence. We move on to use a historical perspective drawing on the pioneering work of Almond and Verba (1963) in *The Civic Culture* to identify the core features of dimensions of the rise of anti-politics in Great Britain. What is revealed is that the issue is less about a loss of trust in politicians and more about a loss of faith by citizens – in particular, those with lower socio-economic status – in their capacity to influence the political system and in its capacity to respond. There follows a review of the way that political scientists have attempted to grapple with the issue of political disenchantment. What emerges is a profession that offers some powerful insights, but has little understanding of its own role in the emergence of anti-politics and offers little in terms of solutions. The final section of the chapter attempts to address these problems by arguing for the emergence of a new 'science of the artificial' applied to the study of politics. We need to develop a 'design science' arm to our discipline that could explore the creation and maintenance of an effective political system. This science of the artificial would offer a more engineering perspective focused on a better understanding of how to achieve certain goals, where theoretical and empirical investigation link to the tasks at hand.

Reflecting on the rise of anti-politics

Popular political culture in many democracies is deeply 'anti' both politics and politicians (see Stoker 2006, for a review of the evidence from around the world). New phrases have entered the lexicon in recent decades to capture the unsavoury character of politics, with 'sleaze', 'spin' and the faintly exotic 'economic with *l'actualité*' joining the more established 'pork barrel politics', 'gerrymandering' and 'graft'. Events play around this central feature of democracies; some seen as positive, some as negative. So, the election of President Obama in the United States in November 2008 is viewed as a blow for a new type of more open and responsive politics. The row from May 2009 onwards in the United Kingdom over the way that MPs had used and abused the House of

Commons expenses and allowances regime (Kelso 2009) is viewed as confirming – and, indeed, heightening – the sense of anti-politics in that country.

The problem that so many of us and our fellow citizens have with politics might be based, to some degree, in the way that politics is practised – but it also reflects a wider set of social and economic developments connected to rise of an interdependent world. Mass democracy played out in the context of universal adult franchise, and framed by extensive and intrusive mass media and high-speed communication, is a relatively recent phenomenon and one where social actors are in the foothills of understanding their changing roles. We are struggling to come to terms with politics in the context of a globalized and rapidly changing world. Yet, whether your concern is with building communities, global warming or economic competiveness in response to changed conditions, there can be little doubt about the importance of getting the politics right if solutions are to be found and implemented.

We live in a more interdependent world, as Hay argues in the Introduction to this book, and that demands an inter-disciplinary response from the social sciences and beyond. The emerging crisis in politics should concern many disciplines and researchers that have a domestic, regional or global focus. The question of the standing of politics is relevant to the agendas of both theoretically and empirically oriented students of politics and international relations. It is also relevant to those from other disciplines.

Why should the disenchantment of citizens with politics be a matter of concern? One response to that question that I would share with many is that democracy is impossible without politics and that, without democracy, we would lose a range of valued outcomes. These outcomes include a set of checks and balances in the governance of our societies that helps to protect our welfare, a right to be engaged in decisions that affect us and the collective experience of attempting to solve problems with our fellow citizens. Democracy, at a minimum, requires an exchange of views between citizens, processes for holding public leaders to account and a dynamic that leads to the reconciliation of interests. These processes of collective decision-making have politics at their heart. Although all societies, for all time, will fall short of democratic ideals, those societies that find themselves so disappointed by politics and unable to reconcile themselves to its foibles and quirks will lose all prospect of striving towards democratic ideals. Democracy needs politics.

But the connection between democracy and politics goes deeper than has so far been argued. Politics is a precursor to democracy, since its existence reflects a spread of power sufficient to command the reconciliation of a wide range of interests. As Crick (2000: 30–1) comments, politics 'is simply the activity by which government is made possible when differing interests in an area to be governed grow powerful enough to need to be conciliated'. The alternative to politics is the resolution of conflicts of interest through violence or coercion. As interests grow more powerful so the need for politics grows, given the scale of repression that would be required to achieve order through non-political means. Moreover, politics is also a precursor to democracy because it is premised on the assumption than humans can, through their collective action, meet challenges and find solutions to intractable problems. Without that hope embodied in politics, we would be reduced to rely on fate or God's will (Gamble 2000). So, contrary to the view that our democratic ideals have been undermined by the grubby practice of politics, my view is that the emergence of the prospect for politics provides the only base for the development of democratic practices at a societal level, since those practices involve the triumph of non-violent means over coercion and human capability over fate.

The above arguments might convince us as citizens but might not command our attention as political scientists or social scientists. Yet, the crisis in politics should be a focus for us because it reflects a wider set of social and economic developments connected to the rise of an interdependent world. In addition, we are struggling to come to terms with politics in the context of a globalized and rapidly changing world. Equally, whether your concern is with building communities, global warming or economic competiveness in response to changed conditions, there can be little doubt about the importance of getting the politics right if solutions are to be found and implemented.

You might still doubt my claim that disenchantment with politics is the big political issue for mature and new democracies. Perhaps, you might argue that citizens have long been sceptical about politics, and so there is nothing new about the current signs of disenchantment. I think that this is a fair challenge and one that would require an extensive research project beyond those that have already been conducted that hint at widespread current disaffection (again, see Stoker (2006), for a review). In order to answer the question of whether we have entered into a qualitatively different era of disenchantment with politics, we need to introduce some historical perspective. That requires some narrowing of focus.

The decline in Britain's civic culture

In this chapter, my empirical focus is on Great Britain. There are good pragmatic reasons for this choice, as I will outline later. But a focus on Britain is particularly helpful here, in order to identify broader trends because – as the row over Parliamentary expenses, referred to earlier, indicates – there is perhaps evidence to suggest that Britain might, sadly, be a world leader in terms of the extent of the current crisis of confidence in the political class and political practice. It might be reasonable to fear that trends evident in Britain could well prove contagious. In short, I want to present Britain as a case of decline in citizen confidence in politics that is particularly graphic and substantial. The pragmatic element in the choice is that I have the evidence at hand to back up that claim, or at least to support a claim that a decline of some import has occurred in the standing of politics in Britain.

The opportunity for historical comparison is afforded in Great Britain by going back to Almond and Verba's (1963) study of the civic culture of five nations. The book, which became an instant classic, compared Great Britain with the US, Germany, Italy and Mexico. What I show is that, along two crucial dimensions – sense of empowerment to influence decisions and contentment with the political system, the positive assessment of British citizens has dropped markedly, even dramatically, when we compare the late 1950s to the early years of the twenty-first century.

Almond and Verba's (1963) book is well worth revisiting because it provides a more sophisticated analysis than memories of reading it years ago can recall. Above all, it is worth re-reading because it provides a clear picture of the political world of citizens in the 1950s, the decade the UK Political Studies Association was founded. So, it provides a benchmark against which to judge the progression of British political citizenship and the understanding of that progression provided by the political science community. Political culture constituted, for Almond and Verba, the broad orientation of citizens towards their political system and their sense of citizenship, measured by way of attitudinal and behavioural data collected by the first academically driven opinion survey conducted in Great Britain in 1959. Judging by the evidence provided by Almond and Verba, there was a widespread pride in the political system and a strong sense of civic competence among many citizens. This 'feel good' factor about our governance arrangements was widely shared among academic commentators of the time.

Civic culture findings

What famously emerged in the study is a portrayal of a political Britain at ease with itself: citizens deferential and respectful of their leaders, but confident of their role and capacities and the responsiveness of government. Almond and Verba (1963: 455) comment about politics in Great Britain:

> The participant role is highly developed. Exposure to politics, interest, involvement, and a sense of competence are relatively high. There are norms supporting political activity, as well as emotional involvement in elections and system affect. And attachment to the system is a balanced one: there is general system pride as well as satisfaction with specific governmental performance.

British citizens were more deferential than their American counterparts, but this aspect of their culture is balanced by an active and participative orientation towards politics: a blend of activity and passivity that, according to Almond and Verba, allows a civic culture to develop.

Almond and Verba's positive findings about the British political system were not considered surprising but, rather, as a confirmation of what was already the common sense of the age among British political scientists. The book 'produced little reaction as a study of Britain largely because it told most British academics little that they did not think that they knew' (Kavanagh 1980: 127). Some of the two hundred or so British political scientists of that era were perhaps a little bemused by the behavioural research methods of Almond and Verba, but they recognized and agreed with the depiction of the British political culture. The Americans, with their new-fangled techniques, provided quantitative evidence for their own views about the virtues of our system. As Kavanagh (1980: 127) goes on to point out, such was the acceptance of the data and the associated interpretation that the 'the findings of the 1959 survey were still being cited ten years later as though the situation had hardly changed'.

The reception of the civic culture thesis began to change, however, in the 1970s. There were criticisms from academics about the theories underlying the work, in that they sustained a very elitist understanding of democratic practice and a rather individualistic understanding of culture. Almond and Verba gave a fair hearing to many of the theoretical criticisms in their edited book *The Civic Culture Revisited* (Almond and Verba 1980), as well as revising and refining their own original argument. In the same volume, Kavanagh (1980) captured the evidence of a changing mood among British citizens about their political system. The shift away from a supportive civic culture was not complete, but there were clear signs of decay and growing disenchantment with the political system. As Kavanagh notes, after only two decades you might not expect to see a large-scale shift in culture. But a further three decades on, from our vantage point, it is possible to conclude that several key features of the civic world described by Almond and Verba have gone.

Challenges in making comparisons

There are a number of challenges involved in making a comparison between the position at the beginning of the twenty-first century and that of the 1950s. Almond and Verba's (1963) survey covered only Great Britain, rather than the United Kingdom. It was based on a relatively small sample of 963 respondents and it used questions that, given the innovative nature of the work, were far from tried and tested. *The Civic Culture* relied on face-to-face interviews for its survey. Techniques today, in addition, involve surveys conducted over the telephone or through using the Internet. The survey instruments of the first decade of the twenty-first century are generally rather more sophisticated affairs, and there appears to have been a number of substantial problems with the Almond and Verba survey in Britain, including the low completion rate and sample size (Kavanagh 1980: 131–2). The former might have biased results towards the politically literate, and the latter makes analysis within the sample very problematic. Moreover, for the purposes of making comparisons, rarely do you find exactly the same question wording replicated in later surveys to those used by Almond and Verba. There are often differences between surveys in terms of their sampling and framing. Finally, comparing findings from two points in time is not always a reliable way of establishing a trend, since there might be something odd about individual survey findings.

Although there are challenges involved, political scientists and other researchers in Britain have produced enough data and analysis to make a comparison between the world of the 1950s and the world of the 2000s relatively deliverable. Indeed, some explicit comparisons are drawn out in Pattie *et al.* (2004), who undertook a large-scale citizen survey in 2000/01 as part of the Economic and Social Research Council's Participation Programme, and in a working paper produced by my former Manchester colleague Peter John (2008). As a further source and base for comparison, I will use the series of surveys that launched in

2004 – undertaken by the Hansard Society and various partners, and marked under the title *Audit of Political Engagement*. The most recent produced for the Hansard in 2008 relied on a survey of just over 1000 respondents, based on face-to-face interviews, and it drew its sample from Great Britain rather than the United Kingdom (Hansard Society 2008). I will also call on the Citizenship Surveys undertaken since 2001 at regular intervals, funded first by the Home Office and then by the Department for Communities and Local Government (see Cabinet Office (various), for details on these surveys).

A pattern of change

So, what broadly is the pattern of change that you find in Britain? Although it is difficult to be certain, I would argue that, in that British citizens are not now less trusting of politicians or less informed or interested about politics, it is rather that we have lost our confidence in our capacities to influence decisions and in the capacity of the system to respond. British citizens have less confidence in their ability to influence decisions, less pride in the political system, and less belief in the fairness and responsiveness of government.

The first thing to establish in the analysis of civic culture is to point out that Almond and Verba did not find a 'perfect' world of politically engaged, knowledgeable and interested citizens. Here are some key findings from their 1959 survey (see Almond and Verba 1963: 89, 96, 116, 263):

- 1 in 3 claim 'to never follow' accounts of political and governmental affairs
- 2 in 10 can name no party leader or any government ministry
- 3 in 10 'never' talk about politics with friends and acquaintances
- only 1 in 50 claim civic-political activities as a preferred leisure activity
- and, finally, a finding from the survey not reported by Almond and Verba is that 8 in 10 are doubtful of the promises made by candidates in elections. (Kavanagh 1980: 145, fn. 58)

It would be difficult to claim, in the light of these findings, that British citizens were political sophisticates in the 1950s. Knowledge of and interest in politics is arguably at about the same levels as at the beginning of the twenty-first century. The 2008 Audit of Political Engagement (Hansard Society 2008: 13) found about half the population claiming an interest in politics, with 2 in 10 claiming no interest at all. The findings on these issues have remained relatively consistent since the first Audit published in 2004. Again, on issues of knowledge, about half the population in the 2008 Audit claimed that they knew nothing at all or not much about politics and here, too, the findings are fairly consistent stretching back to 2004 (Hansard Society 2008: 14). The British were, and remain, a society where a reasonable proportion could claim to be interested and knowledgeable about politics, but with a large section unable to make that claim. The issue is not, then, about citizens being more knowledgeable or sophisticated in the past. The capacity to feel good about having a well-functioning polity that is considered legitimate by most is not driven by having a sophisticated understanding of politics – in the case of British citizens, at least.

In Britain, it appears that we were already fairly cynical about politicians in the 1950s. The unreported finding, from *The Civic Culture*, expressing citizens' doubts about the promises of politicians indicates a level of scepticism, if not cynicism, about politicians in the 1950s that perhaps was not fully captured by Almond and Verba. By the early 1970s, Kavanagh (1980:145–7) was able to offer findings that hint further at lack of trust in politicians. For example, in one survey 58 per cent agreed with the view that 'people become MPs for their own gain and ambition' and, in another survey, 60 per cent held the view that people involved in politics tell the truth only some of the time. In the twenty-first century, lack of trust in politicians is a strong *leitmotif*. Politicians regularly rank among the lowest occupational groups in terms of the extent to which they are trusted (Pattie *et al.* 2004: 37). A survey (Ipsos/MORI 2009), undertaken for the BBC at the height of scandal over Parliamentary expenses in May 2009, found that the proportion of the population that lacked trust in MPs, in general, to tell the truth had risen from 67 per cent in 2004 to 76 per cent in 2009 – a finding that indicates that the scandal had an effect. But the British had not moved from a high trust to a low trust position. They had not lost trust in national politicians but, rather, had never had it, at least as far back as the 1970s, and there are strong indications that a majority of citizens did not trust national politicians in the 1950s.

The major shifts, when comparing the 1950s with fifty-plus years later, come not over the knowledge of citizens or their trust in politicians, but in their sense that they can influence decisions and that the political system is responsive to them and well-functioning. Almond and Verba (1963: 185) found, in 1959, high levels of believe among British citizens that they could influence politics: 8 in 10 claimed they could do something about an unjust local regulation and 6 in 10 made the same claim about an unjust national regulation. In 2007, only two fifths (38 per cent) of respondents to the Citizenship Survey (Communities and Local Government 2007) felt they could influence decisions in their local area and one fifth (20 per cent) of people felt they could influence decisions affecting Great Britain. Even allowing for some difference in wording, it would appear that in just under fifty years we have moved to a position where now only a minority, rather than a majority, of citizens holds that they can influence politics.

In 1959, nearly half the British survey Almond and Verba (1963: 102) spontaneously mentioned the system of government and political institutions as a matter of pride. As Pattie *et al.* (2004: 45) put it: 'it is very doubtful whether a similar response would be obtained if the same question were repeated in Britain today'. In the 2008, the Audit of Political Engagement (Hansard Society 2008: 22) found only 2 per cent of citizens who felt that the present system of governing Britain works extremely well and could not be improved. Two thirds were of the opinion that the system could be improved 'quite a lot' or 'a great deal'. In the wake of the expenses scandal, Ipsos/MORI (2009) found that three quarters were of the opinion that the system of government could be improved. Almond and Verba (1963: 108–9) found that 8 in 10 expected to be treated equally by government bureaucracy if they raised an issue, and 6 in 10 felt that governmental bureaucracy would give their point of view serious consideration. Pattie *et al.* (2004: 44–5), in their survey at the beginning of the twenty-first century, found under 3 in 10 able to agree with the statement that 'government generally treats people like me fairly'. They conclude: 'it would seem that a very significant decline in public confidence in government has occurred' (Pattie *et al.* 2004: 44). In the 1950s, British citizens felt that that they had a responsive and functioning political system, but that sense that they were empowered within a well-functioning political system has gone.

There is evidence of not only a shift in attitudes, but also of major changes in behaviour. Most obviously, there has been a decline in turnout in national elections, as Table 2.1 shows. By grouping elections, the impact of the salience of issues or the closeness of the election can be ironed out to a degree, and still there remains a substantial increase in those not voting (Dorling *et al.* 2008). In the UK, 9 per cent of all registered electors were party members in 1964 but, by 1992, it was barely 2 per cent, and has remained at a similar low level into the twenty-first century (Webb *et al.* 2002). Table 2.2 suggests that the pattern of change

Table 2.1   *Postwar UK elections and the proportion of non-voters*

Election years	Not voting (%)
1945, 1950, 1951	20.0
1955, 1959, 1964	22.4
1966, 1970, 1974 February	24.4
1974 October, 1979, 1983	26.4
1987, 1992	23.2
1997, 2001, 2005	36.3

Source: Adapted from Dorling *et al.* (2008): 26.

Table 2.2   *Organizational membership, 1959 and 2001*

Year	Percentage with 1 membership	Percentage with 2 + memberships
1959	31	17
2001	17	25

Source: Adapted from Pattie *et al.* (2004: 102).

in organisational memberships related to civic life would appear to be more complex. Comparing 1959, using *The Civic Culture* data, other surveys and their 2001 Citizen Audit, Pattie *et al.* (2004: 102) conclude: 'fewer people are now joining just a single group but there is an upward trend in the number of people belonging to two or more groups'. British citizens are less inclined to join a political party but they are more inclined to engage with a wide range of single issue organizations. In both time periods, it would appear that organizational memberships are reported by only half the population.

A particular pattern of decline in our civic culture has been established by comparing the findings of Almond and Verba's work with that of more recent studies by UK political scientists. There is a further feature of the portrait of change that is worth bringing out: the shift in the pattern of social divides in that culture. Again, difficulties in the way that Almond and Verba conducted their survey limit the certainty that surrounds what can be argued, but it would appear that, compared with 1959, there are now fewer gender differentials but greater differentials between the orientation to politics of professional and managerial sectors, and those with unskilled occupations or vulnerable to unemployment.

Almond and Verba (1963: 388) found that 'men showed higher frequencies and higher intensities than women in practically all the indices of political orientation and activity that we employed'. The 2008 *Audit of Political Engagement* (Hansard Society 2008: 14) found that, whilst women were less likely than men to say they were interested in politics (58 per cent against 45 per cent), on other measures women were just as likely as men to engage, as Table 2.3 shows. Almond and Verba (1963) found some class divides in the sense of civic competence and activism. For example, they found that 9 in 10 professionals felt they could do something about an unjust local regulation, whilst only 7 in 10 of the unskilled were of the same view. In general, across a range of tests of participation and civic competence provided by Almond and Verba, lower-status British groups scored higher than equivalent groups in other nations, including the US. As Kavanagh (1980: 135) explains: 'In Britain such long-established organizations as trade unions, cooperative societies, and the Labour Party have made explicit appeals to the working class and mobilized them into comparatively high levels of political activity.' The evidence presented in Table 2.4, from the 2008 *Audit of Political Engagement*, suggests that the positive effect of these organizations in closing class differences in political participation might be on the wane. In 2007, citizens from professional and managerial social groups were twice as likely as those from unskilled groups to vote, donate to a party or campaign, and four times more likely to have engaged in three or more political activities.

There are other factors in the social divisions that characterize engagement today. Young people are generally less likely to want to engage in formal politics, although it is difficult to tell from Almond and Verba's

Table 2.3   *Gendered differences in political activism, 2007*

Activity	Male (%)	Female (%)
Propensity to vote	52	55
Contacted elected representative in the last two or three years	15	15
Donated to a political party	5	3
Donated to a charity or campaigning organization	39	36
Engaged in three or more political activities in the last two or three years	11	13

Source: Developed from data in Hansard Society (2008).

Table 2.4 *Class differences in political activism, 2007*

Activity	Social grades A and B (%)	Social grades D and E (%)
Propensity to vote	66	34
Contacted elected representative in the last two or three years	16	10
Donated to a political party	7	2
Donated to a charity or campaigning organization	52	24
Engaged in three or more political activities in the last two or three years	21	5

Note: The social class definitions are as used by the Institute of Practitioners in Advertising. A and B social classes include those with professional and managerial jobs; D and E include semi-skilled and unskilled manual workers and those living at the lowest levels of subsistence.

Source: Developed from data in Hansard Society (2008).

work whether that is a change from the 1950s. A range of ethnic minorities that were hardly a factor in *The Civic Culture* are now a vital part of British society, and their engagement in politics also creates a complex pattern of difference.

For now, we can simply confirm that the picture of confident British citizens at ease with their democratic polity – which might have been slightly exaggerated in the account provided by Almond and Verba – is no more. The key attitude shifts are not in the levels of knowledge or the extent to which politicians are trusted. British citizens were not in some golden age of high knowledge and trust in the 1950s but they did, for whatever reason, believe they could influence political decision-making at the local and national level, and had pride in a political system that was seen as responsive and well-functioning. That sense of being able to influence decisions has declined dramatically, as has the sense that the system functions well. A majority of British citizens today are clear that the system is in need of major reform. That shift in perspective is reflected in shifts in behaviour. British citizens are voting less but are – at least, in rough terms – maintaining participation through interest groups. Where the disengagement from political activism is most palpable is among lower-status social groups. In the 1950s, our politics reflected gender divides; now it appears it is heading towards becoming a preserve of the professional and middle classes.

Explaining the rise of disenchantment

There has been a considerable amount of debate in the political science community about the factors that are driving the rise of political disenchantment. I have so far suggested that disenchantment with politics might reflect a sense of frustration because, in an interdependent world, politics has struggled to respond with a new effective practice. In this section, I want to build on these arguments to look in greater detail at the factors behind disenchantment, drawing on the established political science literature. Growing interdependence might provide a trigger to disenchantment, but we need to understand the proximate mechanisms. I propose to use the template provided by Parsons (2007), which distinguishes between structural, institutional, ideational and physiological explanations in political science. We will concentrate on the first three but later will take up the issue of physiological explanation. Having briefly outlined key academic positions, this section turns inwards and asks how far academic researchers are implicated in the rising tide of disenchantment with politics.

Structural explanations focus on the impact of the social context on behaviour. The key argument here is that we have shifted the balance in our politics from a partisan to a valence political world (Clarke *et al.* 2004, 2009; Denver 2005). Valence issues have grown in importance where societal ends are agreed, and the core political issue has become how to judge the relative competence of the parties and politicians to achieve the desired ends. Politics then became focused on the performance of the government and leaders, or what prospective opponents could offer. But this focus on performance, in turn, created a rather shallow form of political exchange in which the allocation of credit or blame in performance politics is at the heart of contemporary democracy. Given the high stakes and uncertainty involved, voters rely heavily on campaign cues and party leader images as guides to electoral choice. In the context of the contingencies of politics, citizens are invited to be spectators in a game of credit-taking and blame-avoidance that inevitably creates the cycles of short-term hope and long-term disappointment that characterize Britain's current political culture.

Institutional studies see institutions as shaping the paths down which we travel. According to my *Why Politics Matters* (Stoker 2006), political parties, lobby organizations and even protest movements have lost their role as mass membership institutions and have atrophied into organizations dominated by professional activists and reduced most citizens into passive recipients of messages or short-term calls for action.

As parties have lost membership, they have become reliant on professional campaigners and organizers, and operate in a way that treats citizens as passive political observers who just need to be mobilized at election times to back the party (Webb *et al.* 2002). Citizen lobby organizations – such as Friends of the Earth – have large scale passive memberships and they, too, rely on professional organizers and experts (Jordan and Maloney 1997). Members fund but the professional politicos in the lobby organizations decide on what to campaign. Citizens are a passive audience to be talked to about particular campaigns through the media, and occasionally galvanized to send in letters or cards of support or join a public demonstration based, often, on rather simplistic messages. Citizens are offered little in terms of depth of analysis or understanding of the issues at stake by these organizations. Even more radical protest organizations tend to be professionalized in the style of behaviour and their use of the media. The occasional engagement by a wider group of citizens in a protest 'event' or rally is in danger of being more a lifestyle statement than a serious engagement with a political debate (de Jong *et al.* 2005).

Hay's book on *Why We Hate Politics* (Hay 2007b) has at its core the logic of ideational explanation. Our political masters have shot themselves in the foot, he argues, by swallowing wholesale the economic analysis of politics, coated in a neo-liberal framing of the limits and failings of the state. The actions and moves of politicians are constantly interpreted by the media through a lens that emphasizes their instrumental, self-interested motivation. The mainstream media is, more than ever, for carrying political messages and generally supports a culture of cynicism. The blame game is conducted based on assumptions of instrumental rationality driving human action and, in particular, the practices of politics. The economic academic analysis of politics has infested the very practice of politics and has undermined its capacity to engage people in collective endeavour.

Structural, institutional and ideational explanations have been briefly summarized. In referring to the work of individual studies, it is clear that, in offering an over-arching explanation, authors tend to combine different elements. The three explanations reinforce one another and help to explain the pattern of change in British politics identified earlier. Citizens in Britain feel less confident in their ability to engage in politics because expressing partisan support for a set of ideas or an ideology is more straightforward than making a judgement about leaders and parties whose attributes and qualities are much more difficult to judge. The feeling that someone in the system was on your side has given way to a sense that they are all the same. The institutional professionalization of politics has reinforced that sense of politics is something done by others, not by ordinary citizens. The spread of neo-liberal ideas has helped to confirm to many citizens that involvement in the public sphere is no place for them and no place to expect to see the civic virtues of the public interest acted out. Politics is for insiders, technocrats, experts and those that know how to play the system. Little wonder that it is seen as a place for activism by the professional and managerial classes, rather than all social groups.

The emphasis on the role of ideas in shaping politics provided by Hay reminds us that we, as a profession – the great purveyors of ideas about politics – might, in part, be implicated in the rise of anti-politics. In a review of, among other works, my book on *Why Politics Matters* and Hay's book on *Why We Hate Politics*, Meg Russell (2008: 656) comments: 'Academics must also help construct the solutions to get us out of the mess we are in. These books begin the process, but there is a great deal more to do.' Generally, her view is that neither of us had produced in our books much in the way of thought-through and potentially viable solutions. On the whole, I think she is right to argue that we are not good at constructing solutions; I would only add that is not only our contributions that are at fault in this respect, but also contributions from political science in general.

As professional political scientists, we can provide strong critiques of the solutions offered by governments. The UK's PSA, in 2007, published a series of essays (PSA 2007) that picked apart *The Governance of Britain* Green Paper published earlier that year (HM Government 2007). We can also offer solid and well-argued critiques of the analysis and solutions provided by independent inquiries into the state of our politics.

Bale *et al.* (2006) offer a biting critique of the Power Inquiry (2006) led by Helena Kennedy QC, arguing that it was naively populist in tone, ignored evidence presented by the few academic political scientists it consulted, and produced a mish-mash of reform plans that made little sense. More recently, a collection of essays edited by Hay and Stoker, and presented in the September 2009 issue of the journal *Representation*, offers an analysis of the challenges facing politics in Britain, and a critique of the misdirection and timidity of government-sponsored reform efforts – but it offers remarkably little in terms of solutions. Generally, UK political scientists, in common with those elsewhere, are comfortable in the role of outsiders describing, explaining and analyzing the rise of anti-politics and other phenomena. Jon Tonge's role as Chair of Youth Citizenship Commission is a rare exception to this rule (Tonge 2009).

Political scientists do not do politics, they seek to understand it. I do not propose that we abandon that distinction entirely, but I do think we should consider recognizing whether or not there is a blurring at the boundaries. We might well look to politicians, activists or our fellow citizens to dig us out of the hole in which we appear to be in terms of our failing civic culture, but they should not be expected to undertake the task on their own. Russell (2008: 656) argues that '[p]olitical actors do take their cue indirectly to some extent from how politics is understood by the academic community. Ironically ... the more research has told us about politics the more licence we have felt to despise the process ... This lays down a challenge for others in academia to do better and describe, even celebrate, politics as it really is.' We are implicated as foremost manufacturers of ideas about politics.

Russell has taken up this challenge in her own work. Her pamphlet (Russell 2005: 55–8) proposes a new political charter in which politicians are encouraged to be more honest about their mistakes. They would be encouraged to explain the hard choices that need to be made and the constraints faced by decision-makers. They would be asked to be more generous to their opponents, in not making exaggerated or unnecessary attacks, and to campaign responsibly and in a way that does not exploit citizens' distrust. She adds that media coverage and citizens' attitudes to politics will also need to change. But her optimism that such a new political culture could take hold needs to be tempered by a recognition that, when activists undertake their politics, they do so with a mix of motives from passion for a cause to self-interest (Walzer 2004). But, above all, they campaign, demonstrate, bargain, organize and do the mundane work of filling out envelopes and making phone calls in order to win. There are no neutrals in politics, and to ask activists to forgo potentially winning strategies might be asking for too much. Political opponents were never likely to give up the sleaze attacks where they can see advantage, or allow others to show fallibility without sanction.

The danger in the above paragraph is that I am falling back into the trap I am trying to avoid, critiquing others' solutions but offering none of my own. So, in a spirit of fairness, let me criticize my own answers presented in *Why Politics Matters*. I call for reforms to the way representative politics works, to make it more engaging and accessible for citizens. In addition, like many, I argue that there might be ways of re-engaging people in politics directly. We need a new politics for amateurs, I argue, and show how that could be more than a slogan. Work has gone further on that front and Smith (2009) shows how there has been innovation in forms of public engagement worldwide. However, even if we did find ways of drawing in more citizens into decision-making, the bulk of citizens would still remain observers rather than political practitioners. Moreover, the big unknown is how citizens come to understand politics, and whether they could develop a complex and nuanced understanding of its practices. I will return to this in the conclusion of this chapter. For now, I want to argue that the reason why so many of the solutions offered by political scientists are undercooked is that we have failed to develop the design dimension to our scientific work.

A new political science of design

We lack the intellectual founding to design solutions because we have neglected the challenge of design in our academic studies. We can develop a stronger design dimension to our work by borrowing from other disciplines. The crucial insight here is provided by Herbert Simon – a researcher who never respected academic boundaries – who argues that academics who examine the artificial, things that are created by human beings, have attempted to follow models of investigation suited to examining the natural rather than the artificial. Artificial things have functions, goals and the capacity for adaptation. They exist for a purpose, whilst natural things exist. As Simon (1996: 4) writes, 'We speak of engineering as concerned with "synthesis" whereas science is concerned with "analysis". Synthetic or artificial objects – and, more specifically, prospective artificial objects having desired properties – are the central objective of engineering activity and skill. The engineer, and more generally the designer, is concerned with how things *ought* to be – how they ought to be to *attain goals* and to *function*.' We, as political scientists, have too often asked ourselves questions as if we were studying a natural world rather than an artificial one. One road leads to an attempt to establish mechanisms and causes, and the other, whilst not neglecting those concerns, starts by asking about goals and purposes and how they could be achieved. The first road is generally viewed to be the more lauded and its practice is referred to as primary research; the latter, if practised at all, is often as described in semi-pejorative language, as applied social science. Our political system is evidently, though, an artificial human creation. We need to recognize the implications of that when approaching its study.

As Simon points out, the science of design is not a simple derivative of pure science; it is a neglected pathway. It is a different, equally valid, and demanding way of looking at the challenge of academic understanding.

In hankering after academic respectability, political scientists and others have neglected the design dimension of their studies (Simon 1996: 112). In particular, they have almost completely overlooked the issue of the relevance of what they study (Shapiro *et al*. 2004; Peters *et al*. 2009). But, if our political systems are understood as artificial creations, then their relevance becomes their key point. You know what a clock is by understanding that its purpose is to measure the time. You might, in turn, consider how to make it work in challenging conditions such as the cold of the Arctic or the depths of the ocean. My view is that we need a similar reorientation in political science. We need to ask ourselves design questions first, rather than last – if at all.

What would a science of the artificial look like? Or, more particularly, what would a design-oriented political science do? We can only offer the beginnings of a sketch here (see Simon 1996: ch. 6). One issue that needs to be addressed immediately is the objection that, in the design of political systems, there might be no consensus over goals and purposes. But this does not undermine the role of design, although it might add to its complexity. Indeed, it would seem sensible to design in many instances in a way that allows for future flexibility and reform (Goodin 1996: 40–3). However, a first stage involves establishing some representation of the design problem that is not 'correct' but one that can be 'understood by all participants and that will facilitate action rather than paralyze it' (Simon 1996: 143). The process is one where the designer interacts with the participants in a process of reflection. This might involve offering quantitative or qualitative research but, in the end, 'numbers are not the name of this game but rather representational structures that permit functional reasoning' (Simon 1996: 146). Feedback rather than prediction is the key to managing the future for the designer. Building feedback or learning mechanisms is central rather than solely relying on the power of prediction, which is inherently extremely difficult in human societies (for an example of how research might contribute to these feedback processes, see Stoker and John 2009).

A further major challenge is the design of organizations (Goodin 1996). But here we are aided by developments in cognitive psychology derived from the original insight promoted by Simon and, indeed, familiar to political scientists – the reality of bounded rationality in human decision-making (Jones 2001; see also John *et al*. 2009). Individuals are decision-makers constrained by the fundamental human problem of processing information, understanding a situation and determining consequences. There are limits to their cognitive capacity and the world is a complex place to understand. Decision-making is conditioned by the cognitive limitations of the human mind. Individuals reason, but not as heroic choice-makers. When faced with a decision, they do not think about every available option or always makes a great choice that is optimal to their utility, as assumed by mainstream economists. Their cognitive inner world helps them to focus on some things and ignore others, and it is driven by habits of thought, rules of thumb, and emotions. Rationality is bounded by this framing role of the human mind. People will selectively search based on incomplete information and partial ignorance, and terminate that search before an optimal option emerges, choosing instead something that is good enough. This is not to say that the behaviour of agents needs to be judged as irrational. On the contrary, people are rational in the sense that behaviour is generally goal-oriented and, usually, we have reasons for what we do. It is just that rationality rests on the interaction of the cognitive structure and the context in which individuals are operating and, as a result, sometimes they make poor decisions. These, and other fundamental psychological insights, have been largely absent from our political science theorizing and need to be brought to the foreground.

We need a design oriented political science that is prepared to search for solutions. We have largely neglected the intellectual work that would be necessary to create such a science of the artificial. In this section, it has only been possible to stretch what a political science pursuing this pathway would look like. But, if we are going to address the issue of anti-politics that, as this chapter has established, appears to be central to our current political culture, we need to expand our capacity as designers.

Conclusion

We need both to develop the practice and the substantive content of a design science arm to our study of politics. If academic political science is going to help with moves to reconnect citizens with politics, it needs to commit itself to a design oriented approach and pay far greater attention to what citizens make of politics. In responding to the issue of political disenchantment, we need to go back to citizens and ask them how they understand politics. When it comes to reform strategies, we are slightly pitching in the dark.

We do not know enough about the problem to know what the answer might be. The start of good design is having a plausible representation of the problem. As Hay (2007b: 162) argues, in terms of the silent majority:

[we] know very little ... about the cognitive process in and through which [they] come to attribute motivations to the behaviour [they] witness, or how [they] come to develop and revise assumptions about human nature [they] project on to others. If politics depends ultimately on our capacity to trust one another ... then there can be no more important questions for political analysts than these.

We know a fair amount about what kinds of political activity people engage in and what factors drive that activity. We can offer some reasonable evidence-informed insights into issues such as electoral turnout and election outcomes. What political science – and the social sciences in general – is less good at understanding and explaining is what politics means to citizens at the beginning of the twenty-first century. We need to spend more empirical effort in trying to find out what our fellow citizens understand by the practice of politics. We have some helpful starting points. Hibbing and Theiss-Morse (2002) provide one study of US citizens. Van Wessel (2009) produces some interesting and parallel findings in a small-scale study of 20 Dutch citizens. There is scope for a significant amount of further empirical work.

An important new direction in political science is to provide a deeper understanding of what politics means to citizens in order that, in the future, reform will be more effectively informed. As professional students of politics, we should be in a position to help shape future choices – otherwise, in a further sixty years' time we might have nothing of a democratic polity left to study. In order to do that, we need to change our practice. Ours is a science of the artificial – the study of a something created for a purpose: we need to develop a more effective design orientation in order to support a political system that is ailing, if not terminally ill. We need to help design a politics that can deliver the core purposes of engaging citizens, resolving conflicts and responding to the challenges of our interdependent world.

Note

My thanks go to Peter John, Colin Hay and an anonymous referee for comments on an earlier version of the paper on which this chapter is based.

Chapter 3

The Internet in Political Science

HELEN MARGETTS

This chapter addresses the challenge to political science arising from widespread use of the Internet – meaning that, in many countries, large tranches of political, economic and social life have now moved online. The Internet has brought changes to people's information-seeking behaviour and to political communication; facilitates mass mobilization; reconfigures the 'logic' of collective action; provides new possibilities for coordination and collaboration; and has necessitated organizational change in government and other political institutions, with implications for institutional design. The chapter examines how political science has responded to this development – and argues that current trends will require a more sophisticated theoretical, empirical and methodological response in the future.

As an empirical development, the Internet cannot challenge the assumptions, definitions or principles of macro theories, or conceptual frameworks of political science. It does not affect the assumptions of rational choice models, for example. But it does alter the costs and benefits of political actions, reshaping incentives for individuals to act collectively and participate politically. It does not change the definition of what it means to be an institution, but it can alter the viability of certain institutional and organizational forms. It does not change the basic principles of democracy, but it can level the playing field of democratic engagement or introduce new inequalities in popular control. For these reasons, the Internet challenges many of the micro-foundations of political science understanding and has, therefore, important implications for the discipline.

The first section outlines briefly the challenge for political science. The second section considers the current state of understanding of the implications of online activity, looking at how political scientists have considered – and not considered – the significance for political science research and study. The third section outlines the key trends and developments in online activity by both citizens and governments. The fourth section considers how political science might respond to these developments by seeing how they affect some of the key 'puzzles' of political science. How does widespread citizen use of the Internet affect what we know about political knowledge, political participation, collective action, party membership, and interest group size and formation? What are the implications for political equality, one of the central principles of democratic society? How does government use of the Internet, internally and to interact with society, affect the extent to which government is open, transparent and responsive – and what are the implications for public management reform and institutional design. The fifth section looks at implications of all these developments for political science methodologies, and the final part summarizes the results and lays out the key challenges for political science in the future.

The challenge

The twenty-first century has seen some dramatic political developments. In 2008, the United States elected its first black president, with record levels of turnout (particularly among black and first-time voters), community support, popular excitement and fund-raising from the general public. Mass demonstrations took place in Iran in protest at allegedly rigged election results in 2009, both organized and beamed across the world through Internet-based communications. There has been a rise in global political activism, with mass demonstrations against corporate globalization and campaigns to world leaders attracting millions of supporters. In 2003, millions of people were mobilized rapidly across the world to demonstrate against their state's involvement in the Iraq war. In 2006, millions of US citizens protested against changes to US immigration policy, including 500,000 in Los Angeles alone. Collaborative endeavours, such as the user-generated online encyclopaedia Wikipedia and the video-sharing site YouTube have attracted billions of users within two or three years of their conception, with millions contributing time and effort, apparently with common good goals.

  Use of the Internet played a major role in all of these developments. From the late 1990s onwards, an increasing proportion of the population of democracies has conducted significant amounts of their social, economic and political lives online. There has been a steady rise in Internet penetration (now 70 per cent in the UK), and the percentage of time that Internet users spend online has increased. The range of activities carried out online has also extended, from banking, shopping and information-seeking to new activities such as social networking, video sharing and online collaboration, using a range of web-based technologies based on user-generated content, broadly described as 'Web 2.0' technologies. In a context where many more traditional forms of political activity (such as voting and political party membership) appear to be on the decline, online political activities (such as political discussion groups, charitable activism, petitioning, online fundraising, e-mail campaigns, social enterprise and political videos) are flourishing.

These social, economic and political changes pose challenges to social science disciplines. Economists have paid much attention to newly efficient markets, Internet auctions, the transformation of the firm and radically changed business–customer relationships. In sociology, the dramatic rise in the use of online social networking and the Internet for all kinds of social interactions has pushed the study of Internet-based networks to centre stage. Political scientists have devoted rather less attention to online political activity. Various claims have been made in the past for the transformation of political life through technology, from utopian visions of direct democracy and a radical decentralization of political systems to dystopian warnings of the 'control state' through technologically aided bureaucratic expansion. Most of these claims remain unproven; earlier technologies were largely internal to large organizations, having little effect on interactions between citizens and government or other political institutions. In contrast, the Internet and World Wide Web are technological innovations that citizens are using on a massive scale and that, indeed, driving innovation. Transformation of political life is more possible than ever before.

The current state of our understanding in political science

In comparison with the other disciplines noted, political science has been rather silent on the subject of the Internet. At first glance, the answer to the question 'What difference does widespread use of the Internet make to the study of politics?' would be, 'Not much.' If you look at leading introductory textbooks on politics, you will find very little discussion of the Internet: the 2007 edition of Hague and Harrop, for example, has but three mentions bundled together in a section on political communication. Chapters on political culture, political economy, political participation, elections, interest groups, political parties, constitutions, legal frameworks, multi-level governance, legislatures, political executives and public policy and administration make no mention of it. For all these basic institutions and activities of politics, it seems, the authors (and the many other authors to whom they refer) do not consider the Internet at all important. A glance at the burgeoning list of academic 'handbooks' on various aspects of politics further illustrates the point. Katz and Crotty's (2006) *Handbook of Party Politics* has one chapter on political parties online (written by this author), whilst the *Handbook of Public Administration* by Guy Peters and Jon Pierre (2003) has another. Dalton and Klingemann's (2007) *Oxford Handbook of Political Behaviour* has one chapter on e-government and democracy, whilst even sections on modernization and political communication avoid the topic. Meanwhile, Chadwick and Howard's (2009) *Handbook of Internet Politics*, which contains over thirty contributions on a range of topics of the kind discussed here, is largely written either by people from the field of communications, or by political scientists who work solely on Internet-related issues.

Sub-fields of political science where you might expect to see research into Internet-based change are also silent. In particular, mainstream public administration has tended to ignore the huge amount of resources thrown at e-government by liberal democracies during the last decade. Whilst literally hundreds of reports have been produced, and conferences convened, by international organizations and global consultancies, this activity is dominated by practitioners and is largely ignored by the academic mainstream, with a few 'ghettos' of working groups inside professional associations. In general, within each sub-field of political science there has been a tendency towards ghettoization; the 'ghettos' have produced some useful work to be considered in this chapter, much of which is summarized in the *Handbook of Internet Politics*. But, it is argued here, the time is ripe for theoretical development, methodological innovation and rigorous empirical investigation to enter the mainstream.

Meanwhile, outside political science, a number of scholars have made grand claims for the possibilities of the Internet to have a dramatic effect on political life. As with all new technologies, the most prominent voices in the debate have been those who stress utopian or 'dystopian' consequences. In the former category, Yochai Benkler (2006) presents a vision of an online world of peer-produced goods bringing a cornucopia of wealth and freedom. In the latter category, the US lawyer Cass Sunstein

(2009) claims in the book *Republic.com 2.0* that the personalization and specialization of media available to Internet users means that the political interest of an individual will not extend beyond the 'Daily Me', with the exchange of political information taking place in enclaves and 'echo chambers' where participation leads people to more strongly held versions of their earlier views. Whilst inspiring, intellectually interesting and influential, such overarching claims lack empirical testing and political science understanding.

Recent developments and current trends

So, what are the most important developments in the use of the Internet for political science? Citizens, governments, political parties and interest groups have all strongly increased their use of the Internet in the last decade, and there are significant trends in Internet use for politics-related activities that have clear implications for politics and, therefore, for political science research, which will be considered in subsequent sections.

How citizens find out about politics

Looking first at citizens, for the significant proportion of people in most developed nations that use the Internet (over two thirds of UK citizens), information-seeking behaviour has been transformed by the Internet. In the most recent *Oxford Internet Survey*, around half of UK citizens said that they would 'go to the Internet first' (rather than a telephone, directory or personal visit) to find the name of their MP if they did not know it, or to find information on schools or taxes. Nearly 70 per cent of Internet users have used the Internet to look for health information, one of the fastest growing online activities (Dutton *et al.* 2009). These data highlight a fundamental shift in information seeking behaviour and cast new light on what we know about political knowledge, discussed later in this chapter. Another key shift is in news consumption: people (particularly in younger age groups) watch less television and read fewer newspapers, using the Internet for accessing political news, which means that they will be accessing different news sources in different ways, evidenced by the US primary and presidential campaigns (Pew 2009). New sources of news include the online encyclopaedia, Wikipedia: 'Type a candidate's name into Google, and among the first results is a Wikipedia page, arguably as important as any in defining a candidate.

Already, the presidential entries are being edited, dissected and debated countless times each day' (*Washington Post* 2007).

Political communication

Another shift in political life is the way that political communication takes place. Early discussion of the effect of the Internet on political communication focused on whether it makes it easier for 'ordinary people' to participate in communication activities normally restricted to media organizations, with 'news values' that favour state representative and institutional interests (Rheingold 2000; Bimber 2001). Certainly, there is increasing evidence for such a trend, with the growing use of blogs and hugely popular video-sharing sites (such as YouTube). However, there is also evidence of a new type of selection bias, with search engines (particularly Google) acting as key Internet gatekeepers that are just as selective as news organizations, although in a different way. But another key difference in political communication is that various kinds of 'news' are spread through a series of point-to-point connections in online networks, rather than broadcast from central media. An already classic example is a 37-second video of an Iranian girl dying in the midst of the 2009 demonstrations in Tehran, which was taken on a mobile phone and spread virally across the world on the Internet – an image that many have compared to the photograph broadcast in 1972 of a young Vietnamese girl running naked and burning through the streets, arguing that this image could be equivalently influential (Stoltz 2009). Many massive Internet applications with billions of users, such as Wikipedia and YouTube, grew without advertising or any broadcast media at all until their usage was so substantive that they generated media coverage in their own right; news of these innovations was spread virally, in a series of point-to-point communications by means of online networks, from one person to several other people, who in turn told several other people. This shift could have important implications for how mobilizations develop.

Political participation

The Internet has proved itself as a forum for political participation (see Garrett (2006) for a review), with a range of arguments and evidence that 'changes in the cost and variety of sources of information immediately available to Internet users directly affect levels of political participation' (Bimber 2003). A burgeoning fleet of online petitions is signed by millions, mass demonstrations are organized online, and a huge diversity of politically oriented groups operates on social networking sites such as Facebook. It is difficult to quantify the scale of these activities and the extent to which they replace or augment traditional forms of political participation, particularly now that most activities are a mixture of online and offline, but some attempts have been made. Norris (2009), in an analysis of 19 countries, used the *European Social Survey* to analyze the relationship between Internet use and political activism, finding that regular Internet users are significantly more politically active across all 21 indicators of activism captured by the survey, heavily contingent upon the particular forms of participation under analysis. It was not possible to establish any causal effect, but use of the Internet continued to be significantly related to political activism even when controlling for prior social or attitudinal characteristics of Internet users such as age, education and civic duty. After these factors, use of the Internet proved the next strongest predictor of activism, more important than other indicators such as social and political trust or use of any news media (Norris 2009: 135).

Peer production

Another important development comes from the growing use of 'Web 2.0' applications, facilitating what has come to be known as 'peer production' of online goods. It is not well defined what 'Web 2.0' means, but it is based on the idea of 'user-generated' content, typified by Wikipedia, blogs and social networking sites. In the early days of the Internet, most people online largely consumed content, but the growing use of 'Web 2.0' applications means that significant and growing numbers now also produce content in some way, even if only a feedback comment on a travel site or an 'unconscious' contribution to an application such as Google Trends, which shows patterns in the use of search terms. When such production takes place in the pursuit of collective goods, it might be argued that we have a new type of mobilization, although it is arguable that we might term it 'political'. The places where this trend is most marked is, as you might expect, in the provision of online collective goods (such as Wikipedia itself), open source software, and a range of information and entertainment sources with multiple contributors (such as Digg or YouTube). Although these goods cannot exactly be described as public goods, the collaborative activity that has gone into their generation certainly suggests that new types of participation are viable in a way they have never been before. These social innovations represent mobilizations without leaders, where the coordination takes place by means of the technological platform itself. Benkler (2006) labelled this phenomenon 'peer-production', and it is at the heart of his utopian vision for the Internet.

Electronic government

Governmental and political institutions have responded to widespread use of the Internet by increasing their own use of the Internet and related technologies, developing what has become to be known as 'e-government'. E-government may be defined as the use by government of information technology both internally and to interact with citizens, businesses, voluntary organizations and other governments. Defined in this way, e-government has been developing in Britain and the United States for the last fifty years, since the first computers entered the 'back office' of large transaction processing departments (such as the Post Office) in the 1950s. From that time on, most departments and agencies became increasingly reliant on complex networks of information technology systems. Administrative decision-making is crucially dependent on these systems and so is policy-making, as these systems have been shown to be policy critical; and technological innovation opens up new potential for policy innovation (Margetts 1999). But the earlier information systems were largely internally facing, with few implications for how citizens interacted with government, because they were based on technologies used by government but not by citizens. In contrast, the Internet offered real potential for transformation of government's interactions with the outside world, because of its widespread use. From the late 1990s onwards, most governments adopted an 'e-government' strategy, devoting resources to developing an electronic presence and making some or all services available online. All governments now have an electronic 'window'; even the Democratic People's Republic of Korea has an official website. The electronic presence of many governments consists of thousands of websites and, for many Internet users, this is the only part of government with which they will interact. Governments have thrown huge resources at 'electronic government', with most industrialized nations spending up to 1 per cent of GDP on their own information technologies. Increasingly, government information systems drive policy innovation and debate.

Digital divides

Finally, in thinking about trends and their implications it is important to remember the proportion of populations that do not have access to the

Internet, because trends in online participation are likely to exclude them, with potential implications for political equality. The proportion of the UK population that do not have Internet access is around 30 per cent and, of course, in many countries is much higher. There is a certain amount of evidence that, in countries with significant levels of Internet penetration, digital exclusion can reinforce social and economic exclusion, with clear possibilities to introduce political exclusion for some groups (Helsper 2008).

How will – or should – political science develop? Challenges and opportunities

For a true understanding of the implications of the Internet for political science, we need to consider specific theories and debates of political science, and what we 'know' about political behaviour, and then consider the implications of the Internet for them. It is a more modest aim than those of, for example, Benkler or Sunstein, but more likely to succeed. This section reconsiders a number of key puzzles, theories or sub-fields of political science to which political scientists have devoted time, attention and research effort in the light of the developments outlined; political knowledge, voting, collective action, leadership, party membership, citizen-government relationships, public management reform and political equality.

Political knowledge: what is it rational to 'know'?

Trends in information seeking behaviour outlined above bring shifts in the type of political information that we might expect people to retain. There is a long history in political science of measuring indicators of political knowledge, such as knowing (or reporting knowledge of) basic facts about constitutional, institutional and electoral arrangements, and using them as key predictors of political behaviour – and even in defining a political culture (see, for example, Almond and Verba (1963); Dahl (1989) and Dalton and Klingemann (2007) for a review). Such indicators have been used in studies from Almond and Verba's classic study in 1963 to the Hansard Society's Audit of Political Engagement (which started in 2004 and is discussed in this volume by Gerry Stoker) to indicate a growing disengagement with politics in the United Kingdom – for example, particularly among younger groups (Hansard 2008: 32). But the fact that people do not know the name of their political representative or the details of electoral arrangements might no longer be a sign of a declining engagement with politics. For Internet users, it might be a rational response to a changing information environment, where such information can be found out so easily. For non-Internet users, remembering such facts is more rational, because the costs of finding them out, by means of phone calls or a visit to a physical location, could be quite high. Thus, trends in Internet use are bringing not only enhanced capacity for gaining political knowledge (currently misread by conventional political science indicators), but also increasing inequalities through the differential costs of acquiring that knowledge.

Voting: reversing turnout decline?

Voting is the participatory act that citizens are most likely to undertake, and the question of what motivates people to vote is a key question of political science. Declining turnout in liberal democracies, particularly among young people, is a major concern of contemporary politics, discussed in Gerry Stoker's chapter in this volume. So, do the trends in Internet use outlined affect people's incentives to vote?

The best 'bet' for the Internet having a positive impact on turnout is through the provision of political information, hypothesized by political scientists since Anthony Downs (1957) to be positively associated with higher turnout (see Palfrey and Rosenthal 1985; Feddersen and Pesendorfer 1996, 1999; Horiuchi *et al.* 2005). Through changing patterns in information-seeking behaviour and the consequentially far greater range of political information available to the average citizen, the Internet could help to increase turnout. In an Internet-based randomized field experiment, Horiuchi *et al.* (2005) tested this hypothesis by considering the effect of policy information provided through official party websites in the Japanese 2004 elections. The authors found that voters were less likely to abstain when they received such information about both ruling and opposition parties through their websites; these information effects were greater among those voters who were planning to vote but were undecided about for which party to vote. Analyzing 1996–2000 NES data, Tolbert and McNeal (2003) found access to the Internet and online election news positively associated with voting and other forms of political participation. Various studies have found Internet use to be related to political engagement; for example, Johnson and Kaye (2003) and, more recently, Drew and Weaver (2006) have identified exposure and attention to online political information as positively related to campaign knowledge and interest, themselves indications of propensity to vote.

If the Internet does have a positive effect on turnout, it might well pose a challenge to the conventional political science wisdom (Goerres 2007; Wattenberg 2008) that young people turn out to vote less than older groups, particularly when combined with the shift towards information-seeking rather than political knowledge (also associated with turnout) identified in the previous subsection. Age remains the strongest determinant of Internet use and 'today's youth undoubtedly enjoy a special relationship with communication technology in a manner distinct from how it is experienced by other members of other generations' (Lupia and Philpot 2005; Tedesco 2006). The United States, in 2008, appears to have contributed to record levels of registration in these groups and challenged this convention in the actual election.

Reconfiguring 'The Logic of Collective Action' and the ecology of interest groups

The question of what motivates people to mobilize around collective goods is another long-standing puzzle of political science. In particular, political scientists have long debated Olson's (1965) famous argument that large interest groups organizing around public goods will always find it difficult to form because of the costs of organization and the problem of 'free-riders' who obtain benefits of such goods without contributing to the group effort. Most recently, a number of scholars, such as Bimber (2003, 2005) and Lupia and Sin (2003), have reconsidered the logic of participation in the light of widespread use of the Internet – the latter arguing that it affects opportunities and incentives that are relevant to collective action, advantaging some collective endeavours and endangering others (Lupia and Sin 2003: 318).

One line of argument emphasizes the capacity of the Internet and associated technologies to reduce the costs of large-scale organization such that the costs do not grow with group size. In this environment, a small group that does not use the Internet well is likely to fail against a large one that does, so we might expect a re-patterning of interest group ecology. Furthermore, cost reduction in certain types of coordination can also facilitate the creation of completely new types of group that work on the basis of matching heterogeneous individuals with similar or complementary aims across national boundaries. This difference is illustrated in the extreme by some newer kinds of interest group that exist wholly online in the field of global civic activism. Avaaz, for example, is an international civic organization that promotes activism (such as online campaigns and petitions to world leaders) on a number of issues, particularly climate change and human rights. Its stated mission is to 'ensure that the views and values of the world's people inform global decision making', and it claims more than three million members from every country in the world. The online NGO Kiva is the 'world's first person-to-person micro-lending website', which offers potential entrepreneurs in developing countries the chance to enter their profile on the site. Potential donors visit the site, browse profiles, and choose someone to lend to and make a loan; in so doing, they can receive email journal updates and track repayments. Kiva's 270,000 lenders, who hand over money in US$25 increments, have funded 40,000 borrowers in 40 countries and provided US$27 million funding (Knowledge@Wharton 2008). Such a coordinative task would be inconceivable offline. The 'matching' capability of the Internet is also illustrated by the linking up of geographically dispersed diaspora, which is having a substantive effect on foreign policy-making in many states (Westcott 2008), contributing to spatial interdependence (discussed by Mick Moran in this volume).

   Another line of argument suggests that the Internet can increase incentives to participate by increasing 'social information' that individuals receive about the participation of others (Margetts *et al.* 2009). If collective acts take place online, as they increasingly do, then the Internet makes it possible to feed back real-time information to participants about how many other people are participating, which could reduce tendencies to 'free-ride' in large groups. Olson discusses the effect of social pressure to incentivize group members to participate, but discards it for larger groups: 'In general social pressure and social incentives operate only in groups of smaller size, in groups so small that the members can have face-to-face contact with one another' (Olson 1965: 62). But Lupia and Sin (2003) point out that:

> If the members of a latent group are somehow continuously bombarded with propaganda about the worthiness of the attempt to satisfy the common interest in question, they may perhaps in time develop social pressures not entirely unlike those that can be generated in a face-to face group, and these social pressures may help the latent group to obtain the collective good. A group cannot finance such propaganda unless it is already organized and it may not be able to organize until it has already been subjected to the propaganda; so

this form of social pressure is probably not ordinarily sufficient by itself to enable a group to achieve its collective goals.

Lupia and Sin point out that the Internet could revise the ability of large groups to apply such social pressure. Their argument, although analytically elegant, lacks an empirical base; however, early experimental evidence from research carried out by this author has gone some way to substantiate their claims (Margetts *et al.* 2009). The Internet, it seems, could really reconfigure the logic of collective action – a concept central to political science.

Leadership: the end of charisma and coordination?

Another challenge to political science understanding of interest groups relates to leadership. The traditional view of 'leaders' in political mobilizations is that they are 'those people who are able to co-ordinate the members of an interest group or community, setting up an organization or institutional construction and making the provision of collective goods in which the group is interested viable' (Colomer 2009). That is, they provide collective aims, group identification and private incentives able to promote, maintain and enlarge voluntary membership, participation and contribution to a community or group. Such leaders have been hypothesized to require a range of resources from skills, expertise and economic resources to personality traits and characteristics leading to 'heroic leadership' or Weberian 'charismatic leadership'. Various 'non-claims' and claims have been made for the changing nature of 'leadership' in online environments. Mainstream political science assumes that the traditional view of leadership remains untouched by the virtual nature of much of political communication. Some argue that new 'cyberchiefs' are playing an increasingly important role in bringing together 'online tribes', operating by means of a dual mechanism of 'hacker charisma' with Weber's 'value-rational social action': 'the authority of online charismatic leaders derives from an affective attachment based on their extraordinary personal qualities' (O'Neil 2009: 43).

In contrast to either of these accounts, it could be argued that, on the Internet, leadership (in any of these forms) is not so necessary. Rather than receiving some broadcast message through the media or a leader's 'charismatic' appeal, potential participants are likely to receive political messages virally as they spread from person to person (or many people) through online networks. Many of the coordination activities traditionally carried out by activists can be carried out by means of the Internet (or, more explicitly, online applications operating through the Internet such as online petition sites, charitable giving sites, social networking sites, wikis, feedback or pledge sites). These characteristics of online mobilization could lead to a 'minimalist' view of leadership on the Internet derived from work by the economist Thomas Schelling (1978, 2006) as developed by Colomer (1995, 2009). Schelling argues that, in any collective endeavour, there will be one or more 'tipping' points, at which the majority of people think it is worth joining. Each individual will have their own such point ('k'). Schelling argues that we can expect a normal distribution of 'k': a few people, most likely to be 'leaders' or 'starters', will be those for whom 'k' is very low or zero and who will join anyway. Those for whom 'k' is high will be less likely to join a mobilization until some kind of 'winning point' has been reached, where it seems as though the majority of people will participate. It could be argued that the existence of a small number of people with low 'k' ('starters') is what is crucial in online mobilization. Once a 'critical mass' of starters have initiated joining, the mobilization can take place through a series of chain reactions in which enough 'followers' with higher levels of 'k' will join, incentivized by the 'social information' provided through real-time feedback about how many other people have participated (Margetts *et al.* 2009). This author is leading a research team investigating this phenomenon with respect to signing petitions and charitable giving.

Political parties: the end of membership?

The branch of political science that focuses on political parties has placed particular focus on membership as a key characteristic of political parties as organizations, with recent attention focusing on declining membership. Given that virtually all political parties in liberal democracies now have some kind of online presence, we might expect the Internet to impact upon questions of party organization and activism.

Most research dedicated to the relationship between parties and the Internet has concluded that Internet technologies have been used most for campaign coordination and voter targeting, rather than as mechanisms for empowering members or enhancing internal communication channels. Indeed, to some extent the Internet seems to challenge the dominance of parties as articulators of citizens' interests, rather than reinforcing their role. With respect to party competition, there is evidence that the Internet lowers the entry costs for new and smaller parties; on the Internet 'the playing field is ... less unequal than previous media ... while smaller parties do not have the capacity to offer voters and members the technology enriched experience that the large parties can provide, relative to other forms of media it does appear to provide crucial assistance in disseminating an unedited message globally as well as allowing them a new "space" for organizational co-ordination' (Gibson and Ward 2009: 10).

However, trends in Internet use, combined with the decline in party membership, could still throw down a challenge to political science understanding of political parties. It is by now accepted that party membership is inexorably falling, although there is considerable variation across countries (Bartolini 2000; Scarrow 2000; Mair and van Biezen 2001). Claims by this author that parties might use the Internet to fulfil a new ideal type of political party, the 'cyber party' (Margetts 2006), to add to the existing models of 'catch-all', 'caucus', 'mass' and 'cadre' and 'cartel' parties (Mair 1997) have been viewed with some scepticism by political party specialists. But, if parties were able to redefine the notion of membership to a looser type of supporter, in a predominantly online relationship, parties might yet be able to revive themselves. Members of such a party would be more like the 'members' of US parties, in terms of not paying dues and self-selecting themselves to register support when they want to participate in some way (such as vote, or donate money). Such an idea goes back to Duverger (1964: 61), who points to a series of 'concentric circles ... of ... ever-increasing party solidarity', providing a number of categories of party attachment. If parties (and those that analyze them) were to focus on one of the outer concentric circles, accepting the importance of very low levels of solidarity as a form of participation that is still greater than voting, we might yet see a new perspective on political parties. Indeed, as Hediar (2006: 201–2) points out, earlier 'ideal types' of party organization were defined in terms of the significance and meaning of party membership.

Government–citizen interactions: bringing citizens closer to government?

Turning to governments and their interactions with citizens, are there other ways in which conventional political science wisdom or analysis might be challenged? Key candidates for re-evaluation include transparency and principal agent relationships between citizens and professionals.

With regard to transparency, there are a number of ways in which we might expect electronic government to be more 'open' than offline government. Indeed, there are ways in which governmental institutions have become more transparent in ways directly attributable to the Internet, although the examples tend to be quite disparate, where some organization (usually non-governmental) has driven forward a quite specific innovation. In the UK, the social enterprise MySociety has developed a number of standalone innovations that have had quite important effects on British political life. For example, the website www.write-tothem.org makes it very easy for a citizen to find the name of their representative immediately and write to them through an automatically generated pro-forma email; www.theyworkforyou.org provides tailored information about any representative, such as participation and voting records in the House of Commons (and probably, in future, details of their expenses!). These innovations use government information, most of which is already available online from government sites, but are custom built in a way that reflects people's actual online behaviour. Experiments on how people look for and find government-related information (Margetts and Escher 2007; Margetts *et al.* 2009) revealed that people find the UK parliamentary site difficult to use and rarely discover answers to questions about their representative without using the MySociety sites at some point. In the United States also, various moves do seem to be leading to more open government.

The Federal Funding Accountability and Transparency Act (originally sponsored by Obama in 2006) mandated an online database of federal contracts and awards. Since then, more than twenty states have put up some kind of spending database – there is much variation between them: Alaska is a merely a collection of spreadsheets and PDFs, but others, such as the Missouri Accountability Portal, are 'cleanly designed and easy to use. Anyone can log on and see exactly where Missouri's money was going' (*Economist*, 5 February 2009). These examples do more to highlight the potential of the Internet to enhance transparency, rather than represent a systematic challenge to political science. Differences between countries remain; the United States has always had a more open political culture than the United Kingdom. But the Internet could reinforce such differences, and policy-makers link it with transparency; 'President Obama has committed to making his administration the most open and transparent in history and WhiteHouse.gov will play a major role in delivering on that promise' (www.whitehouse.gov). Moves include making all non-emergency legislation available on the White House website for five days, allowing public review and comment before the President signs legislation.

A more viable candidate for substantive remodelling of govern-ment–citizen interactions comes from changing relationships between citizens and professionals. A stream of analysis in public administration models such relationships on the basis of a 'principal–agent' relationship (Moe 1984), characterized by information asymmetries between princi-pal and agent (patient and doctor, for example). Changes in the scale and quality of information available to Internet users can, in some contexts, drastically shift these asymmetries in citizens' favour, particularly in health care where, as noted, high proportions of Internet users look for information online. There is much evidence to suggest that patients tend to be far better informed when meeting with doctors than in the pre-Internet era. Some health organizations have tried to capitalize on this trend: there is a move in the UK health service to introduce 'information prescriptions', pointing patients to accredited sources and requiring patients to research their own condition before drug prescriptions are written (www.dh.gov.uk). Patient groups for people suffering from chronic illnesses have shown themselves to be particularly innovative in using the Internet to share information and accumulate expertise for patients on their conditions. Similar developments are evident in the recent establishment of the UK Tribunals Service, which offers scope for the Internet not only to provide information to citizens about what tribunals do, but also to facilitate citizens – who often lack legal (or other representation) – to understand how tribunals work, lodge appeals online, discover the progress of their appeal, and even obtain a determination of the appeal (Margetts and Partington 2010). Such developments can shift information asymmetries that have long been seen as an inevitable feature of public bureaucracy.

Public management reform: from Weber to new public management to digital-era governance

So, what of government itself in the age of the Internet? Political science thinking on public administration has been characterized by successive overarching models of reform that have promised ever more 'modern' government and have dominated the agenda for a significant period of time. From Weber (1978) came the idea of bureaucracy as the dominant organizational form; the bureaucratic organization of social and economic life according to principles of efficiency on the basis of techni-cal knowledge. Weber's ideas about bureaucracy dominated what Hood (1994) has termed 'progressive era' public administration, which came into favour in the late nineteenth and early twentieth century, including lifetime career service, fixed pay rather than pay related to performance, and a stress on procedure rules. In the early 1980s, another modernization trend emerged in Western public administration. Termed 'New Public Management' (NPM), this cohort of changes represented a shift away from Weberian and Progressive Era administration. NPM has been described extensively elsewhere, with its three core themes of disaggregation, incentivization and competition (Hood 1994; Barzelay 2000; Dunleavy *et al.* 2006; Pollit *et al.* 2007).

Some commentators (including this author) have argued that Internet-based developments can lead to a new 'paradigm' for public administration, replacing NPM, the dominant model for public sector reform throughout liberal democracies during the 1980s and 1990s (Dunleavy *et al.* 2005, 2006). NPM resulted in complex and fragmented administrations in the countries where it was pursued most enthusiastically, such as the United Kingdom. In contrast, digital-era governance (DEG) involves joining up across departments and agencies, client-focused structures, and disintermediation through the digitalization of processes so that, in effect, governmental organizations can 'become' their online presence. As with Weber's model of bureaucracy, DEG is an ideal type, rather than a description of contemporary bureaucracy in any given country. But changes in this direction could have far-reaching effects for how government will look in the future.

Digital-era trends could go further in terms of generating more responsive governments that might take advantage of the potential of Web 2.0 technologies to allow citizens to enter the 'front office ' of government (see von Hippel 2005), 'co-creating' public services – in part, by generating information that was not previously available. Such information can be generated 'unconsciously', through the analysis of electronically generated transactional data for making policy and developing services (data generated by electronic ticketing systems such as the 'Oyster' card in London is used to feedback into design of the transport system, for example). But, increasingly, there is the possibility for it to be more 'consciously' generated by institutionalizing feedback loops, allowing patients to give feedback on care they have received, pupils and parents to give feedback about schools, and so on. Already, with respect to health care, there are a number of UK websites (such as www.patientopinion.org and www.iwantgreatcare.com, developed by health care professionals or social enterprises) that allow such feedback, in the same way that many private sector sites allow customers to write reviews of consumer experiences (restaurants, holidays, shops, and so on). The UK government has now attempted to institutionalize a similar facility in its flagship 'NHS Choices' website at www.nhs.uk. Of course, a critical mass of population is vital to the success of innovations such this (something NHS Choices might not achieve if it continues to bury the feedback facility inside this huge site), but the potential is great. Another example of citizens 'entering the front office' comes from the United States, where the website readthestimulus.org asks for volunteers to read a portion of the next spending bill and flag any spending promises that strike them as strange. As *The Economist* (2009) put it: 'That may seem like citizens doing the government's job. But at least someone is doing it.'

Political equality

Finally, another challenge to political science thrown down by the Internet is the normative question of political equality, a central tenet of most definitions of democracy (Verba and Nie 1987; Beetham 1994). As noted in the previous section, digital divides remain – in terms of both access to the Internet and the skills required to perform many of the activities highlighted as important. So, where I have argued that political knowledge, turnout, collective action, party involvement, open government and institutional design are all influenced by the Internet, we might expect these influences to have a differential effect on groups who use and do not use the Internet. Digital exclusion can have a 'reinforcing' effect on social or economic inequality, as those most in need of services and information online might be the least likely to access it. For example, finding online health information is the fastest growing area of Internet use (Dutton and Helsper 2007) but, in 2009, only 41 per cent of people with a health or disability problem used the Internet, significantly fewer than the proportion of people without a health problem (Dutton *et al.* 2009).

As Internet penetration rises and political institutions conduct more and more of their business online, these inequalities and reinforcement effects could lead to the possibility of residualization, as offline services decline in frequency and quality. However, there are other signals in the data that mitigate against this tendency to unfairness in the digital era, due to evidence suggesting that even non-users might be able to access e-government and other political institutions. The Oxford Internet Survey (2007) found that 73 per cent of non-users thought that, if they needed to use the Internet, they 'definitely' or 'probably' knew someone who would be able to access it for them. For lapsed users, this figure was even higher (88 per cent), suggesting perhaps that lapsing from Internet use could be a rational time-saving response. These figures suggest that for governmental organizations (and perhaps other political organizations such as parties and pressure groups) there could be a partial way around the so-called 'digital divide'. But reaching these people, political organizations of all kinds have to devote resources to identifying digitally-excluded groups and target intermediaries (such as local community groups and more formal institutions, such as the Citizens Advice Bureau).

Illusions of interdependence

At first glance, it might seem that the Internet makes a substantive contribution to interdependence, in all the senses outlined by Moran in his chapter of this book; spatial, institutional and policy interdependence. Indeed, many claims have been made, in this respect, that the Internet era would bring the 'death of distance', the 'virtual state' and even the 'end of the nation-state' (through the simultaneous trends of global networks and 'cyberculture' with new forms of virtual local community and pluralist politics) and the evolution of a global 'information society' or regime (Toffler 1990; Everard 2000; Castells 2000; Rosenau and Singh 2002).

However, a closer reading of the various developments casts doubt on these views. Most Internet effects on interdependence seem to be disparate and specific. As discussed, the Internet does facilitate transnational interest groups, including diaspora, which then have influence on foreign policy-making in various states. Authoritarian regimes find it more difficult to contain resistance from Internet-enabled mobilizations and resort to technologically complex Internet-filtering regimes in the effort to do so (Deibert *et al.* 2008). Internet-based platforms do bring a blurring of organizational boundaries – between e-Bay or Kiva and the various enterprises that have developed from them, for example, and even between government and society, with the new potential for 'open-book' governance. Websites might present a holistic 'front-end' to government and conglomerations of interest groups. But many inter- and, indeed, intra-institutional and organizational disjunctures remain. The Internet does not, by itself, lead to a reshaping of democratic arrangements; interdependence effects can be somewhat illusory – only part of a wider picture. Take the demonstrations in Iran, where the sharing of images and widespread international concern has led demonstrators inside Iran to hope and believe that the outside world will, or can, do something about the democratic crisis inside Iran, which is far from clear. The situation is similar in Burma (Myanmar), one of the most closed societies in the world, where images of the demonstrations of 2007 have faded from the world's screens in the face of authoritarian control. International popular excitement about the Obama phenomenon did not mean that citizens from other states were able to influence the result, although it might have seemed so from media and Internet coverage, and there might have been some limited influence internally from Obama's international recognition and acclaim. There are Internet effects on interdependence, therefore, but they are narrower, more limited and more restricted than the cyber-utopians would argue.

Methodological challenges for political science

The previous section has put forward a number of challenges to political science, and could form the basis of an agenda for researching the effects of the Internet on politics. But to undertake such an agenda, political science faces another challenge – this time, methodological. In understanding changes in political behaviour online, the challenge for political science is to develop new ways of collecting empirical evidence. The studies by Bimber (2003, 2005) and Lupia and Sin (2003) are insightful and analytical, but largely qualitative. In fact, the Internet itself is a rich source of empirical data about political behaviour, offering the possibility of obtaining 'real' data about behaviour rather than responses to opinion surveys (Savage and Burrows 2007). But there are two key challenges to obtaining such data. First, the richest collections of such data are held by search engine companies, but marketing and privacy concerns mean that they are extremely reluctant to release or it or even publish it. Note, for example, the controversy when the US Department of Justice asked Google for a million anonymized records of users of pornographic sites in 2005, or when AOL released the logs of all searches made by 500,000 of their users over three months in 2006. The data was 'anonymized', but did allow at least one individual to be identified, which was described by many commentators as a blatant violation of users' privacy.

Even if such data were available, political activity forms a somewhat small percentage of overall life online, so it can be difficult to analyze aggregate data. Detailed usage statistics of individual websites are the property of the site's owner, who might not be willing to release it. Facilities such as Google Trends allow the observation of general patterns in Internet use and indicate the prevalence of search terms but, again, there can be difficulties in identifying micro-trends. One way to overcome lack of usage data is by 'scraping' the web for data about when people undertook some kind of political activity, which can give detailed over-time data about political mobilization. This author is currently leading a project that involves automatically scraping data from online petition sites and charitable donation sites to obtain diffusion patterns, but such a task involves the use of custom-built software and negotiating the strategies of some websites to avoid being 'scraped' in this way. It can also involve ethical issues (particularly any attempt to scrape names) and legal problems: YouTube and Facebook, for example, have banned the technique on their own platforms.

The structure of the Internet itself as a 'network of networks' and the proliferation of online networks (particularly since the rapid growth in the use of social networking sites) means that network analysis has become an increasingly important methodology with which to understand political communication and discussion (Gonzalez-Bailon *et al.* 2009). There is a long tradition of network analysis in sociology and anthropology (Laumann and Pappi 1976; Knoke 1990), and network analysis methods have been imported to political science, but political science accounts have tended to be descriptive and qualitative (see, for example, Heclo and Wildavsky 1974; Rhodes 1985; Dowding 1995), whereas analysis of online networks can be extremely statistically and technically complex.

Understanding political organizations, including government, on the Internet raises another methodological point. Political science cannot hope to preserve methodological integrity without developing new methods with which to understand online organizations of all kinds. By now, governments, to some extent, 'are' their electronic presence – the only section of government that most people see. Yet, there is a long tradition of looking at government in a technology-free way: 'why does the contemporary public management and public administration literature look like movies or TV programmes showing office life before the late 1980s? Because there is no IT visible' (Dunleavy *et al.* 2006). Now that the Internet and associated IT systems have moved centre-stage in government policy-making and operations, any analysis of governmental organizations needs to consider their information systems, their electronic presence and the type of data that these systems generate. Many interest groups (such as Kiva and Araaz) now operate almost entirely online. Even more traditional groups operate through online networks and undertake a whole range of online activities, whilst running down their 'offline' activities. Political parties might not be transforming themselves into mass membership organizations online, but the Internet has had a dramatic effect on how they interact with supporters, donors and potential voters.

To understand political organizations in this changed environment requires, and would benefit from, the addition of a number of methodologies to political science research. For example, 'webmetric' analysis involves using dedicated software to 'crawl' the web and establish the pattern of links between websites in order to gauge the structure of online networks. For a given organization, such an analysis includes looking at 'inlinks' coming into a website (to indicate the organization's online visibility and centrality), 'outlinks' pointing out to other sites (which indicate how outward looking an organization appears to be) and the navigability of paths of links internal to the domain (see NAO 2007, for an example). Such an analysis can overcome some of the outlined difficulties involved in securing usage data, as inlinks are known to be a constituent element of the famous Google algorithm for which an organization is returned at the top of search results, so they provide some indication of usage. Taking this argument to its extreme, the phenomenon of Wikipedia, an entirely virtual organization, can only be studied with the type of analysis carried out by Loubser (2009), who downloaded the entire edit history of Wikipedia, including all administrator actions. and examined the governance arrangements as they have operated over time, rather than as they were hypothesized to operate by the organization's founders. The task presented a methodological challenge – the data set was so large that the Grid, rather than the Internet, had to be used to obtain and store the data – but provided an unprecedented opportunity to study an organization in its entirety.

Conclusion

The Internet has brought change to political life, and throws a challenge to political science by raising real questions for the micro-foundations of the study of politics – as for all the social sciences. Just as sociologists must take account of online networks where much of social life takes place and economists must look at online commercial behaviour, as political scientists we should take a fresh look at our discipline.

The challenge to political science is theoretical, empirical and methodological. Theoretically, the Internet requires the re-evaluation of some of the long-standing puzzles of political science. Whatever theoretical or conceptual framework is used to study politics, there are likely to be some implications of Internet-based activity for incentives to act politically, for the costs and benefits of participation, for political organization and mobilization, for the ecology of political organizations, for institutional design and for the attainment of normative democratic principles. There is no over-arching theory or model of politics and the Internet that can be observed, and it is perhaps the search for one that has turned political science against incorporating Internet-based developments into the mainstream. Rather, the task should be to look at individual theories and concepts of specific areas of political life and consider change at this micro-level.

Empirically, political science cannot afford to ignore the new types of data being generated by online activity. As noted above, online organizations can only be studied with the type of analysis carried out by Loubser (2009), who downloaded the whole transactional history of a huge organization. Such a task represents not only a challenge, but also an opportunity for political science. Never before has there been an opportunity to study an organization in this way. Now that the Internet and related technologies form such an integral part of all governmental organizations and political institutions, they cannot be studied without taking account of this kind of data. But, similarly, the transactional data about both internal operations and citizen–government interactions that can be available presents an unprecedented opportunity for the study of political institutions of all kinds.

Methodologically, as discussed in the previous section, these developments present a further challenge to political science, involving technical skills and expertise not only from other social science disciplines but also from computer science and even physics, the discipline that has done most to design and to study the structure of the Internet and World Wide Web. Some of the methodologies discussed here (such as webmetrics, network analysis and experiments) should form an increasingly important part of the study of political behaviour and institutions: they require new skills, but present the possibility of rich pay-offs.

Mainstream political science has been slow to recognize the importance of the Internet. It is also notoriously bad at prediction, failing to predict the Obama phenomenon or the Iranian demonstrations (although the signs were there, see Wheeler 2007) or any of the other developments noted in the Introduction. Perhaps it is time to make a connection.

Chapter 4

The New Politics of Equality

JOHANNA KANTOLA AND JUDITH SQUIRES

Introduction

The politics of equality have changed quite profoundly in recent times, with significant theoretical and practical developments changing the ways in which equality is both conceived and pursued. We have witnessed a paradigm shift in equality thinking, with the 'old' politics of equality that focused primarily on the redistribution of material wealth being subject to a sustained period of critique, which has ultimately unsettled the norms of previous equality perspectives and ushered in a 'new' politics of equality.

The impact of social movement activism, coupled with increased migration, growing employment opportunities for women, the emergence of the knowledge economy and multi-level governance converged to place the demand for cultural 'recognition' on the agenda alongside issues of socio-economic equality. Following a lengthy period of contestation between advocates of redistribution and recognition perspectives, a new equality paradigm is emerging, characterized by multi-dimensional equality considerations and horizontal equality measures. The period of paradigm shift has been characterized by a shift from unitary to multiple indicators of inequality; from primarily redistributive considerations to complex concerns with recognition and representation; from welfare policies that focus on the poor to anti-discrimination policies focused on women, ethnic minorities, the disabled and an increasing number of other identity groupings; from output-based indicators of success, to procedural indicators; and from largely national to international and transnational forms of political engagement by equality advocates and professionals.

Following this period of transition, a 'new' politics of equality is emerging, in which the problem of inequality is increasingly cast as a 'horizontal' issue of social inclusion to be addressed through legal and bureaucratic mechanisms, rather than a 'vertical' issue of absolute or relative poverty to be addressed by social welfare policies. Where the old politics of equality aimed for a more equal economic distribution of resources, the new politics of equality strives for greater social inclusion and more equal opportunities to participate in economic markets and political decision-making. In this paradigm, equalities are plural and diversity is to be recognized and celebrated, inequality is multi-dimensional and multiple inequality indicators are needed, common legislative frameworks are appropriate and single equalities bodies are deemed most effective.

This chapter analyzes the changing politics of equality by comparing the 'old' and 'new' politics of equality. It does this by mapping in turn the political context, theorising, and institutional practices that together shape equality politics. The 'old' and 'new' politics have themselves been dynamic. Key developments within what we label the 'old' politics of equality include the shift from a social-democratic concern with equality of outcome to a more pervasive neo-liberal concern with equality of opportunities in policies seeking to address global inequalities; the turn from theories of distributive justice to theories of recognition in conceptualizing equality; and the use of both anti-discrimination and positive action measures as central mechanisms for securing equality in relation to a number of distinct identity groups. Key developments within what we label the 'new' politics of equality include changing state governance structures associated with globalization and the rise of such international actors as the European Union (EU), coupled with the transnationalization and professionalization of equality movements, changing demographics and migration patterns; the theoretical commitment to combining redistribution, recognition and representation through a 'capabilities' approach to inequalities; and the widening of categories of inequality from gender and class to cover multiple inequalities (including race, ethnicity, sexuality, age, and disability), which results in the growing trend away from a separate strands approach towards the creation of single equalities bodies and common equalities legislation.

Our argument is that we are currently in a period of 'exceptional' policy-making with respect to equality policy, in which 'the parameters that previously circumscribed policy options' are reconfigured (Hay 2004: 505). The number of equality reviews currently underway, together with the growing numbers of new equality institutions and new legislative frameworks, signals something of a 'paradigm' shift in this policy area. The appeal to a capabilities approach, coupled with the multi-dimensional equality agenda, presents new normative and institutional challenges to theories and politics of equality.

These developments pose challenges for the discipline of political science. First, the focus on multi-dimensional equality requires those strands of research that were previously pursued in relative isolation – such as multiculturalism, the politics of gender, disability studies and so on – to engage more directly with one another (see Verloo 2006), recognizing their growing theoretical interdependence. Second, the practical emphasis on anti-discrimination legislation and human rights frameworks in state responses to inequalities demands analysis that draws not only on traditional political science methodologies, but also on legal approaches (Skjeie 2007). Third, the central role played by transnational processes and actors in the development of national equality policies highlights the need for multi-level modelling, and a greater interaction between political science and international relations than has often been the case to date.

'Old' politics of equality

This section starts with the ways in which the politics of equality has traditionally been conceived, mapping the shift from 'equality of outcome' to 'equality of opportunities' in policies seeking to address global inequalities. It then turns to the conceptual developments, depicting the way in which theoretical debates on equality moved from theories of distributive justice to theories of recognition as fundamental to equality. Institutional developments are then surveyed, focusing on the extent to which the past decade saw a proliferation of institutional mechanisms, such as quotas and policy agencies, aimed at ensuring presence for and giving voice to previously marginalized groups.

Contextual: increasing global inequalities

It has been common, since the 1990s, to hear social commentators stating that 'equality has gone out of fashion' (Toynbee 2005). Equality, it seemed, had become a redundant value from another era. The emergence of neo-liberalism during the 1970s resulted in increased levels of confidence in the market as the best mechanism for the allocation of resources and a widespread concern that welfare benefits acted as disincentives to market participation (Hay 2004: 507–8). In this context, the social-democratic commitment to equality of outcome as a normative ideal, along with the policy tools that had been developed to realize this ideal, became increasingly marginal (see Letwin 1983). Reductions in top rates of taxation, coupled with a move away from welfare benefit programmes to 'welfare to work' programmes generated greater inequality in the distribution of income from wages and salaries (see, for a UK example, Office of National Statistics (2008)). The changing distribution of wealth since the 1970s was a story of increasing economic inequalities, whilst social policy focused on social integration through paid work and moral regulation rather than poverty alleviation (Levitas 2005). Talk of equality of outcome came to sound like an old politics of envy (Phillips 1999), with the public in advanced industrial democracies generally endorsing the idea of equal opportunities and protection from discrimination, but expressing scepticism about the idea of equal outcomes (Howard and Tibballs 2003: 7).

Yet, whilst equality of outcome fell off the political agenda, there was considerable activity across the globe in relation to anti-discrimination legislation. There have, of course, been some attempts to address income inequality. The United Nations declared 1997–2007 to be the International Decade for the Eradication of Poverty, and many governments around the globe have focused attention on alleviating poverty. Nonetheless, here, social justice is generally perceived to require strategies for raising the poorest above the poverty threshold; it was not concerned with levels of wealth amongst the rich. Significant changes in the socio-economic environment led to different kinds of inequality becoming central public policy concerns. Falling birth rates across Europe, coupled with increased migration, led to a more ethnically diverse workforce, which placed the issue of equal treatment between different racial groups at the forefront of social policy. The reduction of manufacturing jobs and rise in service sector work brought more employment opportunities for women, which accentuated the concern with equal pay for women. Meanwhile, the focus on the knowledge economy made the educational under-performance of disabled people, boys, and certain ethnic minorities of growing concern. This resulted in a paradigmatic shift in equality considerations, placing the issue of 'horizontal equality', or equality between identity groups, on the political agenda, often at the expense of the earlier focus on absolute and relative inequality between social classes.

Since the 1970s, states developed a growing patchwork of legislative instruments to protect against discrimination, much of it focused on discrimination with respect to race or sex. Over the past forty years, countries around the world have introduced a raft of new measures to tackle non-socio-economic inequalities, including those of race, gender and, more recently, disability. The anti-discrimination laws developed during this period operated within a formal equality of opportunity framework by banning direct discrimination on the basis of particular identities, codified as protected grounds. They largely worked within the logic of the market and focused on individual justice rather than structural inequality (Baker *et al.* 2004: 125–9).

Conceptual: theories of distributive equality and the challenge of recognition

Equality concerns, having largely subsided in elite political discourse, re-emerged through a new understanding of equality. Social movements were key agents of the return to the discourse of equality, newly configured. Developing from the civil rights movement in the United States, movements across the globe focused attention on racism, sexism, ageism, and discrimination in relation to disability and sexual orientation, complicating prior equality discourses that had focused primarily on class inequalities (Baker *et al.* 2004: 10). The demands of these egalitarian movements challenged not only elite policy discourse, but also academic conceptions of inequality. The old equality discourse, which had focused on the distribution of material goods, was increasingly cast by radical social movements as overly reductive, and by political elites as unrealistically utopian. The combined critiques of the 'new left' and the 'new right' ushered in the new politics of equality.

Whilst policy-makers generally eschewed equality of outcomes in favour of an opportunities focus, much of the theoretical reflection on equality during this period similarly took equality of opportunity as its point of departure. Ronald Dworkin, renowned egalitarian theorist, states categorically that, 'no one would now seriously propose equality of outcome as a political ideal' (Dworkin 2002: 2), and egalitarian theorists focused their attention on evaluating the relative merits of different forms of equality of opportunity (Swift 2001). The radical conception of equality of opportunity articulated by Dworkin and the 'luck egalitarians' challenged the assumption that inequality is acceptable as long as it is based on talent alone, arguing that the talented and untalented should be equally entitled to rewards given that talent is a matter of luck. They proposed that states should tailor the distribution of scarce goods on the basis of effort and choice, creating equal opportunities to earn income within a market economy (Dworkin 2002: 87).

Yet, this approach to equality was increasingly challenged, both theoretically and practically, during the 1990s, echoing the more practical challenge of the social movements. Whilst some scholars critiqued the central emphasis on choice and market participation (Armstrong 2006), others questioned by distributive focus *per se*. Influentially, Iris Young argued that, whilst there were pressing reasons to attend to the issues of the distribution of wealth and resources, 'many public appeals to justice do not concern primarily the distribution of material goods' (Young 1990:19), but focus on stereotyping and negative cultural representations. She suggested that, in order to pursue these wider goals of equality, one needed to engage with and eradicate oppression – which 'consists in systematic institutional processes which inhibit people's ability to play and communicate with others or to express their feelings and perspectives on social life in context where others can listen' (*ibid*.: 38) – and domination, which 'consists in institutional conditions which inhibit or prevent people from participating in determining their actions' (*ibid*.: 38). Accordingly, Young proposed that mechanisms for the effective representation of all citizens should entail institutional and financial support for the self-organization of oppressed groups, group generation of policy proposals, and group veto power regarding specific policies that affect a group directly (Young 2000: 141–1; see also the chapter by Tariq Modood in this volume).

This challenge to the 'politics of distribution' brought the issue of recognition to the forefront of theoretical debate (Taylor 1992), and suggested that formal anti-discrimination laws needed to be supplemented by positive action measures in order to ensure greater social inclusion for marginalized groups. Anne Phillips' (1995) defence of a 'politics of presence', which required positive action to ensure women's equal participation in national legislatures, developed similar themes – themes that have been echoed in public policy developments across the globe in recent years. The old politics of redistribution now adopted a more discrete role, even for social democratic and socialist governments, which frequently resorted to 'doing good by stealth' (Lister 2001). For example, in the United Kingdom the language of 'opportunity' and 'social exclusion' was used to frame policies such as the alleviation of child poverty and the introduction of a minimum wage. The newly emergent equality politics did not totally supplant the prior concern with redistribution, but they did elicit a 'quiet redistribution', pursued to 'muted applause' (*ibid*.: 66).

Institutional: group representation and equality bodies

Whilst the pursuit of economic equality dropped down the political agenda, inequalities experienced by various identity groups have become of greater policy concern. These equality policies have traditionally been directed at specific groups: women, ethnic minorities, disabled, or sexual minorities. In Europe, too, most countries have traditionally had single-dimensional equality, and discrimination acts that dealt either with gender, race and ethnicity, or with disability. This single-strand approach to equality policy is also reflected in the organizational structures of civil society groups that remain stratified by single-identity categories. These represent a 'vertical' or 'unitary approach' to inequality – namely, foregrounding one category at the expense of others as the most relevant or most explanatory in particular situations of social disadvantage (Hancock 2007: 67). Practically and institutionally, the unitary approach has resulted in different levels and types of provisions for different groups, ranging from the differences in policy-making tools and the scope of legislation to differences in law enforcement agencies and equality bodies.

Gender equality, in particular, has gained a central place on the global political agenda over the last thirty years, with the pursuit of gender equality widely endorsed as a central policy goal by governments and international organizations around the world (Inglehart and Norris 2003). Of course, gender equality can be understood in a range of ways, variously focusing attention on life expectancy and income distribution (Sen 1992), welfare regimes and employment rates (Sainsbury 1999) or political participation (Kenworthy and Malami 1999). Its role as a '*bon mot*' in political discourse generally rested on a presumption that the equality in question was formal equality of opportunity between women and men, particularly within the political arena. Influentially, the United Nations *Platform for Action* stated that 'without the active participation of women and the incorporation of women's perspectives at all levels of decision-making, the goals of equality, development and peace cannot be achieved' (UN 1995: 181).

The active participation of women in decision-making has been pursued by means of three central strategies: candidate quotas, women's policy agencies and gender mainstreaming (Squires 2007). Candidate gender quotas have been adopted in more than one hundred countries and, whilst this has led to the suggestion that 'quota fever' has affected the world (Dahlerup and Freidenvall 2005: 32), scholars offer differing explanations for quota adoption, ranging from women's mobilization and transnational norm dissemination to the strategic incentives of political elites (Krook 2006, 2009). There is also significant divergence in relation to evaluations of their impact, including arguments that the adoption of quotas has led to increases, stagnation, and even decreases in the numbers of women elected. Nonetheless, the widespread adoption of candidate quotas is a clear manifestation of the growing commitment to the use of positive actions measures to promote the political equality of women. Candidate quotas are part of the new, rather than old, politics then, because they aim primarily to recognize women's political under-representation and to secure their improved social inclusion; they aim to counteract institutional processes that reinforce cultural domination, rather than to redistribute material resources that perpetuate economic inequality. The resulting policies focus on levels of 'descriptive' rather than 'substantive' representation: with the number of women present in decision-making arenas, rather than the nature of the decisions made and their impact on the female electorate (Celis *et al.* 2008).

A second key strategy that emerged during this period to address gender equality was gender mainstreaming. Adopted by the United Nations at the 1995 conference on women in Beijing and then taken up by the European Union, its member states and international development agencies, gender mainstreaming is now 'an international phenomenon' (True 2003; Walby 2005a). Best understood as a set of tools and processes that help to integrate a gender perspective into all policies at the planning stage, mainstreaming operates by requiring those involved in the policy process to consider the likely effects of policies on the respective situation of women and men, and then revise proposed policies if necessary, such that they promote gender equality rather than reproduce gender inequality. Whilst the theoretical potential of gender mainstreaming was initially thought to be significant, evaluations of its practical implementation to date have been somewhat more circumspect (Bacchi and Eveline 2004; Teghtsoonian 2004; Daly 2005; Rees 2005). Critics worry that organizations are adopting some of the mainstreaming tools in the absence of an overall gender framework, focusing on the effective implementation of specific techniques of policy praxis and bracketing larger questions about social transformation (Daly 2005: 436). In line with the general features of the new equality politics, there is a targeting of tools here rather than of equality itself. Given that equality of opportunity is so difficult to measure – and, hence, monitor – techniques tend to stand in for outputs as measures of effectiveness. As a result, legitimacy increasingly resides with being seen to adopt the appropriate techniques rather than actually generating greater equality.

In addition to development of the legislative framework to include positive action policies, and the emergence of 'soft law' tools such as gender mainstreaming, gender equality advocates also successfully lobbied for the creation of dedicated policy agencies. Following the United Nations World Conference on Women in Mexico City in 1975 – which recommended that governments establish agencies dedicated to promoting gender equality, and improving the status and conditions of women – women's policy agencies were actively promoted by transnational women's groups and widely adopted by national governments throughout the late 1970s and 1980s (Chappell 2002). By 2004, 165 countries had women's policy agencies (DAW 2004), representing a 'rapid global diffusion' of a state-level bureaucratic innovation that is 'unprecedented in the post-war era' (True and Mintrom 2001: 30). Although the form and remit of these policies agencies differed across European countries, research indicates that they have generally been successful in advancing women's concerns, both substantively and descriptively (McBride Stetson and Mazur 1995; Mazur 2002; Rai 2003; True 2003; Outshoorn and Kantola 2007; Squires 2007). They have done so by establishing effective links between women's movements and the state, and facilitating women's access into decision-making processes (Mazur 2001; McBride Stetson 2001; Outshoorn 2004; Lovenduski 2005, 2007; Haussman and Sauer 2007). All of this indicates that gender equality has become widely accepted as a political goal over recent decades, with many countries and transnational institutions committing themselves to gender equality; conventions have been signed, special bureaucracies and new political and administrative positions created, new policy and legal instruments developed and installed, and progress monitored in newly produced indices and rankings.

   Yet, it is not only gender equality that has grown in public significance; whilst state institutions have been created to promote greater gender equality, multicultural policies have been adopted to respond to the challenges of cultural diversity (Kymlicka 1995; Parekh 2000; Modood 2007) and the demands of other identity groups – including disability (Albert 2004), religious belief (Bader 2003), sexuality (Richardson 2005) and age (Fredman and Spencer 2003) – have all emerged as key political concerns. This is symptomatic of the degree to which contemporary 'equality' policies and theories now tend to focus on issues of cultural and political inequality, rather than inequalities in distributional goods. Those who are considered to be 'unequal' are increasingly seen to be ethnic minorities, disabled, the elderly, gays and lesbians, religious minorities and so on, rather than the poor. Poverty is no longer the focus for the new politics of equality, notwithstanding the fact that many of the minority groups are differentially exposed to poverty. This is particularly evident in the EU's framing of equality, due in large measure to the specific nature of the EU's powers, which lead it to focus on equal treatment in employment (Walby 2004).

Whereas a range of policy tools has emerged to address gender inequality, the other equality strands generally enjoyed fewer provisions. For example, in the EU, serious differences remain in the scope of the anti-discrimination law, with consequences for the equal treatment of individuals. The scope of the Racial Equality Directive adopted in 2000 is wide, covering discrimination in employment, social protection, social advantages, education, and access to and supply of goods and services. By contrast, directives on gender equality cover equal pay, equal treatment in employment and self-employment to pregnancy protection, parental leave, access to and supply of goods and services, and certain social rights, but not education (as in the Racial Equality Directive). The other bases – disability, age, religion and belief, and sexual orientation – are covered only in the Employment Equality Directive and, hence, exist only in relation to the labour market. The same discrepancy can also been seen in terms of equality bodies that are well developed in relation to gender, but less so in relation to other bases of inequality. The Racial Equality Directive 2000 requires member states to establish bodies to monitor and enforce racial and ethnic equality. The Convention on the Rights of Persons with Disabilities and its Optional Protocol adopted by the United Nations General Assembly in December 2006 requires the same for disabilities, but a number of member states have not been able to ratify the Convention because they lack an equalities body that would deal with the rights of disabled. Hence, this vertical approach to equality policies has become subject to increasing scrutiny: perceived by many to be, itself, a source of inequality, providing different levels of provisions to different groups.

The 'new' politics of equality

Although equality politics develop incrementally, we suggest that we can usefully delineate a 'new' politics that is now emerging. In this second section, we focus on the changing nature of the politics of equality – again, focusing on contextual, conceptual and institutional developments in turn. Changing state governance structures, narratives of globalization, coupled with the transnationalization and professionalization of equality movements provide the new context for equality politics. Theories of equality, in turn, increasingly seek to combine redistribution, recognition and representation. Conceptually, this generates a growing concern with issues of 'capabilities' and intersectional discrimination. Institutionally, the changes have resulted in equality reviews and moves towards single equalities bodies and common legislative frameworks.

Contextual: changing patterns of governance

The new politics of equality emerges in a context of changing governance structures, which impact on the question of who has responsibility for ensuring equality compliance and promotion. Some scholars suggest that globalization and transnationalization present activists and practitioners with a depoliticized and remote state at the same time as the role of international actors has increased (Banaszak *et al.* 2003). The impact of internationalization on national-level equality politics is deemed positive in relation to some actors, such as the UN (True and Mintrom 2001), and negative in relation to others, such as the IMF (Rai 2003, 2008). The UN Beijing *Platform for Action* 1995 resulted in a global spread of progressive gender norms, equality bodies and policies, whilst the IMF structural adjustment programmes led to rolling back state services – with detrimental consequences to women. Equality movements, too, have become transnationalized as well as professionalized. Increasingly, transnational advocacy networks, rather than cohesive national movements, now drive forward equality demands in relation to gender and other identity claims (Keck and Sikkink 1998). Transnational feminist advocates have been rather successful in putting pressure on states around the globe to adopt gender regimes that are consonant with newly emerging international policy norms. Such 'boomerang effects' (Keck and Sikkink 1998) depend on close interaction between the international, national and local levels of policy-making. This interaction can lead to national and local interpretations of international minimum standards on equality.

Regionally, the EU is exerting increasing influence in the field of equality politics. The EU is a prime example of a powerful international actor whose standards and norms are spread (Europeanized) to member states and beyond. In equality politics, the EU has become a carrier and promoter of the new politics of equality. For example, the EU directives have triggered and fundamentally shaped the ways that national legislation has been formulated in most member states in the field of anti-discrimination (Bell 2008; Bustelo 2009; Kantola and Nousiainen 2009; Koldinská 2009; Squires 2009). The EU's enhanced role in the field of the new politics of equality has been explained with reference to the economic frame and neo-liberal thinking behind the reforms (Rossilli 2000; Young 2000) where declining labour force and increasing need for workers from outside 'Fortress Europe' necessitate 'diversity management' (Wrench 2005). Effective competition requires the decrease of discrimination that distorts the labour market. On the other hand, a strong human rights frame has emerged in the European level of policy-making. Here, the ratification of the Lisbon Treaty would further strengthen this tendency, in that it would give the Charter of Fundamental Rights of the Union the same legal value as the main treaties, as well as result in the EU itself acceding to the European Convention on Human Rights.

These patterns can change both the practices and priorities of equality campaigners, impacting on the way in which, for example, feminists make their political claims, and the nature of the claims themselves (Kantola and Squires 2008). Changing practices mean that the promotion of equality is now made with appeal to economic indicators, using impact assessments carried out by 'equality experts' (Squires 2007). Equality politics take place in 'project societies' where the states and international actors fund competitive short-term projects as opposed to permanent funding, thus impacting on the practices of movements (Kantola 2009).

Changing priorities are seen in the new language and rhetorical framing of equality, both deploying the logic of the market and located within arguments about increased economic efficiency. For example, in the EU context, claims have to be framed with a language acceptable to EU level policy-making. Here, Hobson *et al.* (2008) argue that the indigenous Saami people have benefited from the funding and lobbying opportunities provided by the EU. Yet, the consequence has been that Saami claims must be framed within the framework of entrepreneurialism, whose individualist and market oriented discourse is in direct contrast with the community-centred values of the Saami people (Hobson *et al.* 2008: 49–50). Projects that aim for the establishment of competitive and profitable outcomes are prioritized at the expense of community-building or empowerment measures. The groups are also differently positioned in relation to the dominance of market-based arguments. Some claims about gender equality are easy to make in market terms (for example, the need to increase women's labour market participation, or reconcile work and family) although such framings continue to be criticized by feminists (see, for example, Stratigaki 2004). The ILGA (International Lesbian and Gay Association) Europe sought too to frame the problems faced by sexual minorities in terms of the internal market and barriers to competition and free movement. Yet, the rights of sexual minorities continued to be hampered by the fact that they are not that easily translated into the market-driven character of the EU (Bell 2002: 92, 97).

Conceptual: equality as redistribution, recognition and representation

Although many equality activists welcome the new-found commitment to equality measures, the growing focus on equality of opportunity amongst diverse identity groups generated a concern that considerations of economic inequality were being marginalized by equality advocates themselves (Fraser 1995; Barry 2001). The shift of attention from class inequalities to gender, racial or cultural hierarchies was argued to polarize economic and political approaches to inequalities, with political approaches appearing to jettison concern with economic issues altogether (Phillips 1999: 15). Fraser influentially proposes a theoretical framework that addresses both the political economy and culture, addressing both redistribution and recognition as equally significant elements of inequality (Fraser 2000), whilst Young has suggested that the two need to be combined with representation (Young 2000). Similarly, Phillips argues that, whilst concern about political equality is high on the agenda, there is a worrying indifference to economic inequality. Indeed, she links the retreat from economic egalitarianism with the emergence of the idea that equality is all about recognition (Phillips 1999; see also Tariq Modood in this volume).

It is in this context that the concern with socio-economic inequality is being re-affirmed, with growing evidence that the increased levels of income inequality have contributed to a range of social ills, from mental health problems to declining social capital being deployed. Research is building up to show not only that poverty can trigger poor mental health, but also that mental health difficulties are greater in countries with high levels of income and social inequality (World Health Organization 2009; Wilkinson 2005). Social epidemiologists argue that levels of equality correlate directly with life expectancy in rich nations: Greece, with half the GDP per head, has longer life expectancy than the United States, the richest and most unequal country with the lowest life expectancy in the developed world. Indeed, recent research suggests that the reason why the people of Harlem live shorter lives than those in Bangladesh is largely attributable not to bad diet, but to stress; the stress of disrespect and lack of esteem (Wilkinson 2005). In other words, there is clear evidence of a direct correlation between income inequality and health inequality, with debate focused on whether it is relative or absolute poverty that best explains this link (Lynch *et al.* 2000).

One feature of the 'new' politics of equality is therefore an emergent acknowledgement that socio-economic inequality might need to be addressed by public policy measures, and that the pre-occupation with equality of opportunity rather than outcome, coupled with a focus on identity-based inequality, might need to be reconsidered.

There is a growing recognition that indicators of inequality are themselves diverse, including life expectancy and physical health, bodily integrity and safety, educational access and attainment, access to paid work, rates of pay, political empowerment, and being treated with dignity (Robeyns 2003: 76–86). Given the fact of human diversity, egalitarianism cannot be reduced to the distribution of one thing, and the process of determining what the criteria of equality are to be is an ineluctably political one for, given existing inequalities, different people are likely to privilege different egalitarian concerns. So, for example, Amartya Sen (1992) criticizes Dworkin's account of the initial equality of resources and Rawls' account of primary goods as neglecting the importance of diversity, in that different people will need different amounts and kinds of goods to reach the same levels of well-being. Social diversity means that the conversion of resources into opportunities will vary from person to person: some people will need more than others to achieve the same capabilities. Differences in age, gender, disability, and so on can mean that two people with the same 'commodity bundle' will have divergent opportunities regarding quality of life. He suggests, therefore, that human diversity 'is no secondary complication (to be ignored, or to be introduced 'later on'); it is a fundamental aspect of our interest in equality' (Sen 1992: xi). In this way, Sen introduces the notion of multiplicity to the distribution process, broadening the focus on equality debates beyond resources to whatever people need to develop their capabilities.

Whilst recognizing the value of pluralizing the measure of inequality, some scholars have found the capabilities approach to be limited by its 'under-specified character' (Robeyns 2003: 67), and have attempted to make it more concrete by specifying a list of human capabilities that might be measured when trying to establish degrees of, for example, gender inequality. Most influentially, Nussbaum offers a cross-national basis for claims to social justice and equality by providing a philosophical justification for a universal account of human capabilities (Nussbaum 2003). Nussbaum's commitment to a universal list is aimed to guarantee a 'minimal conception of social justice' (*ibid.*: 40) that can challenge paternalism. Others emphasize the importance of the procedural aspects of democratic practice (Robeyns 2003: 69) where critical public discussion, or democratic deliberation, is vital to the realization of capabilities (Sen 1999: 153). This participation should not be viewed in 'an unduly narrow and restricted way' in terms of public balloting only (Sen 2004:

7), but should embrace the messy processes of participatory democracy: 'Such processes as participation in political decisions and social choice cannot be seen as being – at best – amongst the means to development ... but have to be understood as a constitutive part of the ends of development' (Sen 1999: 291; 2004).

This suggests that the capabilities that concern us in relation to equality are, themselves, a product of political deliberation: the list of capabilities is culturally and historically specific rather than universal, a product of dialogue and contestation rather than abstract reflection. Moreover, perceptions as to whether these capabilities might reasonably be expected to be evenly realized by all social groups also present an issue of political contestation. In other words, in considerations of equality what comes to count as a norm of evaluation is a product of social deliberation. If this deliberation is delimited to certain groups of participants only, the current (socially constructed) priorities and preferences of these groups are likely to prevail in the devising of the list of capabilities of concern and determining the relative importance assigned to each. This 'capabilities' approach is emerging as a favoured theoretical framework for thinking about the meaning of equality (see, for instance, Cabinet Office 2007), recognizing, as it does, the diversity of values and preferences of individuals (so avoiding the apparent paternalism or equality of outcome), whilst emphasizing that social institutions and policies can enhance/stunt an individual's life changes (so avoiding the apparent individualism of equality of opportunity). For instance, by adopting an aggregative Human Development Index, the Human Development Report of the United Nations Development Programme has shifted the focus of policy discourse from such mechanical indicators of economic progress as GNP and GDP to 'indicators that come closer to reflecting the well-being and freedoms actually enjoyed by populations' (Anand and Sen 2000).

Meanwhile, the turn away from equality of outcome towards equality of opportunity, coupled with the turn away from distributive considerations towards those of recognition, resulted in the pursuit of equality being increasingly focused on the elimination of discrimination, but discrimination in relation to multiple inequality strands. This has not only meant tackling each strand separately (as in the unitary approaches discussed), but also understanding what happens when they intersect – thereby moving the policy and legislative agenda towards 'multiple' and potentially 'intersectional' approaches, or possibly beyond a separate 'strands' approach altogether. This is perhaps the key feature of the new politics of equality.

Feminist theory has long highlighted the need to understand 'intersectionality', a term coined by Kimberly Crenshaw (1991) to address the legal and policy consequences of the discrimination faced by black women. Crenshaw argued that black women are located at the intersection of racism and sexism and their experiences could be reduced to neither. The reliance of anti-discrimination law on a single-axis framework, where claims can be made on the basis of either race or sex but not both, deprives black women of the possibility of seeking justice as black women (*ibid.*: 57).

Importantly, it is the intersection of social structures and not identities to which intersectionality refers (McCall 2005; Weldon 2008; Conaghan 2009) – the pre-given identity categories that human rights discourse, anti-discrimination law, equality policies and institutions presume are thus rendered problematic. Instead, intersectional approaches explore the ways in which domination, subordination and subjects can be constructed in particular locations and contexts (Grabham *et al.* 2009: 2). Foucauldian analyses also highlight that identity groups do not exist prior to inequalities but are constituted in them and are the effects of power relations (Cooper 2004: 49–51). Here, intersectionality can even be argued to have disciplinary functions, as it can act as a governmental discourse that produces more identities (Grabham *et al.* 2009: 199). Other approaches, however, shy away from total deconstruction of categories of inequality highlighting the stable and durable relationships that social categories represent (McCall 2005: 1774). Despite the differences, intersectional approaches rest on the assumption that the relationship between the categories and structures is an open empirical question (Hancock 2007: 64). Focusing on the interaction of different structures of inequality results in fuller and more developed pictures of oppression and discrimination faced by different groups of people (Weldon 2008).

Whilst the issue of multiple inequalities is not new, the current political debate about multiple equality agendas has led to a debate about the relative merit of various equality demands (Phillips 1999; Barry 2001), and significant attention is currently paid to the tensions between the various equality strands, with particular theoretical focus on the relation between feminism and multiculturalism (Shachar 1999; Okin 2000; Phillips 2007; Skjeie 2007). This generates an emerging discussion relating to the differences between inequalities, which may necessitate specific institutional mechanisms for tackling specific discriminations (Verloo 2006). Scholars have argued that the current emphasis on 'multiple discrimination', however, assumes that the categories can be treated similarly, and does not address difficult political and normative issues about which category should be privileged at times of conflict (Squires 2009). Leaving such difficult questions unattended can foster competition, rather than coordination, between marginal groups where groups compete for the title of being most oppressed to gain attention and political support of dominant groups (Hancock 2007: 68, see also Tariq Modood in this volume).

Institutional: towards single equalities bodies and legislation

This multiple discrimination agenda has also had profound institutional consequences for tackling equalities. Some states are increasingly attempting to engage, at both a conceptual and policy level, with the fact that gender discrimination and inequality are shaped in fundamental ways not only by gender, but also by race, ethnicity, class, sexuality and disability.

Scholars are increasingly interested in exploring the potential that these new developments entail for tackling inequalities (Kantola and Nousiainen 2009). The positive assessment could highlight upward harmonization that considering the six strands together has meant for some grounds. For example, the EU Racial Equality Directive provided protection against discrimination in goods and services. This was later extended to protection against discrimination on the basis of gender in goods and services in the EU and later member states. This integrated approach to discrimination is thought to provide 'coherence, consistency, clarity and simplicity concerning individual rights to non-discrimination' as well as 'increased effectiveness and influence of the monitoring and enforcement authorities' (Skjeie 2008: 296). It is also advanced on the grounds that it enables tackling intersectional or multiple discrimination better than single grounds legislation and law enforcement bodies (Kantola and Nousiainen 2008: 18; Skjeie 2008: 296; Squires 2009).

Yet, feminist scholars are cautious about these developments. Feminist concerns about an integrated approach include the worry that the greater emphasis on, for example, race and disabilities will be at the expense of gender issues (Mazey 2002: 229; Kantola and Outshoorn 2007). The integration of the relevant governmental agencies might entail the dispersal of expertise, loss of contact with the specific constituencies, and a diluted approach; or it might be an opportunity for more efficient deployment of resources and a stronger approach (Walby 2005b: 462). Feminists have inquired whether the equality tools needed by diverse disadvantaged groups are sufficiently similar to share institutional spaces and policies, rather than each needing their own (*ibid*.: 462). Mieke Verloo (2006: 222) argues (in relation to gender, race, class and sexuality) that these bases for inequality are so dissimilar that the tools to tackle one form of inequality (for example, gender mainstreaming) cannot simply be adapted for other forms.

An illustration of the practical challenges related to intersectionality comes from the EU, where equality is currently being debated in terms of 'multiple discrimination' (Kantola and Nousiainen 2009). Recent research suggests that the emerging definitions narrow the debate down to discrimination (omitting other measures and tools such as positive action or mainstreaming), assume inherent similarities between the social categories or axis of inequality, and eclipse the issue of class and poverty (Kantola and Nousiainen 2009; Lombardo and Verloo 2009; Squires 2009).

Conceptualizing intersecting inequalities in terms of 'multiple discrimination' means that there is a heightened emphasis on a narrow anti-discrimination frame. This can eclipse developing different proactive measures in relation to multiple discrimination. According to some scholars, positive duties would be more effective than reactive complaints-based approaches as the initiative would lie with policymakers, service providers and employers. The duty to bring about change lies with those with the power and capacity to do so, not with the 'victim of discrimination' (Fredman 2008: 79–80).

A discrimination frame also results in the omission of class. Class-based inequalities can hardly be tackled with an anti-discrimination agenda. For example, in Europe, during recent decades, social and economic inequality has increased. Understanding poverty is fundamental, for instance, to making the situation of the Roma – arguably the most marginalized people in Europe – better (Goodwin 2008, Koldinská 2009). As socio-economic inequalities are dramatically increasing, anti-discrimination law should be considered alongside policies tackling poverty. The European social policies have, however, concentrated on discrimination because of the limited competences that the member states have been willing to delegate to the Union in this field. Under these circumstances, the EU has to enhance its social legitimacy by other means, such as anti-discrimination, as more effective social policies to combat poverty are not available (Kantola and Nousiainen 2009).

A significant number of states in Europe are in the process of changing their institutional arrangements for promoting equality. Several countries have created 'single equalities bodies' that bring law enforcement and implementation under one roof. Britain, for instance, has created an

Equality and Human Rights Commission (EHRC) – which has responsibility for enforcing equality legislation on age, disability, gender, race, religion or belief, sexual orientation or transgender status – and encourages compliance with the Human Rights Act (Lovenduski 2007; Squires 2008, 2009). The new member states in the Central and Eastern European Countries that had no ombudsmen prior to entry to the EU have followed a single equality bodies model from the start for economic and efficiency reasons (Koldinská 2009). Two Nordic countries, Sweden and Norway, which had a strong model of promoting gender equality, are following the same trajectory (Bergqvist *et al.* 2007; Skjeie and Langvasbråten 2009). However, the trend is not completely uniform. Finland, for instance, has opted for separate equalities bodies and Austria, too, has created three separate Ombuds (for women and men; for ethnic belonging, religion/belief, age and sexual orientation; and for equal opportunities with regard to ethnic belonging). It is too soon to evaluate the relative merits of these different institutional responses to the multi-dimensional equality agenda. However, it is clear that there is a general institutional and legislative trend away from vertical approaches to separate strands, towards horizontal approaches that adopt a common equalities framework. Such an approach might come to focus on 'trigger episodes' within a life-cycle, rather than on identity groups; whether it will rely primarily on anti-discrimination measures, or will also embrace positive action measures is as yet unclear.

Conclusion

In this chapter, we have discussed some key differences between the old and new politics of equality in terms of the changing context, concepts and institutions. We have analyzed the context in terms of a shift from social democratic values promoting equality of outcomes to neo-liberal ones favouring equality of opportunity. In the new politics of equality, this shift is intensified through the processes of internationalization and transnationalization, which, in turn, shape the practices and priorities of equality movement activists and practitioners. The conceptual shifts illustrated some key differences in answering questions about equality for whom. We discerned a shift from unitary approaches that favour particular categories such as 'women', 'ethnic minorities', or 'disabled' to multiple or intersectional approaches that look at intersections of structural inequalities, as evidenced in the positions of 'black women', 'young black boys', or 'lesbians'. Theoretical debates have moved from emphasizing either redistribution or recognition to combining both with representation. This synthesis is echoed in the capabilities approach, which seeks to stress the role of human diversity for equality. The contextual and conceptual developments are fundamentally shaping the institutional arrangements of equality policies, creating pressures towards an integrated equalities agenda institutionalized in single equalities bodies and law.

In conclusion, we would like to foreground three challenges that the new politics of equality poses to the discipline of political science. First, given that the new politics of equality is characterized by a focus on multi-dimensional equality considerations, any adequate theoretical or practical analysis of policy-making in this field now requires scholars of multiculturalism, gender, disability, religious belief, sexual orientation, and so on to engage directly with one another's theoretical debates and empirical studies in order to evaluate areas of synergy and tension. To date, these debates have tended to develop in isolation from one another, yet the political implications of anti-discrimination laws that are empowering for some groups (those based on disability and sexuality) whilst narrowing the notion of equality for others (those based on gender) need to be a central consideration for political science in an age of interdependence.

Second, addressing the new politics of equality in this chapter has relied on *interdisciplinary research*, and has drawn on law and politics in particular. With a heightened emphasis on anti-discrimination law, the new multiple inequalities agenda appears to be symptomatic of the judicialization of politics. Certain existing political science methodologies offer valuable tools for analyzing some of the aspects of the new politics of equality: historical institutional can, for instance, help to understand national variations in policy-making. However, methodological and approaches, and expertise from other disciplines – most notably legal scholarship – is also vital to evaluating the impact of the equal frameworks that are emerging.

Third, understanding and studying the new politics of equality requires *comparative research* that accounts for the impact of *the transnational and international levels* and, thereby, undertakes multi-level modelling. Central to the new politics of equality are the ways in which concepts, policies and legal institutions are filtered through different levels of governance from transnational to national and local levels, and back again. This points to the interdependence of the disciplines of political science and International Relations (IR) (see the Introduction to this volume by Colin Hay).

Finally, it is also worth noting that some challenges remain that are far from new. Throughout the chapter, we have highlighted *the interplay of theory and practice*. The need to pursue problem-driven research, which is theoretically sophisticated and methodologically eclectic, (Shapiro 2004) remains central. The current political changes in the equalities framework that transform equalities thinking and institutions point to the need to undertake applied research and to study policy impact. For example, feminist theories about 'intersectionality' and the political emphasis that many states and international actors place on 'multiple discrimination' seem to parallel one another. However, scholars have studied the significant discrepancies between the theory and the practice here, with significant consequences for individuals and groups at the intersections of inequalities. Political theorists and political scientists continue to have much to learn from a more thorough engagement with each other's crafts.

Chapter 5

Civic Multiculturalism and National Identity

TARIQ MODOOD

This chapter discusses a new strand in democratic politics: multiculturalism. In Europe, in particular, this is associated with the response to the mass immigration of the early postwar years. Political science – specifically, political theory – has played a key role in articulating and debating the normative claims of this politics. This has not only led to an acknowledgement of the emergence of new political actors, mobilizations, controversies and agendas, as part of a larger recognition of the diminishing role of class politics. It has also, as this chapter explains, been part of the interrogation of liberalism and the efforts to recast liberal egalitarian values in a less individualistic or ethnocentric politics. I focus on the latest group to adopt the cause of multiculturalism – namely, Muslims – who are not only associated with the decline of support for this politics, but who, as a religious group, pose a challenge for the secularist biases of political science. My purpose is to establish the nature of the political and intellectual challenge that multiculturalism poses, and to present an understanding of it that is also a justification for it as a political ideal.

Multiculturalism

Whilst, during most of the twentieth century, there was a left–right struggle concerning the extent to which citizenship should or should not entail social welfare and economic rights, illustrated in Marshall's well-known typology (Marshall 1992 [1950]), by the end of the century it was citizenship as identity that had moved to the top of political agendas (Joppke 2008: 534). The fundamental question had become: 'What is the identity of citizenship itself, and what does it imply for other identities that citizens might have or want

109

to have?' Or, 'How should the state and citizens relate to diversity?' Historically, modern states have created a national citizenry, where democratic rights and membership in a single nation have gone together. But, after the Second World War, nationalism was associated with militarism, colonialism and racism. Space was thus created for minority nations (such as the Quebecois or Scots) to challenge the dominant nationalism of the state, and for assimilation – the traditional formula for dealing with immigrants – to seem an illiberal response to the mass immigration from the developing world into the developed economies. At the forefront of this challenge to mono-nationalism was multiculturalism, together with Europeanism in western Europe and, in the context of a later globalization, an internationalism or cosmopolitanism. Multiculturalism – the political accommodation of minorities – is thus seen as part of socio-political processes leading to the lessening of importance of the nation-state and national identity that has been characterized as 'post-national' (Habermas 2001). Whilst migrant and second generation politics in Europe was initially based on mobilizing co-ethnics and opposing racism and xenophobia, a Muslim political subject has come to the fore in the way that few politicians or social scientists anticipated, let alone desired, at the birth of multiculturalism.

The term 'multiculturalism' emerged in the 1960s and 1970s in countries such as Canada and Australia, and, to a lesser extent, Britain and the United States. The policy focus was often initially on schooling and the children of Asian/black/Hispanic post/neo-colonial immigrants, and multiculturalism meant the extension of the school, both in terms of curriculum and as an institution, to include features such as 'mother-tongue' teaching, non-Christian religions and holidays, *halal* food, Asian dress, and so on. From such a starting point, the perspective developed to meeting such cultural requirements in other social spheres, and the empowering of marginalized groups. In Canada and Australia, however, the focus was much wider from the start and included, for example, constitutional and land issues. It has been about the definition of the nation. This was partly because these countries had a continuous and recent history of ethnic communities created by migration, usually from different parts of Europe, and because there were unresolved legal questions to do with the entitlements and status of indigenous people in those countries. Moreover, in the case of Canada, there was the further issue of the rise of a nationalist and secessionist movement in French-speaking Quebec. Hence, the term 'multiculturalism' in these countries came to mean, and now means throughout the English-speaking world and beyond, the political accommodation (by the state and/or a dominant group) of all minority cultures defined first and foremost by reference to race or ethnicity; and, additionally but more controversially, by reference to other group-defining characteristics such as nationality, aboriginality or religion – the latter being more controversial not only because they extend the range of the groups that have to be accommodated, but also because some of the latter groups tend to make larger political claims and so tend to resist having their claims reduced to those of immigrants.

Whilst, in North America, language-based ethnicity was seen as the major political challenge (Francophones in Canada, Hispanics in the United States), in western Europe, the conjunction of the terms 'immigration' and 'culture' now nearly always invokes the large, newly-settled Muslim populations. So, though 'multiculturalism' can have diverse meanings in different parts of the world, in Britain, and western Europe generally, it has come to mean the political accommodation of post-immigration communities of non-European descent, primarily from the former colonies and sources of cheap labour (as Turkey is to Germany). In this chapter, I shall confine myself to this concept. Whilst multiculturalism was becoming an influential view in the last decade of the twentieth century (exemplified in the title of a book by Nathan Glazer, *We Are All Multiculturalists Now* (1997), an erstwhile fierce opponent of affirmative action), during that decade, too, anxieties about the integration of Muslims were also developing. The terrorist attacks of 9/11 and their aftermath were blamed on multiculturalism and were said to have killed multiculturalism.

Academic argument has, however, no less than popular feeling been important in the formulation of multiculturalism, with the study of post-colonial and post-immigration societies and political theory at the forefront. If Rawls' *A Theory of Justice* (1971), the founding text of contemporary Anglo-American political theory, was Kantian in its philosophical approach and centred on the mid-twentieth century problem of distributive justice, Rawls and his critics came both to depart from that philosophical approach and to highlight a different set of political problems. In his next major book, *Political Liberalism* (Rawls 1993), in terms as resonant of the seventeenth as of the twentieth century, Rawls centres on the problem of pluralism: the question of how individuals of different moral beliefs could be persuaded to believe in, and affirm, the basic principles of justice in a constitutional regime. Interestingly, the focus on the limits of pluralism is imagined principally in terms of the political reconciliation of opposed *religious* views of the world, seeking a publicly recognized 'overlapping consensus' of common principles that would enable a workable framework of political decision-making (Favell and Modood 2003). The prominence of political theory in multiculturalism is to be partly understood in terms of the internal dynamic within the discipline. The generation of political theorists following Rawls came to define their questions more in terms of the nature of community and minority rights than in terms of distributive justice (see Kantola and Squires in this volume), no less than their social theory peers defined it in terms of difference and identity rather than class conflict, and, in each case, the intellectual framework lent itself to multiculturalism, even when the term itself was not favoured. The dominant axes of recent applied philosophical enquiry centred around the reconciliation of liberalism with communitarianism, universalism with the value of ethnic and cultural belonging, or equality with membership in a specific national society. Whilst, for most political theorists, academic liberalism has been the primary reference point, Bhikhu Parekh has offered a philosophical multiculturalism grounded in an analysis of human nature and culture, and which elaborates the intrinsic value of diversity as more fundamental than the accommodation of minorities (Parekh 2000).

Drawing on the political theory of multiculturalism, I would like to respond to the above-mentioned death of multiculturalism by restating a conception of multiculturalism. This I situate squarely within an understanding of democratic citizenship and nation-building. It offers, I suggest, a prospect of winning back the lost support for multicultural politics (see also Modood 2007).

Difference and equality

Multiculturalism gives political importance to a respect for identities that are important to people, as identified in minority assertiveness, arguing that they should not be disregarded in the name of integration or citizenship (Young 1990; Parekh 1991; Taylor 1994). Sociologically, we have to begin with the fact of negative 'difference': with alienness, inferiorization, stigmatization, stereotyping, exclusion, discrimination, racism, and so on; but also the senses of identity that groups so perceived have of themselves. The two together are the key datum for multiculturalism. The differences at issue are those perceived either by outsiders or group members to constitute not merely some form of distinctness, but a form of alienness or inferiority that diminishes or makes difficult equal membership in the wider society or polity. There is a sense of groupness in play, a mode of being, but also subordination or marginality, a mode of oppression – and the two interact in creating an unequal 'us–them' relationship (see Modood 2007). The differences in question are in the field of race, ethnicity, cultural heritage or religious community; typically, differences that overlap between these categories, not least because these categories do not have singular, fixed meanings.

Multiculturalism refers to the struggle, the political mobilization, but also to the policy and institutional outcomes and to the forms of accommodation in which 'differences' are not eliminated or washed away but are, to some extent, 'recognized'. In both of these ways, group assertiveness and mobilization, and through institutional and policy reforms to address the claims of the newly settled, marginalized groups, the character of 'difference' is addressed; ideally, a negative difference is turned into a positive difference, though in most contemporary situations something of each is likely to be present simultaneously.

It should be clear from the above that the concept of equality has to be applied to groups and not merely individuals (for example, Parekh 2000). Different theorists have offered different formulations on this question. Charles Taylor (1994), for example, argues that, when we talk about equality in the context of race and ethnicity, we are appealing to two different, albeit related, concepts, which slightly altering Taylor's nomenclature, I will call *equal dignity* and *equal respect*. Equal dignity appeals to people's humanity or to some specific membership such as citizenship, and applies to all members in a relatively uniform way. A good example is Martin Luther King Jr's demand for civil rights. He said black Americans wanted to make a claim upon the American dream; they wanted American citizenship in the way that the constitution, theoretically, is supposed to give to everybody but, in practice, failed to do so. We appeal to this universalist idea in relation to anti-discrimination policies where we appeal to the principle that everybody should be treated the same. But Taylor, and other theorists in differing ways, also posits the idea of *equal respect*. If equal dignity focuses on what people have in common – and so is gender-blind, colour-blind, and so on – equal respect is based on an understanding that difference is also important in conceptualizing and institutionalizing equal relations between individuals (see Kantola and Squires in this volume).

This is because individuals have group identities, and these might be the ground of existing and long-standing inequalities such as racism, for example, and the ways that some people have conceived and treated others as inferior, less rational and culturally backward. Whilst those conceptions persist, they will affect the dignity of non-white people – above all, where they share imaginative and social life with white people. Such negative conceptions will lead to direct and indirect acts of discrimination; they will eat away at the possibilities of equal dignity. They will affect the self-understanding of those who breathe in and seek to be equal participants in a culture in which ideas of their inferiority – or even simply their absence, their invisibility – is pervasive. They will stand in need of self-respect and the respect of others, of the dominant group; the latter will be crucial, for it is the source of their damaged self-respect and it is where the power for change lies (Du Bois 1999).

The interaction and mutuality between these two kinds of equality runs the other way too. Equal respect presupposes the framework of commonality and rights embodied in equal dignity. Hence, it is quite wrong to think of the latter in terms of universalism and the former as a denial of universality. For not only does the concept of equal respect grow out of a concern with equal dignity; it only makes sense because it rests on universalist foundations. It is only because there is a fundamental equality between human beings or between citizens that the claim for respect can be formulated. As Taylor says, there is a demand for an acknowledgement of specificity, but it is powered by the universal that an advantage that some currently enjoy should not be a privilege but available to all (1994: 38–9). Hence, we must not lose sight of the fact that *both* equal dignity and equal respect are essential to multicultural-ism; whilst the latter marks out multiculturalism from classical liberal-ism, it does not make multiculturalism normatively particularistic or relativist.

Some implications for liberal citizenship

Multiculturalism arises within contemporary liberal egalitarianism but it is, at the same time, in tension with, and a critique of, some classical liberal ideas. Specifically, it has four major implications for liberal citi-zenship. First, it is clearly a collective project and concerns collectivities and not merely individuals. Second, it is not colour/gender/sexual orien-tation 'blind', and so breaches the liberal public–private identity distinc-tion that prohibits the recognition of particular group identities in order that no citizens are treated in a more or less privileged way or divided from each other. In many ways, these two challenges to classical liberal-ism are not specific to multiculturalism. Whilst individual rights are fundamental to liberal democracies, much of social democratic egalitari-anism would be impossible if we did not also recognize groups in various ways. Examples that predate multiculturalism would include trades unions in relation to collective bargaining; the Welsh language as one of the national languages of Wales; the women's section in the Labour Party; or state funding for Christian schools. These examples could be multiplied, and they suggest that a liberal democratic polity undertakes in many different ways to recognize and empower diverse kinds of groups. The next two implications for liberal citizenship are less obvious and more controversial. The first of these is that multiculturalism takes race, sex and sexuality beyond being ascriptive sources of identity, mere categories. Liberal citizenship is not interested in group identities and shuns identity-based politics; its interest in 'race' is confined to anti-discrimination and simply as an aspect of the legal equality of citizens. Strictly speaking, race is of interest to liberal citizenship only because no one can choose their race; it is either a biological fact about them or, more accurately, is a way of being categorized by the society around them by reference to some real or perceived biological features, and so one should not be discriminated against on something over which one has no control. But if, as I have argued, equality is also about celebrating previously demeaned identities (for example, taking pride in one's blackness, rather than accepting it as a merely 'private' matter), then what is being addressed in anti-discrimination, or promoted as a public identity, is a chosen response to one's ascription – namely, pride, identity renewal, the challenging of hegemonic norms and asserting of marginalized identities, and so on. Of course, this is not peculiar to race/ethnicity. Exactly, the same applies to sex and sexuality. We may not choose our sex or sexual orientation, but we choose how to live with it politically. Do we keep it private or do we make it the basis of a social movement, and seek public resources and representation for it? In many countries, the initial liberal – and social democratic and socialist – response that the assertions of race, political femininity, gay pride politics, and so on were divisive and deviations from the only political identity that mattered (citizenship; and/or class, in the case of socialists) soon gave way to an understanding that these positions were a genuine and significant part of a plural, centre-left egalitarian movement.

Marginalized and other religious groups, most notably Muslims, are now utilizing the same kind of argument, and making a claim that religious identity – just as gay identity, and just as certain forms of racial identity – should not just be privatized or tolerated, but should be part of the public space (Modood 2005; Modood and Ahmad 2007). In their case, however, they come into conflict with an additional fourth dimension of liberal citizenship. Strictly speaking, this additional conflict with liberal citizenship is a version of the third (rather than a fourth) difficulty but, for many on the centre-left, this one, unlike the previous three, is seen as a demand that should not be conceded and so has to be treated differently. One would think that, if a new group were pressing a claim that had already been granted to others, then what would be at issue would be a practical adjustment, not fundamental principle. But, as a matter of fact, the demand by Muslims – for not only toleration and religious freedom, but also for public recognition – is, indeed, taken to be philosophically very different to the same demand made by black people, women and gays. It is seen as an attack on the principle of secularism, the view that religion is a feature, perhaps uniquely, of private and not public identity.

Hence, it is commonly found in the op-ed pages of the broadsheets that Muslims (and other religious groups) are simply not on a par with the groups with which I have aligned them. It is argued that woman, black and gay are ascribed, involuntary identities, whilst being a Muslim is about chosen beliefs, and that Muslims therefore need or ought to have less legal protection than the other kinds of identities. I think this is sociologically naïve (and a political con). The position of Muslims today, in countries such as Britain, is similar to the other identities of 'difference' as Muslims catch up with and engage with the contemporary concept of equality. No one chooses to be or not to be born into a Muslim family. Similarly, no one chooses to be born into a society where to look like a Muslim or to be a Muslim creates suspicion, hostility, or failure to get the job for which you applied. Of course, how Muslims respond to these circumstances will vary. Some will organize resistance, whilst others will try to stop looking like Muslims (the equivalent of 'passing' for white); some will build an ideology out of their subordination, others will not, just as a woman can choose to be a feminist or not. Again, some Muslims might define their Islam in terms of piety rather than politics; just as some women might see no politics in their gender, whilst for others their gender will be at the centre of their politics.

I reject, therefore, the contention that equality as recognition (uniquely) does not apply to oppressed religious communities. Of course, many people's objections might be based on what they (sometimes correctly) understand as conservative, even intolerant and inegalitarian views held by some Muslims in relation to issues of personal sexual freedom. My concern is with the argument that a commitment to a reasonable secularism rules out extending multicultural equality to Muslims and other religious groups.

I proceed on the basis of two assumptions. The first is that a religious group's views on matters of gender and sexuality, which of course will not be uniform, are open to debate and change; and the second is that conservative views cannot be a bar to multicultural recognition. For example, it is clear that 'moderate' Muslim public figures in Britain are divided about homosexuality (Modood and Ahmad 2007) in the same way that all religions seem to be divided today. Those who see the current Muslim assertiveness as an unwanted and illegitimate child of multiculturalism have only two choices, if they wish to be consistent. They can repudiate the idea of equality as identity recognition and return to the 1950s liberal idea of equality as colour/sex/religion, etc., blindness (Barry 2001); or they must appreciate that a programme of racial and multicultural equality is not possible today without a discussion of the merits and limits of secularism (Levey and Modood 2009).

Multicultural citizenship

Just as social democrats have a notion of positive equality around socio-economic equality, what is called 'social citizenship', I would like to make a parallel case for positive equality in connection with the symbolic dimensions of public culture. Citizenship is not merely a legal status and set of rights, but is amplified by a certain kind of politics. I have nothing specific to say about the former – the basic, foundational levels of citizenship – except that they are necessary (in the way of skeleton to a living body) to all wider meanings of citizenship. T.H. Marshall (1992 [1950]) famously conceptualized a wider citizenship as a series of historical-logical developments, each necessary to later stages, by which legal rights such as *habeas corpus* were gradually extended to include rights of political participation and then, later, to social rights – such as the right of citizens to receive health care funded by the citizens as a whole. These developments were a long process of centuries, involved a history of political struggles, not least in extending the body of citizenry, the rights-holders, from an aristocratic male elite to all adults. With some plausibility, it has been argued that, through egalitarian movements such as the politics of difference, the second half of the twentieth century has seen the emergence of a fourth stage, in the form of a demand for cultural rights (Roche 1992; Turner 1993), whilst also seeing an erosion of some social rights. Social citizenship has certainly not been accultural; rather, it has been informed by an assumption of cultural homogeneity, such as its support of a male breadwinner model of the nuclear family (Lister 2003). The homogeneity has been particularly exposed by social change and change in attitudes, and critiqued by feminists whose work – as with the public–private distinction – others have built upon. I would, however, here like to outline an understanding of this historically developing citizenship – which has not been a simple linear process – in terms of certain over-arching characteristics, rather than by types of rights; as Marshall, I believe the citizenship I speak of is particularly informed by British history, though it can be seen at work in many other places, too.

Non-transcendent or pluralist

Citizens are individuals and have individual rights, but they are not uniform and their citizenship contours itself around specific groups of people with specific cultures and histories. Citizenship is not a monistic identity that is completely apart from or transcends other identities important to citizens; in the way that the theory – though not always the practice – of French republicanism demands. The creation of the United Kingdom created new political subjects (for my purpose, citizens – though strictly speaking, for most of the history of the United Kingdom, subjects of the Crown) but did not eliminate the constituent nations of the United Kingdom. So, a common British citizenship did not mean that one could not be Scottish, English, Irish or Welsh, and so allowed for the idea that there were different ways of being British – an idea that is not confined to constituent nations, but also included other group identities. The plurality, then, is ever present, and each part of the plurality has a right to be a part of the whole and to speak up for itself and for its vision of the whole.

Multilogical

The plurality speaks to each other and it does not necessarily agree about what it means to be a citizen; there can be a series of agreements and disagreements, with some who agree on X whilst disagreeing on Y, whilst some who disagree on X might agree and others disagree on Y, and so on. But there is enough agreement – and, above all, enough interest in the discussion – for dialogues to be sustained. As the parties to these dialogues are many, not merely two, the process is more aptly described as multilogical. The multilogues allow for views to qualify each other, overlap, synthesize, modify one's own view in the light of having to co-exist with that of others, hybridize, allow new adjustments to be made, new conversations to take place. Such modulations and contestations are part of the internal, evolutionary, work-in-progress dynamic of citizenship.

Dispersed

Related to citizenship not being monolithic is that action and power are not monopolistically concentrated, and so the state is not the exclusive site for citizenship. We perform our citizenship and relate to each other as fellow citizens, and so get to know what our citizenship is, what it is composed of – not only in relation to law and politics, but also civic debate and action initiated through our voluntary associations, community organizations, trades unions, newspapers and media, churches, temples, mosques, and so on. Change and reform do not all have to be brought about by state action, laws, regulation, prohibitions and the like, but also through public debate, discursive contestations, pressure group mobilizations, and the varied and (semi-)autonomous institutions of civil society.

Even with such a brief sketch of citizenship, the deep resonance that exists between citizenship and multicultural recognition should be clear. Not only do both presuppose complementary notions of unity and plurality, and of equality and difference, but the idea of respect for the group self-identities that citizens' value is central to citizenship. Moreover, seeing citizenship as a work-in-progress and as partly constituted, and certainly extended, by contestatory multilogues and novel demands for due recognition, as circumstances shift, means that citizenship can be understood as conversations and re-negotiations, not only about who is to be recognized but also about what is recognition, about the terms of citizenship itself. At one point, it is the injuries of class that demand civic attention; at another, there is a plea for dropping a self-deluding 'colour-blindness' and of addressing racialized statuses through citizenship. The one thing that civic inclusion does not consist of is an uncritical acceptance of an existing conception of citizenship, of 'the rules of the game' and a one-sided 'fitting-in' of new entrants or the new equals (the ex-subordinates). To be a citizen, no less than to have just become a citizen, is to have a right to not only be recognized, but also to debate the terms of recognition (Benhabib 1992; Fraser 1992).

Muslims and identity

How does this relate to Muslim identity politics – one of the central sources of anxiety and disillusionment about multiculturalism? British Muslim identity politics was virtually created by the *Satanic Verses* affair of the late 1980s and beyond (Modood 1992). Muslims began to make demands for recognition and civic inclusion within a polity that had, up to that point, misrecognized them (as black or Asian), or had kept them invisible and voiceless; a polity that was struggling to recognize gender, race and ethnicity within the terms of citizenship but was not even aware that any form of civic recognition was due to marginalized religious groups. The conflict that erupted led many to think of themselves for the first time as Muslims in a public way, to think that it was important in their relation to other Muslims and to the rest of British and related societies. This is, for example, movingly described by the author, Rana Kabbani, whose *Letter to Christendom* begins with a description of herself as 'a woman who had been a sort of underground Muslim before she was forced into the open by the Salman Rushdie affair' (Kabbani 1992: ix). Such shocks to Muslim identity are hardly a thing of the past. The present situation of some Muslims in Britain is well captured by Farmida Bi, a New Labour Parliamentary candidate in 2005, who had not particularly made anything of her Muslim background before the London bombings of 7 July 2005 ('7/7') but was moved by the events to claim a Muslim identity and found the organization Progressive British Muslims. Speaking of herself and others as 'integrated, liberal British Muslims' who were forced to ask 'Am I a Muslim at all?', she writes: '7/7 made most of us embrace our Muslim identity and become determined to prove that its possible to live happily as a Muslim in the west' (Bi 2006). It might be thought that, whilst Kabbani is speaking of a Muslim identity in reaction to a liberal intelligentsia, Bi is distancing herself from fellow Muslims and currying favour with white Britain. I do not believe that there is much of a difference here. Both are reacting to a polarization and public stereotyping of Muslims by rejecting the assumption that one has to choose between being Muslim and being 'western' or British. Each is seeking a middle ground from which to challenge the stereotype without having to sign up to someone else's conception of what it is to be British.

This sense that circumstances dictate that one must speak up as a Muslim (and a Briton) is, of course, nothing necessarily to do with religiosity. As with all forms of difference, it comes into being as a result of pressures from 'outside' a group, as well as from the 'inside'. In this particular case, both the 'inside' and the 'outside' have a powerful geopolitical dimension. The emergence of British Muslim identity and activism has been propelled by a strong concern for the plight of Muslims elsewhere in the world, especially (but not only) where this plight is seen in terms of anti-imperialist emancipation and where the UK government is perceived to be part of the problem – tolerant of, if not complicit in or actively engaged in, the destruction of Muslim hopes and lives, all too often, civilian. That British, American and Australian (perhaps, to some extent, most western) Muslims are having to develop a sense of national citizenship, to integrate into a polity that has a confrontational posture against many Muslim countries and is at war or occupying some of them in what is perceived by all sides to be a long-term project, is an extremely daunting task, and one has to say that success cannot be taken for granted. Moreover, domestic terrorism, as well as political opposition, has unfortunately become part of the context. The danger of 'blowback' from overseas military activity is, as events have shown, considerable and capable of destroying the movement towards multicultural citizenship.

One of the reasons why I do not think we should simply give up and pursue a less attractive political goal is that I am impressed by how many British Muslims have responded, and are responding, to the crisis – namely, with a concern to stand up for their community through civic engagement; with a refusal to give up neither on their Muslim identity nor being part of democratic citizenship. Despite this dependency on overseas circumstances outside their control – and so where one might anticipate passivity and a self-pitying introspection, many British Muslims exhibit a dynamism and a confidence that they must rise to the challenge of dual loyalties and not give up on either set of commitments. Ideological and violent extremism is, indeed, undermining the conditions and hopes for multiculturalism, but, contrary to much public discourse, this extremism has nothing to do with the promotion of multiculturalism but is coming into the domestic arena from the international.

Navigating groupness

Multiculturalism has been broadly right and does not deserve the desertion of support from the centre-left, let alone the blame for the present crisis. It offers a better basis for integration than its two current rivals – namely, 'social cohesion' and 'multiculture' (Meer and Modood 2009). For, whilst the latter is appreciative of a diversity of interacting lifestyles and the emergence of new, hybridic cultures in an atmosphere of 'conviviality', it is at a loss as to how to deal sympathetically with the claims of newly settled ethno-religious groups, especially Muslims, who are too readily stereotyped as 'fundamentalists' (Modood 1998). Nevertheless, it is a major challenge, especially strong in recent sociology and social theory. The core argument is that groups such as Muslims are internally diverse; groups are composed of individuals, there are no essential group characteristics, no group monism and so to talk about groups is theoretically facile and usually masks a political motive (Brubaker 2005; Modood 2007: 90–8). It has to be admitted that we do sometimes work with crude ideas of groups, but that is not the same as saying that the groups that multiculturalists speak of do not exist. We do perhaps need looser concepts of groups, but the issue is to do with the nature of social categories, not multiculturalism *per se*. In this sense, all group categories are socially constructed, but it is clear that people do have a sense of 'groupness' (to which they feel they belong or from which they are excluded). One of the reasons we cannot ignore the communitarian conceptions of difference is that minorities often see and describe themselves as sharing a group identity through such categories as 'Jewish' or 'Muslim' or 'Sikh', amongst others. If we accept that these are no less valid than categories of 'working class', 'woman', 'black' or 'youth', it appears inconsistent to reject some group categories simply because they are subject to the same dialectical tension between specificity and generality to which all group categories are subject. This is not to 'essentialize' or 'reify', however, since the category of 'Jew' or 'Muslim' or 'Sikh' can remain as internally diverse as 'Christian' or 'Belgian' or 'middle-class', or any other category helpful in ordering our understandings.

Neither is it to deny that power relations can exist within minority groups, or that there can be issues about equality in relation to 'minorities within minorities' (Eisenberg and Spinner-Halev 2005), especially in relation to gender (Phillips 2007). Political maturity could mean that, when we seek Muslim voices or civic participants, we will not seek exclusively one or even a few kinds of Muslims. This is easier to achieve at the level of discourses, more difficult in terms of institutional accommodation – but not impossible. After all, it seems to work to some degree in relation to other groups; for example, the Jews. A variety of Jewish people can be taken to represent a particular strand of Jewish opinion and might be consulted as such, whether as organizations such as a federation of synagogues or the Board of Deputies, or as individuals. So, we must not set the bar too high for new groups of ethnic and religious minorities. To take the severe view that for a group to enjoy public representation they must all agree, otherwise no representation is possible, is either to use double standards or to succumb to an essentialism about that group. Moreover, it is a positive virtue that there is internal variety within any group and that (organized) members of any one group will want to locate themselves in different parts of the representational landscape – secular, religious, close to government, distant from mainstream political parties – for that is true integration; new groups should have similar opportunities to old groups and will not need to conform to a special minority perspective. They will spread themselves across society in ways that suit them, and also create or give rise to new discourses, new patternings in political activity and in social organization. This is not to return to the idea of group representation, but to make it consistent with the understanding of groupness, its variability and transmutations. The result will be a democratic constellation of organizations, networks, alliances and discourses in which there will be agreement and disagreement, in which group identity will be manifested by way of family resemblances, rather than the idea that one group means one voice.

There is a further sociological argument: namely, that communal ethnicities are dissolving in front of our eyes as people, especially young people, interact, mix, borrow, synthesize and so on; it is not communities that people belong to but an urban melange alive to globalized and commercialized forms of recreation (Hall 1992 categorized this phenomenon as 'new ethnicities'). Indeed, this is often what people are thinking of when they say that they like 'diversity' or are in favour of a multicultural society (but not multiculturalism). Much research supports this sociological reading (Back 1996; Cohen 1999; Mac an Ghaill 1999). But research also shows that such 'new ethnicities' and hybridities exist alongside, rather than simply replace, more prioritized identities (Modood *et al.* 1997). Just because we all have multiple identities does not mean that they are all equally important to us. Indeed, marginalized, stigmatized groups – groups that feel that they are always being talked about, stereotyped or are under political pressure (exactly the kind of minorities of concern to multiculturalism) – are likely to be much more wedded to, if not one, then a few identity elements than to luxuriate in multiplicity. This is exactly what we find with groups such as British Muslims, who are more likely to think that it is important to them that they are 'Muslim' and 'British' (typically both) and that these identities have a macro significance that is present in most public contexts (Jacobson 1997; Travis 2002; see also Saeed *et al.* 1999 in relation to 'Scottish' and 'Muslim'). Some people so comfortably meld into their society that they are not marked – by others or by themselves – by 'difference' (or even by conviction, such as socialism or atheism) and so often the question of identities, let alone prioritization, does not even arise. Our specific concern with 'difference' is typically with those based on or linked to racial and ethnic descent in a context when they shape life-opportunities and how people relate to you; are connected to a heritage or important belief system that governs one's personal life and/or is the basis of political debates, alliances, enmities and projects. Typically, the physical basis and the ideational orientation are linked in the way that the social image of a Middle Easterner is linked with Islam or, to use examples from other contexts, women can be linked with feminism, or even working-class people with socialism.

These linkages are, of course, shaped by contemporary contexts and social movements, and are not simply 'given': neither are these identities discrete; many different kinds of syntheses occur (for example, a woman for whom being a black feminist is central to her self-definition). Moreover, we can allow even that that some people, who in the eyes of others have a visible primary identity, might not wish to embrace that identity but, rather, look for ways and means to de-prioritize it in their life; in particular, given that the identities under discussion typically straddle politics and non-politics, some people might seek to depoliticize their identity or, at least, to remove themselves from the political allegiances others, including co-members, foist upon that identity. All of these are matters of contingency and empirical inquiry; none of them is a critique of groupness, old ethnicities or 'identity politics'. Indeed, sociologists have to attend not only to the facts of identity fluidity and group fragmentation, but equally to the simultaneous trend of a hardening of identities and valorising of difference. In an earlier period, this was around a black/white divide, but that has come to be dwarfed by an Islam/West or Muslim/non-Muslim one. An effect of this is not only that young British Muslims are more militant than their parents (that is a common generational feature) or that Muslim identification has increased; rather, also, that there exist more religiously 'conservative' and 'neo-orthodox' interpretations of Islam and what it means to be a Muslim that emphasize difference – for example, the wearing of the *hijab*, preference for Muslim schools and a more authoritarian *sharia* (GfK 2006; Mirza *et al.* 2007). So, whilst there is evidence of strong identity prioritization, it means the presence of groups that cannot be framed in terms of 'new ethnicities' and 'beyond multiculturalism'. Political science must rise to the challenge of simultaneously theorizing fluid and hardening identities, no less than that of becoming alert to the interplay between the religious and the secular and the interdependence between the civic, 'difference' and the national.

National identity and minority cultures

If group difference is a lived form of subjectivity capable of generating political claims that democrats cannot ignore, some advocacy of multiculturalism has, sometimes, overlooked – or, at least, underemphasized – the other side of the coin, which is not only equally necessary, but is also integral to multiculturalism. For one cannot simply talk about difference. Difference has to be related to things we have in common. The commonality that most multiculturalists emphasize is citizenship. I have argued that this citizenship has to be seen in a plural, dispersed and dialogical way and not reduced to legal rights, passports and the franchise (important though these are). I would now like to go further in suggesting that a good basis for, or accompaniment to, a multicultural citizenship is a national identity.

We, in Europe, have tended to overlook the fact that, where multiculturalism has been accepted and worked as a state project or as a national project – Canada, Australia and Malaysia, for example – it has not simply been coincidental with but has been integral to a nation-building project, to creating Canadians, Australians, Malaysians, and so on. Even in the United States, where the federal state has had a much lesser role in the multicultural project, the incorporation of ethno-religious diversity and 'hyphenated Americans' has been about country-making, civic inclusion and making a claim upon the national identity. This is important because some multiculturalists, or at least advocates of pluralism and multiculture (the vocabulary of multiculturalism is not always used) – even where they have other fundamental disagreements with each other – argue as if the logic of the national and the multicultural are incompatible: partly as a result, many Europeans think of multiculturalism as antithetical to, rather than as a reformer of, national identity.

This has resulted in critiques of multiculturalism across the political spectrum as a discourse of a 'failure of integration' has come to be dominant. Across Europe, there is a renewed emphasis on national identity, including by those who, a decade or so ago, were emphasizing the narrowness of national belonging in favour of transnational Europeanism. Or, alternatively, without explicit intention, two civic identities are being promoted simultaneously: 'native' Germans, French, Dutch, and so on are told that they should be thinking of themselves as Europeans, whilst those of extra-European descent in the same countries are being urged to think and act more German, French, Dutch, and so forth. Whilst some supporters of multiculturalism see the emphasis on 'social cohesion' as anti-minority and old-style assimilationism, if not racist (Bagguley and Hussain 2008; McGhee 2008), this might be an over-reaction, at least in the case of government policy in some countries such as Britain (Meer and Modood 2009). What it does suggest is that some analyses that were predicting a 'post-national' trend were rather short-sighted. For example, Soysal has argued that an international discourse of human rights, rather than specific national conceptions of citizenship, was rightly determining the status of migrants; and this was lessening the gap between citizens and non-citizens and, so, lessening the value of national citizenship (Soysal 1994). This was exaggerated for the late twentieth century (Koopmans and Statham 2001) and does not seem to hold for the first decade of this century, but there is also an intriguing related argument. Christian Joppke (2008) has argued that, both normatively and actually, the discourses of national identity are strengthening liberalism at the expense of nationalism since 'the decoupling of citizenship and nationhood is the incontrovertible exit position for contemporary state campaigns for unity and integration, especially with respect to immigrants' (*ibid.*: 543). He argues that, whilst some politicians and some states are talking of privileging majority culture as *Leitkultur*, for example in Germany and Denmark, this movement is bound to fail. For first, when states come to give content to their national identities, they invariably end up listing universal principles such as liberty, equality, fairness, human rights, tolerance and the like. So, whilst many states are appealing to a national identity, the content they give it is neither ethnic nor cultural (language, history or religion) but, rather, liberal principles. The symbolic form might be 'particularistic', but the content is universal – and it has to be this way because, if it were more particularistic (for example, Christian), it would fail in its purpose of integrating immigrants, especially Muslims. His argument is that 'the typical solution to the problem of collective identity across Europe today is the one pioneered by Republican France, according to which to be national is defined in the light of the universalistic precepts of human rights and democracy (*ibid.*: 541).

Second, he continues, even where some politicians and states do emphasize particularistic aspects of national identity – such as for example, Lutheranism, or Christianity more generally – their own constitutional courts are required to uphold universalistic principles, especially non-discrimination. This is interpreted as the non-privileging of one culture over another, and so the courts strike down particularistic legislation and support appeals of discrimination from minority individuals and groups, supported by the European Court of Human Rights. Joppke acknowledges that, as a matter of fact, there is a discourse in several countries – typified by Germany, the Netherlands and Denmark – in which a universalist liberalism is used in an exclusionary particularistic way by arguing that liberalism is 'our culture' and that some others, such as Muslims, cannot become part of the 'We' because they are not sufficiently liberal (*ibid.*: 541–2). But he thinks these exclusionary uses of liberalism have to appeal to the liberal principle of non-discrimination between cultures (as long as liberal norms are observed) and so he thinks they will self-destruct. Some liberals might aggressively enforce liberal norms (this is his reading of the ban on the headscarf in state schools in

France), but they must do so within liberal constraints (in a non-discriminatory way, by not targeting an ethnic group or religions but by applying universal rules) and they must promote liberal principles and not a specific national culture.

Joppke's argument, however, is quite misleading. It might be the case that European states might not be framing anti-Muslim laws and policies by explicit statutory reference to Muslims; but a general rule that is acknowledged to be targeted to changing Muslim behaviour (such as the French ban on the wearing of 'ostentatious' religious apparel in state schools) is not about protecting liberal rights but, rather, about promoting a perceived national culture. Moreover, a close study of nine European countries reveals that national identities cannot be completely universalized or liberalized; rather, some degree of particularity is both pragmatically necessary but also justifiable within a variety of political orientations, including reference to national cohesion, republicanism and interculturalism, as well as multicultural citizenship (Modood and Meer, 2009). That is to say, where we are currently witnessing various political projects of remaking and updating national identities, they are not being de-particularized. Moreover, countries such as Spain and Greece retain a strong orientation toward *ius sanguine* in, for example, coupling citizenship with a dominant ethnicity; but, were an opposing trend to develop, this would not have to empty out the historical-cultural character of nationality but, instead, include minority ethnicities. The latter, therefore, need not be about being blind to minority ethnic groupness but, on the contrary, seeking to pluralize, and not empty, cultural content. For the dominant ethnicity to de-monopolize the state and the citizenship by not making cultural assimilation a condition of full citizenship, of full social acceptance, is to respect, not blank out, the varied ethnicities of fellow citizens.

Moreover, it does not make sense to encourage strong multicultural or minority identities and weak common or national identities; strong multicultural identities are a good thing – they are not intrinsically divisive, reactionary or fifth columns – but they need a framework of vibrant, dynamic, national narratives and the ceremonies and rituals that give expression to a national identity. It is clear that minority identities are capable of having an emotional pull for the individuals for whom they are important. Multicultural citizenship requires, therefore, if it is to be equally attractive to the same individuals, a comparable counterbalancing emotional pull. Many Britons, for example, say they are worried about disaffection amongst some Muslim young men and, more generally, a lack of identification with Britain amongst many Muslims in Britain. Yet, surveys over many years have shown Muslims have been reaching out for an identification with Britain. For example, in an NOP survey (Channel 4 2006) 82% of a national sample of Muslims said they felt very strongly (45 per cent) or fairly strongly (37 per cent) that they belonged to Britain. Of course, there is considerable anger and fear around these issues, especially in relation to the aggressive United States–United Kingdom foreign policies and terrorism. Whilst I do not feel that we are at all close to undoing the mess we have got into with these policies, to not build on the clear support there is for a sense of national belonging is to fail to offer an obvious counterweight to the ideological calls for a *jihad* against fellow Britons.

It is therefore to be welcomed when politicians of the left show an interest in British national identity. A leading example of this is Gordon Brown, the UK Prime Minister. He has argued for the need to revive and revalue British national identity in a number of speeches (most notably, Brown 2006). Brown wants to derive a set of core values (liberty, fairness, enterprise, and so on) from a historical narrative yet such values, even if they could singly or in combination be given a distinctive British take, are too complex, and their interpretation and priority too contested, to be amenable to be set into a series of meaningful definitions. Every public culture must operate through shared values, which are both embodied in and used to criticize its institutions and practices – but they are not simple and uniform, and their meaning is discursively grasped as old interpretations are dropped and new circumstances unsettle one consensus and another is built up. Simply saying that freedom or equality is a core British value is unlikely to settle any controversy or tell us, for example, what is 'hate speech' and how it should be handled. Definitions of core values will either be too bland or too divisive, and the idea that there has to be a schedule of value statements to which every citizen is expected to sign up is not in the spirit of a multilogical citizenship. The national identity should be woven in debate and discussion, not reduced to a list. For, central to it, is a citizenship and the right to make a claim on the national identity in which negative difference is challenged and supplanted by positive difference. We cannot afford to leave out these aspects of multicultural citizenship from an intellectual or political vision of social reform and justice in the twenty-first century. Rather, the turning of negative difference into positive difference should be one of the tests of social justice in this century.

So, I cannot conclude on a clear note of optimism. But we do need some optimism and self-belief, if we are to even limit the damage that is currently being done to our multicultural politics and prospects. The twenty-first century is going to be one of unprecedented ethnic and religious mix in the West. In the past, multicultural societies have tended to only flourish under imperial rule. If we are to keep alive the prospect of a dynamic, internally differentiated multiculturalism within the context of democratic citizenship, then we must at least see that multiculturalism is not the cause of the present crisis but, rather, part of the solution.

Chapter 6

The Character of the State

HELEN THOMPSON

The global financial crisis has posed important questions about what states are and what they do in modern politics. Most immediately, it appears to have produced a world in which states do rather more in the economic sphere than they have been doing for the past thirty years. But, just as significantly, it has exposed some fundamental questions about the political problems that define states as entities, both in themselves and in relation to each other in an interdependent world. In so doing, the crisis has thrown up some serious challenges to scholarly analysis of the state, so much of which, over the past two decades, has been shaped by the discourse of globalization.

If the era of globalization was supposed to be primarily defined by the economic retreat of the state, the state during the financial crisis appears to have ripped up the script and reasserted itself as the only agent capable of preventing an economic collapse. Whilst it has been a commonplace that globalized finance was the predominant force driving the state's retreat, it is precisely in financial sectors where the state has come to the fore. A significant number of states have taken complete or partial ownership of banks and other financial corporations, provided them with capital, insured their loans, and guaranteed their toxic assets. Beyond the financial sector, states have printed money, bailed-out car firms and mortgage-holders, and engaged in vast borrowing to finance fiscal stimuli. These acts have pushed the state firmly back into the allocation of resources. Governments have decided whether banks should lend capital at home or abroad, which firms to rescue, and where the burden of economic loss between citizens as debtors should lie.

Meanwhile, a dominant political narrative has emerged that the crisis happened because markets had done too much and states too little, and that states in future must be more active, especially in the financial sector. The conjunction of what states practically did in response to the crisis and the narrative that the crisis would not have happened if they had previously done more appears to have created among many citizens a new set of political expectations about what states should do and express. It has produced a political backlash against globalization and a new collective emotion amongst many citizens that the state must be an agent of justice, and even retribution, in economic outcomes. Put differently, the financial crisis placed a political burden of economic populism onto states of a kind of which they had seemed to rid themselves from the 1980s.

However, there is also a complex set of issues brought out by the unfolding of the financial crisis that must qualify this picture of a state resurgent against the older forces of globalization. They suggest that the financial crisis has not significantly changed the character of the state but, rather, exposed the limitations of many of the claims that globalization-focused scholars made about it. Much of what was true about states prior to the crisis – and what they now face after it – remains the same, and has, indeed, endured through all kinds of economic change. States have long had more power than they deploy much of the time and, during the years leading up to the financial crisis, states had regulatory power that they did not use. How much power states exercise has long turned on the political judgement of governments, and the political actions of states were as much a cause of the crisis as the dealings of financial markets. States have always had fiscal problems and, when states engage in large-scale borrowing, what follows in the medium- to long-term is fiscal balancing of the kind that will certainly ensue over the next decade. And when states intervene in specific areas at times of crisis, they invariably swell general political expectations about what states should do and, over time, these tend to clash with the fiscal imperatives that confront states, as they will in the political era we have now entered.

In thinking about what the financial crisis reveals about both the character of the state and the limitations of the existing scholarly debate about it, we can also see some of the more general challenges that states face, and reflect on the analytical apparatus that might be necessary to capture them. The financial crisis is emblematic of some of the most difficult challenges states face because it was a practical problem that confronted a very large number of states simultaneously, the responses of individual states had direct consequences for others, and it exposed distributional issues between states about burden-sharing in dealing with common predicaments. It is also revealing about the prospects for transnational political spaces as sites for managing the problems of interdependence. The European Union (EU) is the most politically significant of these spaces simply because, here, in some areas, there has been a genuine shift of decision-making authority beyond the nation-state. In looking at the fallout of the financial crisis for the EU, we can see something about the ways in which the state is best conceptually conceived in relation to aspirations to transnational governance, and how many of the inherent political problems that states face are recreated in any authoritative political site that tries to go beyond them.

The remainder of this chapter sets out, in general terms, some of the most significant recent conceptual and empirical debates about the state, and then asks what challenges the financial crisis and its fallout for transnational governance cast on these debates. The first section considers arguments about the state's economic discretion, the state as a site of power and sovereignty in the international sphere, and the state as an agent of political identity and bearer of political expectations. The second section analyzes these debates in light of the financial crisis and its broader implications, and the problems facing the EU as a site of transnational governance. It argues that these real-world developments expose some of the limitations of the arguments that the state has been in retreat or diminished, and of the analytical parameters within which these debates have been constructed. The conclusion suggests some ways in which analysis of the state might constructively develop.

Globalization and the economic discretion of the state

According to the globalization thesis, the economic transformations of the past three decades made the state less powerful and relevant, and did so for both developed-country states and those developing-country states integrated into the international economy (Ohmae 1990; Cerny 1995; Strange 1996; Held *et al.* 1999). Put schematically, this thesis stated that globalization forced states to share power with other economic actors and stripped states of the capacity to shape economies according to distinct political purposes, and that consequently differences between national economies were eroding. On specific policy matters, advocates of the globalization thesis made two large claims. First, they argued that, from the 1970s, states lost power over capital and, as a result, had to pursue macro-economic policies with an anti-inflationary, anti-expenditure, and anti-tax bias. Second, they claimed that the expansion of international trade and the integration of production across state borders left states with an imperative to implement investment-friendly economic practices, especially in regard to labour markets. The political consequence of both developments was that states could not redistribute wealth.

Sceptics about globalization variously argued that there was rather less of it than the rhetoric around it would suggest (Hirst and Thompson 1999), that states still have considerable economic power (Weiss 1998; Moseley 2003), that governments have used those powers to sustain what were still politically distinct economies (Garrett 1998; Hall and Soskice 2001; Rodrik 2007), and that states themselves created the financially liberalized world that is the central fact of an apparently globalized economy (Helleiner 1994). Others argued that, so far as states did not do things in the economic sphere that they previously had, it was not because they were constrained by the reality of globalization but, rather, an acceptance of the narrative that globalization existed (Hay 1999, 2006). On particular matters of economic policy, the sceptics stressed that the empirical evidence frequently did not support the globalization thesis. Whilst the methods of taxation that the state deployed had changed, states were raising roughly the same level of overall revenue as they did during the post-Second World War years (Swank 2002; Steinmo 2003). Consequently, states could still maintain high levels of public expenditure (Hay 2008). The welfare state, especially in Europe, proved robust. It was not, the sceptics concluded, a liability to foreign investment and it has not been sacrificed to fiscal retrenchment. States also, the sceptics suggest, maintained distinct national labour markets and they were, in part, able to do so because governments used the power of the state to cultivate high-skill and high-productivity workforces. Some developing-country states also demonstrated that it is possible for states to control short-term capital flows, the presence of which, and the difficulties they pose for exchange-rate management, having been taken by most globalization advocates to be the most significant constraint on macroeconomic policy-making (Rodrik and Kaplan 2002).

Whilst there has been much intellectual disagreement about what the state could do over the past three decades, and what it was normatively desirable for it do, there was, nonetheless, some convergence in charting the political implications of what at least rich-country states in practice tended to do. The political corollary of the practical dimunition of the state by the reality of globalization and of the contingent eclipse of the state by the narrative of globalization was the state as the suppressor of the expectations of its citizens (Thompson 1999; Hay 2006). States acted over the last thirty years to curtail hopes of any more redistribution of wealth and the notion that the state stood as an indirect guarantor of employment or national economic solidarity. Whilst these two theses arrived at a broadly similar point in describing what, from the 1980s, at least some states came to do, the different causal explanations of what produced this phenomenon is politically significant. Was the state suppressing reasonable political expectations when they could have decided otherwise, or were there real-world limits on what the state could be expected to do, such that the imaginative allure of the postwar European promise of citizenship based on economic entitlements and some measure of redistributive justice had, as a matter of necessity, to be permanently jettisoned?

Globalization and the state in the international sphere

The primary theoretical debate in international relations between realism and its critics is, at its centre, a discussion about the state and its weight. Whilst realists have insisted that states remain the decisive political actor in an anarchic world defined by competition between them, the different critics of realism have argued that the state is only one of many actors in the international sphere and that the international arena is neither practically nor ideationally defined by relations between states and an anarchic problem. The structure of this theoretical debate has been matched in a more empirical debate about whether the state still has sovereignty, and how viable both the practice and idea of sovereignty remain if globalization is real. Many have argued that states have lost sovereignty and that now, at best, they share it with the regional and international organizations, non-governmental actors, or global networks (Rosenau 1990; Wallace 1999; Brown 2002; Slaughter 2004). Others have argued that these arguments rest on a confusion concerning the nature of sovereignty. Internal and external sovereignty are not the same thing, and external sovereignty is not something that all states have. It is a claim by a state to be the sole author of laws within its territory, or, put differently, a claim against intervention by other states (Thompson 2006b). However, for many states, such as Afghanistan or those in Central America, that has rarely been a coherent aspiration. Those states that, today, lack external sovereignty were always weak and easily penetrated by foreign powers. By contrast, those states that have enjoyed external sovereignty for most of the past few centuries have retained that sovereignty. Powerful states have asserted themselves as states into international organizations and do not sacrifice authority when they either delegate activities they previously undertook to other actors, or choose to participate in international networks (Clapham 1999; Krasner 1999; Thompson 2006a). It is hard to see any way in which the United States had conceded an iota of legal sovereignty during the years of 'globalization'.

The EU has been a particularly important part of the debate about whether there has been a shift away from the state towards sites of transnational governance because it is a historically distinctive kind of political entity that clearly goes beyond the legally strictly demarcated territory of states and the imaginative language of modern nationhood. However, the decisive question for the future of transnational governance is whether the EU has, as a transnational political space, the capacity to transcend the political character of states as sites of authority and power that require legitimation.

Globalization and the state as an agent of political identity

The question of the relationship between globalization and the state has produced a third general debate about whether the state is any longer an agent of political identity. The discourses of global cosmopolitanism, neo-medievalism and regionalism have challenged the notion that the nation-state remains the decisive form of modern political identity. Some have argued that globalization is producing the political flourishing of something like global civil society or cosmopolitan governance (Held 1995; O'Neill 2000; Archibugi 2004). Others have suggested that it has created a multiplicity of political identities across different territorial spaces (Linklater 1998; Falk 2000), or the possibility of a pan-regional political consciousness (Waller and Linklater 2003). In part, these are normative arguments that suppose that political identity has moved beyond the state because the state was always an artificial constraint on the possibility of political community, and suggest that globalization offers the possibility of something more humanly authentic. But, in part, these arguments are also empirical, and posit that political identity has shifted because globalization has made it progressively more difficult for states to undertake those economic things in which they engaged from the middle of the twentieth century to forge an idea of national citizenship.

Communitarians of different kinds have resisted these approaches and argued that states still express specific identities that belong exclusively to their own citizens and which these citizens cannot readily change. They have insisted that cosmopolitans empirically underestimate the continuing political significance of particular, culturally grounded, human communities whilst they themselves reject the normative desirability of subjecting those communities to the moral demands of a universal politics. States, and something akin to nation-states alone, according to the communitarians, can deliver on the promise of citizenship (Kymlicka 1989; Miller 1995; Walzer 1995).

The academic separation of international political economy, international relations, comparative politics and political theory has frequently turned the three broad debates about the state and globalization into discrete analytical topics. But the question of the state as an agent of political identity brings into sharp focus the reality that the issue of how far the state changed in recent decades, or might still be changing, turns on understanding its cumulative experience as a single entity confronted with a set of problems and having to operate in a domestic and international context simultaneously. If globalization did make it impossible for the state to undertake certain economic acts, and those acts were what had constituted postwar citizenship and were why citizens expressed their political identities through nation-states, then nation-states could no longer be the agent of that identity and had to shred the expectations of those citizens that they might be. If states and transnational sites of governance were sharing sovereignty, or the whole notion of sovereignty were redundant, and, at the same time, the communitarians were right and citizens could only conceive of their political identity within the bounded existing political communities demarcated by nation-states, then new transnational sites of governance have the same political problem as states, albeit manifested in a different form. The financial crisis and its implications are illuminating not only because they seem such a decisive rebuttal of the argument that the state was economically dying under the weight of globalization, but also because they demonstrate how deeply the question of what kind of political identity the state sustains matters in understanding what states do and can do, and whether they can be replaced with transnational political spaces.

The financial crisis and the state: economic discretion

Certainly, in some senses the financial crisis demonstrated what, economically, states had not been doing and where they had left markets mostly to their own devices. Collateralized debt obligations and mortgage-backed securities, the losses on which from the summer of 2007 cascaded through the balance sheets of financial corporations around the world, were unregulated derivatives with the capacity to wreak financial destruction. Many of those corporations that issued and bought these financial derivatives operated through what was effectively a shadow banking system, largely beyond the reach of states' financial regulators. These were financial entities, such as investment banks, hedge funds, structured investment vehicles, money-market funds, and non-bank mortgage lenders. They were not banks, but acted like them in the ways they lent money. They were not formally supported by a national central bank as lender of last resort, they did not have deposit insurance, and they were not regulated as banks. Moreover, shadow banking was also, in part, a deliberate attempt to escape state regulation: much shadow banking activity was off-balance sheet activity of banks that were tightly regulated.

Nonetheless, the ways that governments responded to the financial crisis exposed the limitations of much of the argument that globalization had reduced the economic agency of states, and vindicated those who insisted that states were still crucial economic actors and that the constraints invoked by governments were at least, in part, self-created. Over the last months of 2008, the American government placed the huge mortgage corporations Fannie Mae and Freddie Mac into conservatorship, took large stakes in the insurance company AIG and Citigroup, and prompted Congress to pass a US$750 billion programme to buy assets and equity from financial corporations. The British government nationalized two banks and took large stakes in all but one of the country's largest banks. The Icelandic government nationalized all its large banks, and the German, Spanish, Belgian, Dutch and Luxembourg governments all took some banks into full or partial state ownership. The Irish government guaranteed all deposits, and other EU states followed suit. Virtually everywhere across America and Europe, governments acted to insure bank lending and central banks lent directly to banks. Together, these moves amounted to an attempt by western governments to use the power of the state to recapitalize their banking systems and act as their guarantors. The American government went even further, taking control of much of the shadow banking system by guaranteeing money market funds, orchestrating two investment bank takeovers, and forcing the remaining investment banks into commercial banks with access to formal protection.

Neither have governments confined themselves to using the state's resources to bail out financial corporations. Various governments have bailed out car firms, and the German government established a 'German Economy Fund' with loan guarantees for non-financial corporations. In February 2009, the Obama administration announced a plan to subsidize monthly payments for some mortgage-holders and a programme to allow five million others to restructure their loans at a lower interest rate.

As for macro-economic policy, governments and central banks similarly undertook acts deemed either impossible or irresponsible, according to the old assumptions about what was possible in a globalized economy. Governments in most states pushed emergency fiscal stimulus packages without acting as if the volume to be borrowed was a constraint, either in raising the immediate money or in risking putting downward pressure on their currencies. In the United States, the Obama administration used the fiscal stimulus in its first budget proposal to Congress as justification for a wider expansion of the American state, primarily in regard to health care. States that tried to depoliticize monetary policy by handing authority to central banks have found that politicians could not simply use hands-off rules to disengage in this area, even if the setting of interest rates remains the formal prerogative of central banks. For example, the Icelandic government changed the law so that it could fire the chair of the country's central bank. In Britain, the Bank of England could only make aggressive cuts in interest rates in the autumn of 2008 by ignoring the inflation target set by the government (Hay 2009). Having reduced interest rates to their effective floor, both the Federal Reserve Board and the Bank of England began, effectively, to print money by buying government bonds and the assets and securities of financial corporations with their own money. The British Chancellor made publicly clear that the final decision of the Bank to do so belonged to him. Even more potently, the notion that there is a singular, and ultimately politically incontestable, common good in monetary policy has been destroyed by the overt demonstration of the large difference in consequences for some citizens over others of a radical shift in monetary policy over a period of a few months. When some groups acquire substantial gains from interest rate cuts and others are made worse off, governments cannot plausibly say that monetary policy works according to some kind of rule-based automatic pilot to which there can be no tenable alternative.

This range of actions by governments has involved states in an extensive way in the allocation of resources and capital. In providing financial support to banks, they have tried to ensure that banks lend primarily to domestic firms and households. For example, new financial regulations introduced in Switzerland explicitly exclude domestic lending from minimum capital requirements. In bailing out some corporations and households sinking under debt and not others, governments have chosen to distribute the resources of the state selectively, just as central banks in their monetary policy have directed the banks to net borrowers and away from net savers. When some banks in Britain initially proved unwilling to pass on the interest rate cuts that produced that outcome, the government used the state's financial muscle to ensure that they did. States have not only demonstrated the power they possess to act, but also that there is a significant space for a political contest about how the powers of the state might be used.

As well as states using their power so emphatically to act, the dominant political narrative that emerged out of the crisis projected, accurately or not, that unfettered markets had caused the crisis and that the state could have averted the disaster. States that had largely succeeded at suppressing political expectations about what they could do economically, and for what they were responsible, found themselves confronting waves of public anger. Protests took place in many European countries. In the first months of 2009, police violence, following demonstrations, led to the resignation of the Icelandic government, whilst riots led to the collapse of the Latvian government.

Nonetheless, the financial crisis did not straightforwardly strengthen the state. In borrowing as much as they have, some states are carrying huge short- to medium-term fiscal burdens. The failure, in early 2009, of two German auctions for bonds demonstrated that markets will not necessarily accommodate however much governments wish to borrow. Even if they can, this borrowing will ultimately have to be paid for with fiscal retrenchments. For perhaps the next decade, governments will almost certainly have to cut back on the services states provide, including the entitlements of the welfare state. Meanwhile, most governments have been reluctant to make banks in any way part of the state itself. Where they have taken partial or total ownership of banks, they have not made them subject to political control. When, for example, the British government created UK Financial Investments, the Treasury described it as 'an arm-lengths company' to manage the government's investments in the financial sector on a 'commercial basis' (IIM Treasury 2008). Whilst the British government repeatedly said in 2008 and 2009 that it wanted the banks in which UK Financial Investments had shares to return to lending at 2007 levels, it eschewed direct action to force them to do so.

The state has not made a comeback from relative economic impotence. Neither the political narrative that the financial crisis demonstrated the folly of states doing too little nor the globalization thesis that rendered states impotent in the face of financial markets stand up to empirical scrutiny in examining the causes of the financial crisis. The absence of effective regulation of significant parts of the financial sector was not a matter of the lack of practical agency, but the consequence of a specific political will of politicians in various countries.

For example, in the United States, there was a lengthy political debate, going back to 2003, about whether to regulate the two huge, congressionally-charted but privately-owned mortgage corporations, Fannie Mae and Freddie Mac. These two corporations issued vast quantities of mortgage-backed securities that other financial firms purchased, and held massive investment portfolios of these securities. Until the summer of 2008, they were lightly regulated and had to abide by minimum capital requirements far lower than other financial corporations. One set of politicians, including the Bush administration and a group of Republicans in Congress, pushed to create a tough new regulator, believing that the two corporations were running risks that jeopardized the whole American economy. A competing set of politicians from both parties, but predominantly constituted by Democrats, opposed that move, denying that the two corporations posed a financial risk and arguing that what mattered was that they delivered homeownership (Thompson 2009). By the time Congress passed a bill in July 2008, putting in place some modest new regulation, the two corporations were almost certainly insolvent. The reformers failed, in part because the two corporations orchestrated a systematic lobbying effort backed with a flow of campaign contributions to construct a political support structure in Congress. It was not unstoppable financial markets or the constraints of globalization that left Fannie Mae and Freddie Mac under-regulated and free to borrow and lend recklessly. It was a choice of those who had the authority to create a powerful state regulator and choose not to do so.

Similarly, various governments competed over having under-regulated financial sectors. The New Labour government wanted to establish London as the premier deregulated financial sector in the world. In New Labour's first term, it created a new, financial regulatory structure in the Financial Services Authority that was more liberal than that in any other major economy. When the Americans tightened their accounting regulations with the Sarbanes–Oxley Act, the British government used the absence of such regulatory rules to encourage financial business to London. The calculated weakness of the British state's regulatory financial structure also allowed much of the shadow banking system to go through London, and evade the domestic regulator. The British financial sector was under-regulated because the British government embarked upon an economic strategy that depended on the success of the financial sector. Those governments that eschewed more regulation did not do so because financial globalization made regulation impossible, but because they wanted to procure political gain from economic growth.

Just as significantly, the housing and financial booms were fundamentally dependent on the state in a range of different ways. Both the Clinton and Bush administrations pursued policies that directed money to subprime lending because they wanted to increase home ownership, especially among minorities. In doing, they acted on a political premise about home ownership that has operated in American politics since the 1930s – namely, that the power of the state can be used to push those with capital to lend more for mortgages. The American housing boom was, in significant part, financed by east Asian central banks. In particular, they bought the bonds and securities of Fannie Mae and Freddie Mac, which made possible these corporations' issuance of mortgage-backed securities that then cascaded around western and Asian banks. They also bought sufficient other dollar assets, including American Treasury bonds, to allow the Federal Reserve Board to keep interest rates at a very low level during the boom years. That flow of cheap capital across the Pacific arose because of the exchange rate policies that the east Asian governments, especially China, systematically decided on in the wake of the Asian financial crisis.

Much of what the financial crisis has played out about the state in western countries was already in place in another form in other parts of the world, especially east Asia. The east Asian states had, for some time, been deeply engaged with one aspect of financial risk. This primarily took the form of the exchange rate risks that states must navigate in regard to trade and cross-border capital flows. It was because of the fall in the value of the dollar after 2002, and the resulting desire to find a higher return on the bonds that it was buying, that the Chinese government lent so much to Fannie Mae and Freddie Mac. It was also because of the consequences of exchange rate risks that several east Asian states, including China, created sovereign wealth funds. After the American sub-prime crisis first spread into the broader financial sector in the second half of 2007, sovereign wealth funds rode to the rescue, injecting capital into various western commercial and investment banks. The American and European states had to begin their large-scale intervention from the autumn of 2008 precisely because the sovereign wealth funds that had done the job of recapitalizing American and European financial sectors in the second half of 2007 and early 2008 were no longer willing to do that.

Put differently, prior to the crisis, states in east Asia were systematically allocating resources to cope with the problem of financial risk, and they were doing so in ways that had large-scale consequences for how much capital there was available to western financial sectors and how that capital was allocated. They were willing to finance much of the housing boom because of the expectations created by the American government and Congress about the creditworthiness of Fannie Mae and Freddie Mac. Both the state in east Asia and the state in the United States were party to the hugely disproportionate international allocation of capital to the American housing sector in America between 2002 and 2007. This interaction between different states, and the economic outcomes it produced, had complex roots in the ways in which the Asian states had responded to the exercise of monetary and financial power by the United States in the 1990s, and the historical engagement of the American state with home ownership since the New Deal. It has also created serious dilemmas for the future of the American and Chinese states: the American has had to take upon itself the burden of maintaining the two large mortgage corporations on which the American housing market has long depended, and the Chinese is left holding a massive dollar portfolio on which, eventually, it will have to accept a large currency loss. How these problems for the two states play out over time will have profound consequences for the entire political and military international order in which states have to operate.

Transnational governance

The financial crisis has graphically demonstrated the economic interdependence of states that the discourse of globalization did something to capture whilst simultaneously showing just why, contrary to the claims of some globalization theorists, there is no *a priori* or plausible theoretical reason to suppose that such interdependence will politically translate into transnational structures of governance to address the problems it generates. The existing international economic institutions were not set up to deal with a global financial crisis. Whilst the International Monetary Fund could deal with those relatively poor and small states struggling for foreign currency to service debt, it was irrelevant to the problems facing the world's richest and largest states. Meanwhile the one state that could act as the creditor of last resort, the United States, acted on a politically selective, state-by-state basis, with the Federal Reserve limiting currency swap guarantees to the other G7 members, South Korea, Singapore, Brazil and Mexico.

As the most developed site of transnational governance in the world, the EU has been challenged more directly than any other by the fallout of the financial crisis. The response of the EU as a collective entity has demonstrated just how difficult it is for transnational political organizations to move beyond the state when any significant redistribution of scarce resources is required to achieve political commonality. The crisis brought to the fore a raw political reality about the financing of the EU that frequently lay hidden under cheap European rhetoric and was ignored in much of the academic literature. At the moment in October 2008 when the EU governments had to decide on their first moves to try to stabilize banks, the German government rejected the French proposal for a common bailout based on pooled resources. The reason for this German retreat to the nation-state was made explicit in terms rarely heard in today's politics. As the German Finance Minister, Peer Steinbrück put it:

> We as Germans do not want to pay into a big pot where we do not have control and do not know where German money might be used. (*The Economist* 2008)

Or, in other words, taxes to pay for the borrowing that this common bailout expenditure would require had to be raised nationally from citizens who vote in national elections. So long as states have, virtually, the sole authority to raise revenue, and those who exercise that power have to compete exclusively for votes from those on whom those taxes are levied, there will be severe limits to commonality in any policy area that involves a direct economic cost on citizens within any transnational political organization. This has implications beyond economic policy itself, not least for the prospects of binding international agreements to reduce carbon emissions.

Yet, at the same time, the financial crisis exposed the problem of how transnational sites of governance can be sustained at all without some obligations that cut across nation-states and their claim on revenue raised from their own citizens. The Maastricht Treaty forbade bailouts for indebted members. But the absolute primacy of the nation-state in matters of debt within the euro-zone has left the economically weakest members paying twice the rate of interest on the bonds they issue of the German government, and increased the risk that a euro-zone member state might default. Any individual default would hurt all those states issuing bonds in euros, and almost certainly produce a swift depreciation of the euro. However, if, to avert that risk, the euro-zone states were to issue common bonds, they would raise the cost of borrowing for, and the long-term tax burdens of, the most creditworthy states. Politically, this would recreate the common bailout problem as a permanent structural feature of the EU. At that point, the either euro-zone would break and the nation-state would reassert itself in monetary matters, or an EU state would have to be established with the sole authority to issue debt and raise taxes, which would require a shift in the political representation of citizens to match that fiscal capacity. However, in moving to that option, the EU would create something more akin to a large European state than anything that transcended modern statehood as the primary form of political authority. In this sense, transnational sites of governance could decisively replace existing nation-states, but they would not repudiate the essentially political character of the state in doing so.

The same problem manifests itself in the position of some of the east European states within the EU. During the financial crisis, they suffered from weak currencies, unsustainable external debt denominated in foreign currencies and, in some cases, huge current account deficits. Whilst most of the capital that fuelled the pre-crisis booms came from within the EU, the IMF, not the EU, provided most of the credit that staved off a meltdown in the most debt-ridden states. In early March 2009, the Hungarian government pushed for a large collective EU rescue plan for the east European members, but most other EU states rejected the plea. Again, however, this kind of distributive issue cannot simply be resolved in the medium term within the existing framework of a 27-member Union by the assertion of nation-statehood against transnational claims. Populist anger in the richer EU states might make European redistribution politically impossible, but populist anger in the poorer states, if these economies fall even further behind west European living standards, might also make these states' continuing EU membership acutely difficult. Transnational sites of governance that are grounded neither in economic convergence nor in a political willingness of citizens to support the redistribution of economic resources across existing state borders might be unsustainable.

The state as the agent of political identity and expectations

All of these issues about the state, whether that be for individual states or the future of transnational sites of governance, come back in one way or another to that of the state as an agent of political identity and, as such, a bearer or suppressor of political expectations. In responding to the economic fallout of the financial crisis, citizens in various countries expressed anger at their own states and expected them to act. Those political expectations became part of the domestic context in which governments then decided how to act to deal with the crisis. Expectations that many states had apparently successfully suppressed for a long period were let loose, and created renewed political problems for states. Contrary to the globalization thesis, the state had not decisively removed itself in Europe and America from the burden of acting as an agent of aspirations about distributive justice or even retribution against the wealthy.

Over the medium to long term, states might be able to suppress these expectations but, so long as they persist, such expectations create two different kinds of problems for states. Some governments, not least that of the United States, found it difficult to persuade legislatures to authorize expenditures for the size of financial bailouts and recapitalization required – a problem that was dramatically demonstrated by the defeat of the first version of the Emergency Economic Stabilization Act in the House of Representatives. Although, when the Obama administration assumed office, there was no evidence that the American financial sector had been stabilized, the first economic act of the new President was to ask Congress to finance another fiscal stimulus, not more money for banks. Once the expectation that states should be punishing banks took hold, it proved politically difficult for governments to provide as much capital at an effective rate of interest as banks required in order to have a commercial incentive to restore lending. The British government's insistence that the state receive a higher dividend rate from the banks in which it became a part owner than they could possibly earn from lending illustrates the problem clearly. Politically, the state had both to punish banks and make them act like banks again.

Yet, neither is it possible for states simply to yield to an imperative of collective political expectations and try to use their power to align economic outcomes to those passions. The political emotion let loose by the financial crisis was not monolithic and is ridden with conflict, overt and latent. Clearly, the crisis produced at least a clash between the short-term interests of those citizens who were net-savers and net-debtors, as well as those working in different sectors of the economy. The state cannot possibly, at any given moment, act as a guardian of all its citizens' material interests. It has to side with some over others and, if it is prudent, actively try to persuade those who are the losers that, whatever the intrinsic strength of their grievance, their being a political loser is a long-term economic necessity. Of course, that is a political challenge facing states that is actually there to varying degrees at all times, and many non-western governments never had the luxury of the illusion that the conjunction of economic prosperity and liberal democracy would wish the problem away. For some time, however, it has not been as exposed a political challenge for western states as the financial crisis made it.

The problem states face in confronting political expectations has also now been created in a sharp form for the EU, as a site of transnational governance. The Union's existence is based on a rhetorical promise that there is something beyond the separateness of the provisions of individual statehood when, in practice, the states with the most material resources available to achieve that do not have the political capacity to provide them. Consequently, the EU has to suppress political expectations about what, as a transnational site of governance, it can provide, whilst relying on the whole idea that commonality is possible to legitimate the authority it does have. The deep reluctance of politicians to commit resources to transnational sites of governance, or to accept international purchase on domestic decision-making, suggests that the state still matters as an agent of national political identity. In this sense, arguments about the triumph of cosmopolitan or even regional identities have been proven to imagine something that – at least, as yet – does not exist in a politically significant way. Citizens' expectations still centre on what nation-states can do, and national political identity is a severe constraint on the relatively richer governments accepting redistribution between states or transnational decision-making. This clearly has implications that go well beyond the financial crisis, not least for the possibility of using transnational sites of governance to enhance environmental security. However, neither has the fallout of the financial crisis vindicated the communitarian position about political identity. Communitarians put too much emphasis on a moral consensus of citizens within states for which empirical evidence does not exist, and too little on the clash of interests within states and the ways in which states' relation to these conflicts and their implications for representation shape not only a territorially-bounded political identity, but also the character of the state itself.

Conclusions: future intellectual agendas on the state

The dominance, in recent years, of the 'globalization' discourse within academic debates about the state has distorted our understanding of it as a political entity, after the efforts of various scholars in the 1980s to 'bring the state back in' (Evans *et al.* 1985). The limitations of the globalization discourse were exacerbated by the academic separation of international relations from international political economy, from comparative politics, from political theory, when the state is a central subject of inquiry in all these areas. The debates within each field have been too discrete and have come at different aspects of the state's character, empirically and normatively, without a clear conception of the state as the complex political entity that it is.

Whatever else they are, states are sites of authority and power. But it is also true that it is what governments choose to do with the power of states, and the consequences this has for the political problems states face in legitimating that authority and power, that reveal most clearly what states are like and how they might respond to the dilemmas of today's world. States do have considerably more economic power, and the diplomatically and military most powerful states are more robust in the face of international organizations and networks than the variants of globalization literature supposed. However, this does not tell us anything in itself about how states will, in practice, act in response to which political imperatives.

To understand actual state behaviour, we have to conceive of states as confronting a fundamental political problem of legitimating rule that arises out of the clash of interests and beliefs among their citizens. This manifests itself in various ways, but does so particularly starkly in states' fiscal predicaments. This is where questions of economic discretion, power, sovereignty and political identity about the state come together. They expose the domestic conflicts through which the state must navigate its way or risk its authority, and they set clear limits on the possibilities of transnational governance. Looking at what happens to states after they borrow, or guarantee private corporations' debt, and then have to find political ways to service that debt, and the consequences this can have for relations between states, in and out of formal international organizations, would be a particularly constructive line of future inquiry.

Whatever the focus, in moving forwards scholars of the state need to engage with the question of the relation between the kinds of the general empirical and theoretical claims that they might wish to make and the experience of statehood, both across the world today and of states in the past. Too much of what, through the discourse of globalization, was said to be the case of the state in general in recent years was insensitive to the evidence from non-western states and careless about the historical specifics. If general truths are to be offered about states today, then the lines of analytical investigation must be broader and more comparative than they have been recently, and they must locate the state simultaneously in the domestic and international contexts in which it operates.

Chapter 7

Economic Interdependence and the Global Economic Crisis

JOHN RAVENHILL

Introduction: the great recession and global economic interdependence

At the time of writing (mid-2009), the global economy is embroiled in its most severe downturn since the Great Depression of the 1930s. Overall global production is expected to fall in 2009, the first time this has happened since the 1930s. The World Trade Organization (2009) predicts that global trade will fall by 9 per cent, the largest contraction since 1945. Developing economies face shrinking export markets, lower prices for their commodity exports (a drop of more than 40 per cent), and a halt to inflows of public and private capital. The World Bank (2009a; 2009b) warns that the global recession will increase the number of people living in poverty by 65 million in 2009, and further delay realization of the Millennium Development Goals. The International Monetary Fund (IMF) (2009) estimates that the crisis-induced write-downs of bad loans by financial institutions will total around US$4 trillion – imposing a potentially massive burden on the public purse for the re-capitalization of these institutions.

The recession poses not only an enormous practical challenge for governments, but also calls into question some conventional wisdom in our theorizing of the global political economy. The challenge to governments had several dimensions. The immediate one is how effectively to counter the most severe downturn in more than half a century. It is not simply a matter of substantial falls occurring in employment but, rather, that the very foundations of the financial system in several of the world's largest economies had been undermined. Governments in Washington and London find themselves unexpectedly assuming effective ownership of some of the world's leading financial institutions. Governments are being called upon to provide enormous injections of taxpayers' money to prop up ailing financial institutions and manufacturers.

This is a crisis not simply in the sense of a major economic downturn that poses a management challenge to governments: it is also a challenge to belief systems – how governments conceive of effective and appropriate economic management. The origins of the recession in poor lending practices by financial institutions challenge the fundamental tenet of the prevailing orthodoxy of neo-liberalism, the idea that the role of the state should be minimized and that self-regulating markets would produce optimal economic outcomes (see also the chapter by Helen Thompson in this volume). It also seems to spell the end, at least in the short run, to the dominant role of monetarism in central banks' monetary policies (with its fixation with targeting low levels of inflation, in part by avoiding government deficits), and a return to Keynesian approaches (associated with the running of government deficits to provide a stimulus to economies suffering less than full utilization of resources).

The recession is further evidence that we live in a truly interdependent global economy. One reason for its severity is that, unlike previous postwar downturns, all regions of the world are in economic decline simultaneously. The extent of the recession, and the rapidity with which all regions of the world are affected, again, poses both practical and conceptual challenges. For the global financial institutions (the International Monetary Fund, the World Bank), the cessation of private and public lending poses a severe challenge to their efforts to minimize the impact of the recession on developing economies (and exposes the inadequacies of their existing funding). The extent of the crisis suggests that it was not only a matter of a quantitative increase in interdependence, but also a qualitative change. As the World Trade Organization (WTO) has noted, the rapid spread of the recession worldwide has been caused, in part, by the increasing presence of global supply chains in countries' trade: with components crossing national frontiers many times before a manufactured product reaches its final destination, a decline in the major global markets quickly affected trade – and then employment – in other parts of the world.

For some commentators, the global recession is as significant a challenge for the field of international political economy (IPE) as the demise of the Soviet Union and the end of the Cold War had been for realist approaches to the study of international relations. The recession has taken most commentators by surprise, coming after a sustained period of expansion in global output and trade – one that, unusually, had been accompanied by low rates of inflation. But although few accurately predicted the timing of the recession (and it is an unrealistic expectation of what social sciences can deliver to expect this), the causes of the crisis are ones that will be familiar to all students of the history of the global economy (albeit with some new twists reflecting aspects of contemporary financial globalization).

Something old, something new ...

The recession was triggered by the bursting of an asset price bubble – in this instance, the inflated US housing market. The term 'bubble' was coined in the UK in 1720 following the crash of the South Sea Company, and the passing in that year of the so-called 'Bubble Act' – more formally, 'An Act to Restrain the Extravagant and Unwarrantable Practice of Raising Money by Voluntary Subscription for Carrying on Projects Dangerous to the Trade and Subjects of the United Kingdom'. As in previous crises, the bursting of the bubble caused panic among investors, whose uncertainty over whether they could recoup their money caused them to flee the market (Kindleberger (1978) remains the classic discussion of these phenomena). Investor panic had significantly exacerbated the previous major financial crisis – that which afflicted east Asia in 1997/98 (Noble and Ravenhill 2000; Radelet and Sachs 2000). And, as with previous crashes, the bubble was associated with behaviour that was either outside the law or certainly contrary to its spirit, and the bursting of the bubble with calls for improved regulation.

Globalization of finance did introduce some elements to the contemporary crisis that had not been seen before. The growth of financial intermediation, of which an important aspect was the securitization of mortgage debt, had two important consequences. The first was that what began as a national problem (defaults on US mortgages) was quickly transformed into a global crisis because of its impact on investors in mortgage-backed securities; second, the complexity of the new financial instruments exacerbated the problem of panic because of the uncertainty created in transactions among financial institutions (for discussion of the complexities of what the IMF calls 'structured financial products', see International Monetary Fund 2008: ch. 2).

The new financial instruments had been marketed globally by American and European investment banks – with the consequence that, once the bubble burst, various institutional investors, ranging from local councils in Australia and Norway to the London Metropolitan Police's pension fund, suffered significant losses. A contributing factor here was that, in a low-inflation environment, investors had been attracted to financial instruments that offered potentially higher rates of return than those available on more familiar investments and, in doing so, had either discounted or not understood the risks involved. Once panic set in, financial institutions were reluctant to lend to one another – and, here, another dimension of financial globalization entered the equation: the increasing dependence of bank lending on funds borrowed in the international wholesale market, rather than on their own deposits or capital. The extreme case was that of Iceland, where the country's banks had been the main source of the country's international debts, which were estimated in 2008 to amount to US$276,622 for every resident: in 2008/9, the three largest Icelandic banks had €11 billion of debt obligations maturing (Brogger 2008). When no new financing was forthcoming, the banks collapsed. In turn, the drying up of global bank lending quickly fed into the 'real' economy when companies were denied the credit they required to maintain their operations (including trading); a collapse in consumer spending reinforced the downward spiral.

If many of the dimensions of the global recession were familiar to students of IPE, it did, nonetheless, cast new light on existing questions and raised new ones relating to the characteristics of contemporary global interdependence, and to the challenges of providing effective governance to the global economy. The effects of the recession noted in the opening paragraph of this chapter were spread across all of the principal subject areas of global political economy: trade, finance, investment, production, issues relating to development/poverty eradication, even extending to everyday politics (Hobson and Seabrooke 2007). They posed practical challenges to national governments, and regional and global institutions alike. They challenged a number of prevailing orthodoxies about what makes for effective economic governance. The recession, therefore, provides a particularly useful lens through which to view the state of the field of IPE. In this chapter, I first examine what recent developments have added to our understanding of the forces of globalization, and the extent to which they constrain the policy options of states. I then turn to issues relating to the regulation of the global economy, the variety of forms of global governance, and how responses to the recession might affect the balance between public and private regulatory authorities. Finally, I look at how recent developments in the global economy might impact on how we go about studying interdependence.

Globalization: how new, how constraining?

Globalization – which I understand as the forces (both economic and political) that have permitted the integration of economic space – has been the dominant metaphor in much of the literature of international political economy over the last two decades. Debate has focused on two broad sets of issues: first, is there anything new in the interdependence that characterizes the contemporary global economy; and, second, how constraining are the effects of globalization on states?

The contemporary recession provides further strong evidence that the economic interdependence of the current period is unprecedented. It was the case that in previous major economic downturns, as might well be the case in the medium term with the current recession, less developed economies were frequently the worst affected – as happened, for instance, under the gold standard (Eichengreen 1985). But arguments that suggest that the world economy was more closely interconnected in the 'golden era' between 1870 and 1914 than in the contemporary era (Thompson *et al.* 2009) are guilty of failing to compare like with like, of mixing apples and oranges (Bordo *et al.* 1999).

In particular, the amount of mobile capital in private hands today is unprecedented, as is the speed with which it can be moved across frontiers. In its most recent triennial survey of central banks, the Bank for International Settlements (BIS) (2007) estimated that the *daily* turnover in foreign exchange markets in 2007 was US$3.2 trillion. This is equivalent to roughly one quarter of the *annual* value of global trade. It dwarfs the assets available to the IMF (which stood at approximately US$250 billion before the G20 decision in April 2009 to raise its funding), and the foreign exchange holdings of all national governments (in April 2009, China had the world's largest holdings, at slightly under US$2 trillion; those of Japan were roughly half this amount; those of the euro-zone, collectively, half those of Japan; whilst those of the United Kingdom were US$64 billion). The total global holdings of foreign exchange reserves amounted to US$7.2 trillion, not much more than the value of two days' trading in foreign exchange markets. It only takes a relatively small fraction of the foreign exchange in the hands of private traders to be mobilized against an individual currency for the defences available to a government (whether from national, regional or multilateral sources) to be overwhelmed.

To the unprecedented mobility of international finance and the ever-more-creative and complex instruments that financial institutions have constructed, any consideration of the novel aspects of contemporary globalization must add the extent of cross-national linkages through production networks. Whilst it might be the case that few firms are truly multinational in their operations, let alone in their shareholders and management (Rugman 2005), and the internationalization of production is not an invention of the twentieth century, the extent to which geographically fragmented global production chains dominate contemporary manufacturing is unprecedented and a distinguishing characteristic of the contemporary global economy (Dicken 2007; Thun 2008). It has fundamentally transformed the character of international trade – with manufactures constituting a substantial majority of the exports of less-developed economies, considered in aggregate. We are moving towards a tightly integrated global factory, brought about by changes in technology, and by government actions to liberalize trade and investment flows. It remains one that is ultimately dependent on consumer demand in North America and Europe. The speed with which integrated financial markets and production networks spread the recession in 2008 quickly demolished an emerging myth – that the rapidly developing East Asian region had the capacity to disengage from the global economy because of the increasing demand from China for the exports of its neighbours. In reality, because East Asian economies are so heavily dependent on foreign trade (and, through the ultimate export of assembled products from China, on extra-regional markets), they were among the first to suffer large downturns in the recession.

Sophisticated students of globalization have long rejected the notion that there is anything inevitable or irreversible about the processes that have driven contemporary global interdependence (McGrew 2008). The last great recession – in the 1930s – showed how long-standing patterns of economic integration could quickly unravel. The increasingly integrated (and deregulated) global financial system has been prone to crises that have been of mounting frequency and intensity (Bordo and Eichengreen 2002). The bursting of the dot.com bubble at the end of the last century, and the uncertainties created by the terrorist attacks in the United States on 11 September 2001 ('9/11'), temporarily interrupted the upward trend in such conventional indicators of economic interdependence as foreign direct investment and trade flows. The contemporary crisis has already caused a more severe downturn in these indicators than the events at the turn of the century – and, given the extent of the damage in most of the world's largest economies to the financial system and to national accounts (squeezed by a pincer movement of lower revenues from taxation and the need for increased expenditures to recapitalize banks and for welfare payments to the unemployed), the effects are certain to be longer-lasting. How long it will take, before economic growth will be restored, will depend on the effectiveness of national and international efforts. Here, we move to an especially interesting set of issues that relate not only to the governance of the global economy, but also to national responses to the forces of global integration/disintegration – and, in particular, to how the recession will affect governments' ideas of how to construct a response to the pressures emanating from enhanced interdependence.

One thing is certain: the recession undermined triumphalist notions that governments have learned to master the factors driving business or economic cycles more generally (contrast Weber 1997), or that they could be resolved through leaving them in the hands of unregulated markets. A striking feature of the early governmental response to the recession was the acknowledgement of the inadequacies of previous policy approaches, particularly in the area of financial sector regulation ('Major failures in the financial sector and in financial regulation and supervision were fundamental causes of the crisis', admitted the G20 leaders in the communiqué from their London summit – (G20 2009a: para. 13).

Such admissions and apparent dramatic shifts in policy – seen in the revival of Keynesian approaches to economic stimulation, for example – underline the arguments of astute observers that an understanding of agency, and how the ideas that agents hold about how to construct their responses to globalization, must be a central part of understanding this complex topic (Hay 2002a, 2008).

With major financial institutions on both sides of the Atlantic effectively under governmental ownership, we have moved a long way very quickly from the market exuberance of the three decades before 2008. Whilst Willem Buiter (2008), a Professor of European Political Economy at the LSE, might have been premature in proclaiming the 'end of American capitalism as we knew it', the recession might prove to be a critical juncture not only in economic policies, but also in the underlying conceptual frameworks that political elites adopt in attempting to understand the world around them. The rejection of prevailing orthodoxy was summed up in an article by the Labor Prime Minister of Australia, Kevin Rudd (2009), a member of the right wing of his party and, thus, hardly a radical in the spectrum of political opinion of the day:

> From time to time in human history there occur events of a truly seismic significance, events that mark a turning point between one epoch and the next, when one orthodoxy is overthrown and another takes its

place ... Not for the first time in history, the international challenge for social democrats is to save capitalism from itself ... The current crisis is the culmination of a 30-year domination of economic policy by a free-market ideology that has been variously called neo-liberalism, economic liberalism, economic fundamentalism, Thatcherism or the Washington Consensus.

If advocates of neo-liberalism were placed on the defensive by the crisis, the early responses of governments soon demonstrated that there were significant divisions about priorities in responding to the recession that, in turn, were linked to deeper philosophical divisions about how serious an indictment the crisis provided of the economic philosophies that had prevailed in the previous three decades. Here, the principal fault line was between, on the one hand, continental European economies (supported by the larger developing economies that were given a voice through the G20), which placed emphasis on the need to improve regulation of financial institutions, and, on the other hand, Britain and the United States, which gave priority to calls for additional fiscal stimulation. At least on the surface (and there is little information available about the interactions among the governments at the G20 summit), this division appeared to coincide with that put forward in the literature on 'Varieties of Capitalism' – between the 'Liberal Market Economies' of the United Kingdom and the United States, and the 'Coordinated Market Economies', of which Germany is seen as the archetype (Albert 1993; Hall and Soskice 2001).

The key thrust of the varieties of capitalism literature, which has been dominant in shaping the agenda in the study of comparative political economy over the last decade, has been to deny that globalization imposes such a straitjacket on governments that they must all respond in the same way – whether in corporate taxation, industrial policies, or welfare expenditures (Weiss 1998; Mosley 2002; Swank 2002; Gourevitch and Shinn 2005). Government policies will exhibit a considerable degree of 'path dependency': existing domestic institutional configurations shape the range of policy choices from which governments can choose. As might have been predicted from this literature, it was the coordinated market economies that placed the greatest emphasis on the need for additional regulation.

The simple dichotomy put forward in the varieties of capitalism literature has justifiably been criticized for obscuring differences between countries aggregated into the same category (Crouch 2005a, 2005b; Hay 2008). Nonetheless, the underlying point in this literature remains valid:

that globalization's impact on states is 'more complex and contingent than many observers claim' (Kahler and Lake 2003: 2). This statement is as true for the recession as it is for the second 'golden age' of globalization that preceded and, for some commentators, precipitated it. What remains to be seen is whether the demand for greater harmonization of regulation, particularly in the financial sector, will generate new sources for convergence not only of policies, but also of institutions across countries. As one would anticipate, the early signs in the United States are that there will be considerable opposition to any move towards a more coordinated market economy, once the immediate exigencies of bailing out bankrupt institutions are completed. And the divisions also carried over to prescriptions about what needed to be done at the global level to ensure such crises did not develop again. Even in the Anglo-American world, however, in the words of the eminent American economist, Barry Eichengreen (2009), 'one incontrovertible lesson [learned] is the need for more vigorous regulation of financial institutions and markets. Light-touch Anglo-Saxon style regulation failed its crucial test, and everyone is now agreed on the need for a more heavy-handed approach.'

Regulating the global economy

Diversity is the most striking characteristic of the institutions constructed to govern the global economy. Supranationalism – where governments have pooled their sovereignty and transferred regulatory authority to an international institution – is very rare indeed. Reaching agreement on rules within inter-governmental institutions – especially in the regulation of finance – has also proved difficult. Private (and public–private) networks are responsible for a great deal of international regulatory activity: elsewhere, national rules (sometimes emulated by others or imposed on them) frequently prevail (Kahler and Lake 2009).

Many of the problems in the governance of the global economy were evident before the onset of the global recession. Recent developments have, nonetheless, reinvigorated efforts to fashion more effective regulatory institutions. A key question remains: What makes for effective institutional design? One of the important issues here is membership and the ways in which decision-making procedures are fashioned to deal with the twin problems of numbers and diversity.

The WTO is the most important international economic institution where membership is universal (or, more accurately, open to all countries whose trade policies are acceptable to existing members), and where members nominally have equal voting rights (although the institution has always operated on the basis of consensus). Yet, the WTO has had great difficulty in reaching new compacts on international trade – with many observers pointing to the increasing diversity of its membership as a principal reason for its problems. Many developing economies were unhappy at the results of the bargain they signed on to during the Uruguay Round of GATT negotiations, and at the subsequent failure of developed economies to make any substantial reductions to their agricultural subsidies. Consequently, they were reluctant to enter any further agreements that might impinge on domestic policy autonomy – with good reason, according to critics of the Doha Round proposals (Wade 2004).

For some, the risk is that the 'bicycle effect' will come into play: the argument that if the riders of the WTO do not continue to pedal energetically to generate forward momentum, then the wheels of the global trading system, to mix metaphors, will fall off. The immediate response to the global recession by some industrialized economies in implementing measures that had the effect of raising levels of protection to domestic industry seemed to provide ammunition for these concerns. Yet, the lack of progress in global talks should not obscure the significance of other achievements within the global trading system, most significantly, the work of the Dispute Settlement Mechanisms (DSMs) that the WTO was endowed with following the Uruguay Round negotiations (Barton *et al.* 2006). This legalization of the trade regime has helped to move outcomes away from being determined purely by relative power considerations. Less-developed economies have not always had the resources to make full and effective use of the DSMs (Narlikar 2003). But the enlarged operations of the Advisory Centre on World Trade Law, established in 2001 with the support of ten industrialized economies in order to provide legal advice to developing economies and training for their officials, form an important step towards their more effective participation in these mechanisms. And the WTO has placed a great deal of emphasis in recent years on its 'aid for trade' programme of providing technical assistance to less-developed members. New groupings of developing economies in the Doha Round negotiations have helped to increase the influence of the larger players among them – but questions remain about whether the cohesion of developing economies will hold in the face of their heterogeneous interests.

The lack of progress in global trade talks has contributed to the proliferation of trade agreements at the bilateral and mini-lateral levels – ranging from largely inconsequential bilateral agreements between countries located in different geographical areas that are insignificant trading partners for one another (for example, Singapore and Peru), to negotiations between two existing regional groupings (for example, the EU and Mercosur), to the far more consequential geographical extension of the EU itself. The jury is still out on the issue of whether these agreements damage or contribute to global trade liberalization – either directly (through their own discriminatory provisions) or indirectly (by diverting attention and scarce governmental resources away from the global level).

With the exception of the EU, there is little evidence, to date, that these preferential trade agreements have had any significant impact on the global economy. Several factors explain this: tariff levels, even in many developing economies, are already low so that the advantages conferred by any agreement are small and are frequently swamped by other factors, such as changes in exchange rates; businesses often do not perceive the potential benefits from the provisions of these arrangements to offset the costs of complying with them; in few of the agreements do governments go beyond the commitments that they have made at the WTO, especially in 'new' trade areas such as services; and, as noted, many of the agreements link countries that are relatively unimportant partners for one another (Ravenhill 2008b, 2008c). One thing is clear from the proliferation of agreements, however, as a long tradition of political economy literature would predict (Hirschman 1980): bilateral and mini-lateral arrangements that involve markedly unequal economic partners produce outcomes that favour the stronger parties. The major players – Europe, Japan, and the United States – have been able to make use of such agreements to impose outcomes that have proved impossible to secure at the global level (on the Latin American experience in negotiations with the United States, see Shadlen 2005).

In the global governance of finance, no pretence of membership equality has ever existed. Voting rights in the IMF are determined by the size of a country's quota: despite periodic adjustment, current quotas remain a better reflection of the relative weight of economies in the world in 1944 than today. The EU, in particular, is substantially over-represented – to a considerable extent, at the expense of the rapidly developing economies of Asia. The Fund, however, has never played the role that the architects of the Bretton Woods system intended for it. With the reliance on the US dollar as the principal reserve currency, the Fund had no control over the creation of international reserves in the global financial system. Industrialized economies, moreover, have never permitted it to play a significant role in overseeing exchange rates (and macroeconomic balances). After the Fund's Interim Committee decided, at its Jamaica Meeting in January 1976, to give its blessing to the abandonment of fixed but adjustable parities, the Fund effectively left exchange rate management in the hands of (what turned out to be) a particularly volatile market. To the extent that any coordination of exchange rates took place, this was managed by the G7 (Canada, France, Italy, Germany, Japan, the United Kingdom and the United States). After the industrialized economies recovered in the late 1970s from the first oil price shock, the IMF's only clients were debt-afflicted developing economies. But, even here, its business had largely dried up by 2005: developing economies were increasingly unwilling to go to the Fund for financing because of the conditions it attached to its lending; many had substantially increased their foreign exchange reserves following the East Asian financial crises of 1997/98. With most developing countries benefiting from high commodity prices in the mid-2000s, the Fund was making few loans and actually began to make some staff redundant.

Other areas of global finance were regulated primarily by official representatives of industrialized economies – especially from their central banks, coordinated through the BIS – or delegated largely to private agencies (in the case of accounting standards, for instance, see Mattli and Buthe (2005); on credit rating agencies see Sinclair (2005)). Here, issues of representation, the appropriateness of standards, and enforcement arise. In the case of the prudential principles to govern private bank finances, the key actor has been the Basel Committee on Banking Supervision (BCBS), which was set up by the central bank governors of the Group of Ten countries at the end of 1974, and comprises officials from Belgium, Canada, France, Germany, Italy, Japan, Luxembourg, the Netherlands, Spain, Sweden, Switzerland, the United Kingdom and the United States. Notably absent from this grouping were representatives of developing economies: Japan was the only 'non-Western' country participating until March 2009, when the BIS invited Australia, Brazil, China, India, Korea, Mexico and Russia to join the Committee. Here, it is important to recall that the BCBS sets standards – the most important of which are the Basel Principles on Capital Adequacy, which are intended to apply to all banks, worldwide. Not surprisingly, governments in some developing economies have complained that the circumstances of their domestic financial institutions were not fully taken into account when the principles were developed. Enthusiastic implementation of regulatory principles is unlikely when authorities do not have 'ownership' of them.

An important concern when the responsibility for regulation is delegated to private authorities is to whom these authorities are responsible; or, to pose the question another way: Who regulates the regulators?

Governments often delegate responsibility for regulation to private actors when they believe that the costs of undertaking the regulatory activities themselves are excessive (private actors might be far better informed, have easier access to information, and so on) or if governments want to shift responsibility for blame to other actors should anything go awry. But problems can arise when these private actors, who might wield enormous power (and have the capacity, as do the ratings agencies, to impose significant costs on others), face conflicting motivations in carrying out their responsibilities. Such problems were evident in the behaviour of the credit-ratings agencies in their handling of the complex securities created by investment banks. Staff felt under pressure to provide these securities with a favourable rating because the banks issuing them were important paying clients of the agencies, even though they had significant doubts about the risks involved with these new financial instruments (for excerpts of revealing testimony before the US House Oversight Committee, see Bardeesy 2008). Private and public interest and imperatives were in direct conflict – and, as is typical in such cases, private interest won out. Although ratings crises have occurred before, as Sinclair (2005) describes, the credibility of the ratings agencies has seldom been undermined to the extent that has occurred in the current crisis.

If the credibility of some private agencies as effective regulators has taken a beating during the recession, this was nothing compared with the dramatic loss in faith that has occurred in the capacity of markets to be self-regulating. Of particular note here were the remarks made by Alan Greenspan, the former Chairman of the US Federal Reserve, in hearings before the US Congress where he acknowledged that he had erred in rejecting calls to regulate the risky financial instruments that US banks were issuing, and that his faith in deregulation had been shaken (*New York Times* 2008). As with the credit rating agencies, principal–agent issues were at the root of many of the failures of institutions to police themselves: these were encapsulated in the divergence of interest that occurred between risk-takers, on the one hand, (who were rewarded for short-term results), and, on the other, the long-term interests of firms, shareholders, and most employees. Whilst an almost universal decline in confidence in markets and in private regulatory agencies has occurred, one can anticipate considerable resistance – in particular, in the United States – to efforts to shift responsibility for regulation to inter-governmental forums.

One of the key questions arising from the recession for students of political economy is whether the global economic institutions can/should be given a more central role in global economic governance, more akin to that envisaged by the founders of the Bretton Woods system.

Several major developments in international regulation have come in the immediate responses to the recession. The IMF has been revitalized – with a commitment made to triple its own resources (to US$750 billion), and to allow it to issue US$250 billion in Special Drawing Rights to top up the international reserves of its member states. It has been permitted to open contingency lines of credit (flexible credit lines) to try to forestall crises in countries that are starting to experience financial difficulties, rather than waiting until after the damage has been done before resources are disbursed. Such pre-emptive action will require governments to seek assistance at an early stage (which might be problematic, in that the very act of seeking assistance can be seen by markets as a signal that the country is running into problems). The increase in resources for the Fund has been accompanied by a major shift in its approach to financial crises. The emphasis is now on expansionary government policies, in complete contrast to the requirement for contraction that accompanied lending to debt-afflicted Latin American, African and east Asian economies in their successive crises in the 1980s and 1990s. A pertinent question for students of political economy is how well-equipped the Fund is to play this new role, which goes against the orthodoxy that the Fund has preached for several decades. We know from the experience of other agencies – for example, that of the World Bank, when efforts were made to move its mission from building infrastructure to poverty alleviation – that such radical shifts in orientation are difficult to effect in the face of resistance from staff whose training and incentive structure are focused on the institution's previous mission (Ayres 1983).

The recession has brought about an acknowledgement by the industrialized economies of the shift in global economic power that has occurred over the last decade. This had already been forced on the World Trade Organization, where the requirement for consensus gave a blocking veto to India and Brazil, sometimes supported by China, in the Doha Round negotiations. Quota reform is to continue at the IMF, which will reduce the voting rights of European states and enhance those of East Asian economies, India, and Brazil (albeit still leaving them with quotas in the Fund substantially below their current shares in global output and trade). Perhaps more importantly, the central role given to the G20 – as opposed to the G7/G8 – in the response to the crisis appeared to signal a new willingness on the part of industrialized countries to admit key developing economies to their informal decision-making clubs. As noted above, this new direction was also reflected in the expansion of the membership of the Basel Committee on Banking Supervision in March 2009.

The G20 meeting in London in April 2009 also gave birth to a new international regulatory agency, the Financial Stability Board. This will build on the existing Financial Stability Forum, a grouping established in 1999 aimed at information exchange and the promotion of international cooperation in financial supervision and surveillance, and which comprised representatives of central banks, finance ministries, and national and international financial supervisory agencies. The new agency was tasked with assessing vulnerabilities affecting the financial system and overseeing action to address them, monitoring market developments, promoting and coordinating information exchange among authorities responsible for financial stability, and advising on best practice (G20 2009b).

Sceptics will enquire how effective information exchange will be in meeting the desire for improved regulation of financial markets unless this is backed by clearly specified rules and sanctions. It remains to be seen whether the recession will bring about a major shift in regulatory authority to international institutions – gaining at the expense of markets, private actors and national authorities. It does seem certain, however, that other countries will be less willing than in recent years to accept templates for national regulations drawn up in western capitals, when it has been the very ineffectiveness of their regulations that was at the root of the crisis.

The crisis has also raised questions about the future role of the US dollar in the global financial system. For some commentators, the root of the US sub-prime mortgage problem lay in the easy domestic availability of cheap money – a situation that arose, in part, because of global trade imbalances. The significant trade surpluses run by East Asian economies (and, to a lesser extent, by oil exporters and by Germany), and the willingness of many countries to re-cycle these surpluses through the acquisition of US securities (especially Treasury bills), fed Americans' demand for inexpensive credit. Throughout the postwar era, the stability of the global financial system has depended on confidence that foreigners have had in the US dollar. The demise of the dollar as the principal reserve currency was frequently predicted, even before the current crisis – Kirshner (2008) noted that expectations about a fundamental change in the role of the dollar were increasingly widespread and 'fundamentally plausible'. The attractiveness of the dollar as a safe haven, however, was vividly illustrated at the onset of the recession, when it appreciated rapidly against all other major currencies. But the upheavals in the US financial system – coupled with the costs to the US Treasury of recapitalizing banks (and car companies and their suppliers), which are likely to lead to an even-larger trade deficit – might finally persuade other governments to seek other locations for investing their surpluses and to promote alternatives to the dollar as reserve currencies. Should they do so, profound consequences will follow not only for the US capacity to run its macroeconomic policies largely without international constraint, but also for the global political economy and for the global *political* role that the United States can play. The volume of dollars in foreign hands, however, would suggest that radical change is unlikely – a dramatic sell-off of the dollar will only depreciate the value of countries' other holdings of the currency. Complex interdependence, indeed.

Global economic interdependence and the study of IPE

The study of IPE, as with much of political science, is typically events-driven: writers respond to the major developments of the era. To suggest that the great recession will have a major effect on scholarship is a safe bet. To predict exactly in which directions new scholarship will go is more hazardous.

The field of IPE has become increasingly fragmented in recent years. At one end of the spectrum is what Lake (2006) has termed 'open economy politics', the essential innovation of which, he claims, was to deduce the interests of actors from economic theory – that is, from the distributional implications of various economic policies (Lake 2009). The approach is a variant of the rational choice analysis that has become dominant in many American departments of political science in the last two decades. As with the discipline of economics, the objective is to hold constant as many variables as possible whilst investigating a single hypothesis about causation. At the other extreme are various 'critical' approaches to the study of IPE that consciously eschew causal analysis and positivist methods, are holistic in their approach, and not shy about their normative preference – which is to seek systemic transformation. And, between these two poles, is a vast array of scholarship that is empirically-based and usually concerned with incremental development of theoretically-informed arguments (Ravenhill 2008a). With the 'open economy politics' dominating IPE in many American universities and leading American journals, concerns have been expressed – not only by critics outside the United States, but also by some of the 'founding fathers' of IPE in the United States – that the field has become increasingly introverted, and excessively focused on narrow questions that are susceptible to modelling (see *Review of International Political Economy*

(2009), especially the contributions by Cohen; Katzenstein; and Keohane).

What effects will recent developments in the global economy have on these various approaches to IPE? It certainly opens up the possibility for exploring large questions again, in all of the areas listed above. Those who are sceptical about the utility of rational choice approaches will surely take much comfort from the events that produced the great recession. For here, rather than the behaviour of rational actors, with full knowledge of their interests and how best carefully to calculate the optimal means of pursuing them, we saw a classic response to the bursting of an asset bubble: herd-like behaviour by actors who panicked – not least because they simply were unaware, given the complexities of the financial instruments that they and other actors had invested in, of the extent of the liabilities to which they and others in the market were exposed. For those particularly concerned with the micro-foundations of the global economy, the crisis is likely to foster an interest in the 'behavioural economics' approach that assumes, contrary to the orthodoxy of neoclassical economics, that individuals operate with 'bounded rationality' and with imperfect information.

Liberal institutionalists will see the recession as validating their claims for stronger institutions. 'Broadly speaking', write Mattli and Woods (2009: ix), 'two related factors explain the latest global financial fiasco: inadequate regulation that generated a mismatch between private reward and public risk; and failure of regulators to comply with their supervisory duties'. Elsewhere, the same authors assert that 'what is needed is a hefty global regulatory framework' (*The Guardian* 2008). Regulators, they argue, were conned by overpaid bankers into applying a light touch to the oversight of the new financial instruments. An effective response to the crisis requires new international regulatory authorities to monitor existing watchdogs, and a judicial institution that would have compulsory jurisdiction to enable governments to bring cases against countries that had failed to implement systems of regulations that met agreed international standards. The key issues for advocates of this approach relate to effective institutional design, and what political coalitions can be fashioned to construct the international institutions empowered to deliver preferred outcomes.

For others, however, the origins of the crisis lay not in inadequate regulation, but in the contradictions of the capitalist system itself. After a period of marginalization following the end of the Cold War, Marxist analysts are restating their claims that they have the tools to provide a better understanding of the contradictions of global capitalism. Robert

Brenner, a Marxist economic historian at UCLA, was one of the few commentators who had predicted the severity of the crisis (Brenner 2002, Brenner and Jeong 2009). The revival of Marxist analysis was even picked up by the mainstream US journal, *Foreign Policy*, with the long-time editor of the *Socialist Register*, Leo Panitch (2009), recounting how sales of *Das Kapital* have shot up since the onset of the recession.

One might also expect to see some revival of dependency approaches – for, if anything confirmed how economic growth in less developed economies is 'conditioned' by that in the industrialized world, it was surely this crisis. The current problems less-developed economies face – unlike the debt crises that afflicted Latin America in the 1980s, Africa for most of the previous quarter of a century, and East Asia in 1997/98 – are not at all of their own making. Few financial systems in developing economies had any significant exposure to the new financial instruments that packaged the sub-prime mortgage debt. The crisis was quickly transmitted to them from outside as the markets for their exports collapsed, and flows of capital dried up.

Yet others will see their call for a return to other classics of political economy vindicated by the current crisis. Adam Smith, after all, provided us with a sophisticated understanding of the potential vices, as well as virtues, of the self-seeking behaviour of individuals in the marketplace (Watson 2005, 2008). Yet, it is not clear – except at a very general 'philosophical' level in pointing to relevant questions to pose – what guidance the classics provide to coping with the current challenges.

Many IPE scholars in the UK have long resisted the typical approach in American universities to see IPE as a sub-field of international relations – a position long-rejected, for instance, by one of the leading journals in the field, *New Political Economy*. The significance of the interaction between the domestic and the international, between work in comparative and international political economy, has been re-emphasized by the recession: the argument that the relevant field of study is political economy (without any prefatory adjectives) has surely been strengthened.

Conclusion

The contemporary global recession is, one would hope, a once-in-a-lifetime phenomenon – one that is likely to create a major disjuncture with what has gone before. At least, on the surface, it seems to spell the end of some of the key points of the ideology that has dominated political thinking about and policy-making on globalization in the last quarter of a century. Neo-liberalism, Reaganism or Thatcherism, and the Washington Consensus all appear to have suffered a terminal loss of credibility. We seemed to be poised on the verge of a new era of Keynesian fiscal stimulus – a world in which greed is no longer perceived to be good, and where governments have signalled their willingness to enter into new arrangements for regulating the global economy. Old-fashioned social democracy seems, at least in the short term, to have returned to the ascendancy.

Good intentions have never guaranteed the realization of desired outcomes in world politics, however. The area of international finance is full of complexities and of competing national interests: it is one that has been essentially ungoverned at the multilateral level throughout the postwar period. And, as David Held's chapter in this volume makes clear, global governance in other issue areas is in trouble.

Much work remains to be done on understanding the specific circumstances in which particular forms of regulatory authorities have worked well. Are there areas where regulation is best left in the hands of private actors, where principal–agent problems do not arise or can be overcome? Is regulation best carried out at the national, regional or global level? In a situation where much of the information about what is happening in the financial system is in the hands of private actors, will the proposed new regulatory agencies overcome the problems that have beset their predecessors? This agenda suggests that political economists in the future might benefit from closer collaboration with their colleagues in the field of public policy.

Will states be able to regain control of a global financial market where the bulk of assets is in private hands? Whilst the efforts to extend the participation in the select group that makes key decisions on global trade and finance can be welcomed, such action carries its own risks: will it simply institutionalize fundamental differences in approach so that stalemate ensues on many important issues? And how will the other 170-plus members of the international community react to the institutionalization of a new power elite? These questions suggest a full agenda for a new generation of students of international political economy.

Chapter 8

The Challenge of Territorial Politics: Beyond Methodological Nationalism

CHARLIE JEFFERY AND DANIEL WINCOTT

Introduction: why a new direction? The challenge of territorial politics

Political community, political institutions and public policies all lie at the heart of the study and practice of politics. A founding member of the Political Studies Association, looking back from 1950, might reasonably have detected a long-run trend over the previous two hundred years of European history as these three elements – political community (that is, how citizens claim identity, participate politically and express solidarity), institutions and policies – became increasingly integrated and consolidated on a single spatial scale; that of the nation-state. This trend is the subject of compelling narratives about the political modernization of Europe (Marshall 1992 [1950]; Tilly 1975; Rokkan 1999; Zürn and Leibfried 2005). These tell a largely common story about the intertwined processes of state formation and national integration culminating, after the Second World War, in mass democratic, national welfare states. Sixty years on, the world looks rather different. Oceans of ink have been spilt on the challenges that globalization and European integration pose to Europe's nation-states, which can appear fragile and threatened. Many scholars declare that territoriality and borders are now defunct; some suggest that modernization has simply 'jumped' to a more cosmopolitan 'scale', shifting from the nation-state to the European or global level (Beck 2000). Our focus here, however, is on a second set of changes: the (re)assertion of the sub-state territorial politics of stateless nations and 'regions'.

As decades – even centuries – of political centralization on and within

167

the nation-state came to a head, this trend always took a variety of forms in particular institutional and cultural settings. In turn, these diverse tendencies spawned counter-tendencies so that, as Keating (1998: ix) notes, territorial effects have been a 'constant presence in European politics'. But if there is something old and enduring about territorial politics, evidence is now accumulating behind a new claim: that the current trend is away from centralization and the nation-state, and might have been moving in this direction for some time. The territorialization of politics within the state is a major new – or renewed – challenge to the theory and practice of politics in Europe. Perhaps the clearest evidential support for this view is provided by the 'regional authority index' compiled by Gary Marks *et al.* (2008a, 2008b). It shows that, whilst the extent of regional political authority remained constant between 1950 and 1970, it has grown significantly since then, with 29 of 42 mainly European Union (EU) and OECD states becoming more 'regionalized', and only two (marginally) less so.

As with state formation and nation-building, the tendencies that make up this decentralizing 'turn' can be diverse: they move to distinct rhythms, often unfold unevenly, and sometimes lag behind their initial causes. We explore two aspects of this 'turn' – relating, respectively, to (sub-state) elections and social policy – in greater detail later. For now, it is sufficient to ask this question: Do these cases provide evidence for an 'unravelling' (Zürn and Leibfried 2005: 17) of the same underlying logics that once underpinned the centralization on the nation-state?' Alternatively, the emergence of a more robust and widespread sub-state electoral tier might reflect a shared underlying logic of democratization: for example, during the 1960s forms of 'peripheral mobilisation' (Rokkan and Urwin 1983) sprang up in many parts of Europe in the context of wider social and political movements that all took 'democracy' as a watchword. However, as we shall see below, these changes had only limited impact on nation-state level electoral behaviour. Only much more recently has a sub-state electoral tier has emerged, with significant institutional changes in the UK in 1999, Belgium in 1995, France in 1982, Spain in 1980s and Italy after 1970 (at least, for the fifteen ordinary regions). The three long-standing federal states (Austria, Germany, Switzerland) alone have held 'regional' elections in all parts of the state extending back at least to the Second World War.

If the growth of welfare in the first half of the twentieth century has become associated with a centralist, nation-statist logic, its continued expansion into new areas of social service and the development of novel welfare rights, particularly since the 1960s (again, often in the name of democratization), might also have created pressure for a rescaling of public policy towards the sub-state level. Changes in gender roles and family forms created new demands for the provision of care, both through the market and state policy. The best of the literature on 'new social risks', which has recently grown up around these issues, suggests that 'time matters' in their emergence (and policy responses to them): Bonoli (2007) traces their first appearance back to the 1960s. These issues touch on intimate areas of life that might carry particular cultural sensitivity and do not have the same centralizing logic as, say, social security payments. Equally, the emergence of new social demands represents a change in the political opportunity structure, which some sub-state actors have sought to exploit.

We do not seek to recruit all of the factors that have helped to strengthen sub-state politics to a simple narrative of the changing territorial logic of democratization and/or welfare. There are, of course, significant differences in the timing of, and dynamics behind, the emergence of sub-state elections. Welfare dynamics are still more complicated. As far as we can tell from the existing (rather fragmented) evidence base, it appears public attitudes that tend to support state-wide social provision. Moreover, pressures of cost-containment and retrenchment arguably contribute at least as much to decentralization as do new rights and services: nation-states have often sought to offload difficult choices onto other levels of government.

Addressing these aspects of territorial politics requires a reconsideration of key theoretical and conceptual aspects of political analysis. We seek to contribute to this new direction for political science by:

1. Rejecting the implication of much contemporary analysis that social and political life should be understood primarily as an inexorable movement in an ever-more encompassing direction. So, for example, whilst many theorists of globalization (Scholte 2005) and modernization (Beck 2000) take some note of sub-state phenomena, they tend to reduce them to minor adjunct effects of their primary concern with the 'supraterritorial'. Michael Keating – a leading theorist of Europe's territorial politics – goes so far as to argue that 'modernisation paradigms' have helped to define ' territorial effects … out of existence' (1998: ix; cf. 2009). So, the study of two pillars of political modernization – elections and the welfare state – has focused largely on the endogenous dynamics of nation-state politics. In these and other areas, conventional understandings of modernization, focused on the nation-state, might have directed political scientists'

attention away from important sub-state dynamics, disguising their character and hiding their full extent.

2. Recognizing the 'constant presence' of 'territorial effects' in European politics (*ibid*.: ix). Some of the classic theories of European political development can contribute to a renewed appreciation of these territorial effects. We re-interrogate some of these classics to retrieve their engagements with territoriality, drawing on recent work by Caramani (2004), Bartolini (2005), Ferrera (2005) and Mitchell (2006).

3. Recognizing the grip of 'methodological nationalism' (broadly defined as the naturalization of the equation of society, state and nation) on the political science imagination and its contribution to distracting political science from myriad, often gradual 'real world' developments that have slowly coalesced into a 'turn' to devolution and decentralization. Political science has been slow to take up this vibrant social theory debate, but has much to learn from (and to contribute to) the critique of 'methodological nationalism', particularly those strands within it that seek to retrieve the complex engagements of the classics with the nation-state (Chernilo 2007).

4. Recognizing, *along with* our emphasis on territorial politics within the state, the continuing importance of the nation-state. It is no part of our argument that the nation-state has become obsolete or irrelevant. For example, statewide elections and statewide welfare remain crucially important. Our concern is to open up a new direction in political analysis better attuned to the *multi-scaled* quality of contemporary political life. (The EU level is equally important: Hooghe and Marks (2009a, 2009b) present an ambitious theorization of the EU regional-level that brings identity issues to the fore).

The challenge for political practice

If our conceptual baggage has held us back from recognizing the extent (or even the existence) of a decentralizing 'turn', what does this mean for the relationship between theory and practice? Grappling with this issue, Ulrich Beck, (a leading critic of methodological nationalism) sometimes depicts the problem primarily as one of practice. He sees 'congruence between the perspectives of actors and social science observers' and understands it as problematic because it 'transforms practical categories uncritically into analytical ones'. By asserting that the 'concepts informing the actions of social agents and state actors are tacitly transposed into … conceptualization and empirical investigation' (Beck and Grande

2007: 174), Beck seems to claim both that something like methodological nationalism saturates public life and that the work of analysis is wholly secondary to, and derivative of, the world of practice. However, in relation to territorial politics we are struck by something rather different: the decentralizing 'turn' encompasses significant shifts in the practice of 'real world' politics, at the level of grass-roots social and political mobilization, and increasingly in political institutions and public policies. That is, social agents and state actors have not, in practice, always been entranced by the nation-state: a multiplicity of innovations and activities has taken place on a variety of other scales. Admittedly, many of these have been hidden and slow-moving (or with significant consequences some time after the mobilization of causes). Even so, our claim is that, in general, political science has been poorly equipped to recognize or deal with them. The challenge of territorial politics seems to have slipped below the radar of mainstream political science. Whilst much has been written about particular aspects of sub-state territorialization, very few overarching accounts of political change give real weight to territorial questions (though see Keating, 2001; Marks and Hooghe, 2003; Greer, 2006). Mainstream theories, methods and disciplinary habits still prioritize understandings of the 'nationalisation' of politics within the 'nation-state', which itself is understood as the primary unit of analysis. Those theories, methods and habits appear, at the very least, incomplete in the face of the territorial challenge. This dissonance between how most political science is done (with its focus on the nation-state) and what happens in (sub-state) politics requires us to confront the central, yet ambiguous conceptual role the nation-state has taken in social and political analysis (on which, see Keating 2009: 299).

Methodological nationalism, 'modernization' and territorial politics

It is worth pausing here briefly to trace the emergence of the idea of 'methodological nationalism'. The phrase was coined by Herminio Martins (1974) in the context of a critique of postwar social theory, and has spread to social and political analysis more broadly. Martins hinted at the elusiveness – the ubiquitous yet invisible quality – of the nation-state within social theory. He juxtaposed a definition – the assumption that the nation-state was 'the terminal unit and boundary condition for the demarcation of problems and phenomena for social science' (1974: 276) – to the observation that methodological nationalism had marginalized nationalism research. Initially, he described the latter as an 'odd paradox', but eventually concluded that it was 'not a paradox at all but another symptom of the same methodological ... situation'. In a sense, then, methodological nationalism displays 'banal' features that resemble Billig's (1995) characterization of western nationalism in general: at once forgotten or taken-for-granted, but also omnipresent and regularly reinforced at a subliminal level. Methodological nationalism might even be styled as the form taken by banal nationalism within the academy.

If the nation-state is conceptually elusive, the same can be said of the critique of methodological nationalism. As this critique spills over from social theory to the study of politics and international relations, political analysts need to interrogate it carefully. We argue that the debate around methodological nationalism (Brubaker 2004; Chernilo 2007) has both important insights for the study of territorial politics, but also pitfalls that need to be avoided. Many of these pitfalls have to do with the way that theories of modernization have been treated in the critique of methodological nationalism. Modernization and methodological nationalism are intimately intertwined: the critique of the latter initially 'arose in the context of the decline of Parsonian sociology' – a key source of modernization theory – and was 'to an important extent, also a critique of Parsonianism' (Chernilo 2007: 78). Our particular focus is on the account of modernization inspired by Stein Rokkan's macro-historical political sociology, key elements of which – such as his influential 1967 paper with Lipset (Lipset and Rokkan 1967a) – were developed within a Parsonian framework. Recently, 'cosmopolitan' critics have targeted Rokkan's work as a particularly egregious example of methodological nationalism (Beck and Grande 2007: 122). The targeting of Rokkan appears misdirected. He helped to develop innovative concepts for comparative analysis of states, distinguishing different forms of federalism and, alongside the (otherwise largely residual) 'unitary' category, identifying certain 'union' states. This concept has been taken up in the context of critical assessments of the character of the UK state, not least as analysts seek to make sense of processes of devolution and decentralization (see H. Mitchell 1996, J. Mitchell 2006; Rhodes *et al.* 2003).

More generally, Rokkan's work on processes of state-formation and nation-building was preoccupied with questions of centrality and peripherality. It also foreshadowed the territorial challenge described above. Rokkan saw the student protests of the late 1960s as marking an 'unfreezing' of politics, reflected in part in the (re)activation of territorial identities within European states. For Rokkan and Urwin (1983: 118), that re-activation 'shook to the core the concept, held for much of the twentieth century, of the nation-state as the norm for territorial organisation'.

We propose to shake up the nation-state concept further by recovering and renewing the emphasis on territorial politics within the Rokkanian tradition. First, we interrogate the critique of methodological nationalism, before turning in greater detail to two key fields of study within the Rokkanian tradition: elections; and welfare. In each case, we show that research driven by inherited assumptions about the nation-state offers only a skewed perspective on the territorial dimensions of contemporary politics. Equally, we show that some newer work exploring elections and welfare at territorial scales *within* the state has still not freed itself from the problems associated with methodological nationalism. Our final concern, therefore, is to outline a research agenda in which sub-state territorial political processes are conceived in their own right, rather than as less important reflections, or subordinate functions of state-wide (or, indeed, trans-state) politics.

Beyond 'methodological nationalism'

Social theorists began to grapple with the ambiguous (ubiquitous yet invisible) status of the nation-state at least as early as the 1970s, but for a quarter of a century 'methodological nationalism' generated relatively little grip. The idea did not wholly disappear: influential social theorists and globalization analysts referred to methodological nationalism in the 1970s, 1980s and 1990s. Typically, however, they did so only in passing (Smith 1979, 1983; Cerny 1997) or as a conceptual staging post (Scholte 1993, 1996, 2005). But, since the turn of the millennium, interest in methodological nationalism has grown significantly, particularly through Ulrich Beck's work, (2000, 2002, 2003, 2004, 2007; Beck and Sznaider 2006; Beck and Grande 2007; see also Chernilo 2006, 2007). For Beck, methodological nationalism takes

> the following ideal premises for granted: it equates societies with nation-state societies, and sees states and their governments as the cornerstones of a social sciences analysis. It assumes that humanity is naturally divided into a limited number of nations, which on the inside, organize themselves as nation-states and, on the outside, set boundaries to distinguish themselves from other nation-states. It goes even further: this outer delimitation, as well as the competition between nation-states, represents the most fundamental category of political organization [and] the social science stance is rooted in the concept of nation-state. It is a nation-state outlook on society and

politics, law, justice and history, which governs the sociological imagination. (2002: 51–2)

In large part, we agree. Beck's complaint – that the *presumption* that social and political life is naturally encompassed by nation-states – precisely identifies the blinkering of political science to the enduring significance of sub-state social mobilization and political contestation. But we fear that the critique of methodological nationalism might itself generate conceptual problems. Some analysts wholly repudiate the inherited corpus of social theory and political science. These tendencies can be detected in the seminal contributions on methodological nationalism from the 1970s. Whilst Anthony Smith made only passing reference to methodological nationalism, he depicted its influence within 'the sphere of theory' as sweeping: the 'study of 'society' today is almost without question equated with the analysis of nation-states … the principle of 'methodological nationalism' operates at every level in the sociology, politics, economics and history of mankind in the modern era' (Smith 1979: 191). But Beck's general indictment of existing theory, and his linked political and intellectual project to replace methodological nationalism with a new methodological 'cosmopolitanism', worries us more. Keeping these concerns in mind, we identify three issues that collectively offer a more robust basis for our move 'beyond methodological nationalism'.

Looking inside the state

First, critics of methodological nationalism generally focus on *trans*-state phenomena; for example, seeking to reveal new forms of trans-state territorial community. Within migration studies, anthropologists Andreas Wimmer and Nina Glick Schiller (2003: 579) complain that the nationalized focus on 'processes within nation-state boundaries … left no room for transnational and global processes that connected national territories'. Equivalent concerns have emerged in international relations and political science, particularly as scholars explore globalization and European integration (Scholte 1993, 1996, 2005; Cerny 1997; Grande 2006; Egeberg 2008; Stone 2008).

This anti-nationalizing focus on *trans*-state processes sets out a fruitful path for research. However, either it says little about what happens *within* the state, or interprets sub-state changes as merely responses to trans-state transformations. For example, European integration research has often understood 'sub-national mobilisation' (Hooghe 1995) or sub-state governments' roles in 'multi-level governance' (Marks 1993) as contingent on EU-level political processes. Where the enduring political significance of territory (at both state and sub-state levels) *is* acknowledged, it is largely interpreted as a secondary manifestation of globalization, (Scholte 2005: 235). Such views can appear as modernization redux, with the globe displacing the nation-state (cf. Caramani 2004: 31–2) as the scale towards which the organization of social life expands inexorably. They also risk reproducing the devaluation of territorial politics within the state, but at one further remove. As in 'methodologically nationalist' scholarship, the possibility that territorial communities or institutions within the state 'may themselves and from the "bottom up", actively seek to, and succeed in' (Jeffery 1996: 214) recalibrating multilevel relationships both within and beyond the state is effaced. *Our first concern in moving beyond methodological nationalism is therefore to give due weight to sub-state structures and the possibility of agency at this scale.*

Territory, nation and state

Our second concern hints at a paradox: the critique of methodological nationalism might itself reflect, embody or promote methodological nationalism. This paradox is captured in the term itself, from Martins onwards, in which 'nationalism' denotes the state, a set of political *institutions* rather than the collective goals of a *community*. Though there might be a broad pattern of territorial co-terminosity of state and society, it is flecked by multinational statehood, stateless nationhood and other forms of distinctive territorial community within and across state boundaries. Equally, the form of (nation-)statehood itself is also variegated and contingent as state structures flex to accommodate diverse territorial communities. Over twenty years ago, Keith Banting and Richard Simeon saw territorial claims emerging as the 'major sources of demands for constitutional change', superseding earlier debates driven by class (1985: 11). These new territorial claims posed fundamental questions about the organizational scale of political community. They point to the (increasing?) territorial diversity of society and mutability of statehood; there is and has been no necessary correspondence between the two.

Beck's predilection for epochalist reasoning also elides 'nation' and 'state'. Essentially, he argues that we need new methods and concepts for new times – methodological nationalism is obsolete and needs to be replaced by a more up-to-date approach. His preference is for a 'methodological cosmopolitanism' which, he suggests, allows us to understand our contemporary condition better *and* helps to call this new social order fully into being. Ironically, however, Beck's binary contrast accepts a mythological image of the nation-state during its heyday as an internally harmonious and complete, or 'fully achieved', social formation. By 'equating all previous social theory with methodological nationalism', Beck effectively has 'no option but to *understand the nation-state itself from a methodologically nationalistic standpoint*' (Chernilo 2007: 18), and to accept the legitimacy of methodological nationalism 'before' globalization. Others have argued convincingly that the adoption of a singular nation-state focus was *always* inappropriate. Wimmer and Glick Schiller (2002: 302) note that transnational forms of social and political organization *have always existed* but methodological nationalism left them 'hidden from view' (cf. Keating 1998: ix).

As we 'look for' territorial effects, unlike those who sweepingly repudiate earlier social and political scholarship for its methodological nationalism, we acknowledge the historic importance of processes of state-formation and nation-building. Rather than rejecting the relevance of the nation-state, *our second concern in moving beyond methodological nationalism, is to gather-up theoretical threads – particularly from European macro-historical political sociology – and weave them with new strands of scholarship into a more sensitive understanding of the territorial differentiation of the nation-state*. That sensitivity is necessary for clearer focus on the pervasiveness and vigour of contemporary territorial politics. But it also needs to be retrospective, alert to Keating's 'constant presence' of territorial differentiation, even during in the first decades after the Second World War. For example, some recent work starts to challenge the assumption that welfare policies ever had a seamless, statewide scope (Wincott 2006; Jeffery 2009a). Moving beyond methodological nationalism is a revisionist project of historical reinterpretation, as well as a forward-looking analysis of contemporary statehood.

Knowing territorial politics within the state

Our third set of problems concerns what, exactly, Beck and others mean by 'methodology'. Sometimes they appear more concerned with ontology and epistemology (broadly, 'what is out there to know', and 'what we can hope to know about it') than methodology ('how ... we go about acquiring knowledge' – Hay 2002b: 64; 2007a; Bates and Jenkins 2007). Beck's complaint is that the question 'What is out there to know' has so often been answered with reference to nation-statehood that other forms and scales of social and political organization have been neglected. Identifying aspects of Beck's critique of 'methodological' nationalism as properly ontological and epistemological might help us to think more precisely about the specifically *methodological* implications of nation-state dominance.

Many key research resources were developed under/by the nation-state (often as states constructed their administrative apparatus), or by international organizations of nation-states. Typically, as states collect 'statistics' and 'other systematic information' they take 'national population, economy and society as their given entity of observation' (Wimmer and Glick-Schiller 2002: 306). Etymologically, 'the term statistics shares common roots with 'state' and has always been a largely state-driven activity' (Scholte 2005: 87). Even where state (and inter-state) institutions have not played a primary data-generating role, the data-basis for comparative analysis has often been constructed to produce 'statewide' scale information. In all these respects, the 'banal' assumption has prevailed that the nation-state is the natural scale of interest to analysts. Whilst this has facilitated outstanding comparative research, it has made the exploration of non-nation-state questions difficult, and often impossible. A set of presuppositions about what it is important to know has, it seems to us, set and limited our methodological choices. Over time, initial choices can compound themselves, through the benefits of generating ever longer series of the same data. So, whilst we know a lot about the postwar nation-state and continue to develop data on it, the development of data and methodologies appropriate to understanding territorial politics within the state has remained limited. *Moving beyond methodological nationalism, our third concern is not only to challenge the received wisdom of the limited importance of territorial politics within the state, but also to stress that understanding it properly will need appropriate, and new, data sources and analytical methods.*

The discussion above has allowed us to accumulate a manifesto:

- to recognize territorial agency within the state
- to accept that state and society are (and have been) territorially differentiated
- to develop data sources and research methodologies better attuned to understanding the properties and consequences of territorial differentiation.

Next, we move on to illustrate to how this manifesto might be developed by exploring two features of contemporary democracy – electoral democracy and welfare provision – considering the extent to which they are now partly 'de/re-nationalized' to sub-state scales. In both cases, we do so with reference to the Rokkanian tradition in comparative political sociology. Our concern is to explore the potential of that tradition to provide insights into how, to what degree, why, and with what implications, contemporary democracy has been rescaled.

The territorial politics of elections

Rokkan's foundational contribution (especially Lipset and Rokkan 1967), followed by those who have developed his approach (including Bartolini and Mair 1990; Mair 1997; Bartolini 2000; most recently Caramani 2004), has fundamentally shaped the European tradition of elections analysis. In this tradition, scholars interpret the mobilization of the class cleavage as homogenizing Europe's previously confessionally and territorially divergent polities. As electorates within nation-states became fully mobilized, state-wide electoral logics tended to 'freeze' patterns of party alignment and to replace these territorially-based with functionally-based party competition for control of state-wide institutions.

Not that the Rokkanian tradition ignored the territorial dimension of electoral competition. Identifying 1968 as a turning point, Rokkan and others (Rose and Urwin 1975; Rokkan and Urwin 1982; Hearl *et al.* 1996; Deschouwer 2008) sought evidence for a 'peripheralisation' of statewide electoral competition to exemplify the 'unfreezing' of politics. But none of them found it: 'electorally, contemporary peripheral mobilisation has not been very successful' (Rokkan and Urwin 1983: 165); 'analysis of those regionalist movements which have contested national elections on at least three occasions since 1945 pointed towards extreme steadiness at the national level' (Urwin 1982: 431); 'the cumulative regional inequality of voting behaviour is also declining through time' (Rose and Urwin 1975: 42).

There is a sense here of confounded expectation; Rokkan assumed that renewed peripherality would reshape statewide electoral competition, and seems surprised (disappointed?) that it did not. By contrast, Caramani's work implies that the search for a growing territorial differentiation of electoral competition was misdirected. His analysis of territorial patterns of voting behaviour within states led him to question

the many conclusions reached in recent works about processes of territorialization and 'new' regionalism ... Even though there has been a strong trend to institutional decentralization in all countries, new federal structures did not lead to the regionalization of voting behaviour in the last few decades … the period since World War II has witnessed a fundamental stability of the territorial configurations of the vote in Europe. (Caramani 2004: 291)

In its own terms – an analysis focused on elections to statewide parliaments – Caramani's conclusion is entirely valid. But we should not draw the inference that it also justifies the almost overwhelming concern of social-scientific electoral analysis with statewide elections, overlooking the possibility that elections to *sub-state* parliaments might be, or have become, an arena for patterns of voting behaviour that diverge from the 'nationalized' patterns of statewide elections. Work on sub-state elections is still relatively novel, not least, as we have seen, because in many cases they were only introduced recently: before the late 1990s there was limited regional electoral experience or data for comparative analysis.

Rokkan's hypothesis on the peripheralization of electoral competition could be tested against this data, but scholars tended to use a framework of presumptive 'nationalization' when they first focused on sub-state elections. Often, these studies self-consciously 'borrowed' from pioneering studies of European Parliament (EP) elections, which were conceptualized as 'second-order' national elections, where 'less' was 'at stake' (Reif and Schmitt 1980: 9). A casual remark by Reif and Schmitt (*ibid*.: 8) – 'various sorts of regional elections' are also 'second order' – prompted some scholars (for example, in Hough and Jeffery 2006a) to apply this framework in the regional context. Their finding was that mostly 'sub-state elections do indeed appear to be second order, subordinate to voters' considerations of state-level politics' (*ibid*.: 252). But this might be a self-fulfilling prophesy: using an 'off the peg' approach, which imports the assumption that other electoral competitions are subordinate to statewide politics, pre-empts alternative possibilities. Addressing sub-state elections *on their own terms* might, in other words, generate a different or at least more nuanced picture.

The literature offers two alternative lenses on sub-state elections. The first – long-standing, largely North American, and mostly ignored in European research – conceptualizes sub-state political institutions as focal points for territorially defined interests (Cairns 1977). A rich, if contested, US tradition suggests that voters differentiate their voting in state and federal elections according to the functional responsibilities of each government level (for example, Stein 1990; Atkeson and Partin 1995: 99; Leyden and Borrelli 1995; Ebeid and Rodden 2006). Similarly, Cutler (2008) shows that 'valence' judgements on parties' provincial-level issue profiles and perceived competence shape Ontario provincial election outcomes. The common focus is on *institutional* structure: federal systems make possible a 'split-level democratic citizenship' (Cutler 2008: 502). Electors can make different, unconnected, voting decisions based on the issues at stake at various levels. Few attempts have been made to deploy these institutional approaches for European sub-state elections, and early UK examples have produced inconsistent findings. Curtice (2006) found that voter decisions in 2003 did not serve to hold the Scottish government accountable for its record, whereas Denver *et al.* (2007) and Johns *et al.* (2009) see the 2007 election as largely determined by valence evaluations of government and opposition in Scotland.

The second alternative lens on sub-state elections is primarily European and focuses on the centre-periphery cleavage within a broadly Rokkanian lineage. Richard Wyn Jones and Roger Scully tentatively identify a pattern of 'multi-level voting' to explain post-devolution evidence that Welsh (and Scottish) nationalist parties do better in devolved than UK elections (Trystan *et al.* 2003; Scully *et al.* 2004; Wyn Jones and Scully 2006): 'the complex nature of identities in nonstate nations such as Scotland and Wales ... provides, in elections to devolved institutions, an alternative national focus within which many voters may locate their electoral choices' (Wyn Jones and Scully 2006: 130). Paterson *et al.* (2001: 44) develop a similar analysis, focused more on territorial interest than identity: 'voters revealed that what they are looking for in a Scottish election are parties that are willing to use the devolved institutions to promote Scotland's interests'. Hough and Jeffery (2006b: 137) find equivalent patterns in post-communist eastern Germany, as do Pallares and Keating (2003: 250) in Spain, depicting 'dual voting' with 'a vision of statewide parties based on ideological criteria and one of the non-statewide party based on regional interests'.

Overall, evidence is accumulating, first, that in regions with marked territorial identities voters use regional elections distinctively, for reasons of identity, interest or both and, secondly, that sub-state institutions can provide a focal point for political activity. These findings challenge 'second order' readings of sub-state elections and point to an uncoupling of sub-state voting behaviour from statewide elections. Both elements emphasize *agency* at the sub-state scale, a level that can become the main locus of contestation over central political issues such as economic development, education, health and welfare. The substance of citizenship is increasingly coming to be differentiated by territory (Jeffery 2006, 2009b).

Territorial differentiation of voting behaviour and election outcomes has wider significance for contemporary political practice. How sub-state electorates vote and governments form can determine the formation of statewide governments (as in Belgium – de Winter *et al.* 2006) or statewide government-opposition relations (as in Germany, via the operation of a territorial second chamber, the Bundesrat – Lehmbruch 1976, 1998), with major implications for parties operating across the state. They need to attune their organizational structures and electoral strategies to competition in different territorial arenas, whilst maintaining the credibility of their statewide platform. And in all states with significant 'regional' elections, sub-state voting behaviour directly influences the substance of (statewide with sub-state) intergovernmental relations. No decentralized political system has a perfect divide between governmental functions across levels; all require coordination and cooperation between governments. How sub-state electorates vote thus imposes (greater or lesser) constraints on statewide government. In some cases – where sub-state outcomes prompt constitutional reform – these electorates can even challenge the scope of functions exercised by statewide institutions. The election of the SNP government in Scotland, for example, has prompted debate about moving powers from the UK to the Scottish Parliament, including independence. So, voter behaviour in sub-state elections can fundamentally change the practice of contemporary democracy, at sub-state *and statewide* scales.

Our claim is not that conventional causalities (sub-state politics as a function of statewide politics) have simply been reversed. Rather, we highlight the territorially differentiated and multi-scalar nature of contemporary democracy, with complex interactions and interdependencies across these scales. There remain problems – often to do with data – in how we can *know* this multi-scalarity. Analysis of sub-state elections provides an example. Most existing work compares regional elections and behaviour in national elections within those regions using blunt-edged aggregate data. These data might reveal broad trends, but offer limited scope to explain them, particularly where aggregate-level indicators fail to discriminate between hypotheses. For example, second-order, territorial identity and institutional theories all suggest that the SNP should do relatively well in Scottish Parliament elections, and the Labour Party relatively worse but, for quite different reasons (variously, voters use those elections to protest against the UK-level Labour government; the SNP better encapsulates a sense of Scottishness than UK-wide Labour; the SNP is (currently) judged to offer a more competent government for Scotland than Labour).

Systematically unpacking aggregate-level trends and causal testing of competing theoretical accounts requires individual-level voter behaviour data. Compared with statewide elections, carefully designed, scholarly sub-state election coverage is not good (particularly outside Spain, the UK and France). Where data does exist it is not widely used. Sixty-eight German Länder election studies (for 9/16 Länder with varying time series) are available; we are not aware of any use of these data to analyze voter decisions in Länder elections or to compare them with voting behaviour in federal elections. The limited availability and usage of this sort of data underscores our argument that past methodological choices create path dependencies that narrow the scope and ambition of contemporary political science. Though interest in territorial politics within the state is growing (with research networks on territorial politics among the most active in the UK Political Studies Association, the European Consortium for Political Research, the American Political Science Association, and the International Political Science Association), available data resources are generally ill-fitted for this analysis.

Rescaling welfare

Whilst the welfare state occupies a central place in Rokkan's macro-historical framework (forming its fourth stage after state formation, nation-building and mass democratization), his influence on welfare research is less obvious than on electoral studies. The welfare state rightly takes centre-stage in narratives of nation-state integration, particularly the construction of citizen affiliation to the nation-state. Instead, for welfare, T.H. Marshall has come to hold the canonical position (particularly his short essay on 'Citizenship and Social Class'). Marshall's conception of social citizenship is entirely 'contained' within the nation-state, a 'national' framing that breaks the surface of his famous essay on isolated occasions: 'the citizenship whose history I wish to trace is, by definition, national. Its evolution involved a double process of fusion and of separation. The fusion was geographical, the separation functional' (1992: 9).

The degree to which Marshall and Rokkan shared an understanding of nation-state construction as function replacing territory (or geography) is striking, but not surprising. Marshall exercised a clear and early intellectual influence on Rokkan (see Kuhnle and Rokkan 1979; Flora 1999), especially concerning the social rights of citizenship, read as a strategy 'to maintain territorial-national unity' under pressure from class conflict (Kuhnle and Rokkan 1979: 509; see Wincott 2009, for a discussion). If

Rokkan did not himself develop an extended analysis of welfare, Flora and Alber (1981) present a classic account of welfare within a Rokkanian–Marshallian frame, which rightly stresses the movement from welfare localism to nation-state social citizenship.

But, whilst comparative welfare analysis more generally has engaged with territoriality, it has done so in a particular, limited way. Where territorial diversity has had strong institutional expression – particularly in the form of federal structures – it has been shown to retard welfare state development. This argument has garnered a good deal of empirical support (Swank 2002), but recent research into the welfare history of federal states has added nuance to the basic argument (Obinger *et al.* 2005). The retarding effect of democratic federalism occurs only where it *precedes* major welfare programmes. A territorial dimension is almost entirely missing in scholarship on non-federal states, which are sweepingly assumed to be 'unitary' in character. For example, welfare scholars generally saw the UK as a unitary and centralized state, with a homogenous population. Its long-standing territorially-based differentiation – with particularly distinctive arrangements for Scotland and Northern Ireland – were largely ignored. This led to a misunderstanding of the impact of devolution, blamed for introducing territorial inequalities into welfare (Bogdanor 1999; Swank 2002), when some aspects of welfare provision had always varied geographically (Wincott 2006).

Comparative welfare research has used encompassing conceptions of welfare, whilst operationalizing them in constrained and undifferentiated ways. That is, it has tended to focus on a handful of welfare state indicators, generalizing from these the character of the welfare state as a whole – and, sometimes, even the wider political economy regime. Partly, this reflects the use of undifferentiated (especially OECD) nation-state-scale data. Moreover, scholars' *concepts* were only ever imperfectly operationalized. For example, although Esping-Andersen's famous analysis of welfare regimes used specially gathered data (which is not in the public domain), it operationalized welfare state regimes in terms of a handful of transfer payments, focused on standard (typically male) workers, rather than the wide range of payments and services generally considered part of the welfare state. Moreover, these employment-related operationalizations were often stretched even further – in the form of the 'Keynesian welfare state' – to include large swathes of the political economy.

By contrast, the Rokkanian approach opens space for a more nuanced and differentiated analysis: scholars stress the importance of different 'types' of welfare policy – particularly the distinction between social transfers and social services (Flora 1986; Alber 1995; Ferrera 2005), and thus begin to shift perspective on the territorial politics of the welfare state. Followers of Rokkan also associate transfers – the most direct means of inter-individual redistribution – with class politics and a homogenizing, centralizing logic. By contrast, the politics of social services are tied up more with region and religion. Although far from identical, this focus on policy 'types' shares some features with classic US analyses (Lowi 1964; Peterson 1995) that have also been adapted for policy analysis under UK devolution (Mitchell 2004; Wincott 2006). The US scholars contrast the centralizing logic of redistribution (which Lowi, in particular, associated with class) with 'distributive' (Lowi) policies or 'developmental' ones (Peterson) both linked to localities.

Characteristically, however, Rokkanians add a temporal dimension to the analysis. The new wave of social services that were developed from the 1960s, Alber argues (1995), initially prospered in those states where central state authority was not challenged or compromised by religiously or territorially-based groups. One example concerns early childhood education and care policies. Provision in this area was a site of struggle between the (broadly successful) centralizing French state and the Catholic Church as early as the nineteenth century. Together with Sweden – also often seen as a state that concentrated political power – French provision of education and care was unusually well-developed by the early 1970s. However, particularly in France, the encroachment of a 'tentacular' state apparatus provoked a sharp response, such as the creation of autonomous *crèches sauvages* – an important, if relatively little-noticed, product of 1968 – and, ultimately, wide-ranging decentralization processes. Albeit over a longer period, Swedish early childhood provision also generated new territorial political dynamics.

Expansion of social services is often linked to changing patterns of 'caring', but other policy pressures can also create decentralizing pressures. For example, the turn towards welfare 'activation' might create opportunities for sub-state policy entrepreneurs to 'claim' this policy field. Equally, the logic of activation requires the direct involvement of welfare professionals 'close' to their clients, in contrast to the operation of classically Weberian bureaucracies delivering transfer payments, providing a logic of affinity between this function and a sub-state (rather than state-wide) scale.

Although his primary focus is on the disorganization of the nation-state by European integration (cf. Bartolini 2005), Ferrera's discussion of 'welfare regionalism' (2005) expands Rokkanian welfare analysis. It picks up the structural difference between social transfers and social services (Flora 1986), as well as emergent trends in socio-demographics and 'feedback' effects of new forms of welfare from the 1960s (Alber 1995). Crucially, the welfare regionalist analysis starts from pressures within regions and internal to public welfare dynamics (Ferrera 2005: 167–75), before moving on to consider the EU and international/global context for these developments (*ibid.*: 175–82). His 'long territorial parabola' of social protection describes a local-national-regional movement as its main trajectory (*ibid.*: 167).

The diverse territorial implications of various welfare policies have significant implications for political practice, whether from 'bottom up' citizens' perspectives, or those of governments and policy-makers. Although existing regional-level public attitudes data are limited and fragmented, they indicate that many – and, typically, most – citizens see welfare as a statewide function. Nevertheless, aspects of welfare provision can become detached from the nation-state and relocated as a sub-state function in public perceptions; for example as a consequence of 'welfare nationalist' projects that use social policies to bolster sub-state identities and affiliations (*ibid.*: 175–182; McEwen 2006; Henderson 2007; Beland and Lecours 2008). Equally, inter-regional economic disparities might become politicized and challenge older practices of statewide welfare risk-sharing (Jeffery 2006). More generally, the introduction of sub-state tiers of government is likely to change opportunity structures, leading – even by default – to a shift in the locus of territorial political mobilization (Gallega *et al.* 2005; cf. Chibber and Kollmann 2004). Equally, these pressures interact with neoliberal logics in complex ways, as some central states have offloaded welfare responsibilities to other levels of government (Ferrera 2005: 173–4). 'Welfare regionalism' can be implicated in the 'new politics' of welfare retrenchment (Pierson 2001), which Keating (1998) has called the 'decentralisation of penury'.

These complex interactions require a reconsideration of the conceptual apparatus of comparative welfare research, including a more critical disaggregation of the generalized concept of the 'national welfare state'. Moreover, as with electoral analysis, in addition to conceptual innovation, we believe that making sense of an emergent 'welfare regionalism' requires novel data and new methods. The re-scaling of welfare provision, with differential implications across various domains of welfare policy, requires territorially disaggregated data. Moreover, we need to gain better grip on territorially-based identities, at sub-state as well as nation-state levels (and beyond), to make sense of the connections between identity/public attitudes and welfare provision. Even where Rokkanians explicitly link welfare to a richly textured analysis of state-formation and nation-building, 'nationalization' is basically conceived as the homogenization of the social substance within states. The intuition that state social protection secured public affiliation to particular states – or even played a key role in popular *identification* with nation-states – is widely shared. Whilst broadly comparative cross-state research on public attitudes and welfare is flourishing, relatively little specifically addresses the link to 'national' identification. Moreover, looking back to the period when Ferrera's 'arc' was 'rising' from the local to the 'national', it might be hard to reconstruct the data that we would need to test hypotheses about national (state) identification processes. Some of the data we require for the sub-state level is starting to become available, through a patchwork of unconnected surveys in different states (reported in Jeffery 2006), but also in more systematic, tailored surveys on welfare attitudes across different territorial scales.

Conclusion

We have set out a manifesto for a new direction of research on sub-state territorial politics, consciously confronting the restrictive legacies of a half century or more of 'methodological nationalism'. Our examples – the territorial politics of sub-state elections and welfare – have been restricted for space reasons. But (re-)new(ed) territorial dynamics are equally evident in other areas: such as regional economic development (for example, Keating *et al.* 2003; Goodwin *et al.* 2005), or education (for example, Ozga and Alexiadou 2002; De Rynck and Dezeure 2006); mechanisms of interest aggregation at sub-state scales, such as parties and party systems (Swenden and Maddens 2008; Hepburn 2009a; Stefuriuc 2009) or interest groups (Keating *et al.* 2009); institutional change, such as territorial constitutional reform (Benz and Behnke 2009) or sub-state/state/EU relationships (Piattoni 2009; Carter and Pasquier 2010), providing findings that underline our critique of (existing critiques of) methodological nationalism.

First, sub-state territorial actors (voters, parties, interest groups, governments) pursue goals that are defined within a territorial frame, and are not simply reflections of the goals pursued on a statewide scale. In some cases, the actors are the same on several scales (for example, the voter or the party) but they (consciously) act differently to attune action to scale. In others (such as governments) the actors are different – and autonomous – at each scale, while also being bound by the partisan inter-dependencies of governmental functions.

The mix of autonomy and interdependence confirms, second, that the 'nation-state' operates in a territorially differentiated way. There appears to be more territorial differentiation now than fifty years ago, although scholarly neglect might have hidden enduring territorial effects. Systematic attention to territorial differentiation has begun only in the last decade. We do not claim, with methodological 'cosmopolitans' such as Beck or with proponents of a 'Europe of the regions' (cf. Lynch 1996; Hepburn 2009b), that territorial differentiation means that the nation-state has been, or should be, supplanted. But political science does need to take what happens at sub-state scales more seriously and to understand better – perhaps the most neglected element hitherto – how statewide politics is shaped by sub-state politics.

A multi-scaled approach, third, challenges how we perform political science: disentangling the relationships among new or strengthening sub-state institutions, policy development on sub-state scales, and the pressures created by patterns of social and political change poses important comparative challenges for territorially-oriented analysis. It is not enough, as discussion of sub-state elections confirms, to adapt the logic of analysis for statewide politics to sub-state scales. These logics can swamp and disguise autonomous, sub-state dynamics. To reveal the nature and effects of political contestation at sub-state scales requires greater methodological subtlety. It also requires more and better data. Existing data resources collected over decades at and for the statewide scale have powerful legacies. More or less by default, they help to import 'nationalizing' logics into analysis of sub-state politics. Given the growing significance of sub-state elections, as well as the centrality of 'social citizenship' to welfare analysis, territorially disaggregated public attitudes data will be central to addressing these challenges, but vast sunk costs in existing surveys conducted at the 'nation-state' scale raise the opportunity cost of new investments in better sub-state datasets. Persuading research funders to refocus, or add to, existing data portfolios will be hard.

Equally, however, without a proper understanding of the sub-state level, we might misconstrue state-wide dynamics in policy and politics. Even in relation to voting, where state-wide elections seem to be largely contested on a state-wide basis, regional dynamics can influence the nation-state level – either routinely, though such institutions as the *Bundesrat* in Germany, or more dramatically where elected regional governments are committed to independence. The politics of welfare might be more systematically misunderstood by dint of a neglect of the sub-state level. In contrast to the aggregative logic on the cosmopolitan critics of methodological nationalism, the emphasis we place on territoriality on a variety of different scales leads us to stress the disaggregation of macro-concepts such as the 'Keynesian welfare state' or its alleged nemesis 'globalization'. Thus, for example, as well as insights into the territorial aspect of social policy, linking the analytical distinction between transfers and services to questions of the comparative timing and sequence of welfare state development might have unsettling consequence for the conventional wisdom about the golden age of the welfare state – and, indeed, about globalization itself.

Our final points concern the Rokkanian tradition: its association with understandings of political modernization *qua* 'nationalization' – as made by 'cosmopolitans' such as Beck, and evident in some successor analysis from the mid-1960s to the early 1980s – can be made too glibly. Rokkan was centrally concerned with territorial politics within the state, and always recognized that 'nationalization' was tempered by the persistence of the periphery. One of our concerns – reflected elsewhere in recent work by Bartolini (2005), Ferrera (2005) and others – has been to recover and give fuller substance to this aspect of the Rokkanian tradition. Rokkan's work, collated posthumously in *State Formation, Nation-Building and Mass Politics in Europe* (Rokkan 1999), is widely regarded as one of the most influential and powerful analyses of the evolution and consolidation of (European) democracy. But one of the central foundations of that work – the politics of the 'periphery' and its interrelationship with the politics of the 'centre' – has been partially 'hidden from view' (Wimmer and Glick Schiller 2002: 302) by political scientists' collective preoccupation with politics at the centre. We risk misunderstanding contemporary democracy – how citizens engage in political processes, on what scales they pursue collective goals, how we aggregate interests, how we legitimize democratic institutions – because of this partial and skewed perspective. For these reasons, we need a new direction in political science that takes territorial politics within the state seriously, and develops the data and methods to understand it effectively.

Chapter 9

New Security Challenges in an Interdependent World

STUART CROFT

'New Security Challenges' and 'global interdependence' are frequent themes in security analyses since the collapse of the Soviet Union some twenty or so years ago. They are important issues: what is security without globalized ideological and military threats? How might a range of security issues be managed collectively, recognizing that issues such as HIV/AIDS or climate change are issues that affect all communities? Around such questions, the sub-field of international security has revolved. But, whilst accepting that these questions are important, it is also the case that two important issues can become masked. First, that much that occurs in the contemporary security context is far less novel than is often proclaimed. Second, perhaps even more importantly, the claims that security is a field of interdependence hides the important dynamic of power relations; issues might be shared ones in security terms, but the stakes might affect parties very differently indeed.

International security seems uniquely demanding, threatening, and novel: the dangers of war, terrorism, climate change, and weapons of mass destruction must be urgent and important. And so, international security is an issue area that becomes, from time to time, all-consuming in political life; the debates over entry into the war in Iraq being a perfect example, mobilizing politicians, other political elites, but also the general public into debating and campaigning on an issue. If security threats are novel, what does that mean for our ways of understanding how to address security, and what does it mean for decision-makers in the security field? Security seems to be connected in a variety of issue areas: a concern with a terrorist organization might connect into international trade (smuggling of goods and weapons), into international finance (control of terrorist finances), and into development issues (how to support the development of regions beset by terrorism). Security issues seem interdependent; and so, logically, there are demands for those issues to be met in an interdependent fashion. Security challenges – such as in the environment, or in terrorism – exhibit a range of global, regional and local dimensions, creating demands that can only be met by the recognition of mutual dependencies.

This chapter examines international security in three ways. The first section examines the way in which contemporary security issues are framed on global policy agendas. The second section assesses the way in which contemporary security issues, over many decades, have come to frame the way in which international security is understood and interpreted, as least in the English-speaking world. The third section reads the academic study of international security through the prism of the key schools of thought, both those based in the United States, and those elsewhere that frame security in different ways.

Contemporary security concerns

The daily life of politics in democratic countries tends to be dominated by arguments over resources, positioning of groups in political debates, electoral concerns, and the drive of personal battles. These dominate our media coverage, political speeches, and the texts of political discourse. But they are framed by concerns that somehow, somewhere, there are threats to 'us'. Politics – international and domestic – are framed by threat images, and by preparations for enhancing our security. The American 'Department of Homeland Security's overriding and urgent mission is to lead the unified national effort to secure the country and preserve our freedoms' (DHS 2008). On launching the British National Security Strategy, Gordon Brown told the House of Commons that 'The primary duty of government – our abiding obligation – is, and will always be, the safety of all British people and the protection of the British national interest' (Brown 2008).

That which threatens 'us' inevitably changes over time. Sometimes, the threat is the policies of other states, which requires defensive investment, as during the Cold War. Or perhaps the threat is so great that it needs to be pre-empted; a case made in the preparations for the war in Iraq in 2003. The threat might also be weapons themselves – particularly in the nuclear age, vast investment has been made against the threat of accidental launches of missiles, or against the dangers that such weapons might fall into 'the wrong hands'. Or the threat might be of non-state actors, which has been particularly noticeable since the attacks on the

United States in September 2001. And then again, the threat might be environmental, with climate change often seen as a security challenge. Politicians, and public discourse, has been framed by these four sets of challenges to security – states, weapons, non-state actors, and climate – throughout the first decade of the twenty-first century. It is vitally important to understand the implications of framing an issue as being one of security; that carries with it claims to its importance (as no political leader would want to be seen to be taking risks with security), and it means that significant resources will be devoted to that issue. Consider immigration, for example, framed as a security issue – with connotation of threats being brought with immigrants (of crime, to our way of life, of terrorism, and so on) – and immigration as a political and economic issue (addressing generation gaps, skills gaps, and the like).

Crucially for our understanding of security in the contemporary world, that frame of four sets of challenges has been contextualized by two claims. The first is that this is new; we face a novel combination of these challenges for the first time in human history. Of course, that is not an uncontested position; but it is a claim that is deeply embedded in politicians' discourse. A second claim that can be found in the discourse of political leaders is that, given the uniqueness of the challenges, they can only be faced together; meaning not only that states must combine their efforts to address them, but also that these challenges are, themselves, impossible to address separately. Interdependence lies at the heart of the contemporary security debate in both of these senses. How, then, have these four security challenges been framed as key elements of political debate, and how have they affected the way in which security is studied and taught?

In relation to the first challenge, whereas the state-level of concern is not the same in terms of intensity and focus as it was during the Cold War, the first decade of the twenty-first century has nevertheless been marked by the international security focus on a number of states, famously described as the 'axis of evil' by President George W. Bush. Whatever ones views about the validity of the Iraq War, Iraq under Saddam Hussein had fought wars with a number of its neighbours whilst, elsewhere, there have been tensions and security fears between other states. In 2006, the then Russian president, Putin, announced that a dozen nuclear capable aircraft would from that point be permanently airborne; increasing, amongst some, the sense that a threat to Russia has re-emerged; a sense strengthened by the Russia–Georgia war of August 2008. Those nuclear aircraft would, in part, be aimed against Europe; as Putin put it, in response to American plans to deploy anti-missile technology, 'What kind of steps are we are going to take …? Of course we are going to acquire new targets in Europe' (cited in Blomfield 2007).

In terms of the second challenge, that of powerful and destructive weapons, it has been a decade in which the realities of the new nuclear relationship between India and Pakistan (which emerged from nuclear tests in 1998) have been the subject of debate about stabilization. The end of the Cold War has not meant the end of fears about nuclear weapons. Given the density of population in the sub-continent, the *Natural Resources Defense Council*, for example, have calculated that, superimposing Hiroshima casualty data onto ten cities would lead to 2.8 million deaths, and another 1.5 million serious injuries. An accidental or unauthorized launch of a weapon just against, for example, Mumbai, would lead to nearly half a million deaths (NRDC 2002). In 2006, North Korea conducted a nuclear test, deemed by Tony Blair to be a 'completely irresponsible act' (cited in Naughton and Knight 2006), not least due to fears that North Korea's leadership is irrational (see Roy 1994 for a historical overview). But underlying all of this has been a long concern in the West of Iranian plans to develop nuclear weapons. President Obama illustrated his concern with the danger of nuclear weapons when he committed America to seek a peaceful and secure world without nuclear weapons in April 2009.

The third challenge, that of non-state actors, has in many ways come to be the leitmotif of international security in the first decade of the twenty-first century. President Bush created a 'war on terror' from the attacks on the United States in September 2001. In a detailed report from the *Congressional Research Service*, Amy Belasco calculated that all aspects of this 'war' had cost the United States US$864 billion, in terms of monies authorized by Congress between 2001–08 (2008). That figure is roughly the equivalent of the gross domestic product of the Netherlands in a single year. Counter terrorism has come to dominate Western countries' security strategies and this, in turn, has led to significant changes in legal regimes. In Britain, the original Counter Terrorism Strategy ('CONTEST') was established in 2003 based on four workstreams: *Pursue*, to prevent terrorist attacks; *Prevent*, to stop people becoming terrorists; *Protect*, against terrorist attack; and *Prepare* for the consequences of attack. Post-11 September 2001 ('9/11') terrorism is deemed to be more serious than the IRA terrorism of the past. It is deemed to be more serious in its scope – as it could emerge from many different parts of the world – and in that with which it threatens, with continual references to the dangers of terrorists securing weapons of mass destruction. Whereas the IRA (mostly) would give warnings before bombs detonated, the new international terrorists are (sometimes) suicide bombers. As Gordon Brown put it, 'This new form of terrorism is different in scale and nature from the terrorist threats we have had to deal with in recent decades. It is intent on inflicting mass casualties without warning, motivated by a violent extremist ideology, and exploits modern travel and communications to spread through a loose and dangerous global network' (2009a: 4). Yet, this 'new form of terrorism' is, at the same time, thought of in spatial terms; Gordon Brown spoke a great deal in 2009 about the border areas between Afghanistan and Pakistan: 'They are the crucible for global terrorism. They are the breeding ground for international terrorists. They are the source of a chain of terror that links the mountains of Afghanistan and Pakistan to the streets of Britain' (2009b). Of course, the claim that there is a 'new type of terrorist threat' legitimizes the claim that there need to be 'new types of response' to it; whether that be enhanced police powers, tighter immigration rules, greater investments in counter terrorism resources, or deeper involvement in the affairs of other countries.

The final category of threat is that which comes from change to the environment. In the first part of the twenty-first century, there is much discussion – for the first time in recorded human history – of the phenomenon of 'climate security'. The basic proposition is that significant change in the climate will, by definition, have impact upon security. One view is that this is a generic point; rising temperatures will lead to increasing desertification, for example, through which we will inevitably see mass migrations of peoples. Or it will lead to rising sea levels, and the disappearance of whole countries (low-lying island states such as the Maldives), or the habitable parts of populous countries (rising sea levels would devastate Bangladesh, for example, a country of 140 million people, in which 20 per cent of the country is within one metre of sea level currently). During 2007, a bill entitled the Climate Security Act was introduced into the United States' Senate; it was not passed, but sought to connect a reduction in greenhouse gas emissions to a system of capping the amount allowed to polluters, who would also be able to trade their allowances. Another view is that it is the effect of climate change that will lead to conflict between peoples and states. As the website of the pressure group Climate Security Now (a joint initiative of Friends of the Earth and Voters for Peace) put it: 'warming means war'. Climate security, as a concept, has become a powerful analytic, campaigning, legislative and political tool (see Barnett 2003). And, of course, it has proved a useful way of maintaining defence and other budgets in the post-Cold War period.

Four sets of policy agendas that, when taken together, comprise the set of issues that are the focus of contemporary security. Of course, they are not met simply by policies and responses at the state level. Just as those sets of challenges arise from a variety of different sets of actors – state and non-state – so policy responses to them arise not only at the state level, but also in, by and through international organizations such as the United Nations and NATO, through non-governmental agencies, and also through a number of other non-state actors. Thus, security can be conceived of in an interdependent fashion: that we are all interdependent in the way that security challenges impact upon us (think about climate change, for example), and can only address these problems in an interdependent fashion.

Security, of course, has not always been thought of as interdependent. The term 'national security' was coined to encapsulate a very different way of thinking; a way of imagining security relations that were defined by the social realities of a zero sum game, rather than that of a positive sum game, which underpins that notion of 'security in an interdependent world'. Hans Morgenthau, author of one of the key elements of the international security canon – *Politics Among Nations* – wrote of national security as the integrity of the nation's territory and institutions: that is, the state both physically and ideationally. For Morgenthau, security was concerned with the power of the state and, as such, it was a zero sum game: for one state to gain security, it would be necessary for another to lose it. Morgenthau wrote *Politics Among Nations* in 1948, and the tenor of the book shows the deep shadow of the wars of the 1930s and 1940s. But, in that context, states – and particularly the United States – developed 'national security' architectures; and those architectures have had to be adapted to the pressures of different ways of thinking. During the 1970s, the idea of interdependence became central to political debates – and security was no exception. Security could now be obtained not in a zero sum fashion, but in a positive sum game. A good example was the advent of arms control, in which states agreed to limitations (far more often than they agreed to reductions) in their stockpiles in order to reassure others that they were not threatening. Such reassurances provided an interdependent security framework, different to the origins of the national security framework. And, from the 1980s, the new idea of globalization became influential, in security as in so many other sectors. Globalization might be deemed to have advantages in terms of freedoms (freer flows of peoples, goods, and finance) but, in the world of security, these all have a downside: a globalized world is believed to be more vulnerable to the movement of terrorists; to the smuggling of weapons of mass destruction; and to the movement of terrorist finances to support their military operations).

One of the key elements of thinking about 'security' in the framework of an 'interdependent world' is connected with the concept of mimesis – essentially, adapting to dominant norms and patterns of behaviour. This is not to suggest that there is anything particularly new about this. States have tended to be mimetic in relation to security ideas, particularly in the period since the end of the Cold War. Ideas and practices spread and take root in different contexts from those in which they began. Here, we have a different notion of globalization: not one based on the freer flow of peoples, goods and finances but, rather, one in which the dominant political, social, cultural and economic power – the United States – sees its ideas and practices (and interests) spread globally. The United States introduced its 'National Security Act' first in 1947; other states moved from 'war offices', 'ministries of defence', and other security institutions in the same direction: by the early twenty-first century, France had its 'White Paper on Defence and National Security'; Britain had its 'National Security Strategy'; those states that had not followed suit, were under pressure so to do – with, for example, Germany's CDU/CSU parliamentary grouping calling for the establishment of a National Security Council in 2008. Ideas of this sort are often referred to as mimetic isomorphism, and come in a variety of forms (see Mizruchi and Fein 1999). One example frequently studied is the transfer of American ideas on security institutions to south-east Asia (Katsumata, forthcoming).

Ideas and practices concerning security tend to flow from the United States and, certainly, there is a larger community of scholars writing about security issues in the United States than anywhere else in the world – possibly even more than write of security in the senses described here than the rest of the world put together. Those ideas are often – but not always, as shown later – amplified elsewhere in the English-speaking world; and now, often, scholars from other language backgrounds seek to publish their ideas predominantly in English. These ideas and practices, together, have helped to comprise an Anglophonic pattern of understanding that comprises international security. In this sense, examining Anglophone International Security Studies – as this chapter does – simply means to reflect on the meanings of security, and the schools of thought within international security studies, as represented in the English language. But perhaps we should have cause for thought. If there is an academic field of study so related to key issues of political practice – that is, capable of being presented largely through English language sources – what does that mean? Is it that other countries/societies/cultures are less concerned with international security? A quick examination of global insecurities – which predominantly lie outside the Anglophone in terms of everyday lived experience – would surely convince us that this is not so. Perhaps it represents a consolidation of power and resources invested in these issues? There might well be rather more to that. E.H. Carr – retrospectively constructed into one of the 'founding fathers' of the sub-discipline of international relations and the field of security studies – said that international relations in the English speaking countries were essentially about 'how to run countries from positions of strength'; and Michael Cox put it that the subject was seen as 'an ideology of control masking as a proper academic discipline' (2001: xi). It is certainly worth considering, when reading and writing about particular security issues, how this might look in 'Arabic' security studies or to Chinese security specialists. Yet, this having been said, it is Anglophonic work in international security studies that predominates and, as such, will be the focus of the next section.

The evolution of Anglophone international security studies

The study of international security in the Anglophone world has been interpreted as travelling through a series of waves, and those waves have been very much linked to that which is deemed to be the key challenges faced in the 'real world.' That is, although there has, of course, been a good deal of intellectual debate in and for its own sake, a great deal of the terrain of the field of international security has been framed by the ways in which security challenges have been deemed to impact upon the Western polity.

It is a point that can be demonstrated over the course of the twentieth century; the focus on international cooperation and peace following the conclusion of the First World War; the rise of realist explanations of security dilemmas before, during and after the Second World War; the emphasis on 'scientific' social science to prosecute the Vietnam War. Actual conflict and the content of international security studies have necessarily been interwoven: 'necessarily' in the sense that the scholar does not stand aloof from society but is, of course, embedded within, subject to social concerns and fears; 'necessarily' also in that prestige has been accorded to those who could speak to governmental and media demands, and that prestige has, in more recent times, also connected to the ability to secure research funding throughout the Anglophone world.

These factors have undoubtedly impacted upon the ways in which security has come to be defined, at least in the mainstream.

To understand contemporary new directions in the study of international security, then, it is important to reflect upon the means by which it became composed of its current subject matter, and the compelling pressures that drive an intellectual field in particular ways. Of course, this is so for very many of the social sciences. What makes the study of international security distinctive, along with (perhaps) criminology, is that its core business is to understand the dynamics of 'othering' – the means by which alliances, states, communities, tribal/ethnic/racial groups become identified as a threat to the core identity.

The study of international security itself has three 'others' in the Western lexicon from which, in its contemporary form, the field seeks to define itself in contradistinction. The first is the received history of the Cold War. Security studies during the Cold War is often deemed to have been a 'simple' process, one that required very little input from other disciplines. In the Anglophone world, international security was about the 'adversarial relationship' between the Americans and Soviets, articulated through arms races and arms control, strategic stability and regional competition. The research questions set for the study of international security were thereby limited and, essentially, could be answered without recourse to other disciplines, even mainstream political science, although sometimes a nod in the direction of international history was made. The 'simplicity' of that period is contrasted with the 'complexity' of contemporary international security, in which the research questions set for the field require the importation of expertise from economists, sociologists, anthropologists, geographers and others to understand, for example, the dynamics of 'global terrorism' or insecurity in central Africa. Even if one holds that there is still something distinct about international politics – as would, for example, Kenneth Waltz – there would still be an expectation that the international security scholar would be engaged in dialogue about particular issues with experts from these other disciplines.

The second 'other' is that believed to have dominated in the United States – in particular, in the 1960s when, for many, the study of international security (and other disciplines, such as anthropology) became subsumed by the 'need' to 'win' the Vietnam War. A lack of critical distance is the assumed fault; with a view that this lesson must always been kept at heart. Analysis might (for some, should) be connected to a governmental policy agenda, but must not be subsumed by it. This sounds like a tenet of 'critical security studies', but it is not only found there; a strong example of this would be the resistance of many in the

American neo-realist community to the Bush Administration's arguments in favour of commencing the war in Iraq. In the January/February 2003 issue of *Foreign Policy*, just as the preparations for war were nearing completion, John J. Mearsheimer and Stephen Walt wrote of 'An Unnecessary War', illustrating this desire for critical distance.

The final 'other' from which contemporary international security studies seeks to secure itself is the analytical failures of the end of the Cold War, and its immediate aftermath. Scholarship in international security did not contain any significant grouping of scholars who 'predicted' the end of the central component of the field; indeed, many would hold that it did not contain any such views at all. Of course, international security was not the only field discomfited in this way; Soviet Studies was naturally even more so. And yet, the traditional refuge for many social scientists – that 'their' form of social science did not lend itself to prediction – was generally not available as so much work in the field had taken the form of analysis leading to advocacy, based precisely upon particular predictions. This failure of prediction was compounded by the rush away from the study of security at the end of the Cold War; many argued that without that Cold War there was no core to the field, and that it would necessarily diminish significantly in the 'new world order.' Of course, the field was 'saved' by killings: in former Yugoslavia; in Rwanda; on 9/11. The conclusions drawn from this were: be aware of 'naivety' that widespread killings and the threat of them would be something of the past; and be alive to the existence of change in any analysis about the future. This final 'other' – connected, as it is, to the failure of social scientific prediction – echoes the agonies that economists have been going through in the light of the international financial crisis of 2008 onwards which, as with the failure to see the end of the USSR, was not prefigured. Whether social science can 'predict' in this sense is an important issue for legitimate debate. What is perhaps easier to accept is that there is more room for imaginative work.

The disciplinary lessons learned by the collective that we describe as international security scholarship are thereby threefold: recognize the complexity of contemporary international security, and therefore recognize that other disciplines might have some contribution to make; establish and defend a critical distance from governmental power structures in debating and advocating policy lines; and, finally, the need for the avoidance of naivety and to be alert to change. Of course, there are different perspectives on all three elements; and, of course, some of these have been important in debates framing international security in the past. But one challenge for the future is clearly how to entrench these insights in new and differently charged political circumstances.

None of this is fixed; it is entirely probable that the field of international security studies will be reformed at various moments in the future. But it is a reasonable way of understanding the dominant expectations in Anglophone international security in the twenty-first century, because one issue has come to dominate the way in which that field has developed: the advent of international terrorism as a global phenomenon. Of course, there is much debate as to whether there really is something new in this rise to a global phenomenon; as to whether it is global at all; as to whether the phenomenon is worthy of such effort, when insecurity is so much more apparent in other sectors connected, for example, to poverty and underdevelopment. But a quantitative assessment of the amount of work published over the course of the period since 2001 would certainly bear out the assumption that contemporary international security studies is dominated by the study of terrorism.

Such a reading of the nature of contemporary international security studies would seem to emphasize the engagement of the field with empirical security issues that are high on the agenda of governments, international organizations, sometime non-governmental organizations, but also with the media. But that is only one side of the story. For more than twenty years, a vigorous theoretical 'debate' has developed – clearly closely linked to, and often (but not always) as a sub-set of that in international relations theory – within which the empirical cases have been framed. International security can sometimes be accused of being a field obsessed with the empirical during the Cold War (partly unfairly, given the significant development of realist/neo-realist theory and oddly, also, given the parallel strong strand of normativity). In the last twenty years, however, international security studies has seen the rise of theoretical contestation. Heuristically, this debate is often linked to the publication of Barry Buzan's *People, States and Fear* in 1983. This book symbolized, and further opened, a debate about the very nature of security itself, although it was the second edition of the book, published in 1991, that produced the greater impact upon the structure of the field. Amongst many other arguments, Buzan suggested that security could be analyzed by sectors – military, political, social, economic and environmental – and (also through the second edition and other works) that there were different levels at which security dynamics operated: individual, collective, state, regional and global. In this way, traditional strategic studies was placed into a wider category of international security studies; strategic studies was but one approach (focusing on the military sector, and the state/regional/global levels) rather than *the* approach. Also encompassed within the new wider category would be scholarship previously seen to be the polar opposite of strategic studies – notably, peace studies. And these debates have impacted upon policy debates: it is normal, now, for political leaders to speak of security in a variety of sectors, with 'climate security' being one such manifestation.

It is the work of Buzan that, rightly, is placed centre stage in the reconceptualization of security. Buzan's work – in particular, *People, States and Fear* – has taken on the status of being part of the canon of work that students must know if they are to be recognized as legitimate and engaged students of international security. Of course, Buzan was not alone in working to open the debate: other important contributions were made by scholars such as Caroline Thomas (1987). But, in this sense, it was Buzan's work that has been admitted to the canon, alongside other important and symbolic texts, such as Clausewitz's *On War* and Waltz's *Theory of International Politics*.

This broadening of the debate about security (McSweeney 2008, especially ch. 3) became the origin of a particularly important element of the contemporary debate about international security in the Anglophone world – and it is the separation of American international security from European international security theory (Waever 1998). Of course, such a crude geographical rendering cannot catch all of the complexity of the work in international security; and it also ignores work emanating from other important intellectual centres of Anglophone work; for example, in Australia and Canada. But it does establish the core strands of contemporary international security and, as such, is the frame for the next section, which examines the nine different ways in which 'security' is defined and deployed in the literature in international security studies.

Different meanings of security

Barry Buzan introduced W.B. Gallie's notion of the 'essentially contested concept' to the study of security in the early 1980s and, in so doing, opened up a range of debates about the meaning of security. By 'essentially contested concept', Gallie meant that a concept could be widely recognized and agreed upon as encapsulating a particular field, but that there is and can be no agreement about the most appropriate instantation of that field. So, although there is widespread recognition of that field described by the term 'security', there is no agreement as to the proper (and improper) use of that term, and the debate can therefore not be resolved by an appeal to empirical evidence. For example, how could there be evidence for us to decide whether climate change should be understood as a security issue or not?

As a consequence of the opening of this debate, one assumption that is widely shared in the field – and that contrasts very strongly with the form of the field in the 1980s, when Buzan introduced the term – is the view that, for many, the meaning 'security' is constructed by those that speak the term, and that its content changes over time and place. This, of course, means that there is no objective reality to security (which is not to hold that there are no material realities, since security practices frequently lead to real people dying in real places). Although not all would accept this epistemological position by any means, the overwhelming majority of those that do not would accept that such a position can be held from within the field of international security. It is a significant change. In the fiftieth anniversary edition of *International Organization*, the three high-profile (American) guest editors went out of their way to describe that which comprised legitimate research and that which did not (Katzenstein *et al.* 1999). Postmodernist research was not deemed to be legitimate; and little of it had been, or would be, published in the high-profile *International Organization* because, '*IO* has been committed to an enterprise that postmodernism denies: the use of evidence to adjudicate between truth claims.' And so they conclude that 'postmodernism falls clearly outside of the social science enterprise, and in international relations research it risks becoming self-referential and disengaged from the world, protests to the contrary notwithstanding' (*ibid.*: 38). This was not a denunciation of all reflectivist thought – critical constructivism, with its strong focus on discourse, was deemed to be valid – but was an attempt to set boundaries around what could and could not be seen to be legitimate research in the field. Yet, a mere seven years later, the American International Studies Association announced the launch of its fifth journal, *International Political Sociology* that many saw as filling exactly this intellectual space. Edited by Didier Bigo and R.B.J. Walker, the first issue of the journal included pieces by Michael Dillon on 'Governing Terror: The State of Emergency of Biopolitical Emergence' and Vivienne Jabri on 'Michel Foucault's Analytics of War: The Social, the International, and the Racial'.

The intellectual space for understanding and researching 'security' has thus broadened and changed dramatically – even in just the last ten years, let alone from the 1980s – and the debate over the essentially contested status of the concept of security continues. It would be wrong to ask the question: Is this due to intellectual debates; or to real world pressures? It is simply not possible to separate the two in the way in which such a dichotomy would suggest. Bloodshed in Bosnia and Rwanda, and starvation in the developing world have, by necessity, been issues upon which there has had to be empirical, theoretical and policy reflection. But it has developed on the basis of a distinction between the work that predominates in the United States, on the one hand, and largely in Europe and the rest of the Anglophone world, on the other. This distinction should not be overly drawn: 'American' style security analysis takes place in Britain with writers such as Adrian Hyde-Price; 'European' style security studies research takes place in the United States, with James Der Derian being a good example. The point is not to make hard and fast rules. Rather, it is to highlight the different emphasize in the intellectual orientation of the mainstreams of work in international security in the two spheres.

Security studies in the United States

The American mainstream is dominated – to different degrees – by four different theoretical ideas of what security actually is. There are two forms of realism – traditional, and neo in character – that comprise an umbrella within with there is a whole host of sub-realist formats. A neo-conservative reading, whilst post-George W. Bush is hardly the mainstream, is nevertheless worth considering, given the impact it has had on policy practice and given how widely these ideas predominated on the political right of American politics. The final conceptualization is that of the liberals, who would disagree firmly with the realist formulations, but find themselves (often, uncomfortably) connected to neo-conservative thought.

Realist formulations of understanding security are often read retrospectively into great classical works of history and political theory. Thus, for example, it is sometimes said that it is not possible to understand Thucydides' great *History of the Peloponnesian War* written in Ancient Greece as anything other than a realist treatise; full of structural analysis (of an international anarchy between states, rather than of the power of gods), of pessimism about human nature, and of cynicism about idealism. In *War and Change in World Politics*, Robert Gilpin (1981) asserted that we had learnt little more to add to Thucydides in the two-and-a-half thousand intervening years (pp. 226–7). In political theory, realists would raise in importance the work of Machiavelli as indicative of the strand of thinking along with Clausewitz. These works – particularly Hobbes, Clausewitz and Thucydides – comprise that which Edward Kolodziej (2005: 48) called 'the foundations of security studies'.

These authors had to be read into a particular school of international relations and, heuristically, the authors first credited with self-consciously constructing the field of political realism were E.H. Carr and Hans Morgenthau. On security, Morgenthau's *Politics Among Nations* came with a handy six-point guide to realism; three of which points are particularly important. The first was that there were objective laws of politics, rooted in (an unchanging) human nature; second, that international politics is concerned with 'interest, defined as power'; and third, power of humans over others is thereby at the heart of the theory. Security, then, is a by-product of the search for power over others. When a state has significant power over others, it will have a degree of security (Lott 2004: 10–12).

This formulation of security as a product of power was, to many, unsatisfactory. In the classic piece on this, John Herz wrote of the security dilemma as follows:

> where groups live alongside each other without being organised into a higher unity ... there has arisen what may be called the 'security dilemma' ... Groups or individuals living in such a constellation must be, and usually are, concerned about their security from being attacked ... Striving to attain security from such an attack, they are driven to acquire more and more power in order to escape the impact of the power of others. This, in turn, renders the others more insecure and compels them to prepare for the worst. Since none can ever feel entirely secure in such a world of competing units, power competition ensues, and the vicious circle of security and power accumulation is on. (Herz 1950: 157)

Morgenthau's classical realism would lead not to security but, rather, to insecurity, unless a particular state could achieve hegemony in its area. It is interesting that Morgenthau wrote of America's Monroe Doctrine – the policy of keeping European powers out of Latin America during the nineteenth century – as a positive example of classical realism. Herz was more concerned of the dangers of the security dilemma in the middle of the twentieth century, when the nuclear age had dawned.

In response to this (and other criticisms) of classical realism, Kenneth Waltz published what, to date, has become the most important text for theorizing international security: *Theory of International Politics* (1979). Waltz's invocation of 'neo-realism' abandoned the classic realist's dependency on the objective reality of human nature and, instead, instituted an emphasis on structural constraint on agents. Here, although all states are in the same situation – that of international anarchy – not all states have the same capability for managing that situation. Whereas, for Morgenthau, international politics was about power, for Waltz, it is about security: 'Internationally, the environment of states' action, or the structure of their system, is set by the fact that some states prefer survival over other ends obtainable in the short run and act with relative efficiency to achieve that end' (*ibid*.: 93).

Although neo-realism has come to play a significant role in the study of international security, this should not be read as an argument that says that there are no classical realists. With regard to contemporary studies of international security, the framework of realism contains at least two large strands of work. Contemporary neo-classical realists seek to incorporate non-structural explanations for state behaviour; for example, why states behave differently according to whether their motivations are *status quo* or revisionist; or why states fail to balance. Important authors include William Wohlforth and Randall Schweller (Schweller 2004). Neo-realist authors have worked to develop particular concepts within the framework that Waltz established thirty years ago. John J. Mearsheimer, for example, has developed the notion of offensive realism, in which a distinction is made between great powers and others. Mearsheimer argues that, for great powers, there is always a drive not to balance, but to achieve hegemony. 'Given the difficulty of determining how much power is enough for today and tomorrow, great powers recognize that the best way to ensure their security is to achieve hegemony now, thus eliminating any possibility of a challenge by another great power' (Mearsheimer 2001: 35). Mearsheimer applies this logic to China, worrying that US trade and engagement with that country runs the risk that China might prove a challenge to American security in the future. For Mearsheimer, China's growth has led a number of states in the region to look to closer ties with the United States, increasing America's role as an offshore balancer. Other neo-realists, such as Stephen Walt, welcome this: 'Offshore balancing is the ideal grand strategy for an era of US primacy. It husbands the power upon which US primacy rests and minimizes the fear that US power provokes. By setting clear priorities and emphasizing reliance on regional allies, it reduces the danger of being drawn into unnecessary conflicts and encourages other states to do more to help us' (Walt 2005: 223).

One of the issues that has bound together all of the above-mentioned analysts – be they neo-realist or neo-classical realist – in relation to contemporary security issues has been opposition to the war in Iraq. Indeed, many of these scholars signed a petition against the War, using language very much like that of Barack Obama during the 2008 election campaign: that Iraq was the wrong war and a distraction from the campaign against Al Qaeda (Thinkprogress 2008). Whereas the distinctions within the different strands of realist thought are distinctive and important, there are still powerful commonalities, and significant collective differences with neo-conservative thought. For realists of all hues, the Iraq War was a mistake, and a neo-conservative one at that. Those intellectually implicated in the drive to war in Iraq are to be found amongst the neo-conservatives, the next group for analysis.

Neo-conservative security studies is, oddly, a relatively undefined field – oddly, given the focus on neo-conservatism before and during the Iraq War (for exceptions, see Williams 2005; and Rapport 2008). Irving Kristol, one of the key figures in neo-conservatism, identified four factors in relation to foreign and security policy. First, that patriotism is a good, natural and healthy phenomenon, and should be encouraged. Second, world government – and institutions that tend in this direction – must be opposed because, with world government, comes the possibility of world tyranny. Third, it is crucial to be able to identify allies, friends and enemies on ideological grounds. The United States is an ideological power, every bit as much as the Soviet Union was. And fourth, that this inevitably means that the 'national interest' has an ideological component every bit as much as material interests. Therefore, 'no complicated geopolitical calculations of national interest are necessary' (Kristol 2003). Security, therefore, is only achievable with ideologically like-minded states and is threatened by ideological foes, regardless of where they are geographically situated. In a critical review of US policies in the 1990s, William Kristol and Robert Kagan (2004) argue that: 'In the face of the moral and strategic challenges confronting it, the United States engaged in a gradual but steady moral and strategic disarmament. Rather than seeking to unseat the dangerous dictatorships in Baghdad and Belgrade, the Clinton administration combined empty threats and ineffectual military operations with diplomatic accommodation.'

The fourth strand of work in security studies – in the United States, in particular – focuses on liberal approaches. Harking back very much to the work on 'interdependence theory' that came to the fore during the 1970s, neo-liberal institutionalist work argues that there is no analytical distinction between the realms of security and the economy, and that institutions help to create a focus on absolute, rather than relative, gains. Under the former, everyone gains, and that is the focus – all are happy in a region if everyone's GDP is growing. Under the latter, one state is not content if its GDP is rising more slowly than that of its neighbour. But institutions help mitigate this absolute gains concern, and allow states to develop a longer-term, and more cooperative, focus (Keohane and Martin 1995). And, crucially, institutions play a key informational role, which, in turn, significantly reduces the incentives to cheat. Given that both neo-realists and neo-liberal institutionalists agree that security analysis should be about states seen as rational egoists operating in an anarchical world, where cooperation can only take place if there are clear gains to be made, it is possible to construct comparative research programmes on the impact of both sets of theoretical claims (Wolf 2002).

In additional to neo-liberal institutionalism, liberal approaches to security also contain important work on the 'democratic peace.' This holds that democratic states – either because of the norms in operation, or due more directly to the nature of the political system – do not go to war with each other. Of course, there is a clear linkage here with the neo-conservative thinkers. If the democratic peace holds, then the clear policy prescription is one of supporting global democratization (for a development of this from within democratic peace theory, see Russett 1994). And, of course, this is one of the key policy prescriptions for neo-conservatives, although the latter would tend to see threats more directly and, hence, the responses as being more military in nature.

The theoretical ideas and research agendas discussed comprise the sets of issues that a graduate student, for example, should expect to face in the United States, and in some departments in Canada. The study of international security elsewhere in the Anglophone world, however, is more likely to be dominated by a focus on four different approaches to security issues: in terms of human security; in terms of the Welsh school (emphasis on emancipation); the Copenhagen school (working on securitization); and the Paris school (emphasizing the technologies of insecuritization).

Security studies in the rest of the Anglophone world

Outside the United States, the study of security might well involve many of the approaches outlined (although perhaps not neo-conservatism), but it is more likely to focus on one or more of the main 'alternative', or 'critical', perspectives on security. Three of these perspectives are very relevant to emerging European schools of thought: the Copenhagen school; the Paris school and the Welsh school. The fourth perspective relates to work on human security that has taken place in a variety of locations within and beyond the Anglophone world.

Human security seeks to focus on the individual rather than the state. It has long been noted that human security might well be threatened by the policies and actions of the citizens' own state – whether that be in terms of repression and denial of human rights, or inequitable social and economic systems leading to poverty and underdevelopment. Anyone examining the politics and society of Zimbabwe in the first decade of the twenty-first century would be struck that the key insecurity for Zimbabweans was the policy and action of their own government. Human security was brought dramatically to the fore with the publication of the United Nations Development Programme's Human Development Report (UN 1994), which argued that human security would be secured by pursuing policies that ensured 'freedom from want' and 'freedom from fear'. The Report sited security in seven different fields: economic (basic income), food, health, environmental, personal (safety from attack), community (freedom from attack based on ethnicity or other collective identity markers), and political (provision of human rights). Human security does not in itself comprise a theory; rather, it is a set of commitments that differs significantly from realist approaches to security on the grounds of the key referents (humanity versus states), scope (seven fields of security, rather than merely military), actors (non-governmental organizations and civil society, rather than state agency), and means (development, rather than military strategies such as arms competition or deterrence).

Human security is therefore a 'critical' approach to security, in that it seeks to set out a means of understanding security that is distinctive from the (largely American) mainstream. The three other schools of thought are similarly critical; although they also all share certain commitments to focus on actors other than the state, all view reality as socially constructed, and all – in different ways – focus on the impact on people.

The most popular of these schools of thought – measured solely in quantitative terms in relation to outputs – would be the Copenhagen School. Particularly in *Security – A New Framework for Analysis* (Buzan *et al.* 1997), the school posits that security should be understood in terms of distinctive fields (military, economic, environmental, social, political and, perhaps in the near future, religious); that it can be seen to operate in different ways in different parts of the planet (hence a focus on regional security complexes); and that issues are drawn into security debates – they are 'securitized' – by speech acts by powerful figures (often, but not necessarily, political leaders speaking on behalf of the state). Once securitized, the issue is taken out of the realm of normal democratic politics and will be subjected to 'emergency measures'; those emergency measures would only be possible because of the securitizing claim that the issue is of such importance that the survival of the political unit is at stake.

Copenhagen School theory is set up as value-free; that is, there is no normative agenda to engage in, for example, securitization research. The purpose is for the analyst to engage in a process of identifying where and how such securitization takes place. It is clear that this is somewhat controversial within Copenhagen School circles; Ole Waever, for example, has expressed a preference for desecuritization over securitization – that is, he argues that it is morally preferable for issues to be taken out of the realm of security than for them to be put in. The second European school of security, the Welsh School, draws heavily on the Frankfurt School for its philosophical underpinnings. For Welsh School analysts, traditional security studies is too narrow and restrictive; it is the case, they hold, that patriarchy is as dangerous for world politics as anarchy is for realists. At the heart of a structure of analysis that puts people at the centre of its analysis, the Welsh School calls for a focus on emancipation: a demand that people be freed of structural constraints that, in direct and indirect ways, lessen lives. And it is an approach determinedly very different from the (American) mainstream. As Ken Booth puts it in the clearest text on the School – *A Theory of World Security*: 'The answers of traditional security studies are confined to the trinity of statism, strategy and the status quo: this book replaces that trinity with security, emancipation and community' (Booth 2007: 29), and the purpose is to produce a world security in which: 'The greater the level of security enjoyed, the more individuals and groups (including human society as a whole) can have an existence beyond the instinctual animal struggle merely to survive' (*ibid.*: 4–5).

The third and final 'European' school of international security is the most recent, and is sometimes referred to as the 'Paris School.' Proponents of this perspective argue that a field of security (in a Foucauldian sense) has been developed by the merging of policing and other matters of 'internal' security with that of external security. It is therefore a construction of governmental processes; whether it be the search for new roles for large departments at the end of the Cold War, or the development of new political projects – such as the construction of a home affairs mandate within the European Union. Thus, as one of the key proponents of the school, Didier Bigo, would hold: 'Security is in no sense a reflection of an increase of threats in the contemporary epoch – it is a lowering of the level of acceptability of the other; it is an attempt at insecuritization of daily life by the security professionals and an increase in the strengths of police potential for action' (Bigo 2001: 111).

These schools of thought are not hard and fast and, often, the ascribing of geographical labels to them is somewhat controversial, as it implies exclusion as much as it implies coherence. Two of the schools are, nevertheless, continental European in identification – but they still form part of the Anglophone approach to international security, in that so much of the work published has been in English, and has been aimed at mainstream publishing houses and journals.

Conclusion

International security as a field of study is therefore highly contested, but a field in which the impact of 'real world events' is felt particularly strongly. Working in the field requires the scholar or student to make decisions about what is important theoretically, as well as empirically. And it requires key decisions about concepts. Is security really something that should be thought about as purely interdependent in character? The West might worry about climate change as summers alter and growing patterns become less predictable; but Bangladeshis will drown and the Maldives will disappear as seas rise. The risks are hardly borne equally. Despite the attacks of 2001, the 'West' still offers a lifestyle that, in terms of security as discussed in this chapter, is far in advance of that on offer to the rest of the world. The West might worry about threats in the rest of the world, and respond to it by seeking to close borders. Where is interdependence in an interdependent world?

Of course, this is not to argue that we should discard interdependence; but it is to argue that it needs to be carefully interrogated. In security terms, many parts/peoples of the world are in a dependent situation – dependent on the policies and actions of others. And 'interdependent security' implies that there can be an agreement as to a core meaning; but it is not clear where common ground on interdependent security can be found between, for example, a Russian nationalist, a central African warlord, or a member of al Qaeda. There is a danger that calls to 'interdependent security' are calls by those in the West to see things as the West does; 'danger', because such calls rarely seem persuasive to those who understand their interests differently.

Thus, what is crucial is to understand that much that occurs in the contemporary security context is far less novel than is often proclaimed. Indeed, it is a useful exercise to ask: Why is this issue being described as 'new'? To whom is it new, and why? In addition, the claim that security is a field of interdependence hides the important dynamic of power relations. That security issues might be shared does not always mean that the impact is equal.

This might seem complacent, in a world of novel and uniquely dangerous security threats and challenges; and, indeed, if security is seen as uniquely pressing and dangerous in the contemporary world, then that is so. It has become commonplace for analysts and politicians to hark back to the 'simpler' times of the Cold War. But in those 'simpler' times, enough nuclear weapons to destroy the entire world many times over were on (by today's standards) very short fuses. Security issues are always immediate, unique and pressing: that is the nature of an issue being defined in terms of security. What is required, analytically, is precision on terms, epistemologies and policy prescriptions, rather than merely a replication of the language of contemporary security.

Chapter 10

Global Challenges: Accountability and Effectiveness

DAVID HELD

The paradox of our times can be stated simply: the collective issues with which we must grapple are of growing cross-border extensity and intensity and, yet, the means for addressing these are weak and incomplete. Three pressing global issues highlight the urgency of finding a way forward.

First, insufficient progress has been made in creating a sustainable framework for the management of climate change, illustrating the serious problems facing the multilateral order. Second, progress towards achieving the Millennium Development Goals has been slow and, in many places, lamentably so. Underlying this fact is, of course, the material vulnerability of over half the world's population. Each year, some 18 million people die prematurely from poverty-related causes. This is one third of all human deaths – 50,000 every day, including 29,000 children under five years old. And, yet, the gap between rich and poor countries continues to rise, and there is evidence that the bottom 10 per cent of the world's population has become even poorer since the beginning of the 1990s. Third, the threat of nuclear catastrophe might seem to have diminished, as a result of the end of the Cold War, but it is only in abeyance. Huge nuclear stockpiles remain, nuclear proliferation among states is continuing, new generations of tactical and nuclear weapons are being built, and nuclear terrorism is a serious threat.

These global challenges are indicative of three core sets of problems we face: those concerned with sharing our planet (global warming, biodiversity and ecosystem losses, water deficits), sustaining our life chances (poverty, conflict prevention, global infectious diseases) and managing our rulebooks (nuclear proliferation, toxic waste disposal, intellectual property rights, genetic research rules, trade rules, finance and tax rules) (cf. Rischard 2002). In our increasingly interconnected world, these global problems cannot be solved by any one nation-state acting alone. They call for collective and collaborative action – something that the nations of the world have not been good at, and that they need to be better at if these pressing issues are to be tackled adequately.

The limits of current global governance arrangements

Whilst complex global processes connect the fate of communities to each other across the world, global governance capacity is under pressure. This is so for two reasons. First, the multilateral order, founded after the Second War World, was designed in a different era and, above all, as a set of institutions to help constrain political violence and the conditions under which war might be considered legitimate. Many of today's global challenges do not fit readily into these priorities. Second, the extensity and intensity of many pressing problems today, from climate change to the regulation of global financial markets, sharply increases the governance capacity required. Accordingly, problem-solving capacities at the global and regional levels are weak for a number of deep underlying reasons. Many of these follow from the nature and form of the postwar settlement itself, and the subsequent development of the multilateral order.

Among the spectrum of international organizations are those whose primary concerns are technical; the Universal Postal Union, the International Civil Aviation Organization, the World Meteorological Organization, for example. These agencies have tended to work effectively, often providing extensions to the services offered by individual nation-states (Burnheim 1985: 222). To the extent that their tasks have been sharply focused, they have usually been politically uncontroversial. At the opposite pole lie organizations such as the World Bank, the International Monetary Fund (IMF), the United Nations (UN) Education, Scientific and Cultural Organization (UNESCO) and, of course, the UN itself. Preoccupied with central questions of war and peace, and of resource allocation, these bodies have been highly politicized and controversial. Unlike the smaller, technically based agencies, these organizations are at the centre of continual conflict over aspects of their nature and form, and over the policy that they generate or fail to develop.

The difficulties faced by these more contested agencies and organizations stem from many sources, including the tension between universal values and state sovereignty built into them from their beginning. Many global political and legal developments since 1945 do not simply curtail sovereignty, but support it in many ways. From the UN Charter to the Rio Declaration on the environment, international agreements often serve to entrench the international power structure. The division of the globe into powerful nation-states, with distinctive sets of geopolitical interests, was embedded in the articles and statutes of leading inter-governmental organizations (IGOs) (see Held 1995: chs 5 and 6). Thus, the sovereign rights of states are frequently affirmed alongside more universal principles. Moreover, whilst the case can be made that universal principles are part of 'the working creed' of officials in some UN agencies such as the United Nations Children's Fund (UNICEF), UNESCO and the World Health Organization (WHO), and NGOs such as Amnesty International, Save the Children and Oxfam, they can scarcely be said to be constitutive of the conceptual world and working practices of many politicians, democratic or otherwise (Barry 1998: 34–5).

Second, the reach of contemporary regional and international law rarely comes with a commitment to establish institutions with the resources and authority to make declared universal rules, values and objectives effective. The susceptibility of the UN to the agendas of the most powerful states, the partiality of many of its enforcement operations (or lack of them altogether), the underfunding of its organizations, the continued dependency of its programmes on financial support from a few major states, the weaknesses of the policing of many environmental regimes (regional and global) are all indicative of the disjuncture between universal principles (and aspirations) and their partial and one-sided application. Four deep-rooted problems need highlighting (see Held 2004: ch. 6).

A first set of problems emerges as a result of the development of globalization itself, which generates public policy problems that span the 'domestic' and the 'foreign', and the interstate order with its clear political boundaries and lines of responsibility. A growing number of issues can be characterized as intermestic – that is, issues that cross the *inter*national and do*mestic* (Rosenau 2002). These are often insufficiently understood or acted upon. There is a fundamental lack of ownership of many problems at the global level. It is far from clear which global public issues – such as global warming or the loss of biodiversity – are the responsibilities of which international agencies, and which issues ought to be addressed by which particular agencies. The institutional fragmentation and competition leads not only to the problem of overlapping jurisdictions among agencies, but also to the problem of issues falling between agencies. This latter problem is also manifest between the global level and national governments.

A second set of difficulties relates to the inertia found in the system of international agencies, or the inability of these agencies to mount collective problem-solving solutions faced, as they are, with uncertainty about lines of responsibility and frequent disagreement over objectives, means and costs. This often leads to the situation where the cost of inaction is greater than the cost of taking action. Bill Gates recently referred to the developed world's efforts in tackling malaria as 'a disgrace': malaria causes an estimated 500 million bouts of illness a year, kills an African child every thirty seconds, and costs an estimated US$12 billion a year in lost income; yet, investment in insecticide-treated bed nets and other forms of protective treatment would be a fraction of this (Meikle 2005: 22). The failure to act decisively in the face of urgent global problems not only compounds the costs of dealing with these problems in the long-run, but it can also reinforce a widespread perception that these agencies are not only ineffective, but also unaccountable and unjust.

A third set of problems arises because there is no clear division of labour among the myriad of international governmental agencies; functions often overlap, mandates frequently conflict, and aims and objectives too often get blurred. There are a number of competing and overlapping organizations and institutions, all of which have some stake in shaping different sectors of global public policy. This is true, for example, in the area of health and social policy, where the World Bank, the IMF and the WHO often have different or competing priorities (Deacon 2003); or, more specifically, in the area of AIDS/HIV treatment, where the WHO, Global Fund, UNAIDS and many other interests vie to shape reproductive health care and sexual practices.

A fourth set of difficulties relates to a democratic deficit, itself linked to two interconnected problems: the power imbalances among states, as well as those between state and non-state actors, in the shaping and making of global public policy (see Held 2004). Multilateral bodies need to be fully representative of the states involved in them, and they rarely are. The main problem can be qualitative: 'how well various stakeholders are represented' (Kaul *et al.* 2003: 30). Having a seat at the negotiating table in a major IGO or at a major conference does not ensure effective representation. For, even if there is parity of formal representation (a condition often lacking), it is generally the case that developed countries have large delegations equipped with extensive negotiating and technical expertise, whilst poorer developing countries frequently depend on one-person delegations, or even have to rely on the sharing of a delegate. In addition, where there is a clear case for dialogue and consultation between state and non-state actors, conditions to make it happen are often only partially met in multilateral decision-making bodies.

Underlying these institutional difficulties is the breakdown of symmetry and congruence between decision-makers and decision-takers (see Held 1995: pt I). The point has been well articulated recently by Kaul and her associates in their work on global public goods. They speak about the forgotten *equivalence* principle (see Kaul *et al.* 2003: 27–8). At its simplest, the principle suggests that those who are significantly affected by a global good or bad should have a say in its provision or regulation; that is, the span of a good's benefits and costs should be matched with the span of the jurisdiction in which decisions are taken about that good (see Held 2004: 97–101). Yet, all too often, there is a breakdown of 'equivalence' between decision-makers and decision-takers, between decision-makers and stakeholders, and between the inputs and outputs of the decision-making process. To take some topical examples: a decision to permit the 'harvesting' of rain forests might contribute to ecological damage far beyond the borders that formally limit the responsibility of a given set of decision-makers. A decision to build nuclear plants near the frontiers of a neighbouring country is a decision likely to be taken without consulting those in the nearby country (or countries), despite the many risks for them.

A number of significant governance innovations have been made in recent decades to address such issues, yet the global governance system remains, too often, weak and/or fragmented. Moreover, there has been a complex 'unbundling' of sovereignty, territoriality and political forces (Ruggie 1993). This unbundling involves a plurality of actors, a variety of political processes, and diverse levels of coordination and operation, with complex and uneven implications for accountability and effectiveness. Specifically, it includes:

- different forms of intergovernmental arrangements – for example, in the World Bank, IMF and WTO – embodying various levels of legalization, types of instruments utilized and responsiveness to stakeholders
- an increasing number of public agencies – for example, central bankers – maintaining links with similar agencies in other countries and, thus, forming transgovernmental networks for the management of various global issues
- diverse business actors – that is, firms, their associations and organizations, such as international chambers of commerce – establishing

their own transnational regulatory mechanisms to manage issues of common concern
- non-governmental organizations (NGOs) and transnational advocacy networks – that is, leading actors in global civil society – playing a role in various domains of global governance and at various stages of the global public policy-making process
- public bodies, business actors and NGOs collaborating – for example, on a range of development issues, in order to provide novel approaches to social problems through multi-stakeholder networks.

There is evidence that the politicization, bureaucratization and capacity limits of multilateral institutions have been important factors in driving the expansion of new forms of global governance, since powerful governments have sought to avoid either expanding the remit of existing multilateral agencies or creating new ones. Another factor that has been significant has been the normative shift towards 'self-regulation', as the private sector has sought to pre-empt or prevent international public regulation whilst governments have sought to share the regulatory burden with non-state actors.

Key political challenges

The postwar multilateral order is threatened by the intersection and combination of political, economic and environmental crises. Moreover, the very nature and form of globalization creates a delicate and complex system of structural global vulnerability. As is evident, the world we are in is highly interconnected. The interconnectedness of countries – or the process of 'globalization', as it is often called – can be measured by mapping the ways in which trade, finance, communication, pollutants and violence, among many other factors, flow across borders and lock the well-being of countries into common patterns (Held *et al.* 1999b). The deep drivers of this process will be operative for the foreseeable future, irrespective of the exact political form globalization takes. Among these drivers are:

- the changing infrastructure of global communications linked to the information technology (IT) revolution
- the development of global markets in goods and services, connected to the new worldwide distribution of information

- the pressure of migration and the movement of peoples, linked to shifts in patterns of economic demand, demography and environmental degradation
- the end of the Cold War, and the diffusion of democratic and consumer values across many of the world's regions, alongside some marked reactions to this
- the emergence of a new type and form of global civil society, with the crystallization of elements of a global public opinion.

Despite the fractures and conflicts of our age, societies are becoming more interconnected and interdependent. As a result, developments at the local level – whether economic, political or social – can acquire almost instantaneous global consequences, and vice versa. If we link to this the advances in science across many fields, often now instantly diffused through global communication networks, it is clear that the global arena has become both an extraordinary potential space for human development, as well as for disruption and destruction by individuals, groups or states (all of whom can, in principle, learn the lessons of nuclear energy, genetics, bacteriology and computer networking, among other things).

There are many reasons to be concerned about this. From the point of view of accountable and effective global governance, four distinct reasons are worth stressing: solidarity, social justice, democratic consent and policy effectiveness. It is important to clarify each of these because they provide a map of the dimensions we need to keep in mind for thinking about the nature and adequacy of governance at the global level. By solidarity, I mean not mere empathetic recognition of another's plight but, rather, the willingness to stand side-by-side with others in the creation of solutions to pressing collective problems. Without solidarity between rich and poor, developed and developing countries, the Millennium Development Goals (MDGs) will not be met and, as the former Secretary-General of the United Nations (UN) Kofi Annan simply put it, 'millions of people will die, prematurely and unnecessarily'. These deaths are all the more poignant because solutions are within our grasp. As far as challenges such as global warming and nuclear proliferation are concerned, we need to add to the definition of solidarity a focus on our own sustainability, never mind that of citizens of the future. Contemporary global challenges require recognition of, and active participation in, the forces that shape our overlapping communities of fate.

A second reason to focus on global challenges is social justice. Standards of social justice are, of course, controversial. To make my argument as accessible as possible, I will, following Thomas Pogge, take social justice to mean the fulfilment of human rights in an institutional order to the extent that it is reasonably possible (Pogge 2006). Of course, most argue that social justice requires more, and so it can claimed with some confidence that an institutional order that fails to meet these standards cannot be just. Accordingly, it can be reasoned that, insofar as our existing socio-economic arrangements fail to meet the MDGs, and the broader challenges of global warming and the risks of nuclear proliferation, they are unjust, or, simply, beyond justice.

The third reason is democratic consent. Democracy presupposes a non-coercive political process in and through which people can pursue and negotiate the terms of their interconnectedness, interdependence and difference. In democratic thinking, 'consent' constitutes the basis of collective agreement and governance; for people to be free and equal, there must be mechanisms in place through which consent can be registered in the determination of the government of public life. Yet, when millions die unnecessarily and billions are threatened unnecessarily, it can clearly be held that serious harm can be inflicted on people without their consent and against their will. The recognition of this reveals fundamental deficits in our governance arrangements that go to the heart of both justice and democracy.

Finally, the failure to act sooner rather than later on pressing global issues generally escalates the costs of dealing with them. For instance, it has been estimated the costs of inaction in dealing with communicable diseases in Africa are about 100 times greater than the costs of corrective action, and that these costs grow on a year-by-year basis (Conceição 2003). Similar calculations have also been undertaken in areas of international financial stability, the multilateral trade regime, and peace and security, all of which show that the costs of deficient provision of global public goods are extremely large and outweigh, by significant margins, the costs of corrective policies. And yet we, too, often stand paralyzed in the face of urgent collective challenges, or actively engage in the reproduction of political and social arrangements that fail to meet the minimum standards that solidarity, justice and democratic consent require.

Global economic governance: problems and opportunities

These points are well illustrated by reflecting on key elements of global economic priorities and their impact on governance arrangements. For the last twenty-five years, the agenda of economic liberalization and global market integration – or the Washington Consensus, as it is sometimes called – has been the mantra of many leading economic powers and international financial institutions. The standard view of economic development has maintained that the path to economic and social well-being is economic liberalization and international market integration. As Martin Wolf put it, 'all else is commentary' (2004: 144). But is this true? There are strong grounds for doubting that the standard liberal economic approach delivers on promised goods and that global market integration is the indispensable condition of development. Moreover, their forceful implementation by the World Bank, IMF and leading economic powers has often led to counter-productive results, at national and global levels.

Countries that have benefited most from globalization are those that have not played by the rules of the standard liberal market approach, including China, India and Vietnam (Rodrik 2005). In addition, those that have – for example, the Latin American and the Caribbean countries – have done worse judged by the standards of East Asia and their own past. In other words, the link between growth, economic openness and liberalization is weaker than the standard liberal argument suggests. The widespread shift among developing countries to greater openness has coincided with a slowdown in the rate of world economic growth compared with earlier in the postwar period, from 2.7 per cent in 1960–78 to 1.5 per cent from 1979–2000 (Milanovic 2005).

The link between growth and poverty reduction is also not as close as the liberal argument would predict. Accounts of this type generally assume a catch-up or convergence story whereby poorer countries, opening their markets and liberalizing, are expected to grow faster and richer so that income differentials narrow over time. However, the evidence to support this is controversial, at best. In the first instance, outside the phenomenal development of China and, to some extent, (urban) India, the reported number of people living below the World Bank poverty line of US$1 per day has actually risen in the two decades since 1981 (see Wade 2006). In addition, there is a near perfect correlation between a group's relative standing at the beginning of the 1990s and its real cumulative income gains in the years that followed (see Pogge 2006). The evidence shows that gains at the bottom of the global income hierarchy were minimal or even negative, as the first (that is to say, bottom) percentile lost 7.3 per cent and the second gained only 1 per cent. Moreover, the World Bank's measure of absolute poverty – based on US$1 per day – is, to a large extent, arbitrary. If you take the figure of US$2 per day, you can actually show the reverse trend (see Held and Kaya 2006).

Examining and evaluating trends in income inequality between countries, it is clear that much depends again on how, in particular, China's economic success and subsequent reduction in poverty is treated. If China is excluded from consideration, inequality between countries can be shown to have increased since 1980, identified as an important date because it is often claimed to be the moment when income inequality between countries reached its peak. Of course, there is much to be said for including China in the account but, then, it has to be borne in mind that China's success has depended significantly on a host of factors, not all of which fit neatly into the liberal argument. For example, China has staggered and regulated its entry into the global market; tariffs have been cut, but after economic take-off, particularly heavily in the last 10–12 years; capital movements have remained tightly regulated; and FDI is locked into partnerships, often with significant political controls.

None of this is to argue that trade and international capital flows do not provide important potential gains to many countries. The question, rather, relates to what conditions trade and capital flows (and what kinds of trade and capital flows) are introduced to maximize benefit. Thinking of globalization as either an inextricably positive force or the opposite is likely to miss the core conditions for successful development and political change. The choice is not between globalization in its liberal free market form and no globalization. Rather, what is at issue is the proper form globalization should take – that is, how it should be governed.

This critical issue cannot be resolved within the terms of the Washington Consensus because its thrust is to enhance economic liberalization and to adapt public policy and the public domain to market leading institutions and processes. It thus bears a heavy burden of responsibility for the common political resistance or unwillingness to address significant areas of market failure, including:

- the problem of externalities, such as environmental degradation
- the inadequate development of *non*-market social factors, which alone can provide an effective balance between 'competition' and 'cooperation', and thus ensure an adequate supply of essential public goods such as education, effective transportation and sound health
- the under-employment of productive resources (for example, in the pharmaceutical industry) in the context of the demonstrable existence of an urgent and unmet need (for example, the provision of anti-virals for the treatment of AIDS/HIV).

The Washington Consensus has weakened confidence in public authority and in that authority's ability – locally, nationally and globally – to govern and provide urgent public goods. Economic freedom is championed at the expense of social justice and environmental sustainability, with damage to both. It has, moreover, confused economic freedom and economic effectiveness. The question (and it is, of course, a big question) is: How can markets, democratic choices about public goods and a concern with basic universal standards such as human rights and environmental protection be pursued systematically and simultaneously? What follows constitutes some first steps in addressing this question.

To begin with, bridges have to be built between international economic law and human rights law, between commercial law and environmental law, between state sovereignty and transnational law (Chinkin 1998). It is as if all these things refer to separate domains and do not speak to each other, with the consequence that entrenched interests trump social and environmental considerations, among other urgent matters. What is required is not only the firm enactment of existing human rights and environmental agreements together with the clear linking of these with the ethical codes of particular industries, but also the introduction of new terms of reference into the ground rules or basic laws of the free market system. Precedents exist in the social chapter of the Maastricht Agreement, and in the attempt to attach labour and environmental conditions to the NAFTA regime, that are helpful in this regard.

At stake, ultimately, are three interrelated transformations. The first would involve engaging companies in the promotion of core universal principles, as the UN's Global Compact does at present. To the extent that this led to the entrenchment of human rights and environmental standards in corporate practices, that would be a significant step forward. But if this is to be something other than voluntary, and therefore vulnerable to being ignored, then it needs to be elaborated in due course into a set of more codified and mandatory rules. Thus, the second set of transformations would involve the entrenchment of revised rules and codes on health, child labour, trade union activity, environmental protection, stakeholder consultation and corporate governance in the articles of association of economic organizations and trading agencies. The key groups and associations of the economic domain would have to adopt in their very *modus operandi* a structure of rules and procedures compatible with universal social requirement, and be held accountable for them. Now, of course, it can be countered that poorly designed regulatory structures can harm employment levels, but Scandinavian countries show that it is possible to be both business-friendly and welfare-orientated.

There are several possible objections to the scheme set out. However, most of these are misplaced (Held 2004). The framework of human rights, democratic standards and environmental values is sound because it is preoccupied with the equal liberty and equal development possibilities of all human beings, and is consistent with the universal principles enshrined in the post-1945 multilateral order. But it has to be conceded that, without a third set of changes, the advocacy of such standards descends into *high-mindedness* because it fails to pursue the socio-economic changes that are a necessary part of such a commitment.

At a minimum, this means that development policies must be linked to:

- promoting the development space necessary for national trade and industrial incentives, including infant industry protection (and recognizing that 'one size' in economic policy does not fit all)
- building robust public sectors, capable of nurturing political and legal reform
- ensuring long-term investment in health care, human capital and physical infrastructure
- challenging the asymmetries of access to the global market, which are often hypocritical and indefensible
- ensuring the sequencing of global market integration into a framework of fair rules for trade and finance
- taking steps to match the movement of labour to the movement of capital – including creating a system of temporary work permit schemes of three to five years to allow for economic migration within an agreed multilateral framework
- increasing developing country participation in the running of the international financial institutions
- moving the headquarters of the IMF and the World Bank, on a rotating basis, to developing countries.

In addition, if such measures were combined with a turnover tax on financial markets, and/or a consumption tax on carbon emissions, and/or a shift of the priorities from military expenditure (now running at US\$1,000 billion per annum globally) towards the alleviation of severe need, direct aid amounts only to some US\$50 billion dollars per annum globally, then the development context of the Western nations and Northern nation-states could begin to be accommodated more adequately to those nations struggling for survival and minimum welfare.

The UN budget is US\$3.8 billion per annum plus peacekeeping, but the United States and Europe each spend vastly more annually on chocolate and bubble gum, alcohol, cars, pet food and so on. The expenditure on each of these items dwarfs the amounts available for direct poverty alleviation and for dealing with urgent diseases. The United States and its allies went to war after 9 September 2001; 9/11 was a serious matter, a crime against the United States and a crime against humanity. But, every day, ten times as many people die as were lost on 9/11: of poverty, malnutrition and poverty-related diseases – and yet, there is no war or, better

Figure 10.1 *UN core budget, 1996–97 to 2006–07 (US bn dollars)*

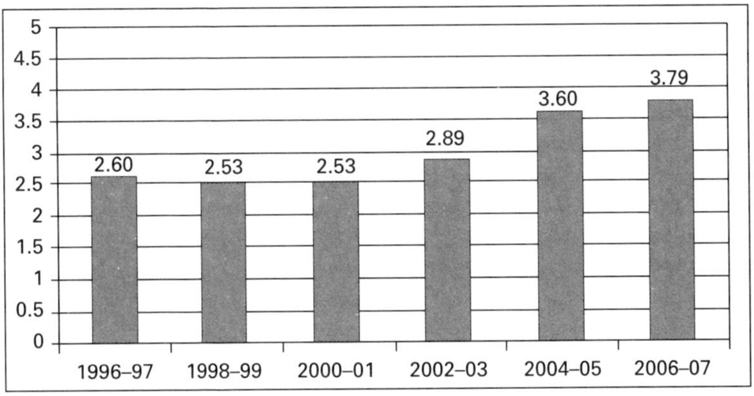

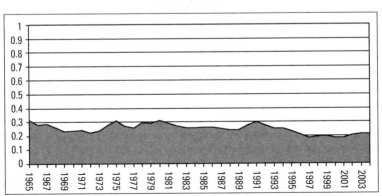

Sources: Data for 1996–2005 drawn from UN (2005); data for 2006–2007 drawn from UN (2006).

Figure 10.2 *International aid as a percentage of Gross National Income (world)*

Source: Based on data drawn from World Bank (2006).

Figure 10.3   *Amount that world ODA as a percentage of GNI would have to be multiplied by to equal world military expenditure as a percentage of GDP, 1989–2004*

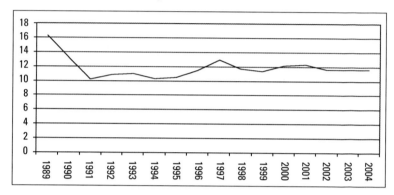

Note: According to data from the World Bank, in 2004, world ODA as a percentage of GNI would have to be multiplied by 11.58 times to equal military expenditure as a percentage of world GNP.

Source: Calculations based on data drawn from World Bank (2006).

Figure 10.4   *Ratio of military expenditure to ODA, selected countries, 2004*

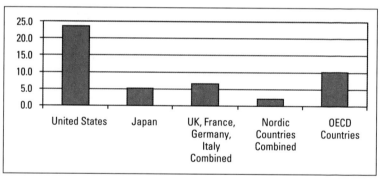

Note: In 2004, the United States spent 23.7 times the amount spent on ODA on military expenditure – this figure dwarfs comparable figures for the rest of the world.

Sources: Data and chart adapted from Worldwatch Institute (2006). Figures are extracted from Stockholm International Peace Research Institute (2005) and from OECD (no date).

still, decisive social change in relation to these life and death issues. The resources are available, but the question is political will and choice, especially those of elite political actors who have the capacity to act otherwise. Figures 10.1 to 10.5 and Table 10.1 disclose some interesting detail in this regard.

Figure 10.5 *Global consumption priorities (US$ billion)*

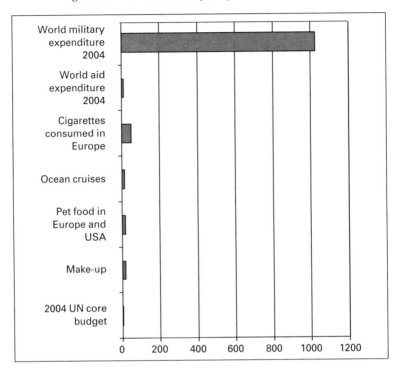

Sources:
1   2004 UN core budget –1.804, based on UN core budget figure for 2004–05, divided by
    2. See UN (2005);
2   Make-up – 18, Worldwatch Institute (2004): table 1-6;
3   Pet food in Europe and USA – 17, Worldwatch Institute (2004): table 1-6;
4   Ocean cruises – 14, Worldwatch Institute (2004): table 1-6;
5   Cigarettes consumed in Europe – 50, Shah (no date) (This report is based on data from
    the 1998 UNDP Human Development Report.);
6   World aid expenditure 2004 – 8.731, figure of 8,730,715,297, which is based on WDI
    indicators for World GNI and Aid as a Percentage of World GNI, 2004. See World Bank
    (2006);
7   World military expenditure 2004 – 1024, Stockholm International Peace Research
    Institute (2004).

The politics of global governance change

There are many pressing questions that need addressing further, and the
time has come, to say the least, to address them. Surprisingly perhaps, it is
an opportune moment to rethink the nature and form of global governance

Table 10.1   *Comparisons of annual expenditure on luxury items compared to estimated funding needed to meet selected basic needs*

Product	Annual expenditure (US$ billion)	Social or economic goal	Additional annual investment needed to achieve goal (US$ billion)
Make-up	18	Reproductive health care for all women	12
Pet food in Europe and United States	17	Elimination of hunger and malnutrition	19
Perfumes	15	Universal literacy	5
Ocean cruises	14	Clean drinking water for all	10
Ice cream in Europe	11	Immunizing every child	1.3

Sources: Worldwatch Institute (2004) table 1-6. The Worldwatch figures are drawn from the UNDP Human Development Report (1998).

and the dominant policies of the last decade or so. The policy packages that have largely set the global agenda – in economics and security – are failing. The Washington Consensus and Washington security doctrines have dug their own graves. The most successful developing countries in the world, as already noted, are successful because they have not followed the Washington Consensus agenda, and the conflicts that have most successfully been defused (the Balkans, Sierra Leone, Liberia, among others) are ones that have benefited from concentrated multilateral support and a human security agenda (Human Security Centre 2006). Here are clear clues as to how to proceed in the future. We need to follow these clues and learn from the mistakes of the past if solidarity, democracy, social justice and the multilateral order are to be advanced.

In addition, the political tectonic plates appear to be shifting. With the faltering of unilateralism and US foreign policy, uncertainty over the role of Europe in global affairs, the crisis of global trade talks, the emergence of powerful authoritarian capitalist states (Russia, China), the growing confidence of leading emerging countries (China, India and Brazil), and the unsettled relations between elements of Islam and the West, business as usual seems unlikely at the global level in the decades ahead. It is highly dubious that the multilateral order can survive for very much longer in its current form.

The political space for the development of more effective and accountable global governance has to be made, and advances are being achieved: by the activities of all those forces that are engaged in the pursuit of greater coordination and accountability of the leading processes of globalization, the opening up of IGOs to key stakeholders and participants, the protection of human rights and fundamental freedoms, sustainable development across generations, and peaceful dispute settlement in leading geopolitical conflicts. This is not a political project that starts from nowhere. It is, in fact, deeply rooted in the political world shaped and formed after the Holocaust and the Second World War. Moreover, it can be built on many of the achievements of multilateralism (from the founding of the UN system to the development of the European Union (EU)), international law (from the human rights regime to the establishment of the International Criminal Court) and multilayered governance (from the development of local government in cities and sub-national regions to the dense web of international policy-making forums).

The story of our increasingly global order is not a singular one. Globalization is not, and has never been, a one-dimensional phenomenon. Whilst there has been a massive expansion of global markets, which has altered the political terrain, the story of globalization is far from simply economic. Since 1945, there has been a significant entrenchment of universal values concerning the equal dignity and worth of all human beings in international rules and regulations; the reconnection of international law and morality, as sovereignty is no longer merely cast as effective power but, increasingly, as legitimate authority defined in terms of the maintenance of human rights and democratic values; the establishment of new forms of governance systems, regional and global (however weak and incomplete); and the growing recognition that the public good – whether conceived as financial stability, environmental protection, or global egalitarianism – requires coordinated multilateral action if it is to be achieved in the long term (see Held 2004). These developments need to be, and can be, built upon.

A coalition of political groupings could emerge to push these achievements further, comprising European countries with strong liberal and social democratic traditions; liberal groups in the US polity that support multilateralism and the rule of law in international affairs; developing countries struggling for freer and fairer trade rules in the world economic order; non-governmental organizations, from Amnesty International to Oxfam, campaigning for a more just, democratic and equitable world order; transnational social movements contesting the nature and form of contemporary globalization; and those economic forces that desire a more stable and managed global economic order. To the extent that the 2007 Bali discussions on a comprehensive 'Global Deal' on climate change were a success, it is attributable to an increasingly effective EU, positive action by key developing countries, and continuing pressures by leading environmental international non-governmental organizations (INGOs). Europe could have a special role in advancing the cause of more effective and accountable global governance (McGrew 2002). As the home of both social democracy and a historic experiment in governance beyond the state, Europe has direct experience in considering the appropriate designs for more effective and accountable suprastate governance. It offers novel ways of thinking about governance beyond the state that encourage a (relatively) more democratic – as opposed to more neoliberal – vision of global governance. Moreover, Europe is in a strategic position (with strong links west and east, north and south) to build global constituencies for reform of the architecture and functioning of global governance. Through inter-regional dialogues, it has the potential to mobilize new cross-regional coalitions as a countervailing influence to those constituencies that oppose reform, including unilateralist forces in the United States.

Of course, this is not to suggest that the EU should broker an anti-US coalition of transnational and international forces. On the contrary, it is crucial to recognize the complexity of US domestic politics and the existence of progressive social, political and economic forces seeking to advance a rather different kind of world order from that championed by the Republican right of the political spectrum (Nye 2002; Held 2004). Despite its unilateralist inclinations in recent years, it is worth recalling that public opinion in the United States (especially that of the younger generation) has been quite consistently in favour of the UN and multilateralism, and slightly more so than European publics (Norris 2009). The 2008 US presidential campaign drew upon some of these cultural resources, and President Barack Obama could become a unique catalyst of change in this regard. Any European political strategy to promote a broad-based coalition for a new global governance arrangement must seek to enlist the support of these progressive forces within the US polity, whilst it must resist within its own camp the siren voices now calling with renewed energy for the exclusive re-emergence of national identities, ethnic purity and protectionism.

Although some of the interests of those groupings that might coalesce around a movement for such change would inevitably diverge on a wide range of issues, there is potentially an important overlapping sphere of concern among them for the strengthening of multilateralism; building new institutions for providing global public goods; regulating global financial markets; creating a new global trade regime that puts the poorest first; ameliorating urgent social injustices that kill thousands of men, women and children daily; and tackling climate change and environmental problems. Of course, how far they can unite around these concerns – and can overcome fierce opposition from well-entrenched geopolitical and geoeconomic interests – remains to be seen. The stakes are very high, but so, too, are the potential gains for human security and development, if the aspirations for global democracy and social justice can be realized.

In sum, the postwar multilateral order is in trouble. Clear, effective and accountable decision-making is needed across a range of urgent global challenges; and, yet, the collective capacity for addressing these matters is in doubt. The dominant policy packages of the last several years have not delivered the goods, and a learning opportunity beckons. We need to build on the universal steps of the twentieth century and deepen the institutional hold of this agenda. Further steps in this direction remain within our grasp, however bleak the first few years of the twenty-first century – post 9/11 – have been. A change of direction in the governance of the world economy, linked to a new direction in the management of human security, would both buttress international law and multilateral institutions, and ensure that the wisdom embedded in the universal principles and institutional advances of the post-1945 era is safe-guarded, nurtured and advanced for future generations.

Rethinking politics in a global age

Politics in a global age unfolds at many levels – local, national, regional and global – and across these. It also unfolds across many sectors of activity, from the commercial and financial to the cultural and ecological. Where politics goes as an activity, political science must follow as a discipline, or risk being marginalized by historical shifts. A discipline of politics that doggedly analyzes political phenomena within the borders of states, or only strays beyond this to compare and contrast politics within different states, is simply not equipped to understand politics, shaped and reshaped by globalization, and the new global collective action problems and risks that confront it.

The growth of complex interconnections and interrelations between states and societies, the intensification of worldwide socio-political processes that link together seemingly distant localities, and the causal shaping of events in one location by those occurring thousands of miles away, raise fundamental questions about the fate of the modern state and about the appropriate locus of the political good in this vast and changing context. The assumption that one can understand the nature and possibilities of political life by an exclusive or primary focus on national structures, processes and forces does not stand up to scrutiny. There can no longer be a valid theory of the state, or of political choices, without an understanding of their wider regional and global settings, and of the ways in which the latter shape the nature and form of the former. At the same time, we need to bear in mind that there cannot be an adequate account or explanation of regional or global politics without understanding the role of states, especially those of powerful geopolitical actors and subaltern players.

Moreover, if political science is to develop the means to grasp this complexity, it needs to develop in a number of different modes, for it faces challenging questions of understanding and explanation, of value and the contestation of norms, and practical calls to action or to improve (more modestly) the policy agenda. The project of political science, therefore, must involve a number of different tasks: first, the empirical-analytical – concerned, above all, with understanding and explanation; second, the theoretical or philosophical – concerned, above all, with conceptual and normative issues (for example, a world in which we are forced to think through the clash of meanings attributed to democracy, social justice and policy effectiveness); and, third, the policy agenda – the question of the feasibility of moving from a current set of problems and policy dilemmas to a better resolution of these. To these three tasks, one must always add the historical – the examination of the changing meaning of political discourse, its key concepts, theories and concerns, over time. Without the historical, it is scarcely possible to imagine, of course, how the insights and failings of past generations can be built into the collective wisdom of the present (see Dunn 1990).

Taken as a whole, the tasks of political science are unquestionably demanding. In the absence of their pursuit, there is always the danger that politics will be left to the ignorant and self-interested, or to those simply with a 'will to power'. Pursuing them systematically obviously creates no guarantees of a better life; but it at least enhances the possibility of a greater understanding of the nature of contemporary political communities, their diverse power centres and sites of conflict, and their dense forms of inter-connectedness. Examining the processes and forces that interweave to determine the fate of each and every one of these, assessing critically the competing claims of political value, and refashioning the meaning of the political good in the face of global challenges are all indispensable elements of a contemporary political understanding – and a platform for action.

Chapter 11

Global Justice

KIMBERLY HUTCHINGS

Introduction

In the 1970s and 1980s, in the context of neoliberal challenges to redistributive welfare states, theoretical debates about justice were largely taken up by arguments about principles of distributive justice appropriate for liberal political communities (Rawls 1971; Nozick 1974). In the 1990s, feminist and multiculturalist politics challenged the assumptions of mainstream theories of justice, and issues of difference and identity, as well as distribution, became the focus of attention in both theory and practice (Young 1990; Kymlicka 1995; Mulhall and Swift 1996; Parekh 2000; see also Kantola and Squires in this volume). Across all of these debates, two matters were taken for granted: first, the assumption that the nation-state was the site within which claims of justice could be articulated and satisfied; and, second, a particular understanding of the disciplinary role of the political theorist, in relation to that of the political scientist, the policy-maker or the activist. In this chapter, I will suggest that disrupting the first of these assumptions has implications for the second. Once discussions about theories of justice shift to the global arena, it becomes harder to sustain the myth of the political theorist as a monological source of authority on the meaning of justice. And it becomes apparent that much closer collaboration between political theorists, scientists and activists is required if principles of global justice are to make sense to a global audience, as opposed to the select company of liberal political theorists and their critics within the western academy.

As is clear from other contributions to this volume, analysts disagree about the extent to which levels of global economic, ecological and political interdependence are, as a matter of empirical fact, new. Within political theory, the question of the relevance of such interdependence to theorizing justice is also contested. Perspectives on global justice vary, from those who argue that the language of justice is never applicable beyond the borders of states (Nagel 2005) to those that argue that the language of justice should always have been understood as global in scope (Singer 2004). In most cases, however, where political theorists have started to think about justice as a global issue, this has been driven by claims about changing empirical realities (Held 1995, 2004; Pogge 2007a, 2008; Caney 2005). Three aspects of global interdependence in particular have been the focus of a growing literature on global justice: global economic inequality, impending ecological catastrophe, and globalized political violence (MacGinty and Williams 2009). For example, political theorists increasingly acknowledge that the gap between rich and poor is embedded within globalized economic relations that are beyond the power of states to regulate or control in isolation. If wealth and poverty depend, to a significant extent, on reciprocal relations with others beyond the state, then it is difficult to sustain the claim that identifying the principles that underpin the just state is the key to resolving economic injustice (Held 2004: 3–12; Pogge 2008: 19–23).

Theorists have also begun to reflect on the emerging global consensus on the unsustainability of current levels of energy consumption and carbon emissions. Non-renewable resources, such as coal and oil, are finite. In parts of the world, the capacity to produce renewable resources (such as food and timber) is becoming exhausted, and desertification is increasing as an effect of climate change. The planet cannot continue to absorb the global warming effects of industrial production and consumption. Again, it would seem that the idea that the state is the sole site of justice makes little sense when states are unable to control such a profound threat to their own populations (Shue 1993; Dower 2007). The same is true of a world in which intervention, on the grounds of justice, in the affairs of states has become an accepted practice. In the post-Cold War period, the Rwandan genocide, and the extremes of violence involved in civil conflicts in Bosnia, Kosovo, the Democratic Republic of Congo, Darfur and elsewhere have been responded to with different types and degrees of 'humanitarian intervention' by the international community, and by the articulation of new international norms such as 'Responsibility to Protect' (Bellamy 2008). This has, again, prompted political theorists to reflect on the need for principles of justice that transcend state boundaries (Wheeler 2000; Brown 2002; Caney 2005; Bellamy 2008).

In what follows, I sketch out two broad trajectories of contemporary theories of global justice. Both of these trajectories originated in debates about justice within the nation-state. The first espouses the view that the shift in focus to global justice does not fundamentally affect the task and resources of the political theorist. The second implies that the move to a global stage has profound consequences for both the task and the resources of the political theorist. In conclusion, I will argue that, even though it is the first of these trajectories that continues to dominate in theory and practice, it is the second trajectory of thinking that will become increasingly important in theorizing global justice in the twenty-first century.

Theorizing global justice: between statism and globalism

Janus-faced justice

John Rawls set the meta-theoretical and substantive agenda for debates about the nature and meaning of justice within the state in his *A Theory of Justice* (Rawls 1971; Daniels 1975). Rawls premised his theory of justice within the state on a hypothetical procedure, in which individuals were imagined engaging in a debate about the principles of justice that should underpin their society. The individuals deciding on principles of justice were rational, self-interested choosers, with general knowledge about human psychology and different forms societies can take, but without specific knowledge of their own characters or of the position they would occupy in the society for which they are selecting the principles of justice (Rawls 1971: 136–47). Rawls's theory of justice, as with other contractualist theories, sees ethical and political principles as legitimated by the choices that individuals either made, or, more commonly, *would have made*, in a hypothetical state of nature or original position. Such theories involve two kinds of assumption: first, assumptions about the parties to the contract; and, second, assumptions about the circumstances and purpose of the contract. Different forms of contractualism build in different assumptions into the contract and its context, and might give rise to more or less libertarian or authoritarian outcomes (see Nozick's response to Rawls, Nozick 1974). But, to the extent that contractualists restrict the authority of the contract to a delimited polity, contractualism underpins a Janus-faced account of justice, in which justice *within* political communities is necessarily distinct from justice *between* political communities.

When Rawls addresses the second face of justice in *Law of the Peoples*, the argument is premised on the pre-existence of delimited political communities that are already ordered according to principles of justice (Rawls 1999; Martin and Reidy 2006). International justice involves a further contract in which the parties are not individuals, but liberal (and later, also other 'well-ordered') peoples. Inter-people political relations are much looser than those characteristic of domestic political community. The primary principle of the law of the peoples on Rawls's account is respect for the freedom and self-determination of liberal peoples. This principle makes non-intervention the starting point for the relation between liberal peoples, and makes any breaching of that self-determination *prima facie* unjust (paternalistic) in the case of liberal states (which, of course, on Rawls's account would already institutionalize principles of distributive justice) (Rawls 1999: 35–43). In his argument, Rawls extends this requirement to all peoples that institutionalize certain standards of rights and accountability in their political system (peoples he terms 'well-ordered'). It is only when it comes to the relation between well-ordered peoples and those that are not well-ordered that global inequality might raise questions of justice across borders (Rawls 1999: 105–13). Rawls allows for the possibility that a case might be made for it being a requirement of justice for affluent, liberal and well-ordered peoples to address the poverty of non-liberal 'burdened societies'. But this should only be with a view to enabling those societies to become well-ordered, and would not involve major redistribution of global wealth but, rather, aid in establishing the right kind of basic structure to nurture indigenous economic development (*ibid.*: 114–15).

Rawls explains different levels of economic development between political communities in terms of their distinctive culture, and plays down the significance of natural resources in the relative success or failure of distinct economies. In his account, there is no recognition that such resources might be the shared responsibility of all of the inhabitants of the planet, or that it might be difficult to draw boundaries between the environment of one people and that of another. For this reason, Rawls's vision of international justice does not recognize that global environmental degradation might be a matter of transnational or global justice. At best, on this account, peoples might have a global obligation to act as responsible stewards of their own environmental resources, not because of what they owe to others, but because of what they owe to themselves as members of a well-ordered society (*ibid.*: 119).

In relation to distributive and environmental justice, from the contractualist point of view, only minimal requirements of justice govern the relation between political communities. These requirements might be somewhat greater when it comes to the relation between well-ordered societies and 'burdened' societies, where poverty and mismanagement make it difficult for those societies to help themselves. In addition to this, however, Rawls also identifies inter-societal requirements of justice between well-ordered and what he terms 'outlaw' peoples. Outlaw peoples have tyrannical and aggressive governments that violate the human rights of their own citizens – in particular, those of security, liberty and equality – but also pose a threat to other political communities (*ibid.*: 80–1). Such violations, on Rawls's account, are so fundamental that they can be identified as *unjust* by liberal and non-liberal well-ordered peoples. For this reason, intervention in their affairs might sometimes be a requirement of justice. The aim of such intervention, however, as with aid to burdened societies, must be to enable outlaw states to become well-ordered, and therefore subscribe to the law of the peoples (*ibid.*: 94–7).

Contractualist thinking is an important element of contemporary actual international norms and policies. Although there is recognition of the need to address poverty and environmental sustainability, the predominant view is that these problems can only be addressed legitimately in ways that respect the right of political communities to give or not to give, to control their own borders, to agree or not to agree to treaties dealing with carbon emissions and so on (Miller 1994; 1995; Cole 2000; Miller and Hashmi 2001). Similarly, when it comes to the circumstances under which intervention into other political communities might be considered legitimate. International law continues to privilege the state's right to manage its own affairs and to permit intervention only in very specific kinds of circumstances (though there is increasing contestation about this, discussed later in this chapter). And international peace-keeping and state-building operations tend to reflect a paternalistic commitment to enabling political communities to become 'well-ordered' in Rawls's sense (Barnett and Snyder 2008). Somewhat paradoxically, therefore, the same theory of justice that has profound critical consequences for justice within the liberal state, largely confirms a conservative attitude towards the *status quo* when it comes to international justice.

Rawls's approach to theorizing justice beyond the state is premised on a particular understanding of the nature and role of political theory. The purpose of political theory, on this account, is to elicit normative principles through rational inquiry, and then to use these principles as a mode of critical engagement with real-world issues. Although in his earlier work, Rawls made claims for the universal validity of his theory of justice, he later became more cautious about this claim and argued, rather, that his theory was a kind of distillation of the principles inherent in liberalism, in the case of *Law of the Peoples* of a liberal international order. His approach to theorizing justice clearly follows a particular disciplinary division of labour. The political theorist's task is to identify principles of justice: it is the task of political science or international relations to determine the extent to which the world actually does, or does not, reflect those principles, and to provide evidence for the institutions and instruments that might best realize them; meanwhile, it is, potentially, the task of policy-makers and activists to work to close the gap between the world as it is and the world as it ought to be. This approach to theorizing global justice raises two questions: first, does it matter whether the empirical assumptions made in *Law of the Peoples* are accurate? Second, does it matter that the presumptive audience of Rawls's claims about justice beyond the state are those that already endorse a liberal paradigm of inter-state relations?

In Rawls's argument, prescriptive consequences follow from a combination of normative principles and empirical assumptions. Rawls makes assumptions about the capacities of peoples to control, and therefore take responsibility for, their own economies and environments, without having to be involved in anybody else's. He also makes assumptions about the possibility and efficacy of using instruments, such as military force, to bring about positive political change. There is, of course, a massive body of work in political science, international relations and other disciplines that investigates and problematizes these empirical premises. But Rawls is able to largely ignore this literature; in part, because he is setting out an ideal of liberal international order, to which the real world might well not live up but, more importantly, because his theoretical starting point does not permit him to think from any perspective other than that of globally predominant liberal international norms. This is because, for Rawls, the second face of justice is parasitic on the first. Even though the principles of international justice seem very different to those applicable to the liberal state, their *difference* follows from the *sameness* of Rawls's theoretical assumptions, originally formulated as part of an inter-liberal conversation about the true meaning of liberal justice.

In both cases, the conversations that Rawls has with fellow liberal theorists position his argument as one amongst others that share a particular history and set of reference points. Contractualist theorists of global justice, such as Rawls, are the avatars of liberal states seeking to deal justly with a world in which not every political community is their mirror. Rawls's liberal peoples are tolerant (within limits) of other less liberal, less well-ordered peoples. But it is one thing to speak to fellow liberals as fellow citizens, and another to speak to them as a global, powerful minority within a much larger global population, whose inheritance from the world of the social contract tradition has been colonialism, imperialism and authoritarianism, rather than liberalism. In turning the face of justice from the world of liberal insiders to the world of non-liberal outsiders, the *same* theoretical position acquires a very different political meaning.

Universal justice

The major opponents of contractualist accounts of global justice in contemporary political theory base their arguments on the idea of fundamental human entitlements. From this point of view, the question of whether global inequality is unjust depends on the nature and status of what count as fundamental human rights (Nickel 1987; Donnelly 1989). In debates over global justice, two kinds of human rights argument conclude that global inequality, where extremes of deprivation are involved for the poor, is unjust. One such argument rests on the straightforward claim that economic rights are as fundamental as rights of liberty and security, and should therefore be regarded as strict entitlements. For thinkers such as Shue, any world in which human rights to subsistence are not guaranteed is an unjust world (Shue 1996). On other human rights accounts, however, fundamental human rights or entitlements alone do not sufficiently account for the nature of the injustice of global inequality. On Pogge's account, just as all human beings have a right not to be murdered and a duty not to murder others, so all human beings have a right not to be extremely impoverished (and therefore hungry, ill and in danger of untimely death) and, correspondingly, all human beings have a duty to refrain from violating this right (Pogge 2007a; 2008). In conditions of economic interdependence, in which past colonialism and present dominance of the institutions governing the global political economy mean that certain rich societies control global economic outcomes, Pogge concludes that this means that the situation is unjust not only because people's rights are violated as such, but also because the rights of the poor are being actively violated by the rich (Pogge 2007b).

Pogge's argument takes direct issue with Rawls's claims that economies of peoples are relatively discrete, and that the primary reason for inequalities in living standards between them are to do with domestic political culture. Along with theorists such as Beitz, Pogge has made the argument that, in the light of global interdependence and common dependence on the earth's resources, Rawls's original position should be re-imagined on behalf of the global population, rather than presuming politics is always already separated into discrete political communities (Beitz 1979: 127–36; Rawls 1999: 115–20; Pogge 2008: 110–14). From this starting point, he argues, compulsory schemes for the global redistribution of wealth would clearly be justified (Pogge 2008: 202–21). And it would be much less obvious that political communities had the right to control membership and block economic immigration (Cole 2000; Miller and Hashmi 2001).

From the point of view of Pogge, common environmental threats are part and parcel of the story of economic interdependence and exploitation that has systematically enriched a global minority at the expense of the global majority (Pogge 2008: 147–8). In general, this would tend to put the onus of addressing ecological harms not only on those who can best afford the costs of the kinds of technological transformations and limitations on consumption that dealing with something such as global warming would involve, but also on those who have done most to inflict environmental damage on the planet as a whole. However, matters become more complicated when it comes to developing economies and the potential tension between ensuring universal economic rights of various kinds and the limitations on economic development necessary to limit environmental destruction. In response to this problem, Shue suggests a scheme in which poor countries should be given autonomy over a certain amount of environmental damage, in the interests of meeting human needs (Shue 1993; de Vita 2007: 124).

Just as human rights arguments are more likely than contractualist approaches to identify global economic relations and global environmental damage as being matters of global justice, so they are more likely to take a view of rights violations as injustices that should be recognized and responded to by all wherever they take place. Whereas non-intervention remains the default principle of Rawls's law of the peoples, human rights arguments undermine the ethical relevance of respect for political community, except insofar as it is based on the respect for fundamental human rights. Large-scale human rights abuses are therefore matters of injustice, not only within the context in which they are taking place, but also for all of humanity (Wheeler 2000; Caney 2005: 226–62). A rights-based global justice requires the capacity of the global community to act effectively to sanction violations of rights wherever they occur. Human rights theories of global justice endorse the idea of 'responsibility to protect' (Bellamy 2008), and call for strengthening the UN and other international institutions and potentially setting up an international military force to undertake global policing functions (Held 1995: 279–80; Kaldor 2003: 109–41; Bellamy 2008).

Although the language of human rights has become deeply entrenched in international governmental and INGO aid and development policies, a human rights view of global economic justice is a long way from the principles currently governing the world economic order. The language of rights has, however, become a key discourse for actors, often humanitarian INGOs, seeking to challenge and transform existing practices in relation to both the global economy and migration. This can be seen in campaigns targeting multinational corporations over child labour or ethical investment; in INGOs lobbying for the reform of institutions such as the UN or the WTO, to make them more genuinely representative of the global population and therefore more responsive to the problem of global poverty; and in the range of INGOs arguing on behalf of the rights of economic migrants, refugees and asylum seekers (Kaldor 2003). Although it remains the case that contractualist principles are deeply embedded in global rules governing intervention, it has been argued that developments since the end of the Cold War suggest a trend towards a more rights-based approach to this aspect of global justice. In particular, the intervention in Kosovo in 1999 and the setting up of the International Criminal Court have been cited as evidence of a changing understanding of justice in the global order (Wheeler 2000).

Human rights theories of justice run counter to the implications of contractualism, and are often identified as the radical globalist 'other' of predominant statist thinking, both within political theory and within the institutions and practices of global politics. So, in what sense do they depart from contractualism in their understanding of the nature and role of political theory? In many ways, there is very little difference. As with contractualist theories, human rights arguments presume that the task of political theory is to identify the principles that provide the critical standard against which actual global economic and political conditions can be judged. In the case of right-based arguments, the justification for this critical standard lies in claims about the moral status of the individual human being, which are understood in different ways by different thinkers, but are always ahistorical and universal. In this respect, human rights theories rest on a stronger claim to universally valid foundations than versions of contractualism, such as that of Rawls, which acknowledge that the contract reflects a particular kind of population and context. The political theorist does not need political scientists or practitioners to identify the principles that should govern global politics. Nevertheless, taking the human being, rather than the contractual political community, as the starting point for political theory opens up the sensitivity of political theory to new kinds of facts. Whereas Rawls selectively drew on accounts of economic development that fitted with his view of the primacy of collective self-determination, theorists such as Pogge are open to taking arguments about economic globalization much more seriously.

Pogge differs from Rawls over the facts, but his theory of justice is nevertheless articulated within the same inter-liberal conversation. It was noted above that contractualist theories of justice were articulated from the point of view of the tolerant liberal state. Human rights theorists take issue with the contractualist account of what can be tolerated. The arguments made by thinkers such as Shue and Pogge are addressed not to the global poor or oppressed, but to the same liberal audience with which Rawls engages. Whereas contractualism speaks explicitly on behalf of liberalism as well as to fellow liberals, human rights thinkers speak, on behalf of everyone, in a liberal idiom and to a liberal audience. There is no requirement for these theorists to speak to the oppressed because the injustice of their situation is a given that 'we' (for which read the rich and powerful) must do something about. Even more than in the case of contractualism, human rights theories are premised on the idea that political theory grasps the truth of the human condition and, on the basis of this confidence, is prepared to battle against the predominant norms underpinning the global order to change the world for the better.

Theorizing global justice: beyond statism and globalism

Critical theory

From the point of view of critical theory, and in contrast to both contractualist and human rights accounts, the question of whether global inequality is unjust is unanswerable *a priori*. Critical theorists follow Habermas in arguing for the inter-subjective grounding of principles of justice in communicative reason (Habermas 1990). On this account, *substantive* principles of justice can only be reached as the result of an inter-subjective agreement, arrived at under *procedurally* just conditions of argumentation, between all those affected by a particular issue. Because of this, critical theory identifies formal and informal democratic mechanisms as central to the meaning of justice. In conditions of economic globalization, the proliferation of international human rights regimes and the growth of transnational political projects such as the EU, where affected populations are rarely confined within the border of a single state, critical theorists accept that the scope of justice in relation to certain issues will transcend state borders and is potentially global. Given the need for *actual* deliberation over principles of justice to take place, this means that critical theorists have had to address the question of whether forums for such deliberation exist and, if they do not, how they could be created and sustained. For critical theorists, therefore, global justice necessarily implies global formal and informal democratic institutions (Held 1995, 2004; Fraser 2005; 2007; Habermas 2006). Formal institutions, such as those envisaged in Held's model of cosmopolitan democracy, allow for the representation of those affected in deliberation over policy; informal institutions, based in global civil society, allow for more direct participation of different publics in opinion formation concerning those issues that directly affect them (Held 1995: 179–180; Fraser 2007; see also Held in this volume).

Forst argues that critical theory provides a way out of the stand-off between predominant statist and globalist approaches to global justice (2001: 170). Because critical theory is not solely concerned with specific outcomes but with practices of justification, in which all those affected have a right to participate, neither statism nor globalism provides an adequate response to contemporary challenges of justice at global and local levels. Forst points out that *actual* practices of justification necessarily happen within particular political contexts and that, therefore, the institutional specifications that follow from the principle of justification are likely to differ depending on the context. To impose a 'thick' globalist account of justice on all contexts is to prejudge the outcome of specific dialogic encounters and, thereby, to violate the conditions for a free and fair debate. However, in order for those conditions to be upheld, a certain kind of global justice is required, what Forst calls a principle of *minimal transnational justice* (*ibid.*: 182). In keeping with the nature of critical theories of justice, this minimal transnational justice is procedural rather than substantive. On the one hand, it ensures that all political communities institutionalize a minimal level of democracy and, on the other, that all political communities have a roughly equal say in questions of global concern.

Critical theory does not claim to be able to identify substantive principles of justice absent in an actual deliberative process in which all affected parties participate, either directly or through representatives. Paradoxically, however, this means that it has strong substantive consequences for the architecture of global governance. For critical theorists, global justice *requires* global democratic mechanisms, whether these are those of formal democratic institutions or more informal civil society mechanisms (Held 2004; Fraser 2005; Habermas 2006). Recently, for example, Fraser has argued for the need for global public spheres in which the views of those affected by the realities of a post-Westphalian world order can be articulated (Fraser 2007). It might be that in such

forums the global redistribution of wealth would be condemned as paternalistic, that control of environmental damage would be delegated to
local communities, or that the dangers of humanitarian intervention
undermining local self-determination would be seen as greater than the
dangers of violations at the local level. But it might also be the case that
opinion formulated in such forums would support a root and branch
reform of the global political economy, more stringent global limitation
of carbon emissions, and the strengthening of international institutions
and global mechanisms to protect human rights. Although, for critical
theorists, these are not questions that can be answered in advance and in
the abstract, there is a requirement to enable the kinds of dialogue
(between those affected) that could provide such answers.

   Although its proponents present critical theory as a way out of the
dead-end of the debate between Rawls and Pogge, there is more common
ground between critical theory and human rights based accounts of global
justice than between critical theory and contractualism. The key difference is that, where the emphasis of human rights theories is on specified
human entitlements, critical theory places its emphasis on participation.
In this respect, it is worth noting that in both global governmental and
civil society sectors there has been an increasing commitment to principles of deliberation and participation in policy formation and implementation. For example, bodies such as the UN and the WTO have
increasingly institutionalized consultative relations with a range of non-
governmental organization (NGO) groups. And development projects are
increasingly required to formalize principles of participation and
accountability in the design and delivery of international aid (Rubenstein
2008; Stein 2008).

   In many ways, critical theory does not appear to change the agenda for
theorizing global justice very much from the alternatives of statism and
globalism. As with both contractualism and human rights theories, it sees
the task of political theory as being to identify principles that can then
provide a critical standard for judging and prescribing for actual global
economic and political relations. As with both of these modes of theorizing also, the prescriptive consequences of the theory depend on empirical assumptions made, for instance, about levels of economic or
ecological interdependence across political communities. There is,
however, something new that is introduced by this mode of theorizing.
Where Rawls and Pogge are at odds over their empirical reading of the
causes and effects of economic inequalities between political communities, they are not obliged to settle this argument as a prerequisite for
setting up the procedure for thinking about global justice. In contrast,

critical theory effectively requires an informed historical analysis before it can begin the process of identifying relevant participants in a global dialogue about economic injustice or, indeed, whether one should take place at all (Fraser 2007).

Critical theory has often been criticized for its utopianism and abstraction, in particular when it comes to enabling actual dialogue between those most powerfully affected by global inequality, ecological destruction or political violence. But, unlike contractualism and human rights theories, it does at least raise the question of who these people are, rather than assume that it already knows who they are. This has a twofold implication: on the one hand, the reliance of normative theory on good political science becomes something much more foundational to critical theory as an approach to global justice. On the other hand – again, in contrast to the alternatives so far considered – critical theory does not simply democratize the idea of justice, it democratizes the process of theorizing about justice. In this respect, it leaves open the possibility of the transformation of assumptions about addressor and addressee that are built into contractualist and human rights theories. The critical theorist who takes critical theory seriously de-centres his or her own position as a truth-bearer either about the essence of liberalism or the essence of humanity and, in doing this, at least potentially de-centres the particular political and ideological history that constructed debates between statists and globalists in the first place.

Feminism

Feminist theories of justice take their starting point from feminist politics, and, following on from this, take a variety of forms. There has been ongoing debate between feminist theorists aiming to re-think existing theories to encompass women and gender (see Okin 1989, on Rawls's theory of justice; MacKinnon 2006, on women's human rights; and Benhabib 1992, on a feminist critique of Habermas). At the same time, feminists, unconvinced by the capacity of contractualist human rights or critical theorists to encompass gender justice, have argued for a feminist ethic of care (Ruddick 1990; Robinson 1999; Held 2006). Others, in turn, have argued for a postmodern or postcolonial understanding of feminist justice, in which gendered injustices are understood as always intersecting with other hierarchies of identity and power (Young 1990; Flax and Okin 1995; Kantola and Squires in this volume). In clashes between these different perspectives, feminist theorists find themselves involved in negotiating with each other between a tendency to universalize and essentialize the meanings of both 'gender' and 'justice', and a decentralization of ethical foundations that potentially undermines the possibility of generalized claims about feminist justice in the world as a whole (Benhabib 1992; Robinson 1999; Nussbaum 2000). Although different feminist theorists settle this negotiation differently within their own work, feminist theories of justice are always marked by a heightened sensitivity to the philosophical and political problems of generalization.

For feminist theorists, the general question as to whether global inequality is unjust means very little unless it is particularized into thinking about 'what' is just or unjust 'to whom' and 'how'. Different women and men experience global inequality differently in different parts of the world. In seeking to break down the task of recognizing global injustice at the theoretical level, feminist perspectives build on the idea of the ethical relevance of history and procedure that characterizes the work of human rights theorists such as Pogge (2008) or critical theorists such as Forst (2001). But they do so in a way that is more specific, concrete and contextual than is the case with these approaches. For example, feminist critiques of global inequality have been informed by human rights arguments that identify lack of the means of subsistence with the violation of basic human rights, and that make a connection between the affluence of some and the poverty of many, historically and currently (Nussbaum 2000; Ackerly 2008). However, from the feminist point of view, to respond to this through schemes of global redistribution will not necessarily rectify injustices that have their roots in gendered institutions of property ownership (modern and traditional) and the gendered organization of reproductive and productive labour (Robinson 1999; Nussbaum 2000; Held 2006). In this respect, feminist responses to distributive justice issues, such as those of critical theorists, emphasize the importance of democratization as essential to justice. In contrast to critical theorists, however, for feminism this is not a matter of enabling a fair debate to arrive at principles of redistribution, but one of re-shaping practices of aid and development to enable greater levels of participation and control in and of those practices by poor women. This requires, amongst other things, working against the 'top down' tendency of much of contemporary humanitarianism, where policy and resources are largely controlled by governmental organizations and NGOs dominated by representatives of the world's rich (Robinson 1999: 157–63; Nussbaum 2000).

In relation to questions of environmental degradation, rather than focusing on outcomes as the site of injustice, feminist environmental ethics has focused on the nature of the relation between human beings and the earth's resources, and sought to show how a hierarchical, gendered understanding of the relation between human beings and the earth's resources is bound up with processes and outcomes when it comes to ecological destruction (Warren 1994). In relation to questions of human rights violations, again, feminists have sought to examine the political relations that structure and enable the violations of bodies in different kinds of ways in political conflict. On examination, the gendered structures through which killing and injuring are rendered meaningful and legitimate are inextricably entwined with a range of injustices that might not necessarily be addressed when killing and injuring stops (Ruddick 1990; Cockburn and Zarkov 2002).

Feminism has always been concerned about the interconnection between gender and political violence. In this respect, it differs from the other perspectives considered so far because it does not consider violence simply as one means (amongst others) that can be used to attain political goals (Hutchings 2007). Rather, it understands that the practice of violence itself, as a political means, relies on and reproduces gendered relations of power. From the feminist point of view, this makes the question of the justice of responses to widespread violent violations of human rights – which themselves are deeply gendered – particularly difficult. The experience of women on the ground in conflict situations testifies to the fact that violence against women often does not stop at the point of ceasefire, and that peace agreements rarely take account of women's interests. This means that the boundary between conflict and peace is blurred from the feminist point of view and it is, therefore, harder to arrive at some kind of list of criteria by which to decide when intervention might be justified as opposed to when it might not (Sjoberg 2006). Again, taking their cue from feminist activists, feminist theorists have argued for a multi-level approach to the question of a just peace (Robinson 1999: 142–46).

On the face of it, feminist accounts of global justice are the most aspirational of the perspectives we have considered. In general, it is clear that the principles underlying what counts as just in the current international order do not fundamentally challenge gendered relations of power, their reproduction and effects. However, some recent institutional developments do reflect feminist concerns. The institutionalization of UNSCR 1325, which calls for the integration of a gender perspective into all aspects of peace-making, peace-keeping and peace-building, and the explicit identification of sexual violence as a war crime recognized by the International Criminal Tribunal for the former Yugoslavia (ICTY), International Criminal Tribunal for Rwanda (ICTR) and the International

Criminal Court (ICC), were both the result of active feminist lobbying at the level of global governmental institutions (Hill *et al.* 2003; Spees 2003). So, too, was the recognition by Amnesty International of domestic violence as a violation of women's human rights (Youngs 2003). At the same time, at the civil society level, there are innumerable examples of feminist ideas having an impact on transnational and local women's movements campaigning around economic, environmental and peace issues (Mertus 2000; Helms 2003).

It was suggested earlier in this chapter that critical theory shifts the traditional division of labour between political theory, political science and political action, and that this has particularly significant consequences once the context of debate about justice no longer takes the liberal nation-state – and, therefore, like-minded fellow citizens – for granted. Feminist perspectives on global justice also follow this trajectory, and develop it further. Not only do feminist theories of global justice require specific and contextual knowledge about what is unjust to whom and how, they also actively involve those experiencing injustice – the 'objects', as it were, of theories of global justice – in the formulation of theory. There are fierce debates within feminism about how this can be done without reproducing the politics of toleration entrenched in contractualist and human rights thinking (see, for example, the contrast between Nussbaum 2000 and Ackerley 2008). Nevertheless, however flawed feminist attempts to democratize theories of global justice might have been so far, they go some way to responding to critical theory's aspiration to move political theory from a grounding in monological reasoning to a grounding in inter-subjective communication. In feminist theories of justice, therefore, normative theory no longer operates as the source of moral commands, which it is the task of political scientists and political actors to help to actualize. Instead, normative theory is formulated through collaborative engagement with the knowledge and insights of political scientists and political actors. When the context for this engagement is global economic, ecological and political relations, the normative theorist is obliged to come to grips with his or her own status as the product of a particular history that is not necessarily the same as that of the audience he or she is trying to persuade, or the people he or she is trying to help.

Conclusion: the future of theorizing global justice

Theories of global justice set out to establish the principles and values that ought to govern matters of global concern, such as global economic inequality, planetary destruction and extreme political violence. These principles provide a reference point in relation to which the world may be judged, but also embody goals towards which 'we' ought to strive. Unsurprisingly, in an international order dominated by liberal values, the policies adopted by states and international governmental organizations to the challenges of inequality, global warming and political violence are most closely linked to the assumptions of contractualism. In addition, human rights arguments have played an increasingly important part in the rhetoric and practice of international actors in both governmental and non-governmental sectors since the 1980s – to the extent that it has been argued that this is an example of theory influencing practice and changing the principles of international order (Risse *et al.* 1999; Wheeler 2000). Much of the work done on the question of global justice has pointed to the contradiction between state-based and individual rights-based principles at work in international norms, but also to the way that both are principles inherent in the liberalism that emerged as the dominant international ideology in the wake of the end of the Cold War (Brown 2002).

All of the theories examined recognize that they are idealizations. However, all of them are also linked to principles, institutions and practices already at work in global formal and informal political relations. Contractualists can point to the principle of state sovereignty; human rights theorists to a range of international human rights regimes, exercises in humanitarian intervention and developments such as the setting up of the International Criminal Court. Critical theorists, in turn, can point to transnational deliberative forums at the UN or EU, or feminists to the passing of UN Resolution 1325 as evidence of the actual political significance of the ideas of justice they uphold. And all will argue that their ideals of global justice provide normative discourses that political actors can use to challenge and transform the global *status quo*. All of these theories of justice are global, in the sense that they aim to be global in their scope of application. But to what extent are they global as modes of theorizing?

On the face of it, contractualism and human rights thinking are more obviously global as theoretical discourses than either critical theory or feminism. Not only are they both much more recognized and institutionalized in global political practice, but both are also grounded in what are claimed to be universal truths about human individuals. From the point of view of these perspectives, just as the nature of the just state can be worked out monologically and yet be universally applicable, so too can the nature of the just world. For these theories, there is no need to re-think the mode of theorizing used to address justice in the liberal state in order to grapple with questions of global justice. It is assumed that theories of justice can be formulated in abstraction from actual global economic, ecological and political realities.

In this context, global economic, ecological and political realities only become important in the *application* of political theory, not in its formulation. Understanding such realities is the task of political science, and political theorists will select from the arguments of political scientists in ways that are compatible with their prior normative orientation. The addressee of the discourses of contractualism and human rights theories continues to be a generalized 'reasonable' other, by definition the person who shares similar assumptions. Within these theories, the claims of global justice are formulated in terms of what the rich owe to the poor or the well-ordered to the disordered. The implict 'we' that is the audience of these claims are the rich and the well ordered, those who know what a just society looks like and need to extend those lessons to the rest of the world. On such accounts, global justice is in the gift of the rich and ordered, both because they know what it is and because only they can make it happen.

Critical theory and feminist discourses overlap with elements of contractualism and human rights approaches, but they also bring something new into the picture, in the sense that they both call for the *democratization* not only of global political relations but also of the *process of theorizing global justice*. Where contractualism and human rights theory leave the political theorist in exactly the same place, whether thinking about justice within or beyond the state, critical and feminist theories suggest a radical displacement of the theorist's authority once global justice is in question. Critical and feminist theorists, if taking their own assumptions seriously, must take on board the implications of their own status as political actors in a complex, hierarchical and contested global order. This should not be taken to mean that they cease making claims about justice but, rather, that they acknowledge the contextuality of those claims and that their meaning might not be the same for those listening as it is for those speaking. This means a re-thinking of the traditional division of labour between persons theorizing global justice, those studying global relations of economic and political power, and global political actors, whether in formal or informal sectors.

The idea that predominant ways of executing political theory are too remote from the realities of political life is not new. There are reasons to be sceptical of undertaking political theory as if it were applied ethics, even where justice within the liberal state is in question (Williams 2005;

Geuss 2008). But it seems to me that the problems of liberal political theory become particularly stark and obvious when its concerns move from justice within the liberal state to global justice. In this context, the reliance of the plausibility of the normative priorities of liberalism on a commonality of history and situation between theorist and audience becomes powerfully obvious. Theories of global justice need to speak to a global audience. An exercise in humanitarian intervention on human rights grounds might simultaneously be the prevention of the worst injustice of genocide to one person and the repetition of the worst injustice of imperialism to another. Hierarchies of moral outrage tend to reflect particular histories. Only through engagement between these histories can a global theory of justice be *constructed* as opposed to *discovered*. Current predominant contractualist and human rights approaches to theorizing global justice will, in my view, increasingly be challenged to adapt their thinking in order to speak to a global audience. As this happens, political theorists will increasingly embrace the trajectory that moves beyond statism and globalism, and re-works the division of labour between normative theory, political science and political activism.

References

Ackerly, B. (2008) *Universal Human Rights in a World of Difference*, Cambridge: Cambridge University Press.

Advisory Centre on World Trade Law (no date) Available at http://www.acwl.ch/e/index_e.aspx.

Alber, J. (1995) 'A Framework for the Comparative Study of Social Services', *Journal of European Social Policy*, 5(2): 131–49.

Albert, B. (2004) 'Is Disability Really on the Development Agenda? A Review of Official Disability Policies of the Major Governmental and International Development Agencies', DKaR. Available at: http://www.disabilitykar.net/research/red_pov.html.

Albert, M. (1993) *Capitalism vs. Capitalism: How America's Obsession with Individual Achievement and Short-term Profit Has Led It to the Brink of Collapse*, New York: Four Walls Eight Windows.

Almond, G. and Verba, S. (1963) *The Civic Culture*, Princeton: Princeton University Press.

Almond, G. and Verba, S. (eds) (1980) *The Civic Culture Revisited*, Boston: Little, Brown & Co.

Alvarez, S.E. (1999) 'Advocating Feminism: The Latin American Feminist NGO "Boom"', *International Feminist Journal of Politics*, 1(2): 181–209.

Amin, A. and Thrift, N. (1995) 'Institutional Issues for the European Regions: From Markets and Plans to Socio-economy and Powers of Association', *Economy and Society*, 24(1): 41–66.

Anand, S. and Sen, A. (1995) 'Gender Inequality in Human Development'. Available at http://origin-hdr.undp.org/en/reports/global/hdr1995/papers/sudhir_anand_amartya_sen.pdf.

Anand, S. and Sen, A. (2000) 'The Income Component of the Human Development Index', *Journal of Human Development*, 1(1): 17–23.

Andersen, R., Tilley, J. and Heath, A. (2005) 'Political Knowledge and Enlightened Preferences: Party Choice through the Electoral Cycle', *British Journal of Political Science*, 35(2): 285–302.

Archibugi, D. (2004) 'Cosmopolitan Democracy and its Critics: A Review', *European Journal of International Relations*, 10(3): 437–73.

Armstrong, C. (2006) *Rethinking Equality: The Challenge of Equal Citizenship*, Manchester: Manchester University Press.

Arneson, R. (2001) 'Luck and Equality', *Proceedings of the Aristotelian Society Supplement*, 73–90.

Atkeson, L. and Partin, R. (1995) 'Economic and Referendum Voting: A Comparison of Gubernatorial and Senatorial Elections', *American Political Science Review*, 89(1): 99–107.

Avaaz (no date) Available at www.avaaz.org.

Ayres, R.L. (1983) *Banking on the Poor: The World Bank and World Poverty*, Cambridge, MA: MIT Press.

Bacchi, C. and J. Eveline (2004) 'Mainstreaming and Neoliberalism: A Contested Relationship', *Policy and Society: Journal of Public, Foreign and Global Policy*, 22(2); 98–118.

Back, L. (1996) *New Ethnicities and Urban Culture: Racisms and Multiculture in Young Lives*, London: Routledge.

Bader, V. (2003) 'Taking Religious Pluralism Seriously', *Ethical Theory and Moral Practice*, 5(1): 3–22.

Bagguley, P. and Hussain, Y. (2008) *Riotous Citizens: Ethnic Conflict in Multicultural Britain*, Aldershot: Ashgate.

Baker, J., Lynch, K., Cantillon, S. and Walsh, J. (2004) *Equality: From Theory to Action*, Basingstoke: Palgrave.

Baldwin, D. (1997) 'The Concept of Security', *Review of International Studies*, 23(1): 5–26.

Bale, T., Taggart, P. and Webb, P. (2006) 'You Can't Always Get What You Want: Populism and the Power Inquiry', *Political Quarterly*, 77(2): 195–203.

Banaszak, L.-A., Beckwith, K. and Rucht, D. (2003) 'When Power Relocates: Interactive Changes in Women's Movements and States', in L.A. Banaszak, K. Beckwith and D. Rucht (eds), *Women's Movements Facing the Reconfigured State*, Cambridge: Cambridge University Press.

Bank for International Settlements (2007) *Triennial Central Bank Survey: Foreign Exchange and Derivative Market Activity in 2007*, December, Basle: BIS. Available at http://www.bis.org/publ/rpfxf07t.pdf

Banting, K. and Simeon, R. (1985) 'Introduction: The Politics of Constitutional Change', in K. Banting and R. Simeon (eds), *Redesigning the State. The Politics of Constitutional Change in Industrial Democracies*, Toronto: University of Toronto Press.

Bardeesy, K. (2008) 'Structured by Cows'. Available at http://tbm. thebigmoney.com/articles/juicy-bits/2008/10/22/%E2%80%9C structuredcows%E2%80%9D (accessed 18 November 2008).

Barnett, A., Held, D., and Henderson, C. (eds) (2005) *Debating Globalization*, Cambridge: Polity.

Barnett, J. (2003) 'Security and Climate Change', *Global Environmental Change*, 13(1): 7–17.

Barnett, M. and Snyder, J. (2008) 'The Grand Strategies of Humanitarianism', in M. Barnett and T.G. Weiss (eds), *Humanitarianism in Question: Politics, Power, Ethics*, Ithaca: Cornell University Press.

Barry, B. (1998) 'International Society from a Cosmopolitan Perspective', in D. Mapel and T. Nardin (eds), *International Society: Diverse Ethical Perspectives*, Princeton: Princeton University Press.

Barry, B. (2001) *Culture and Equality*, Cambridge: Polity Press.

Bartolini, S. (2000) *The Political Mobilization of the European Left, 1860–1980*, Cambridge: Cambridge University Press.

Bartolini, S. (2004) 'Old and New Peripheries in the Processes of European Integration', in C. Ansell and G. Di Palma (eds), *Restructuring Territoriality: Europe and the United States Compared*, Cambridge: Cambridge University Press.

Bartolini, S. (2005) *Restructuring Europe: Centre Formation, System Building and Political Structuring between the Nation-state and the European Union*, Oxford: Oxford University Press.

Bartolini, S. and Mair, P. (1990) *Identity, Competition, and Electoral Availability: The Stabilisation of European Electorates 1885–1985*, Cambridge: Cambridge University Press.

Barton, J.H., Goldstein, J.L., Josling, T.E. and Steinberg, R.H. (2006) *The Evolution of the Trade Regime: Politics, Law, and Economics of the GATT and the WTO*, Princeton: Princeton University Press.

Barzelay, M. (2000) *The New Public Management: Improving Research and Policy Dialogue*, Berkeley: University of California Press.

Bates, S.R. and Jenkins, L. (2007) 'Teaching and Learning Ontology and Epistemology in Political Science', *Politics*, 27(1): 55–63.

Beck, U. (1992) *Risk Society: Towards a New Modernity*, trans. M. Ritter, London: Sage.

Beck, U. (2000) *What is Globalization?*, Cambridge: Polity Press.

Beck, U. (2002) 'The Terrorist Threat: World Risk Society Revisited', *Theory, Culture and Society*, 19(4): 39–55.

Beck, U. (2003) 'Toward a New Critical Theory with a Cosmopolitan Intent', *Constellations*, 10(4): 453–68.

Beck, U. (2004) 'Cosmopolitan Realism: On the Distinction between Cosmopolitanism in Philosophy and the Social Sciences', *Global Networks*, 4(2): 131–56.

Beck, U. (2007) 'The Cosmopolitan Condition. Why Methodological Nationalism Fails', *Theory, Culture and Society*, 24(7–8): 286–90.

Beck, U. and Grande, E. (2007) *Cosmopolitan Europe*, Cambridge: Polity

Beck, U. and Sznaider, N. (2006) 'Unpacking Cosmopolitanism for the Social Sciences: A Research Agenda', *British Journal of Sociology*, 57(1): 1–23.

Beetham, D. (1994) 'Key Principles and Indices for a Democratic Audit', in D. Beetham (ed.), *Defining and Measuring Democracy*, London: Sage.

Beitz, C.R. (1979) *Political Theory in International Relations*, Princeton: Princeton University Press.

Beland, D. and Lecours, A. (2008) *Nationalism and Social Policy. The Politics of Territorial Solidarity*, Oxford: Oxford University Press.

Belasco, A. (2008) 'The Cost of Iraq, Afghanistan, and Other Global War on Terror Operations Since 9/11'. Available at http://www.fas.org/sgp/crs/natsec/RL33110.pdf.

Bell, M. (2002) *Anti-Discrimination Law and the European Union*, Oxford: Oxford University Press.

Bell, M. (2008) 'The Implementation of European Anti-Discrimination Directives: Converging towards a Common Model?', *Political Quarterly*, 79(1): 36–44.

Bellamy, A. (2008) 'The Responsibility to Protect and the Problem of Military Intervention', *International Affairs*, 84(4): 615–39.

Benhabib, S. (1992) *Situating the Self: Gender, Community and Postmodernism in Contemporary Ethics*, New York: Routledge.

Benhabib, S. (2002) *The Claims of Culture: Equality and Diversity in the Global Era*, Princeton: Princeton University Press.

Benhabib, S. (2004) *The Rights of Others: Aliens, Residents and Citizens*, Cambridge: Cambridge University Press.

Benkler, Y. (2006) *The Wealth of Networks: How Social Production Transforms Markets and Freedom*, New Haven, CT: Yale University Press.

Benz, A. and Behnke, N. (eds) (2009) 'Federalism and Constitutional Change', *Publius. The Journal of Federalism*, 39/2, Special issue.

Bergqvist, C., Olsson Blandy, T. and Sainsbury, D. (2007) 'Swedish State Feminism: Continuity and Change', in J. Outshoorn and J. Kantola (eds), *Changing State Feminism*, Basingstoke: Palgrave Macmillan.

Bi, F. (2006) 'Alienation: The London Bombs, One Year On', *Open Democracy*, 3 July. Available at http://www.opendemocracy.net/articles/ViewPopUp Article.jsp?id=3&articleId=3704

Bigo, D. (2001) 'The Möbius Ribbon of Internal and External Security(ies)', in M. Albert, D. Jacobsen and Y. Lapid (eds), *Identities, Borders, Orders – Rethinking International Relations Theory*, London: University of Minnesota Press.

Billig, M. (1995) *Banal Nationalism*, London: Sage.

Bimber, B. (2001) 'Information and Political Engagement in America: The Search for Effects of Information Technology at the Individual Level', *Political Research Quarterly*, 54(1): 53–67.

Bimber, B. (2003) *Information and American Democracy: Technology in the Evolution of Political Power*, New York: Cambridge University Press.

Bimber, B. (2005) 'Reconceptualizing Collective Action in the Contemporary Media Environment', *Communication Theory*, 15: 365–88.

Blomfield, Adrian (2007) 'Putin in Nuclear Threat against Europe', *Daily Telegraph*, 5 June. Available at http://www.telegraph.co.uk/news/worldnews/1553593/Putin-in-nuclear-threat-against-Europe.html (accessed March 2009).

Bogdanor, V. (1999) *Devolution in the United Kingdom*, Oxford: Oxford University Press.

Bonoli, G. (2007) 'Time Matters: Postindustrialization, New Social Risks, and Welfare State Adaptation in Advanced Industrial Democracies Comparative', *Political Studies*, 40(5): 495–520.

Booth, K. (2007) *Theory of World Security*, Cambridge: Cambridge University Press.

Bordo, M.D., and Eichengreen, B.J. (2002) 'Crises Now and Then: What Lessons from the Last Era of Financial Globalization', *National Bureau of Economic Research Working Paper*, 8716, Cambridge, MA: NBER.

Bordo, M.D., Eichengreen, B.J. and Irwin, D.A. (1999) 'Is Globalization Today Really Different Than Globalization a Hundred Years Ago?', *National Bureau of Economic Research Working Paper*, 7195, June, Cambridge, MA: NBER.

Braithwaite, J. and Drahos, P. (2000) *Global Business Regulation*, Cambridge: Cambridge University Press.

Breitenbach, E., Brown, A., Mackay, F. and Webb, J. (eds) (2002) *The Changing Politics of Gender Equality in Britain*, Basingstoke: Palgrave.

Brenner, R. (2002) *The Boom and the Bubble: The US in the World Economy*, London: Verso.

Brenner, R.P. and Jeong, S.-J. (2009) 'Overproduction Not Financial Collapse Is the Heart of the Crisis: The US, East Asia, and the World', *Asia-Pacific Journal*. Available at http://www.globalresearch.ca/index.php?context=va&aid=13131.

Brogger, T. (2008) 'Europe Scrambles as Iceland's Banks Fail', *Bloomberg News*, 9 October.

Brown, C. (2002) *Sovereignty, Rights and Justice: International Political Theory Today*, Cambridge: Polity.

Brown, G. (2006) 'The Future of Britishness', Keynote Speech, Fabian Conference on The Future of Britishness, January, London. Available at http://www.fabian-society.org.uk/press _office/news_latest_all.asp?pressid=520.

Brown, G. (2008) 'National Security Statement', Labour Party. Available at http://www.labour.org.uk/gordon_brown_national_security_statement. 19 March (accessed March 2009).

Brown, G. (2009a) in *The United Kingdom's Strategy for Countering International Terrorism* CM7547, March 2009. Available at http://security.homeoffice.gov.uk/news-publications/publication-search/general/HO_Contest_strategy.pdf?view=Binary.

Brown, G. (2009b) 'PM's Speech about the Strategy on Afghanistan and Pakistan', House of Commons, 29 April. Available at http://www.number10.gov.uk/Page19166.

Brubaker, R. (2004) 'In the Name of the Nation: Reflections on Nationalism and Patriotism', *Citizenship Studies*, 8(2): 115–27.

Brubaker, R. (2005) *Ethnicity without Groups*, Cambridge USA: Harvard University Press.

Buiter, Willem (2008) 'The End of American Capitalism as We Knew It', *Financial Times*, 17 September. Available at http://blogs.ft.com/maverecon/2008/09/the-end-of-american-capitalism-as-we-knew-it/.

Burnheim, J. (1985) *Is Democracy Possible*, Cambridge: Polity.

Bustelo, M. (2009) 'Spain: Intersubjectivity faces the Strong Gender Norm', *International Feminist Journal of Politics*, 11(4).

Buzan, B. (1991) *People, States and Fear: National Security Problem in International Relations*, 2nd edn, London: Longman.

Buzan, B., Waever, O. and de Wilde, J. (1997) *Security – A New Framework for Analysis*, Boulder, CO: Lynne Rienner.

Cabinet Office (various) Citizenship Surveys. Available at http://www.cabinetoffice.gov.uk/third_sector/Research_and_statistics/third_sector_research/citizenship_survey.aspx.

Cabinet Office (2007) 'The Equalities Review' 2007. Available at archive.cabinetoffice.gov.uk/equalitiesreview/ (accessed 30 March 2009).

Cairns, A. (1977) 'The Governments and Societies of Canadian Federalism', *Canadian Journal of Political Science*, 10(4): 695–725.

Caney, S. (2005) *Justice beyond Borders: A Global Political Theory*, Oxford: Oxford University Press.

Caramani, D. (2004) *The Nationalization of Politics*, Cambridge: Cambridge University Press.

Carter, C. and Pasquier, R. (2010) 'Europeanisation of Regions as Spaces for Politics: A New Research Agenda', *Regional and Federal Studies*, 19, forthcoming.

Castells, M. (2000) *The Rise of the Networld Society, The Information Age: Economy, Society and Culture*, Volume 1, 2nd edn, Oxford: Blackwell.

Celis, K., Childs, S., Kantola, J. and Lena Krook, M. (2008) 'Rethinking Substantive Representation', *Representation*, 42(2): 99–110.

Cerny, P.G. (1995) 'Globalization and the Changing Logic of Collective Action', *International Organization*, 49(4): 595–625.

Cerny, P. (1997) 'Paradoxes of the Competition State', *Government and Opposition*, 32(2): 251–74.

Chadwick, A. and Howard, P. (2009) *Handbook of Internet Politics*, London: Routledge.

Channel 4 (2006) NOP Survey of Muslims in Britain. Available at http://www.channel4.com/news/microsites/D/dispatches2006/muslim_survey/index.html.

Chappell, L. (2002) *Gender Government: Feminist Engagement with the State in Australia and Canada*, Vancouver: UBC Press.

Chernilo, D. (2006) 'Social Theory's Methodological Nationalism. Myth and Reality', *European Journal of Social Theory*, 9(1): 5–22.

Chernilo, D. (2007) *A Social Theory of the Nation-State: The Political Forms of Modernity Beyond Methodological Nationalism*, London: Routledge.

Chibber, P. and Kollman, K. (2004) *The Formation of National Party Systems*, Princeton: Princeton University Press.

Chinkin, C. (1998) 'International Law and Human Rights', in T. Evans (ed.), *Human Rights Fifty Years On: A Reappraisal*, Manchester: Manchester University Press.

Clapham, C. (1999) 'Sovereignty and the Third World State', *Political Studies*, 47(3): 522–37.

Clarke, H., Sanders, D., Stewart, M., and Whiteley, P. (2004) *Political Choice in Britain*, Oxford: Oxford University Press.

Clarke, H., Sanders, D., Stewart, M., and Whiteley, P. (2009) *Performance Politics and the British Voter*, Cambridge: Cambridge University Press.

Climate Security Now (no date) 'Warming Means War'. Available at http://www.globalclimatesecurity.org/home.

Cockburn, C. and Zarkov, D. (eds) (2002) *The Postwar Moment: Militaries, Masculinities and International Peacekeeping*, London: Lawrence & Wishart.

Cohen, B.J. (2009) 'Striking a Nerve', *Review of International Political Economy*, 16(1): 136–43.

Cohen, G. (2000) *If You're an Egalitarian, How Come You're So Rich?* Cambridge, MA: Harvard University Press.

Cohen, P. (ed.) (1999) *New Ethnicities, Old Racisms*, London: Zed Books.

Cole, P. (2000) *Philosophies of Exclusion: Liberal Political Theory and Immigration*, Edinburgh: Edinburgh University Press.

Colomer, J. (1995) *Game Theory and The Transition to Democracy: The Spanish Model*, Brookfield, VT: Edward Elgar.

Colomer, J. (2009) *The Science of Politics*, New York: Oxford University Press.

Communities and Local Government (2007) Citizenship Survey: April–June 2007, England and Wales. Available at: http://www.communities.gov.uk/documents/corporate/pdf/citizenshipsurveyaprjun 2007.pdf.

Conaghan, J. (2009) 'Intersectionality and the Feminist Project of Law', in E. Grabham, D. Cooper, J. Krishnadas and D. Herman (eds), *Intersectionality and Beyond: Law, Power and the Politics of Location* (Abingdon: Routledge-Cavendish): 21–48.

Conceição, P. (2003) 'Assessing the Provision Status of Global Public Goods', in I. Kaul, P. Conceição, K. Le Goulven and R.U. Mendoza (eds), *Providing Public Global Goods*, Oxford: Oxford University Press.

Cooke, P. and Morgan, K. (1998) *The Associational Economy: Firms, Regions and Innovation*, Oxford: Oxford University Press.

Cooper, D. (2004) *Challenging Diversity: Rethinking Equality and the Value of Differences*, Cambridge: Cambridge University Press.

Cormack, J. and Bell, M. (2005) *Developing Anti-Discrimination Law in Europe*. Available at http://www.migpolgroup.com/multiattachments/3077/DocumentName/legal_comparative1_en.pdf.

Cox, M. (2001) 'Introduction', in E.H. Carr, *The Twenty Years Crisis*, Basingstoke: Palgrave.

Crenshaw, K. (1991) 'Demarginalizing the Intersection of Race and Sex: A Black Feminist Critique of Antidiscrimination Doctrine, Feminist Theory and Antiracist Politics', in K. Bartlett and R. Kennedy (eds), *Feminist Legal Theory: Readings in Law and Gender*, San Francisco: Westview Press.

Crick, B. (2000) *In Defence of Politics*, 5th edn, London: Continuum.

Crouch, C. (2005a) *Capitalist Diversity and Change: Recombinant Governance and Institutional Entrepreneurs*, Oxford: Oxford University Press.

Crouch, C. (2005b) 'Models of Capitalism', *New Political Economy*, 10(4): 439–56.

Curtice, J. (2006) 'Is Holyrood Accountable and Representative?', in C. Bromley, J. Curtice, D. McCrone and A. Park (eds), *Has Devolution Delivered?*, Edinburgh: Edinburgh University Press.

Cutler, F. (2008) 'One Voter, Two First-Order Elections?, *Electoral Studies*, 27(3): 492–504.

Dahl, R.A. (1989) *Democracy and its Critics*, New Haven: Yale University Press.

Dahlerup, D. and Freidenvall, L. (2005) 'Quotas as a "Fast Track" to Equal Representation for Women. Why Scandinavia is No Longer the Model', *International Feminist Journal of Politics*, 7(1): 26–48.

Dalton, R. and Klingemann, H. (2007) *The Oxford Handbook of Political Behaviour*, Oxford: Oxford University Press.

Daly, M. (2005) 'Gender Mainstreaming in Theory and Practice', *Social Politics*, 12(3); 433–50.

Dani, R. (2005) 'Making Globalization Work for Development', Paper presented at the Ralph Miliband Lecture, London School of Economics, 31 January 2007.

Daniels, N. (ed.) (1975) *Reading Rawls: Critical Studies of A Theory of Justice*, Oxford: Blackwell.

Dardanelli, P. (2005) *Between Two Unions: Europeanization and Scottish Devolution*, Manchester: Manchester University Press.

DAW (Division for the Advancement of Women, United Nations) (2004) *Directory of National Machineries for the Advancement of Women*. Available at http://www.un.org/womenwatch/daw/egm/nationalm2004/AideMemoire_18Oct04.pdf.

de Jong, W., Shaw, M. and Stammers, N. (eds) (2005) *Global Activism, Global Media*, London: Pluto.

de Rynck, S. and Dezeure, K. (2006) 'Policy Convergence and Divergence in Belgium: Education and Health Care', *West European Politics*, 29(5): 1018–33.

de Vita, A. (2007) 'Inequality and Poverty in Global Perspective', in T. Pogge (ed.), *Freedom from Poverty as a Human Right*, Oxford: Oxford University Press.

de Winter L., Swyngedouw, M. and Dumont, P. (2006) 'Party System(s) and Electoral Behaviour in Belgium: From Stability to Balkanisation', *West European Politics*, 29(5): 933–56.

Deacon, B. (2003) 'Global Social Governance Reform: From Institutions and Policies to Networks, Projects and Partnerships', in B. Deacon, E. Ollida, M. Koivusalo and P. Stubbs (eds), *Global Social Governance: Themes and Prospects*, Helsinki: Ministry for Foreign Affairs of Finland, Department for International Development Cooperation.

Deibert, R., Palfrey, J., Rohozinski, R. and Zittrain, J. (2008) *Access Denied: The Practice and Policy of Global Internet Filtering*, Cambridge, MA: MIT Press.

Denver, D. (2005) 'Valence Politics: How Britain Votes Now', *British Journal of Politics and International Relations*, 7(3): 292–9.

Denver, D., Johns, R., Mitchell, J. and Pattie, C. (2007) 'The Holyrood Elections 2007: Explaining the Results'. Available at www.scottishelectionstudy. org.uk/paperspubs.htm.

Deschouwer, K. (2008) 'Towards a Regionalisation of Statewide Electoral Trends in Decentralized States? The Cases of Belgium and Spain', in W. Swenden and B. Maddens (eds), *Territorial Party Politics in Western Europe*, Basingstoke: Palgrave Macmillan.

DHS (Department of Homeland Security) (2008) *Strategic Plan*. Available at http://www.dhs.gov/xlibrary/assets/DHS_StratPlan_FINAL_spread.pdf.

Dicken, P. (2007) *Global Shift: Mapping the Changing Contours of the World Economy*, 5th edn, New York: Guilford Press.

Diebert, R., Palfrey, J., Rohozinski, R. and Zittrain (eds) (2008) *Access Denied: The Practice and Policy of Global Internet Filtering*, Cambridge, MA: MIT Press.

Dillon, M. (2007) 'Governing Terror: The State of Emergency of Biopolitical Emergence', *International Political Sociology*, 1(1): 7–28.

Donnelly, J. (1989) *Universal Human Rights in Theory and Practice*, Ithaca, NY: Cornell University Press.

Dorling, D., Vickers, D., Thomas, B., Pritchard, J. and Ballas, D. (2008) *Changing UK. The Way We Live Now*, Report commissioned by BBC Regions and Nations. Available at http://sasi.group.shef.ac.uk/research/changingUK.html.

Dowding, K. (1995) 'Model or Metaphor? A Critical Review of the Policy Network Approach', *Political Studies*, 45(1): 136–58.

Dower, N. (2007) *World Ethics: A New Agenda*, 2nd edn, Edinburgh: Edinburgh University Press.

Downs, A. (1957) *An Economic Theory of Democracy*, New York: Harpers & Row.

Drew, D. and Weaver, D. (2006) 'Voter Learning in the 2004 Presidential Election: Did the Media Matter?', *Journalism and Mass Communication Quarterly*, 83(1): 25–42.

Du Bois, W.E.B. (1999 [1903]) *The Souls of Black Folk Centenary Edition*, H.L. Gates Jr and H. Oliver (eds), London: Norton Critical Edition.

Dunleavy, P. (1995) 'Policy Disasters: Explaining the UK's Record', *Public Policy and Administration*, 10(2): 52–70.

Dunleavy, P., Margetts, H., Bastow, S., Pearce, O. and Tinkler, J. (2007) *Government on the Internet: Progress in Delivering Information and Services Online*, Value for Money Study by the UK National Audit Office, London: Stationery Office, HC 529.

Dunleavy, P., Margetts, H., Bastow, S. and Tinkler, J. (2005) 'New Public Management Is Dead – Long Live Digital-Era Governance', *Journal of Public Administration Research and Theory*, 16(3): 467–94.

Dunleavy, P., Margetts, H., Bastow, S. and Tinkler, J. (2006) *Digital-era Governance: IT Corporations, the State and e-Government*, Oxford: Oxford University Press.

Dunn, J. (1990) *Interpreting Political Responsibility*, Cambridge: Polity.

Dutton, W.H., di Gennaro, C. and Millwood, A. (2005) *The Internet in Britain: The Oxford Internet Survey (OxIS) 2005*, Oxford: Oxford Internet Institute.

Dutton, W.H. and Helsper, E. (2007) *The Internet in Britain: The Oxford Internet Survey (OxIS) 2007*, Oxford: Oxford Internet Institute.

Dutton, W.H., Helsper, E. and Gerber, M. (2009) *The Internet in Britain: The Oxford Internet Survey (OxIS) 2009*, Oxford: Oxford Internet Institute.

Duverger, M. (1964 [1951]) *Political Parties*, Methuen: London.

Dworkin, R. (2002) *Sovereign Virtue: The Theory and Practice of Equality*, Cambridge: Cambridge University Press.

Easton, D. (1957) 'An Approach to the Analysis of Political Systems', *World Politics*, 9: 383–400.

Easton, D. (1965) *A Systems Analysis of Political Life*, New York: Wiley.

Ebeid, M. and Rodden, J. (2006) 'Economic Geography and Economic Voting: Evidence from the US States', *British Journal of Political Science*, 36(3): 527–47.

Egeberg, M. (2008) 'European Government(s): Executive Politics in Transition', *West European Politics*, 31(1): 235–57.

Eichengreen, B.J. (1985) *The Gold Standard in Theory and History*, New York: Methuen.

Eichengreen, B.J. (2009) 'Financial re-regulation, Yes. But Europe's Cacophony of Ideas is Counterproductive', *Europe's World*, Summer. Available at http://www.europesworld.org/NewEnglish/Home/Article/tabid/191/Article Type/ArticleView/ArticleID/21423/language/en-US/Financial reregulationyesButEuropescacophonyofideasiscounterproductive.aspx.

Eisenberg, A. and Spinner-Halev, J. (eds) (2005) *Minorities within Minorities: Equality, Rights and Diversity*, Cambridge: Cambridge University Press.

Escher, T., Margetts, H., Petricek, V. and Cox, I. (2006) 'Governing from the Centre? Comparing the Nodality of Digital Governments', Presented at the 2006 Annual Meeting of the American Political Science Association, 31 August–4 September.

Evans, P., Rueschemeyer, D. and Skocpol, T. (1985) *Bringing the State Back In*, Cambridge: Cambridge University Press.

Everard, J. (2000) *Virtual States: The Internet and the Boundaries of the Nation-State*, London: Routledge.

Falk, R. (2000) 'A New "Medievalism"', in G. Fry and J. O'Hagan (eds), *Contending Images of World Politics*, Basingstoke: Macmillan.

Favell, A. and Modood, T. (2003) 'The Philosophy of Multiculturalism: The Theory and Practice of Normative Political Theory', in A. Finlayson (ed.), *Contemporary Political Thought: A Reader and Guide*, Edinburgh: Edinburgh University Press.

Feddersen, T. and Pesendorfer, W. (1996) 'The Swing Voter's Curse', *American Economic Review*, 86(3): 408–24.

Feddersen, T. and Pesendorfer, W. (1999) 'Abstention in Elections with Asymmetric Information and Diverse Preferences', *American Political Science Review*, 93(2): 381–98.

Ferrera, M. (2005) *The Boundaries of Welfare: European Integration and the New Spatial Politics of Social Protection*, Oxford: Oxford University Press.

Fieldhouse, E., Tranmer, M. and Russell, A. (2007) 'Something about Young People or Something about Elections? Electoral Participation of Young People in Europe: Evidence from a Multilevel Analysis of the European Social Survey', *European Journal of Political Research*, 46(6): 797–822.

Fisher, S., Lessard-Phillips, L., Hobolt, S. and Curtice, J. (2006) 'How the Effect of Political Knowledge on Turnout Differs in Plurality Electoral Systems', Paper presented at the annual meeting of the American Political Science Association, Marriott, Loews Philadelphia, and the Pennsylvania Convention Center, Philadelphia, PA, 31 August.

Flax, J. and Okin, S.M. (1995) 'Race/Gender and the Ethics of Difference: A Reply to Okin's "Gender Inequality and Cultural Differences"', *Political Theory*, 23(3): 500–10.

Flora, P. (1986) 'Introduction', in P. Flora (ed.), *Growth to Limits: The European Welfare States Since World War II*, Berlin: De Gruyter.

Flora, P. (1999) *State Formation, Nation Building and Mass Participation in Europe. The Theory of Stein Rokkan*, Oxford: Oxford University Press.

Flora, P. and Alber, J. (1981) 'Modernization, Democratization and the Development of Welfare States in Western Europe', in P. Flora and A. Heidenheimer (eds), *The Development of Welfare States in Europe and America*, New Brunswick, NJ: Transaction Books.

Forestor, J. (2006) 'Policy Analysis as Critical Listening', in M. Moran, M. Rein and R.E. Goodin (eds), *The Oxford Handbook of Public Policy*, Oxford: Oxford University Press.

Forst, R. (2001) 'Towards a Critical Theory of Transnational Justice', in T. Pogge (ed.), *Global Justice*, Oxford: Blackwell.

Frankel, J.A. (ed.) (1998) *The Regionalisation of the World Economy*, Cambridge, MA: NBER.

Fraser, N. (1992) 'Rethinking the Public Sphere', in C. Calhoun (ed.), *Habermas and the Public Sphere*, Cambridge, MA: MIT Press.

Fraser, N. (1995) 'Recognition or Redistribution? A Critical Reading of Iris Young's "Justice and the Politics of Difference"', *Journal of Political Philosophy*, 3(2): 166–80.

Fraser, N. (2000) 'Rethinking Recognition', *New Left Review*, 3: 107–20.

Fraser, N. (2005) 'Reframing Justice in a Globalizing World', *New Left Review*, 36: 69–88.

Fraser, N. (2007) 'Transnationalizing the Public Sphere: On the Legitimacy and Efficacy of Public Opinion in a Post-Westphalian World', *Theory, Culture and Society*, 24(4): 7–30.

Fredman, S. (2002) 'The Future of Equality in Britain', *EOC Working Paper Series*, 5, Manchester: Equal Opportunities Commission.

Fredman, S. (2008) 'Positive Rights and Positive Duties: Addressing Intersectionality', in D. Schiek and V. Chege (eds), *European Union Non-*

discrimination Law. Comparative Perspectives on Multidimensional Equality Law, London: Routledge.

Fredman. S. and Spencer, S. (eds) (2003) *Age as an Equality Issue*, Oxford and Portland, OR: Hart Publishers.

G20 (2009a) 'London Summit – Leaders' Statement 2 April 2009', London: G20, Communique 2 April. Available at http://www.g20.org/Documents/g20_communique_020409.pdf.

G20 (2009b) 'London Summit – Leaders' Statement 2 April 2009: Annex 1 Declaration on Strengthening the Financial System', London: G20, Communique 2 April. Available at http://www.londonsummit.gov.uk/resources/en/PDF/annex-strengthening-fin-sysm.

Gallega, R., Goma, R. and Subirats, J. (2005) 'Spain, from State Welfare to Regional Welfare?', in N. McEwen and L. Moreno (eds), *The Territorial Politics of Welfare*, London: Routledge.

Gamble, A. (2000) *Politics and Fate*, Cambridge: Polity.

Garrett, G. (1998) *Partisan Politics in the Global Economy*, Cambridge: Cambridge University Press.

Garrett, R.K. (2006) 'Protest in an Information Society. A Review of Literature on Social Movements and New ICTs', *Information, Communication & Society*, 9(2): 202–24.

Geuss, R. (2008) *Philosophy and Real Politics*, Princeton: Princeton University Press.

GfK NOP Social Research (2006) 'Attitudes to Living in Britain: A Survey of Muslim Opinion'. Available at http://www.gfknop.co.uk/content/news/news/Channel4_MuslimsBritain_toplinefindings.pdf.

Gibson, R. and Ward, S. (2009) 'Parties in the Digital Age – A Review Article', *Representation*, 45(1): 87–100.

Giddens, A. (1990) *The Consequences of Modernity*, Cambridge: Polity.

Giddens, A. (1999) 'Risk and Responsibility', *Modern Law Review*, 62(1): 1–10.

Gilpin, R. (1981) *War and Change in World Politics*, Cambridge: Cambridge University Press.

Gilpin, R. (2000) 'The Retreat of the State?', in T.C. Lawton, J.N. Rosenau and A.C. Verdun (eds), *Strange Power: Shaping the Parameters of International Relations and International Political Economy*, Aldershot: Ashgate.

Glasius, H , Kaldor, M. and Anheier, M. (eds) (2002) *Global Civil Society Yearbook*, Oxford: Oxford University Press.

Glazer, N. (1997) *We Are All Multiculturalists Now*, Cambridge, MA: Harvard University Press.

Goerres, A. (2007) 'Why are Older People more likely to Vote? The Impact of Ageing on Electoral Turnout', *British Journal of Politics and International Relations*, 9(1): 90–121.

Gonzalez-Bailon, S., Kaltenbrunner, A. and Banchs, R.E. (2009) 'The Structure of Political Discussion Networks: A Model for the Analysis of Online Deliberation', *Journal of Information Technology*.

Goodin, R.E. (1996) 'Institutions and Their Design', in R.E. Goodin (ed.), *The Theory of Institutional Design*, Cambridge: Cambridge University Press.

Goodwin, M. (2008) 'Multidimensional Exclusion: Viewing Romani Marginalisation through the Nexus of Race and Poverty', in D. Schiek and V. Chege (eds), *European Union Non-discrimination Law. Comparative Perspectives on Multidimensional Equality Law*, London: Routledge.

Goodwin M., Jones, M. and Jones, R. (2005) 'Devolution, Constitutional Change and Economic Development: Understanding the Shifting Economic and Political Geographies of The British State', *Regional Studies*, 39: 421–36.

Gourevitch, P.A., and Shinn, J. (2005) *Political Power and Corporate Control: The New Global Politics of Corporate Governance*, Princeton: Princeton University Press.

Grabham, E. (2009) 'Intersectionality: Traumatic Impressions', in E. Grabham, D. Cooper, J. Krishnadas and D. Herman (eds), *Intersectionality and Beyond: Law, Power and the Politics of Location*, Abingdon: Routledge-Cavendish.

Grabham, E. (with Herman, D., Cooper, D. and Krishnadas, J.) (2009) 'Introduction', in E. Grabham, D. Cooper, J. Krishnadas and D. Herman (eds), *Intersectionality and Beyond: Law, Power and the Politics of Location*, Abingdon: Routledge-Cavendish.

Grande, E. (2006) 'Cosmopolitan Political Science', *British Journal of Sociology*, 57(1): 87–111.

Greer, S. (ed.) (2006) *Territory, Democracy and Justice*, London: Palgrave Macmillan.

Guardian, The (2008) 'Watching the Watchdogs: The Only Way to Avoid Future Financial Crises is to Push for Robust Global Regulatory Oversight', 19 December.

Habermas, J. (1990) 'Discourse Ethics: Notes on a Programme of Philosophical Justification', in F. Dallmayr and S. Benhabib (eds), *The Communicative Ethics Controversy*, Cambridge, MA: MIT Press.

Habermas, J. (2001) *The Postnational Constellation: Political Essays*, Cambridge, MA: MIT Press.

Habermas, J. (2006) *The Divided West*, Cambridge: Polity Press.

Hague, R. and Harrop, M. (2007) *Comparative Government and Politics: An Introduction*, 7th edn, Basingstoke: Palgrave Macmillan (published in North America as *Political Science: A Comparative Introduction*, 5th edn).

Hall, P.A. and Soskice, D.W. (eds) (2001) *Varieties of Capitalism: The Institutional Foundations of Comparative Advantage*, Oxford: Oxford University Press.

Hall, S. (1992) 'New Ethnicities', in J. Donald and A. Rattansi (eds), *"Race", Culture and Difference*, London: Sage.

Hancock, A.-M. (2007) 'When Multiplication Doesn't Equal Quick Addition: Examining Intersectionality as a Research Paradigm', *Perspectives on Politics*, 5(1): 63–79.

Hansard Society (2008) *Audit of Political Engagement 5. The 2008 Report*, London: Hansard Society.

Hausmann, M. and Sauer, B. (eds) (2007) *Gendering the State in the Age of Globalization. Women's Movements and State Feminism in Post Industrial Democracies*, Boulder,CO and London: Rowman & Littlefield.

Hay, C. (1999) *The Political Economy of New Labour: Labouring under False Pretences*, Manchester: Manchester University Press.

Hay, C. (2002a) 'Globalization as a Problem of Political Analysis: Restoring Agents to a "Process without a Subject" and Politics to a Logic of Economic Compulsion', *Cambridge Review of International Affairs*, 15(3): 379–92.

Hay, C. (2002b) *Political Analysis*, Basingstoke: Palgrave.

Hay, C. (2004) 'The Normalizing Role of Rationalist Assumptions in the Institutional Embedding of Neoliberalism', *Economy and Society*, 33(4): 500–27.

Hay, C. (2006) 'What's Globalisation Got to Do with It?', *Government and Opposition*, 41(1): 1–22.

Hay, C. (2007a) 'Does Ontology Trump Epistemology? Notes on the Directional Dependence of Ontology and Epistemology in Political Analysis', *Politics*, 27(2): 115–18.

Hay, C. (2007b) *Why We Hate Politics*, Cambridge: Polity.

Hay, C. (2008) 'Globalization's Impact on States', in J. Ravenhill (ed.), *Global Political Economy*, 2nd edn, Oxford: Oxford University Press.

Hay, C. (2009) 'Good Inflation, Bad Inflation: The Housing Boom, Economic Growth and the Disaggregation of Inflationary Preferences in the UK and Ireland', *British Journal of Politics and International Studies*, 11(3): 461–78.

Hay, C. and Rosamond, B. (2002) 'Globalization, European Integration and the Discursive Construction of Economic Imperatives', *Journal of European Public Policy*, 9(2): 147–67.

Heald, D. and Jeffery, C. (eds) (2003) *Money Matters. Territorial Financial Arrangements I Decentralised States*, Regional and Federal Studies, 13(4), Special issue.

Hearl, D., Budge, I. and Peterson, B. (1996) 'Distinctiveness of Regional Voting: A Comparative Analysis across the European Community Countries (1979–1993)', *Electoral Studies*, 15(2): 167–82.

Heclo, H. (1978) Issue Networks and the Executive Establishment, in A. King (ed.), *The New American Political System*, Washington, DC: American Enterprise Institute.

Heclo, H. and Wildavsky, A. (1974) *The Private Government of Public Money*, London: Macmillan.

Hediar, K. (2006) 'Party Membership and Participation', in R. Katz and W. Crotty (eds), *Handbook of Party Politics*, London: Sage.

Held, D. (1995) *Democracy and the Global Order: From the Modern State to Cosmopolitan Governance*, Cambridge: Polity Press.

Held, D. (2002) 'Globalization, Corporate Practice and Cosmopolitan Social Standards', *Contemporary Political Theory*, 1(1): 59–78.

Held, D. (2004) *Global Covenant: The Social Democratic Alternative to the Washington Consensus*, Cambridge: Polity Press.

Held, D., and Kaldor, M. (2001) *What Hope for the Future?*. Available at www.lse.ac.uk/depts/global/maryheld.htm.

Held, D. and Kaya, A. (eds) (2006) *Global Inequality: Patterns and Explanations*, Cambridge: Polity.

Held, D. and McGrew, A. (2002a) *Globalization/Anti-Globalization*, Cambridge: Polity.

Held, D. and McGrew, A. (eds) (2002b) *Governing Globalization: Power, Authority and Global Governance*, Cambridge: Polity.

Held, D., McGrew, A., Goldblatt, D. and Perraton, J. (eds) (1999a) *The Global Transformations Reader*, Cambridge: Polity Press.

Held, D., McGrew, A., Goldblatt, D., and Perraton, J. (1999b) *Global Transformations: Politics, Economics and Culture*, Cambridge: Polity.

Held, V. (2006) *The Ethics of Care: Personal, Political and Global*, Oxford: Oxford University Press.

Helleiner, E. (1994) *States and the Re-emergence of Global Finance*, Ithaca, NY: Cornell University Press.

Helms, E. (2003) 'Women as Agents of Ethnic Reconciliation? Women NGOs and International Intervention in Postwar Bosnia-Herzegovina', *Women's Studies International Forum*, 26(1): 15–33.

Helsper, E. (2008) *Digital Inclusion: An Analysis of Social Disadvantage and the Information Society*, London: Department of Communities and Local Government.

Henderson, A. (2007) *Hierarchies of Belonging: National Identity and Political Culture in Scotland and Quebec*, Montreal, Kingston: McGill-Queen's University Press.

Hepburn, E. (ed.) (2009a) *New Challenges for Stateless Nationalist and Regionalist Parties*, *Regional and Federal Studies*, 19(4), Special issue.

Hepburn, E. (2009b) 'Introduction: Re-conceptualising Regional Mobilisation', *Regional and Federal Studies*, 19(4).

Hepple, B., Coussey, M. and Coudhury, T. (2000) *Equality: A New Framework*, Oxford and Portland, OR: Hart.

Herz, J. (1950) 'Idealist Internationalism and the Security Dilemma', *World Politics*, 2(2): 157–80.

Hibbing, J. and Theiss-Morse, E. (2002) *Stealth Democracy*, New York: Cambridge University Press.

Hill, F., Aboitz, M. and Poehlman-Doumbouya, S. (2003) 'Nongovernmental Organizations' Role in the Build up and Implementation of SCR 1325', *Signs: Journal of Women, Culture and Society*, 28(4): 1255–70.

Hill, J. (2004) *Inequality and the State*, Oxford: Oxford University Press.

Hirschman, A.O. (1980) *National Power and the Structure of Foreign Trade*, Expanded edn, Berkeley, CA: University of California Press.

Hirst, P. and Thompson, G. (1999) *Globalisation in Question*, 2nd edn, Cambridge: Polity Press.

HM Government (2007) *The Governance of Britain,* Cm 7170, 3 July. London: Stationery Office.

HM Treasury (2008) News release, 3 November. Available at http://www.hm-treasury.gov.uk/uk_financial_investments_limited.htm.

Hobson, B., Carson, M. and Lawrence, R. (2008) 'Recognition Struggles in Trans-national Arenas: Negotiating Identities and Framing Citizenship', in B. Siim and J. Squires (eds), *Contesting Citizenship*, London: Routledge.

Hobson, J.M. and Seabrooke, L. (2007) *Everyday Politics of the World Economy*, Cambridge: Cambridge University Press.

Hood, C. (1994) *Explaining Economic Policy Reversals*, Buckingham: Open University Press.

Hooghe, L. (1995) 'Sub-national Mobilisation in the European Union', in J. Hayward (ed.), *The Crisis of Representation in Europe*, London: Frank Cass.

Hooghe, L. and Marks, G. (2009) 'A Postfunctional Theory of European Integration: From Permissive Consensus to Constraining Dissensus', *British Journal of Political Science*, 39(1): 1–23.

Horiuchi, Y., Imai, K. and Taniguchi, N. (2005) 'Estimating the Causal Effects of Policy Information on Voter Turnout: An Internet-based Randomized Field Experiment in Japan', Paper presented at the annual meeting of the Midwest Political Science Association, Palmer House Hilton, Chicago, Illinois, 7 April. Available at http://www.allacademic.com/meta/p85172_index.html.

Hough, D. and Jeffery, C. (eds) (2006a) *Devolution and Electoral Politics*, Manchester: Manchester University Press.

Hough, D. and Jeffery, C. (2006b) 'Germany: An Erosion of Federal-Länder Linkages?', in D. Hough and C. Jeffery (eds), *Devolution and Electoral Politics*, Manchester: Manchester University Press.

Howard, M. and Tibballs, S. (2003) *Talking Equality: What Men and Women Think About Equality in Britain Today*, UK: Future Foundation.

Human Security Centre, Human Security Report 2005: War and Peace in the 21st Century. Available at http://www.humansecurityreport.info.

Hutchings, K. (2007) 'Feminist Ethics and Political Violence', *International Politics*, 44: 90–106.

Ikenberry, G.J. (2002) 'America's Imperial Ambition', *Foreign Affairs*, 81(5): 44–60.

Inglehart, R. and Norris, P. (2003) *Gender Equality and Cultural Change*, Cambridge: Cambridge University Press.

International Monetary Fund (2008) *Global Financial Stability Report: Constraining Systemic Risks and Restoring Financial Soundness*, Washington, DC: IMF, April. Available at http://www.imf.org/External/Pubs/FT/GFSR/2008/01/pdf/text.pdf.

International Monetary Fund (2009) *Global Financial Stability Report: Responding to the Financial Crisis and Measuring Systemic Risks*,

Washington, DC: IMF, April. Available at http://www.imf.org/External/Pubs/FT/GFSR/2009/01/pdf/text.pdf.

Ipsos/MORI (2009) *Expenses Poll for the BBC*, J26434 available at http://www.ipsos-mori.com/_assets/pdfs/bbcmpstopline.pdf.

Jabri, V. (2007) 'Michel Foucault's Analytics of War: The Social, the International, and the Racial', *International Political Sociology*, 1(1): 67–81.

Jacobson, J. (1997) 'Religion and Ethnicity: Dual and Alternative Sources of Identity among Young British Pakistanis', *Ethnic and Racial Studies*, 20(2).

Jeffery, C. (1996) 'Conclusions: Sub-national Authorities and "European Domestic Policy"', *Regional and Federal Studies*, 6(2): 204–19.

Jeffery, C. (2005) 'Federalism: The New Territorialism', in S. Green and W. Paterson (eds), *Governance in Contemporary Germany: The Semisovereign State Revisited*, Cambridge: Cambridge University Press.

Jeffery, C. (2006) 'Devolution and Social Citizenship: Which Society, Whose Citizenship?', in S. Greer (ed.), *Territory, Democracy and Justice*, Basingstoke: Palgrave Macmillan.

Jeffery, C. (2009a) 'Devolution, Public Attitudes and Social Citizenship', in S. Greer (ed.), *Devolution and Social Citizenship in the UK*, Bristol: Policy Press.

Jeffery, C. (2009b) 'Territoriale Politik, a-territoriale Wissenschaft und der deutsche Föderalismus 1949–2009', *Jahrbuch des Föderalismus 2009*, Baden-Baden: Nomos.

Jeffery, C. and Hough, D. (2006) 'Devolution and Electoral Politics: Where Does the UK Fit In?', in D. Hough and C. Jeffery (eds), *Devolution and Electoral Politics*, Manchester: Manchester University Press.

John, P. (2008) 'The Civic Culture in Britain and America: Trust, Political Attitudes and Efficacy Fifty Years On', Unpublished manuscript, University of Manchester.

John, P., Smith, G. and Stoker, G. (2009) 'Nudge Nudge, Think Think: Two Strategies for Changing Civic Behaviour', *Political Quarterly*, forthcoming.

John-François, R. (2002) *High Noon*, New York: Basic Books.

Johns, R., Mitchell, J., Denver, D. and Pattie, C. (2009) *Voting for a Scottish Government. The Scottish Parliament Election of 2007*, Manchester: Manchester University Press.

Johnson, T.J., and Kaye, B.K. (2003) 'A Boost or Bust for Democracy? How the Web Influenced Political Attitudes and Behaviors in the 1996 and 2000 Presidential Elections', *Harvard, International Journal of Press-Politics*, 8(3), 9–34.

Jones, B. (2001) *Politics and the Architecture of Choice. Bounded Rationality and Governance*, Chicago: University of Chicago Press.

Joppke, C. (2008) 'Immigration and the Identity of Citizenship: The Paradox of Universalism', *Citizenship Studies*, 12(6): 533–46.

Jordan, G. and Maloney, W. (1997) *The Protest Business? Mobilizing Campaign Groups*, Manchester: Manchester University Press.

Kabbani, R. (1989) *Letter to Christendom*, London: Virago Press.

Kagan, R. (2004) 'America's Crisis of Legitimacy', *Foreign Affairs*, 83(2): 65–87.

Kahler, M., and Lake, D.A. (2003) 'Globalization and Governance', in M. Kahler and D.A. Lake (eds), *Governance in a Global Economy: Political Authority in Transition*, Princeton: Princeton University Press.

Kahler, M. and Lake, D.A. (2009) 'Economic Integration and Global Governance: Why So Little Supranationalism?', in W. Mattli and N. Woods (eds), *The Politics of Global Regulation*, Princeton: Princeton University Press.

Kaldor, M. (1998) *New and Old Wars*, Cambridge: Polity.

Kaldor, M. (2003) *Global Civil Society: An Answer to War*, Cambridge: Polity Press.

Kaltenbrunner, A., Gonzalez-Bailon, S. and Banchs, R. (2009) *Communities on the Web: Mechanisms Underlying the Emergence of Online Discussion Networks*, in the Proceedings of the WebSci'09: Society On-Line, 18–20 March 2009, Athens, Greece.

Kantola, J. (2006) *Feminists Theorize the State*, Basingstoke: Palgrave Macmillan.

Kantola, J. (2009) *Gender and the European Union*, Basingstoke: Palgrave Macmillan.

Kantola, J. and Nousianien, K. (2009) 'Institutionalising Intersectionality: Introducing Issues and Themes', *International Feminist Journal of Politics*, 11(4).

Kantola, J. and Outshoorn, J. (2007) 'Changing State Feminism', in J. Outshoorn and J. Kantola (eds), *Changing State Feminism*, Basingstoke: Palgrave Macmillan.

Kantola, J. and Nousiainen, K. (2008) 'Pussauskoppiin? Tasa-arvo- ja yhden-vertaisuuslakien yhtenämisestä', *Naistutkimus-Kvinnoforskning*, 2(2008): 6–20.

Kantola, J. and Squires, J. (2008) 'From State Feminism to Market Feminism?', Paper presented at the International Studies Association Annual Convention, San Francisco, 26–29 March.

Katsumata, H. (2009) 'Mimetic Adoption and Norm Diffusion: 'Western' Security Cooperation in Southeast Asia?', *Review of International Studies*, forthcoming.

Katz, R. and Crotty, W. (2006) *Handbook of Party Politics*, London: Sage.

Katzenstein, P.J. (2009) 'Mid-Atlantic: Sitting on the Knife's Sharp Edge', *Review of International Political Economy*, 16(1): 122–35.

Katzenstein, P.J., Keohane, R.O. and Krasner, S.D. (1999) '*International Organization* and the Study of World Politics', in P.J. Katzenstein, R.O. Keohane, and S.D. Krasner (eds), *Exploration and Contestation in the Study of World Politics: A Special Issue of International Organization*, Cambridge, MA: MIT Press and IO Foundation.

Kaul, I., Conceição, P., Le Goulven, K. and Mendoza, R.U. (eds) (2003) *Providing Global Public Goods*, Oxford: Oxford University Press.

Kavanagh, D. (1980) 'Political Culture in Great Britain: The Decline of the Civic Culture', in G. Almond and S. Verba (eds), *The Civic Culture Revisited*, Boston: Little, Brown & Co.

Keating, M. (1996) *Nations against the State*, New York: St Martin's Press.

Keating, M. (1998) *The New Regionalism in Western Europe*, Cheltenham: Edward Elgar.

Keating, M. (2001) *Plurinational Democracy. Stateless Nations in a Post-Sovereignty Era*, Oxford: Oxford University Press.

Keating, M. (2009) 'Putting European Political Science Back Together', *European Political Science Review*, 1(2): 297–316.

Keating, M., Cairney, P. and Hepburn, E. (2009) 'Territorial Policy Communities and Devolution in the United Kingdom', *Cambridge Journal of Regions, Economy and Society*, 2(1): 51–66.

Keating, M., Loughlin, S. and Deschouwer, K. (2003) *Culture, Institutions and Regional Development: A Study of Eight European Regions*, Cheltenham: Edward Elgar.

Keating, M. and McEwen, N. (eds) (2005) *Devolution and Public Policy in Comparative Perspective*, Regional and Federal Studies, 15(4), Special issue.

Keck, M. and Sikkink, K. (1998) *Activists Beyond Borders: Advocacy Networks in International Politics*, Ithaca: Cornell University Press.

Kelso, Alexandra (2009) 'Parliament on its Knees: MPs' Expenses and the Crisis of Transparency at Westminster', *Political Quarterly*, forthcoming.

Kenworthy, L. and Malami, M. (1999) 'Gender Inequality and Political Representation: A Worldwide Comparative Analysis', *Social Forces*, 78(1): 235–68.

Keohane, R.O. (2009) 'The Old IPE and the New', *Review of International Political Economy*, 16(1): 34–46.

Keohane, R.O. and Martin, L.L. (1995) 'The Promise of Institutionalist Theory', *International Security*, 20(1): 39–51.

Kindleberger, C. (1978) *Manias, Panics, and Crashes: A History of Financial Crises*, New York: Basic Books.

King, A. (ed.) (1976) *Why is Britain becoming Harder to Govern?*, London: British Broadcasting Corporation.

Kirshner, J. (2008) 'Dollar Primacy and American Power: What's at Stake?', *Review of International Political Economy*, 15(3): 418–38.

Knoke, D. (1990) *Organizing for Collective Action: The Political Economies of Associations*, New York: de Gruyter.

Knowledge@Wharton (2008), 'When Small Wars Make a Big Diference', *Forbes*, 6 March 2008, www.forbes.com/2008/06103.

Koldinská, K. (2009) *International Feminist Journal of Politics*, 11(4).

Kollman, K. (2007) 'Same-sex Unions: The Globalization of an Idea', *International Studies Quarterly*, 51(2).

Kolodziej, E. (2005) *Security and International Relations*, Cambridge: Cambridge University Press.

Koopmans, R. and Statham, P. (2001) 'How National Citizenship Shapes Transnationalism. A Comparative Analysis of Migrant Claims-making in Germany, Great Britain and the Netherlands', *Revue européenne des migrations internationales*, 17(2): 63–100.

Krasner, S. (1999) *Sovereignty: Organised Hypocrisy*, Princeton: Princeton University Press.

Kristol, I. (2003) 'The Neoconservative Persuasion', *Weekly Standard*, 23 August.

Kristol, W. and Kagan, R. (2004) 'National Interest and Global Responsibility', in I. Stelzer (ed.), *The NeoCon Reader*, New York: Grove.

Krook, M.L. (2006) 'Reforming Representation: The Diffusion of Candidate Gender Quotas Worldwide', *Politics & Gender*, 2: 303–27.

Krook, M.L. (2009) *Quotas for Women in Politics: Gender and Candidate Selection Reform Worldwide*, New York: Oxford University Press.

Kuhnle, S. and Rokkan, S. (1979) 'Marshall, T.H.', in D. Sills (ed.), *International Encyclopedia of the Social Sciences, Volume 18, Biographical Supplement*, New York: Free Press.

Kymlicka, W. (1989) *Liberalism, Community and Culture*, Oxford: Oxford University Press.

Kymlicka, W. (1995) *Multicultural Citizenship*, Oxford: Clarendon Press.

La Porte, T. (ed.) (1975) *Organized Social Complexity: Challenges to Politics and Policy*, Princeton: Princeton University Press.

Lake, D.A. (2006) 'International Political Economy: A Maturing Interdiscipline', in B.R. Weingast and D. Wittman (eds), *The Oxford Handbook of Political Economy*, New York: Oxford University Press.

Lake, D.A. (2009) 'Trips across the Atlantic: Theory and Epistemology in IPE', *Review of International Political Economy*, 16(1): 47–57.

Lane, J.-E., Newton, K. and McKay, D. (1991) *Political Data Handbook*, Oxford: Oxford University Press.

Laumann, E.O. and Pappi, F.U. (1976) *Networks of Collective Action: A Perspective on Community Influence Systems*, New York: Academic Press.

Lehmbruch, G. (1976) *Parteienwettbewerb im Bundesstaat*, Stuttgart: Kohlhammer.

Lehmbruch, G. (1998) *Parteienwettbewerb im Bundesstaat*, 2, erweiterte Auflage, Opladen: Westdeutscher Verlag.

Letwin, W. (ed.) (1983) *Against Equality*, Basingstoke: Macmillan.

Levey, G. and Modood, T. (eds) (2009) *Secularism, Religion and Multicultural Citizenship*, Cambridge and New York: Cambridge University Press.

Levitas, R. (2005) *The Inclusive Society? Social Exclusion and New Labour*, Basingstoke: Palgrave Macmillan.

Leyden, K. and Borrelli, S. (1995) 'The Effect of State Economic Conditions on Gubernatorial Elections – Does Unified Government Make a Difference?', *Political Research Quarterly*, 48(2): 275–90.

Linklater, A. (1998) *The Transformation of Political Community: Ethical Foundations of the Post-Westphalian Era*, Cambridge: Polity.

Lipset, S.M. and Rokkan, S. (1967a) 'Cleavage Structures, Party Systems, and Voter Alignments: An Introduction', in S.M. Lipset and S. Rokkan (eds), *Party Systems and Voter Alignments: Cross-National Perspectives*, New York: Free Press.

Lipset, S.M and Rokkan, S. (eds) (1967b) *Party Systems and Voter Alignments: Cross-National Perspective*, New York: Free Press of Glencoe.

Lister, R. (2001) 'Doing Good by Stealth: The Politics of Poverty and Inequality Under New Labour', *New Economics*, 8(2): 65–70.

Lister, R. (2003) *Citizenship: Feminist Perspectives*, New York: New York University Press.

Lombardo, E., Meier, P. and Verloo, M. (2009) 'Stretching Gender Equality to Other Inequalities: Political Intersectionality in European Gender Equality Politics', in E. Lombardo, P. Meier and M. Verloo (eds), *The Discursive Politics of Gender Equality: Stretching, Bending and Policy-making*, London: Routledge.

Lombardo, E. and Verloo, M. (2009) 'Institutionalising Intersectionality in the European Union: Policy Developments and Contestations', *International Feminist Journal of Politics*, 11(4).

Lott, A.D. (2004) *Creating Insecurity: Realism, Constructivism, and US Security Policy*, Aldershot, UK and Burlington, VT: Ashgate.

Loubser, M. (2009) *Organizational Mechanisms in Peer Production: The Case of Wikipedia*, DPhil thesis, University of Oxford.

Lovenduski, J. (ed.) (2005) *Feminism and Political Representation*, Cambridge: Cambridge University Press.

Lovenduski, J. (2007) 'Unfinished Business. Equality Policy and the Changing Context in Great Britain', in J. Outshoorn and J. Kantola (ed.), *Changing State Feminism*, Basingstoke: Palgrave Macmillan.

Lovering, J. (1999) 'Theory Led by Policy: The Inadequacies of the New Regionalism', *International Journal of Urban and Regional Research*, 23(2): 379–95.

Lowi, T. (1964) 'American Business, Public Policy, Case Studies and Political Theory', *World Politics*, 16(4): 677–715.

Lupia, A. and Philpot, T.S. (2005) 'Views from Inside the Net: How Websites Affect Young Adults' Political Interest', *Journal of Politics*, 67: 1122–42.

Lupia, A. and Sin, G. (2003) 'Which Public Goods are Endangered? How Evolving Communication Technologies Affect the Logic of Collective Action', *Public Choice*, 117: 315–31.

Lynch, J., Davey Smith, G., Kaplan, G. and House, J. (2000) 'Income Inequality and Mortality: Importance to Health of Individual Income, Psychosocial Environment, or Material Conditions', *British Medical Journal*, 320: 1200–04.

Lynch, P. (1996) *Minority Nationalism and European Integration*, Cardiff: University of Wales Press.

Mabbett, D. (2005) 'The Development of Rights-based Social Policy in the European Union: The Example of Disability Rights', *Journal of Common Market Studies*, 43(1): 97–120.

Mac an Ghaill, M. (1999) *Contemporary Racisms and Ethnicities*, Buckingham: Open University Press.

MacGinty, R. and Williams, A. (2009) *Conflict and Development*, London: Routledge.

MacKinnon, C.A. (2006) *Are Women Human?: And Other International Dialogues*, Cambridge MA: Harvard University Press.

Mair, P. (1997) *Party System Change: Approaches and Interpretations*, New York: Oxford University Press.

Mair, P. and van Biezen, I. (2001) 'Party Membership in Twenty European Democracies, 1980–2000', *Party Politics*, 7(1): 5–21.

Margetts, H. (1999) *Information Technology in Government: Britain and America*, London: Routledge.

Margetts, H. (2006) 'Cyber Parties', *Handbook of Party Politics*, London: Sage.

Margetts, H. and Escher, T. (2007) 'Understanding Governments and Citizens On-line: Learning from e-Commerce', Paper to the Annual Meeting of the American Political Science Association, Chicago, 30 August–2 September 2007.

Margetts, H., John, P., Escher, T. and Reissfelder, S. (2009) 'How Many People Does It Take to Change a Petition? Experiments to investigate the impact of on-line social information on collection action, Paper to ECPR General Conference, University of Potsdam, Germany, 9–12 September 2009.

Margetts, H. and Partington, M. (2010) 'Developments in E-Government', in M. Adler (ed.) *Administrative Justice in Context*, Oxford: Hart Publishing.

Marks, G. (1993) 'Structural Policy and Multi-level Governance in the EC', in A. Cafruny and G. Rosenthal (eds), *The State of the European Community Volume 2: The Maastricht Debates and Beyond*, Boulder, CO: Lynne Rienner.

Marks, G. (1996) 'An Actor-centred Approach to Multi-level Governance', *Regional and Federal Studies*, 6(2): 20–40.

Marks, G. and Hooghe, L. (2003) 'Unraveling the Central State. But How? Types of Multi-level Governance', *American Political Science Review*, 97(2): 233–43.

Marks, G., Hooghe, L. and Schakel, A. (eds) (2008a) *Regional Authority in 42 Countries, 1950–2006: A Measure and Five Hypotheses, Regional and Federal Studies*, 18(2–3), Special issue.

Marks, G., Hooghe, L. and Schakel, A. (2008b) 'Patterns of Regional Authority', *Regional and Federal Studies*, 18(2–3): 167–81.

Marshall, T. (1992 [1950]) 'Citizenship and Social Class', in T. Marshall and T. Bottomore, *Citizenship and Social Class*, London: Pluto Press.

Martin, R. and Reidy, D.A. (eds) (2006) *Rawls's Law of Peoples: A Realistic Utopia?*, Oxford: Blackwell.

Martins, H. (1974) 'Time and Theory in Sociology', in J. Rex (ed.), *Approaches to Sociology*, London: Routledge & Kegan Paul.

Mason, A. (2006) *Equal Opportunity for All: On Levelling the Playing Field*, Oxford: Oxford University Press.

Mattli, W., and Buthe, T. (2005) 'Accountability in Accounting? The Politics of Private Rule-Making in the Public Interest', *Governance*, 18(3): 399–429.

Mattli, W., and Woods, N. (2009) 'Introduction', in W. Mattli and N. Woods (eds), *The Politics of Global Regulation*, Princeton: Princeton University Press.

Mazey, S. (2002) 'Gender Mainstreaming Strategies in the E.U.: Delivering an Agenda?', *Feminist Legal Studies*, 10: 227–40.

Mazur, A. (ed.) (2001) *State Feminism, Women's Movements and Job Training: Making Democracies Work in the Global Economy*, New York and London: Routledge.

Mazur, A. (2002) *Theorizing Feminist Policy*, Oxford: Oxford University Press.

McBride Stetson, D. (2001) *Abortion Politics, Women's Movements and the Democratic State: A Comparative Study of State Feminism*, Oxford: Oxford University Press.

McBride Stetson, D. and Mazur, A. (1995) *Comparative State Feminism*, London: Sage.

McCall, L. (2005) 'The Complexity of Intersectionality', *Signs: Journal of Women in Culture and Society*, 30(3): 1771–99.

McEwen, N. (2006) *Nationalism and the State: Welfare and Identity in Scotland and Quebec*, Brussels: PIE-Peter Lang.

McEwen, N. and Moreno, L. (eds) (2005) *The Territorial Politics of Welfare*, London: Routledge.

McGhee, D. (2008) *The End of Multiculturalism?*, Maidenhead and New York: Open University Press.

McGrew, A. (2002) 'Between Two Worlds: Europe in a Globalizing Era', *Government and Opposition*, 37(3): 343–58.

McGrew, A. (2008) 'The Logics of Economic Globalization', in J. Ravenhill (ed.), *Global Political Economy*, 2nd edn, Oxford: Oxford University Press.

McNeill, K. (2006) 'Can We Restore Trust?', *Fabian Review*, 118(4): 16–7.

McSweeney, B. (2008) *Security, Identity and Interests: A Sociology of International Relations*, Cambridge: Cambridge University Press.

Mearsheimer, J.J. (2001) *The Tragedy of Great Power Politics*, Boston: W. Norton & Co.

Mearsheimer, J.J. and Walt, S. (2003) 'An Unnecessary War', *Foreign Policy*, January/February.

Meer, N. and Modood, T. (2009) 'The Multicultural State We're In: Muslims, "Multiculture" and the "Civic Rebalancing" of British Multiculturalism', *Political Studies*, forthcoming.

Meikle, J. (2005) 'Bill Gates Gives $258m to World Battle against Malaria', *Guardian*, 31 October.

Mendoza, B. (2002) 'Transnational Feminism in Question', *Feminist Theory*, 3(3): 295–314.

Mertus, J. (2000) *War's Offensive on Women: The Humanitarian Challenge in Bosnia, Kosovo and Afghanistan*, West Hartford, CT: Kumarian Press.

Milanovic, B. (2005) *Worlds Apart: Measuring International and Global Inequality*, Princeton: Princeton University Press.

Miller, D. (1994) 'The Nation-State: A Modest Defence', in C. Brown (ed.), *Political Restructuring in Europe: Ethical Perspectives*, London: Routledge.

Miller, D. (1995) *On Nationality*, Oxford: Clarendon Press.

Miller, D. and Hashmi, S.H. (eds) (2001) *Boundaries and Justice: Diverse Ethical Perspectives*, Princeton: Princeton University Press.

Mirza, M., Senthilkumaran, A. and Ja'far, Z. (2007) *Living Apart Together: British Muslims and the Paradox of Multiculturalism*, London: Policy Exchange.

Mitchell, H. (2006) 'Evolution and Devolution: Citizenship, Institutions and Public Policy', *Publius: The Journal of Federalism*, 36(1): 153–68.

Mitchell, J. (1996) 'Scotland in the Union 1945–1995: The Changing Nature of the Union State', in T. Devine and R. Findlay (eds), *Scotland in the 20th Century*, Edinburgh: Edinburgh University Press.

Mitchell, J. (2004) 'Scotland: Policy Types, Expectations and Devolution', in A. Trench (ed.), *Has Devolution Made a Difference?*, Exeter: Imprint Academic.

Mizruchi, M.S. and Fein, L.C. (1999) 'The Social Construction of Organizational Knowledge: A Study of the Uses of Coercive, Mimetic, and Normative Isomorphism', *Administrative Science Quarterly*, 44.

Modood, T. (1992) *Not Easy Being British: Colour, Culture and Citizenship*, London: Runnymede Trust/Trentham Books.

Modood, T. (1998) 'Anti-Essentialism, Multiculturalism and the "Recognition" of Religious Minorities', *Journal of Political Philosophy*, 6(4): 378–99; reproduced in W. Kymlicka and W. Norman (eds), (2000), *Citizenship in Diverse Societies*, Oxford: Oxford University Press.

Modood, T. (2005) *Multicultural Politics: Racism, Ethnicity and Muslims in Britain*, Minneapolis: University of Minnesota Press; Edinburgh: University of Edinburgh Press.

Modood, T. (2007) *Multiculturalism: A Civic Idea*, Cambridge: Polity.

Modood, T. and Ahmad, F. (2007) 'British Muslim Perspectives on Multiculturalism', *Theory, Culture and Society*, 24(1): 187–213.

Modood, T., Berthoud, R., Lakey, J., Nazroo, J., Smith, P., Virdee, S. and Beishon, S. (1997) *Ethnic Minorities in Britain: Diversity and Disadvantage*, London: Policy Studies Institute.

Modood, T. and Meer, N. (2009) 'Multicultural Citizenship in Europe: The States We Are In', Paper for the EMILE Conference, 'Migration and Diversity Challenges in Europe: Theoretical and Policy Responses', Berlin, 24 September, 2009.

Moe, T. (1984) 'The New Economics of Organization', *American Journal of Political Science*, 28(4): 739–77.

Moore, M. (2003) *A World Without Walls: Freedom, Development, Free Trade and Global Governance*, Cambridge: Cambridge University Press.

Moran, M. (1999) *Governing the Health Care State: A Comparative Study of the United Kingdom, the United States and Germany*, Manchester: Manchester University Press.

Moran, M. (2007) *The British Regulatory State: High Modernism and Hyperinnovation*, 2nd edn, Oxford: Oxford University Press.

Mortimore, R. (1995) 'Politics and Public Perceptions', in F.F. Ridley and A. Doig (eds), *Sleaze: Politicians, Private Interests and Public Reaction*, Oxford: Oxford University Press.

Mosley, L. (2002) *Global Capital and National Governments*, Cambridge: Cambridge University Press.

Mulhall, S. and Swift, A. (1996) *Liberals and Communitarians*, 2nd edn, Oxford: Blackwell.

Münch, U. (2008) 'Materielles Abweichungsrecht der Länder und föderative Asymmetrien in der bundesdeutschen Bildungspolitik', *Jahrbuch des Föderalismus 2007*, Baden-Baden: Nomos.

Murphy, C. (2000) 'Global Governance: Poorly Done and Poorly Understood', *International Affairs*, 76(4): 789–803.

Nagel, T. (2005) 'The Problem of Global Justice', *Philosophy and Public Affairs*, 33(2): 113–47.

NAO (National Audit Office) (2007) *Government on the Internet: Progress in Delivering Information and Services Online*, HC 529 Session 2006–7, London: Stationery Office.

Narlikar, A. (2003) *International Trade and Developing Countries: Bargaining Coalitions in GATT and WTO*, London: Routledge.

Naughton, P. and Knight, S. (2006) 'World Searches for Response to North Korea's Nuclear Test', *The Times*, 9 October. Available at http://www.timesonline. co.uk/tol/news/world/asia/article666501.ece.

New York Times (2008) 'Greenspan Concedes Errors on Regulation', 24 October. Available at http://www.nytimes.com/2008/10/24/business/economy/24 panel.html? (accessed 26 April 2009).

Nickel, J.W. (1987) *Making Sense of Human Rights: Philosophical Reflections on the United Nations Declaration of Human Rights*, Berkeley, CA: University of California Press.

Noble, G.. and Ravenhill, J. (eds) (2000) *The Asian Financial Crises and the Global Financial Architecture*, Cambridge: Cambridge University Press.

Norris, P. (2009) 'The Impact of the Internet on Political Activism: Evidence from Europe', in C. Romm and K. Setzekorn (eds), *Social Networking Communities and E-Dating Services*, I-Global.

Nozick, R. (1974) *Anarchy, State and Utopia*, Oxford: Blackwell.

NRDC (Natural Resources Defense Council) (2002) 'The Consequences of Nuclear Conflict between India and Pakistan'. Available at http://www.nrdc.org/nuclear/southasia.asp.

Nussbaum, M. (2000) *Women and Human Development: The Capabilities Approach*, Cambridge: Cambridge University Press.

Nussbaum, M.C. (2003) 'Capabilities as Fundamental Entitlements: Sen and Social Justice', *Feminist Economics*, 9(2/3): 33–59.

Nye, J.S. (2002) *The Paradox of American Power*, Princeton: Princeton University Press.

O'Neil, M. (2009) *Cyber Chiefs: Autonomy and Authority in Online Tribes*, London: Pluto Press.

O'Neill, O. (2000) 'Bounded and Cosmopolitan Justice', *Review of International Studies*, 26(5): 45–60.

Obinger, H., Liebfried, S. and Castles, F. (2005) *Federalism and the Welfare State. New World and European Experiences*, Cambridge: Cambridge University Press.

OECD (no date) 'Aid Rising Sharply, According to Latest OECD Figures'. Available at www.oecd.org/dac.

Office of National Statistics (2008) Available at http://www.statistics.gov.uk/cci/article.asp?id=2083.

Ohmae, K. (1990) *The Borderless World*, London: Collins.

Okin, S.M. (1989) *Justice, Gender and the Family*, New York: Basic Books.

Okin, S.M. (2000) 'Is Multiculturalism Bad for Women?', in S.M. Okin, J. Cohen, M. Howard and M.C. Nussbaum (eds), *Is Multiculturalism Bad for Women?* Princeton: Princeton University Press.

Olson, M. (1965) *The Logic of Collective Action*, Cambridge: Harvard University Press.

Osborne, D. (1988) *Laboratories of Democracy*, Boston, MA: Harvard Business School Press.

Outshoorn, J. (ed.) (2004) *The Politics of Prostitution: Women's Movements, Democratic States and the Globalisation of Sex Commerce*, Cambridge: Cambridge University Press.

Outshoorn, J. and Kantola, J. (eds) (2007) *Changing State Feminism*, Basingstoke: Palgrave Macmillan.

Ozga, J. and Alexiadou, N. (2002) 'Modernising Education Governance in England and Scotland: Devolution and Control', *European Educational Research Journal*, 1(4): 676–91.

Oxford Internet Survey (2007) Available at http://corinnadigennaro.com/2007/07/25/oxford-internet-survey-2007.

Palfrey, T.R. and Rosenthal, H. (1985) 'Voter Participation and Strategic Uncertainty', *American Political Science Review*, 79(1): 62–78.

Pallares, F. and Keating, M. (2003) 'Multi-level Electoral Competition: Sub-state Elections and Party Systems in Spain', *European Urban and Regional Studies*, 10(3): 239–55.

Pallares, F., Montero, J. and Llera, F. (1997) 'Non State-wide Parties in Spain: An Attitudinal Study of Nationalism and Regionalism', *Publius: The Journal of Federalism*, 27(4): 135–69.

Panitch, L. (2009) 'Thoroughly Modern Marx: Lights. Camera. Action. *Das Kapital.* Now', *Foreign Policy*, 1 May, 172.

Parekh, B. (1991) 'British Citizenship and Cultural Difference', in G. Andrews (ed.), *Citizenship*, London: Lawrence & Wishart.

Parekh, B. (2000) *Rethinking Multiculturalism: Cultural Diversity and Political Theory*, Basingstoke: Macmillan.

Parsons, C. (2007) *How to Map Arguments in Political Science*, Oxford: Oxford University Press.

Paterson, L., Brown, A., Curtis, J., Hinds, K., McCrone, D., Park, A., Sproston, K. and Surridge, P. (2001) *New Scotland, New Politics?*, Edinburgh: Polygon.

Pattie, C., Seyd, P. and Whiteley, P. (2004) *Citizenship in Britain*, Cambridge: Cambridge University Press.

Payne, A. (2003) 'Globalization and Modes of Regionalist Governance', in D. Held and A. McGrew (eds), *The Global Transformations Reader*, Cambridge: Polity.

Peters, B. and Pierre, J. (2003) *Handbook of Public Administration*, London: Sage.

Peters, G., Pierre, J. and Stoker, G. (2009) 'The Relevance of Political Science', in D. Marsh and G. Stoker (eds), *Theories and Methods in Political Science*, Basingstoke: Palgrave Macmillan.

Peterson, P. (1995) *The Price of Federalism*, Washington, DC: Brookings.

Pew (2009) 'Newspapers Face a Challenging Calculus', 26 February 2009, Pew Research Center Publications at http://pewresearch.org/pubs/1133/decline-print-newspapers-increased-online-news

Phillips, A. (1995) *The Politics of Presence*, Oxford: Clarendon Press.

Phillips, A. (1999) *Which Equalities Matter?*, Cambridge: Polity Press.

Phillips, A. (2007) *Multiculturalism without Culture*, Princeton: Princeton University Press.

Piattoni, S. (2009) 'Multi-level Governance: A Historical and Conceptual Analysis', *Journal of European Integration*, 31(2): 163–80.

Pierson, P. (2001) *The New Politics of the Welfare State*, Oxford: Oxford University Press.

Pogge, T. (2006) 'Why Inequality Matters', in D. Held and A. Kaya (eds), *Global Inequality: Patterns and Explanations*, Cambridge: Polity.

Pogge, T. (ed.) (2007a) *Freedom from Poverty as a Human Right: Who Owes What to the Very Poor?*, Oxford: Oxford University Press.

Pogge, T. (2007b) 'Severe Poverty as a Human Rights Violation', in T. Pogge (ed.), *Freedom from Poverty as a Human Right: Who Owes What to the Very Poor?*, Oxford: Oxford University Press.

Pogge, T. (2008) *World Poverty and Human Rights*, 2nd edn, Cambridge: Polity.

Pogge, T. and Moellendorf, D. (eds) (2008) *Global Justice: Seminal Essays*, St Paul, MN: Paragon House.

Pollitt, C., Van Thiel, S. and Homburg, V. (2007) *New Public Management in Europe: Adaptation and Alternatives*, Basingstoke: Palgrave Macmillan.

Power Inquiry (2006) *Power to the People. The Report of Power: An Independent Report into Britain's Democracy*, London: Joseph Rowntree Charitable Trust.

Pressman, J. and Wildavsky, A. (1973) *Implementation*, Berkeley, CA: University of California Press.

PSA (2007) 'Failing Politics. A Response to the Governance of Britain Green Paper'. Available at http://www.psa.ac.uk/PSAPubs/PSA%20Response%20 to%20Governance%20Green%20Paper.pdf.

Putnam, R. (2000) *Bowling Alone: The Collapse and Revival of American Community*, New York: Simon & Schuster.

Radelet, S. and Sachs, J. (2000) 'The Onset of the East Asian Financial Crisis', in P. Krugman (ed.), *Currency Crises*, Chicago: University of Chicago Press.

Rai, S. (ed.) (2003) *Mainstreaming Gender, Democratizing the State: Institutional Mechanisms for the Advancement of Women*, Manchester: Manchester University Press.

Rai, S. (2008) *The Gender Politics of Development*, London: Zed Books.

Rapport, D. (2008) 'Unexpected Affinities? Neoconservatism's Place in IR Theory', *Security Studies*, 17(2): 257–93.

Ravenhill, J. (2008a) 'In Search of the Missing Middle', *Review of International Political Economy*, 15(1): 18–29.

Ravenhill, J. (2008b) 'The Move to Preferential Trade on the Western Pacific Rim: Some Initial Conclusions', *Australian Journal of International Affairs*, 62(2): 129–50.

Ravenhill, J. (2008c) 'Regionalism', in J. Ravenhill (ed.), *Global Political Economy*, 2nd edn, Oxford: Oxford University Press.

Rawls, J. (1971) *A Theory of Justice*, Oxford: Oxford University Press.

Rawls, J. (1993) *Political Liberalism*, New York: Columbia University Press.

Rawls, J. (1999) *The Law of the Peoples*, Cambridge, MA: Harvard University Press.

Rees, M. (2003) *Our Final Century*, New York: Arrow Books.

Rees, T. (1998) *Mainstreaming Equality in the European Union: Education, Training and Labour Market Policies*, London: Routledge.

Rees, T. (2005) 'Reflections on the Uneven Development of Gender Mainstreaming in Europe', *International Feminist Journal of Politics*, 7(4): 555–74.

Reif, K. and Schmitt, H. (1980) 'Nine Second-order National Elections: A Conceptual Framework for the Analysis of European Election Results', *European Journal of Political Research*, 8(1): 3–44.

Rein, M. (2006) 'Reframing Problematic Policies', in M. Moran, M. Rein and R.E. Goodin (eds), *The Oxford Handbook of Public Policy*, Oxford: Oxford University Press.

Review of International Political Economy (2009) 16(1), Special issue.

Rheingold, H. (2000) *The Virtual Community*, Cambridge, MA: MIT Press.

Rhodes, R. (1985) 'Power-dependence, Policy Communities and Intergovernmental Networks', *Public Administration Bulletin*, 49: 4–20.

Rhodes, R. (1997) *Understanding Governance: Policy Networks, Governance, Reflexivity and Accountability*, Buckingham: Open University Press.

Rhodes, R., Carmichael, P., McMillan, J. and Massey, A. (2003) *Decentralizing the Civil Service*, Buckingham: Open University Press.

Richardson, D. (2000) 'Constructing Sexual Citizenship: Theorising Sexual Rights', *Critical Social Policy*, 20(1): 105–35.

Rischard, J.F. (2002) *High Noon*, New York: Basic Books.

Risse, T., Ropp, S.C. and Sikkink, K. (1999) *The Power of Human Rights: International Norms and Domestic Change*, Cambridge: Cambridge University Press.

Rittel, H. and Webber, M. (1973) 'Dilemmas in a General Theory of Planning', *Policy Sciences*, 4(2): 155–69.

Robeyns, I. (2003) 'Sen's Capability Approach and Gender Inequality: Selecting Relevant Capabilities', *Feminist Economics*, 9(2/3): 61–92.

Robinson, F. (1999) *Globalizing Care: Ethics, Feminist Theory and International Relations*, Boulder, CO: Westview Press.

Roche, M. (1992) *Rethinking Citizenship: Welfare, Ideology and Change in Modern Society*, Cambridge: Polity.

Rodrik, D. (2005) 'Making Globalisation work for Development',' Ralph Miliband Public Lecture, London School of Economics, 18 November.

Rodrik, D. (2007) *One Economics, Many Recipes: Globalisation, Institutions and Economic Growth*, Princeton: Princeton University Press.

Rodrik, D. and Kaplan, E. (2002) '*Did the Malaysian Capital Controls Work?*', in S. Edwards and J. Frankel (eds), *Preventing Currency Crises in Emerging Markets*, Chicago: University of Chicago Press.

Rokkan, S. (1999) *State Formation, Nation-Building and Mass Politics in Europe: The Theory of Stein Rokkan*, P. Flora, S. Kuhnle and D. Urwin (eds), Oxford: Oxford University Press.

Rokkan, S. and Urwin, D. (1982) 'Introduction: Centres and Peripheries in Western Europe', in S. Rokkan and D. Urwin (eds), *The Politics of Territorial Identity*, London: Sage.

Rokkan, S. and Urwin, D. (1983) *Economy, Territory, Identity. Politics of West European Peripheries*, London: Sage/ECPR.

Rose, N. (1990) *Governing the Soul: The Shaping of the Private Self*, London: Routledge.

Rose, N. (1999) *Powers of Freedom*, Cambridge: Cambridge University Press.

Rose, R. and Urwin, D. (1975) 'Regional Differentiation and Political Unity in Western Nations', *Sage Professional Papers in Contemporary Political Sociology*, 06-007(1).

Rosenau, J.N. (1990) *Turbulence in World Politics*, Princeton: Princeton University Press.

Rosenau, J.N. (1992) 'Governance, Order, and Change in World Politics', in J. Rosenau and E. Czempiel (eds), *Governance without Government: Order and Change in World Politics*, Cambridge: Cambridge University Press.

Rosenau, J.N. (2000) 'Change, Complexity, and Governance in a Globalising Space', in J. Pierre (ed.), *Debating Governance*, Oxford: Oxford University Press.

Rosenau, J.N. (2002) 'Governance in a New Global Order', in D. Held and A.G. McGrew (eds), *Governing Globalization*, Cambridge: Polity.

Rosenau, J.N. and Singh, J.P. (2002) *Information Technologies and Global Politics: The Changing Scope of Power and Governance*, Albany, NY: State University of New York Press.

Rossilli, M. (2000) *Gender Policies in the European Union*, New York: Peter Lang.

Roy, D. (1994) 'North Korea and the Madman Theory', *Security Dialogue*, 25(3): 307–16.

Rubenstein, J.C. (2008) 'The Distributive Commitments of International NGOs', in M. Barnett and T.G. Weiss (eds), *Humanitarianism in Question: Politics, Power, Ethics*, Ithaca: Cornell University Press (2008): 215–34.

Rudd, K. (2009) 'The Global Financial Crisis', *The Monthly*, 42, February.

Ruddick, S. (1990) *Maternal Thinking: Towards a Politics of Peace*, London: Women's Press.

Ruggie, J.G. (1993) 'Territoriality and Beyond: Problematizing Modernity in International Relations', *International Organization*, 47(1), Winter: 139–74.

Rugman, Alan M. (2005) *The Regional Multinationals: MNEs And 'Global' Strategic Management*, Cambridge: Cambridge University Press.

Russell, M. (2005) *Must Politics Disappoint?*, London: Fabian Society.

Russell, M. (2008) 'Review: Who is Afraid of Politics?', *Political Quarterly*, 79(4): 651–6.

Russett, B. (1994) *Grasping the Democratic Peace*, Princeton: Princeton University Press.

Saeed, A., Blain, N. and Forbes, D. (1999) 'New Ethnic and National Questions in Scotland: Post-British Identities among Glasgow Pakistani Teenagers', *Ethnic and Racial Studies*, 22(5): 821–44.

Sainsbury, D. (ed.) (1999) *Gender, Equality and Welfare State Regimes*, Oxford: Oxford University Press.

Savage, M. and Burrows, R. (2007) 'The Coming Crisis of Empirical Sociology', *Sociology*, 41(5): 885–99.

Schelling, T.C. (1978) 'Egonomics, or the Art of Self-Management', *American Economic Review*, 68(2): 290–4.

Schelling, T.C. (2006) 'Some Fun, Thirty-Five Years Ago', *Handbook of Computational Economics*, 2: 1639–44.

Scarrow, Susan E. (2000) 'Parties without Members?: Party Organization in a Changing Electoral Environment', in R.J. Dalton and M.P. Wattenberg (eds), *Parties without Partisans: Political Change in Advanced Industrial Democracies*, Oxford: Oxford University Press.

Scholte, J.-A. (1993) 'From Power Politics to Social Change: An Alternative Focus for International Studies', *Review of International Studies*, 19(1): 3–21.

Scholte, J.-A. (1996) 'The Geography of Collective Identities in a Globalising World', *Review of International Political Economy*, 3(4): 565–607.

Scholte, J.-A. (2005) *Globalization: A Critical Introduction*, Basingstoke: Palgrave Macmillan.

Schweller, R. (2004) 'Unanswered Threats: A Neoclassical Realist Theory of Underbalancing', *International Security*, 29(2), Fall.

Scott, J. (1998) *Seeing Like a State: How Certain Schemes to Improve the Human Condition Have Failed*, New Haven: Yale University Press.

Scully, R., Wyn Jones, R. and Trystan, D. (2004) 'Turnout, Participation and Legitimacy in Post-Devolution Wales,' *British Journal of Political Science*, 34(3): 519–37.

Seidman, H. (1979) *Politics, Position and Power: The Dynamics of Federal Organization*, New York: Oxford University Press.

Sen, A. (1992) *Inequality Re-examined*, Oxford: Clarendon Press.

Sen, A. (1999) *Development as Freedom*, New York: Oxford University Press.

Sen, A (2004) 'Capabilities, Lists, and Public Reason: Continuing the Conversation', *Feminist Economics*, 10(3): 77–80.

Shachar, A. (1999) 'The Paradox of Multicultural Vulnerability: Individual Rights, Identity Groups, and the State', in C. Joppke and S. Lukes (eds), *Multicultural Questions*, Oxford: Oxford University Press: 87–111.

Shadlen, Ken (2005) 'Exchanging Development for Market Access? Deep Integration and Industrial Policy under Multilateral and Regional–Bilateral Trade Agreements', *Review of International Political Economy*, 12(5), December: 750–75.

Shah, Anup (no date) 'Behind Consumption and Consumerism'. Available at http://www.globalissues.org/TradeRelated/Consumption.asp.

Shapiro, I. (2004) 'Problems, Methods, and Theories, or: What's Wrong with Political Science and What to Do about It', in I. Shapiro, R. Smith and T. Masoud (eds), *Problems and Methods in the Study of Political Science*, Cambridge: Cambridge University Press.

Shue, H. (1993) 'Subsistence Emissions and Luxury Emissions', *Law and Policy*, 15(1): 39–59.

Shue, H. (1996) *Basic Rights: Subsistence, Affluence and US Foreign Policy*, 2nd edn, Princeton: Princeton University Press.

Simon, H. (1996) *The Sciences of the Artificial*, 3rd edn, Cambridge, MA: MIT Press.

Sinclair, T.J. (2005) *The New Masters of Capital: American Bond Rating Agencies and the Politics of Creditworthiness*, Ithaca, NY: Cornell University Press.

Singer, P. (2004) *One World: The Ethics of Globalization*, 2nd edn, New Haven: Yale University Press.

Sjoberg. L. (2006) *Gender, Justice and the Wars in Iraq*, Lanham, MD.: Lexington Books.

Skjeie, H. (2007) 'Religious Exemptions to Equality', *Critical Review of International Social and Political Philosophy*, 10(4): 471–90.

Skjeie, H. (2008) 'Multiple Equality Claims in the Practice of the Norwegian Anti-discrimination Agencies', in D. Schiek and V. Chege (eds), *European Union Non-discrimination Law. Comparative Perspectives on Multidimensional Equality Law*, London: Routledge: 295–309.

Skjeie, H. and Langvasbråten, T. (2009) 'Intersectionality in Practice? Anti-discrimination Law in Norway', *International Feminist Journal of Politics*, 11(4).

Slaughter, A.-M. (2004) *A New World Order*, Princeton: Princeton University Press.

Smith, A. (1979) *Nationalism in the Twentieth Century*, Oxford: Martin Robertson.

Smith, A. (1983) 'Nationalism and Social Theory', *British Journal of Sociology*, 34: 19–38.

Smith, G. (2009) *Democratic Innovations*, Cambridge: Cambridge University Press.

Solana, J. (2003) 'The Future of Transatlantic Relations', *Progressive Politics*, 2(2).

Soysal, Y. (1994) *Limits of Citizenship: Migrants and Postnational Membership in Europe*, Chicago, IL: University of Chicago Press.

Spees, P. (2003) 'Women's Advocacy in the Creation of the ICC: Changing the Landscapes of Justice and Power', *Signs: Journal of Women, Culture and Society*, 28(4): 1233–54.

Squires, J. (2007) *The New Politics of Gender Equality*, Basingstoke: Palgrave Macmillan.

Squires, J. (2008) 'Negotiating Equality and Diversity in Britain: Towards a Differentiated Citizenship', in B. Siim and J. Squires (eds), *Contesting Citizenship*, London: Routledge: 129–58.

Squires, J. (2009) 'Intersecting Inequalities: Britain's Equality Review', *International Feminist Journal of Politics*, 11(4).

Stefuriuc, I. (ed.) (2009) 'Government Coalitions in Multi-level Settings: Institutional Determinants and Party Strategy', *Regional and Federal Studies*, 19/1, Special issue.

Stein, J.G. (2008) 'Humanitarian Organizations: Accountable – Why, To Whom, For What, and How?', in M. Barnett and T.G. Weiss (eds), *Humanitarianism in Question: Politics, Power, Ethics*, Ithaca, NY: Cornell University Press.

Stein, R. (1990) 'Economic Voting for Governor and US Senator: The Electoral Consequences of Federalism', *Journal of Politics*, 52(1): 29–53.

Steinmo, S. (2003) 'The Evolution of Policy Ideas: Tax Policy in the 20th Century', *British Journal of Politics and International*, 5(2): 206–36.

Stockholm International Peace Research Institute (2004) *SIPRI Yearbook 2004*, New York: Oxford University Press.

Stockholm International Peace Research Institute (2005) *SIPRI Yearbook 2005*, New York: Oxford University Press.

Stoker, G. (2006) *Why Politics Matters: Making Democracy Work*, Basingstoke: Palgrave Macmillan.

Stoker, G. and John, P. (2009) 'Design Experiments: Engaging Policy Makers in the Search for Evidence about What Works', *Political Studies*, 7: 356–73.

Stoltz, C. (2009) 'Neda and the Power of the Viral Age', *Huffington Post*, 22 June 2009.

Stone, D. (2008) 'Transfer Agents and Global Networks in the "Transnationalization" of Policy', *Journal of European Public Policy*, 11(3): 545–66.

Strange S. (1996) *The Retreat of the State*, Cambridge: Cambridge University Press.

Stratigaki, M. (2004) 'The Cooptation of Gender Concepts in EU Policies: The Case of "Reconciliation of Work and Family"', *Social Politics*, 11(1): 30–56.

Sunstein, C. (2009) *Republic.com 2.0*, Princeton: Princeton University Press.

Susskind, L. (2006) 'Arguing, Bargaining and Getting Agreement', in M. Moran, M. Rein and R.E. Goodin (eds), *The Oxford Handbook of Public Policy*, Oxford: Oxford University Press.

Swank, D. (2002) *Global Capital, Political Institutions, and Policy Change in Developed Welfare States*, Cambridge: Cambridge University Press.

Swenden, W. and Maddens, B. (eds) (2008) *Territorial Party Politics in Western Europe*, Basingstoke: Palgrave Macmillan.

Swift, A. (2001) *Political Philosophy*, Cambridge: Polity.

Taylor, C. (1992) 'The Politics of Recognition', in C. Taylor and A. Gutmann (eds), *Multiculturalism and 'The Politics of Recognition'*, Princeton: Princeton University Press.

Taylor, C. (1994) 'Multiculturalism and "The Politics of Recognition"', in C. Taylor and A. Gutmann, (ed.) *Multiculturalism and 'The Politics of Recognition'*, Princeton: Princeton University Press.

Tedesco, J.C. (2006) 'Web Interactivity and Young Adult Political Efficacy', in J.C. Tedesco (eds), *The Internet Election: Perspectives on the Web in Campaign 2004*, New York: Rowman & Littlefield.

Teghtsoonian, K. (2004) 'Neoliberalism and Gender Analysis Mainstreaming in Aotearoa/New Zealand', *Australian Journal of Political Science*, 39(2): 267–84.

Thinkprogress (2008) Available at http://thinkprogress.org/wp-content/uploads/2008/12/nyt_iraq.pdf.

Thomas, C. (1987) *In Search of Security: The Third World in International Relations*, Brighton: Harvester Wheatsheaf.

Thompson, G., Hirst, P. and Bromley, S. (2009) *Globalization in Question*, 3rd edn, Cambridge: Polity.

Thompson, H. (1999) 'The Modern State, Political Choice and an Open International Economy', *Government and Opposition*, 34(2): 203–25.

Thompson, H. (2006a) 'The Modern State and its Adversaries', *Government and Opposition*, 41(1): 23–42.

Thompson, H. (2006b) 'The Case for External Sovereignty', *European Journal of International Relations*, 12(2): 251–74.

Thompson, H. (2009) 'The Political Origins of the Financial Crisis: The Domestic and International Politics of Fannie Mae and Freddie Mac', *Political Quarterly*, 80(1): 17–24.

Thun, E. (2008) 'The Globalization of Production', in J. Ravenhill (ed.), *Global Political Economy,* 2nd edn, Oxford: Oxford University Press.

Tilly, C. (1975) *Reflections on the History of European State-Making*, Princeton, NJ: Princeton University Press.

Toffler, A. (1970) *Future Shock*, London: Pan Books.

Toffler, A. (1980) *The Third Wave*, New York: Bantam Books.

Toffler, A. (1990) *Power Shift*, New York: Bantam Books.

Tolbert, C.J., and McNeal, R.S. (2003) 'Unraveling the Effects of the Internet on Political Participation?', *Political Research Quarterly*, 56: 175–185.

Tonge, J. (2009) 'Revitalising Politics: Engaging Young People', *Representation: Journal of Representative Democracy*, 45(3): 237–46.

Toynbee, P. (2005) 'Inequality Kills', *The Guardian*, 30 July.

Travis, A. (2002) 'The Need to Belong – But with a Strong Faith', *The Guardian*, 17 June.

True, J. (2003) 'Mainstreaming Gender in Global Public Policy', *International Feminist Journal of Politics*, 5(3): 368–96.

True, J. and Mintrom, M. (2001) 'Transnational Networks and Policy Diffusion: The Case of Gender Mainstreaming', *International Studies Quarterly*, 45: 27–57.

Trystan, D., Scully, R. and Wyn Jones, R. (2003) 'Explaining the Quiet Earthquake: Voting Behaviour in the First Election to the National Assembly for Wales,' *Electoral Studies*, 22(4): 635–50.

Turner, B. (1993) *Citizenship and Social Theory*, London: Sage.

UN (1994) *Human Development Report*, United Nations Development Programme, New York: Oxford University Press.

UN (1995) *Platform for Action and the Beijing Declaration*, New York: United Nations.

UN (1998) *Human Development Report*, United Nations Development Programme, New York: Oxford University Press.

UN (2005) 'General Assembly Adopts 2006–2007 Budget of $3.79 Billion, as Main Part of Sixtieth Session Concludes', Press release, 23 December. Available at http://www.un.org/News/Press/docs/2005/ga10442.doc.htm.

UN (2006) 'Growing Share of UN Resources in Field Operations' UN Factsheet publication, March. Available at http://www.un.org/reform/investinginun/pdfs/factsheet.pdf.

Urwin, D. (1982) 'Conclusion: Perspectives on Conditions of Regional Protest and Accommodation', in S. Rokkan and D. Urwin (eds), *The Politics of Territorial Identity*, London: Sage.

US Census Bureau, 2009 Available at http://www.census.gov/hhes/www/income/histinc/f03ar.html.

Van Wessel, M. (2009) 'Citizens and Problems of Representative Democracy', PSA Conference, Manchester, 7–9 April.

Verba, S. and Nie, N. H. (1987) *Participation in America: Political Democracy and Social Equality*, Berkeley, CA: University of California Press.

Verloo, M. (2006) 'Multiple Inequalities, Intersectionality and the European Union', *European Journal of Women's Studies*, 13(3): 211–28.

Vita, A. de (2007) 'Inequality and Poverty in Global Perspective', in T. Pogge (ed.), *Freedom from Poverty as a Human Right: Who Owes What to the Very Poor?*, Oxford: Oxford University Press.

von Clausewitz, C. (2008) *On War*, with Introductions by Beatrice Heuser, Michael Howard and Peter Paret, Oxford: Oxford University Press (Oxford World's Classics).

von Hippel, E. (2005) *Democratizing Innovation*, Cambridge, MA: MIT Press.

Waddington, L. (2005) 'Implementing the Disability Provisions of the Framework Employment Directive: Room for Exercising National Discretion', in A. Lawson and C. Gooding (eds), *Disability Rights in Europe: From Theory to Practice*, Oxford: Hart.

Wade, R. (2004) 'The Ringmaster of Doha', *New Left Review*, 25: 146–52.

Wade, R. (2006) 'Should We Worry About Income Inequality?', in D. Held and A. Kaya (eds), *Global Inequality: Patterns and Explanations*, Cambridge: Polity.

Waever, O. (1998) 'The Sociology of a So International Discipline: American and European Developments in International Relations', *International Organization*, 52(4): 687–727.

Walby, S. (2004) 'The European Union and Gender Equality: Emergent Varieties of Gender Regime', *Social Politics*, 11(1): 4–29.

Walby, S. (2005a) 'Gender Mainstreaming: Productive Tensions in Theory and Practice', *Social Politics: International Studies in Gender, State and Society*, 12(3): 321–43.

Walby, S. (2005b) 'Introduction: Comparative Mainstreaming in a Global Era', in *International Feminist Journal of Politics*, 7(4): 453–70.

Wallace, W. (1999) 'The Sharing of Sovereignty: the European Paradox?', *Political Studies*, 47(3): 503–21.

Waller, M., and Linklater, A. (eds) (2003) *Political Loyalty and the Nation-State*, London: Routledge.

Walt, S. (2005) *Taming American Power*, Boston: W. Norton & Co.

Waltz, K. (1979) *Theory of International Politics*, London: McGraw-Hill.

Walzer, M. (1995) *The Spheres of Justice: A Defence of Pluralism and Equality*, Oxford: Blackwell.

Walzer, M. (2004) *Politics and Passion*, New Haven: Yale University Press.

Warren, K. (ed.) (1994) *Ecological Feminism*, London: Routledge.

Watson, M. (2005) *Foundations of International Political Economy*, Basingstoke: Palgrave Macmillan.

Watson, M. (2008) 'Theoretical Traditions in Global Political Economy', in J. Ravenhill (ed.), *Global Political Economy*, 2nd edn, Oxford: Oxford University Press.

Wattenberg, M. (2008) *Is Voting for Young People?*, London: Pearson Longman.

Webb, P., Farrell, D. and Holliday, I. (eds) (2002) *Political Parties in Advanced Industrial Societies*, Oxford: Oxford University Press.

Weber, M. (1948 [1918]) 'Politics as a Vocation', in *From Max Weber: Essays in Sociology*, ed. and trans. by H.H. Gerth and C.W. Mills, London: Routledge & Kegan Paul.

Weber, M. (1978 [1922]) *Economy and Society*, 2 volumes, Berkeley, CA: University of California Press.

Weber, S. (1997) 'The End of the Business Cycle?', *Foreign Affairs*, 76(4): 65–82.

Weiss L. (1998) *The Myth of the Powerless State: Governing the Economy in a Global Era*, Cambridge: Polity Press.

Weldon, L.S. (2008) 'The Concept of Intersectionality', in G. Goertz and A. Mazur (eds), *Politics, Gender and Concepts: Theory and Methodology*, Cambridge: Cambridge University Press.

Westcott, N. (2008) 'Digital Diplomacy: The Impact of the Internet on International Relations', *Oxford Internet Institute Working Paper*, 16.

Wheeler, D. (2007) 'Internet and Mobilization in the Arab World: A View from Internet Cafes in Jordan and Egypt', Paper prepared for the 103 Annual Political Science Association Meeting, 30 August–2 September 2007, Chicago, Illinois.

Wheeler, N. (2000) *Saving Strangers: Humanitarian Intervention in International Society*, Oxford: Oxford University Press.

Wilkinson, R. (2005) *The Impact of Inequality: How to Make Sick Societies Healthier*, London: Routledge.

Williams, B. (2005) *In the Beginning was the Deed: Realism and Moralism in Political Argument*, Princeton: Princeton University Press.

Williams, M.C. (2005) 'What is the National Interest? The Neoconservative Challenge in IR Theory', *European Journal of International Relations*, 11(3): 307–37.

Wimmer, A., and Glick Schiller, N. (2002) 'Methodological Nationalism and Beyond: Nation-State Building, Migration and the Social Sciences', *Global Networks*, 2(4): 301–34.

Wimmer, A. and Glick Schiller, N. (2003) 'Methodological Nationalism, the Social Sciences, and the Study of Migration: An Essay in Historical Epistemology', *International Migration Review*, 37(3): 576–610.

Wincott, D. (2006) 'Social Policy and Social Citizenship: Britain's Welfare States', *Publius: The Journal of Federalism*, 36(1): 169–88.

Wincott, D. (2009) 'Citizenship in Space and Time: Observations of T.H. Marshall's *Citizenship and Social Class*', in S. Greer (ed.), *Devolution and Social Citizenship in the UK*, Bristol: Policy Press.

Wolf, M. (2004) *Why Globalization Works*, New Haven: Yale University Press.

Wolf, R. (2002) 'How Partners become Rivals: Testing Neorealist and Liberal Hypotheses', *Security Studies*, 12(2): 1–42.

World Bank (2006) World Development Indicators, *WDI Database*, Washington, DC: World Bank.

World Bank (2009a) 'Swimming against the Tide: How Developing Countries Are Coping with the Global Crisis', Washington, DC: World Bank,

Background Paper prepared by World Bank Staff for the G20 Finance Ministers and Central Bank Governors Meeting, Horsham, United Kingdom on 13–14 March. Available at http://siteresources. worldbank.org/NEWS/Resources/swimmingagainstthetide-march2009. pdf.

World Bank (2009b) 'World Bank Updates Global Economic Forecasts'. Available at http://econ.worldbank.org/WBSITE/EXTERNAL/EXTDEC/ 0,,contentMDK:22122200~pagePK:64165401~piPK:64165026~theSitePK: 469372,00.html.

World Health Organization (2009) Available at http://www.euro.who.int/ mentalhealth/topics/20090309_1.

World Trade Organization (2009) 'World Trade 2008, Prospects for 2009: WTO Sees 9% Global Trade Decline in 2009 as Recession Strikes', Press Release, PRESS/554, Geneva: World Trade Organization, 24 March. Available at http://www.wto.org/english/news_e/pres09_e/pr554_e.pdf.

Worldwatch Institute (2004) 'State of the World 2004: Consumption by the Numbers', 8 January. Available at: http://www.worldwatch.org/node/1783

Worldwatch Institute (2006) *Vital Signs 2006–2007*, Washington, DC: Worldwatch Institute.

Wrench, J. (2005) 'Diversity Management Can be Bad for You', *Race and Class*, 46(3): 73–84.

Wyn Jones, R. and Scully, R. (2006) 'Devolution and Electoral Politics in Scotland and Wales', *Publius: The Journal of Federalism*, 36(1): 115–34.

Xenos, M. and Moy, P. (2007) 'Direct and Differential Effects of the Internet on Political and Civic Engagement', *Journal of Communication*, 57: 704–18.

Young, B. (2000) 'Disciplinary Neoliberalism in the European Union and Gender Politics', *New Political Economy*, 5(1), 77–98.

Young, I.M. (1990) *Justice and the Politics of Difference*, Princeton: Princeton University Press.

Young, I.M. (2000) *Inclusion and Democracy*, Oxford: Oxford University Press.

Young, I.M. (2001) 'Equality of Whom? Social Groups and Judgements of Injustice', *Journal of Political Philosophy*, 9(1):1–18.

Youngs, G. (2003) 'Private Pain/Public Peace: Women's Rights as Human Rights and Amnesty International's Report on Violence against Women', *Signs: Journal of Women, Culture and Society*, 28(4): 1209–29.

Zürn, M. and Leibfried, S. (2005) 'Reconfiguring the National Constellation', in S. Leibfried and M. Zürn (eds), *Transformations of the State?*, Cambridge: Cambridge University Press.

Newspaper publications

Economist, The (2008) 'The EU's Week from Hell', 11 October.

Economist, The (2009) 'Track my Tax Dollars' 5 February.

Financial Times (2008) 17 September.

Forbes (2008) 3 June.

New York Times (2008) 'Greenspan Concedes Errors on Regulation', 24 October.

Washington Post (2007) 'On Wikipedia, Debating 2008 Hopefuls' Every Facet',
17 September.

Index

Key: **bold** = extended discussion or term highlighted in the text; f = figure; t = table.

accountability   5, 7, 16, 214–15, 217, 227, 234, 242, 257, 277
accounting standards   159, 271
Ackerley, B.   246, 250
Act to Restrain Extravagant Practice of Raising Money' (UK, 1720)   150
activists   236
  motives   59
  professional   56–7
  see also   political activism
Advisory Centre on World Trade Law (2001–)   157
Afghanistan   134, 193, 252
Africa   161, 165, 214, 218
age   74, 89, 92, 96–7, 101, 106
agency (sub-state level)   **175, 180**
aid/ODA   222, 223–5f, 238, 242, 244, 275
aid for trade programme (WTO)   157
AIDS/HIV   38, 189, 214, 220
AIG   137
Al Qaeda   205, 209
Alaska   79
Alber, J.   183, 250, 260
Alexiadou, N.   186, 275
Almond, G.   44, **47–55**, 72, 250, 268
Almond and Verba survey (1959)
  key findings   **50**
  substantial problems   49
American Political Science Association   182
Amnesty International   213, 227, 246
Anand, S.   102, 250
Annan, K.   217
anthropology/anthropologists   85, 174, 197

anti-discrimination law/measures   88–91, 93, 97–9, 103, **104–6**, 107, 113, 115, 252, 256
  enforcement   104, 106
  'narrow frame'   105
anti-politics   **44–6**, 58, 62
AOL   84
Arabia   196
arms control   194, 197
asset bubbles   150, 164, 254, 268
assimilation   110, 125
Atkeson, L.   179, 250
Audit of Political Engagement (Hansard Society, 2004–)   50–1, 54, 54–5n, 72, 262
Australia   110, 120, 125, 151, 154–5, 159, 200
Austria   106, 168
authoritarian high modernism   37
authoritarianism   83, 237
autonomy   186–7
Avaaz (online NGO)   75, 251
'axis of evil' (Bush)   191

Bali (2007)   227–8
Ballas, D.   258
'banal nationalism' (Billig)   172, 177, 253
Bangladesh   100, 193, 209
Bank of England   138
Bank for International Settlements (BIS)   152, 159, 251
banking   28, 34
  shadow system   137, 140
'banking crisis' (label)   10
banks
  dependence on wholesale market   151

banks (*cont.*):
    financial support from governments
        138
    nationalization   137, 139
    off-balance-sheet activity   137
    re-capitalization   141, 145 162
    savers versus debtors   138–9, 145
    state ownership   130
Banting, K.   175, 251
Bardeesy, K.   160, 251
Barnett, J.   193, 251
Bartolini, S.   170, 178, 184, 188,
        251–2
Basel Committee on Banking
        Supervision (BCBS)   159, 161
Basel Principles on Capital Adequacy
        159
Bates, S.R.   176, 252
BBC   51, 258, 266
Beck, U.   38, 170–1, 175–6, 187–8,
        252
    on methodological nationalism
        173–4
    understanding of methodology
        176–7
behavioural economics   164
behavioural research   48
Beijing   95
Beitz, C.R.   237, 252
Belasco, A.   192, 252
Belgium   137, 168, 181, 257–8
Belgrade   205
Benhabib, S.   243, 253
Benkler, Y.   67, 71, 72, 253
Bi, F.   120, 253
'bicycle effect'   157
Bigo, D.   201, 208, 253
Billig, M.   172, 253
Bimber, B.   74, 84, 253
Blain, N.   279
Blair, A.C.L., 'Tony'   192
blame game   56, 57, 160
Blomfield, A.   192, 253
bonds   141, 143–4
Bonoli, G. 169, 253
boomerang effects (Keck and
        Sikkink)   98
Booth, K.   208, 253
Borrelli, S.   179, 269

Bosnia   202, 232
bounded rationality   **61–2**, 164
Braithwaite, J.   30, 254
Brazil   142, 159, 161, 226
Brenner, R.   164–5, 254
Bretton Woods system   158, 160
Britain   *see* United Kingdom
Bromley, S.   282
Brown, A.   275
Brown, G.   128, 190, 193, 254
'Bubble' Act (UK, 1720)   150
Budge, I.   263
Buiter, W.   154, 254
Bundesrat   181, 187
'burdened societies' (Rawls)   234–5
bureaucracy   31, 37, 52, 80, 184, 216
bureaucratic theory   32
Burma   84
Bush, G.W.   140–1, 191–2, 198, 202
business cycles   154, 284
Buthe, T.   159, 271–2
Buzan, B.   **199–200**, 201, 255

Cabinet Office (UK)   102, 255
Canada   110, 111, 125, 159, 200,
        206
candidate quotas   **94–5**
'capabilities'   98, **101–2**, 107, 274,
        280
    socially constructed priorities   102
    under-specified character
        (Robeyns)   101, 277
capital   132, 133, 138, 145, 148, 152,
        165, 220, 222
capital allocation   141–2
capitalism   155
    American   154
    literature   155–6
    varieties   155
Caramani, D.   170, 175, 255
    territorial voting behaviour   178–9
Carmichael, P.   277
Carr, E.H.   196, 203, 256
Carson, M.   265
catastrophic interdependence   35
catastrophic problems   41
Catholic Church   184
causation (reciprocal)   6–7
CDU/CSU (Germany)   195

Central Africa 197, 209
Central America 134
central banking 22, 30, 137–9, 141, 149, 159, 162, 215, 251
Central Europe 106
centralization 167–8, 184
centre–periphery 172, 180, 188, 278
Chadwick, A. 67, 255
challenges **2–5**
 civic culture (comparisons) **49–50**
 complexity 18
 contemporary political 23
 global 16
 global (accountability and effectiveness) **5, 211–30**
 global governance arrangements 212
 government–citizen interactions **78–80**
 interdependence 20, 25, 63
 Internet **65–6, 86–7**
 Internet (articulation of citizens' interests) 77
 Internet and political equality **82–3**
 methodological **84–6**
 national security 194
 new politics of equality 90, **107–8**
 political 2
 political science (global age) **229–30**
 political science (micro foundations) 64
 political science (secularist biases) 109
 political science (understanding of political parties) 78
 post-war multilateral order **216–18**
 scholarly analysis of the state 130
 security (interdependent world) **189–210**
 solutions to intractable problems 46
 territorial differentiation (comparative analysis) 187
 territorial politics **170–1**

territorial politics (beyond methodological nationalism) **4, 167–88**
theorizing identities 124
turnout (conventional wisdom) 74
Chancellor of Exchequer (UK) 138
'charismatic leadership' (Weber) 76
Chernilo, D. 173, 255
Chibber, P. 185, 255
children 91, 214, 226t
 child labour 221, 239
 child poverty 93
 childcare 184
China 141–2, 152–3, 159, 161, 196, 204, 219–20, 226
Christianity 126, 184
Citigroup 137
Citizen Audit (2001) 53
citizens
 degree of political engagement (1959, 2008) 50–1
 information-seeking behaviour (politics) **68–9**
 interactions with government **78–80,** 87
 meaning of politics to (need to understand) 63
 newly-acknowledged interdependence 21, 22
 participation in decision-making 50, 51–2, 55, 57–60, 62
citizenship **109–29,** 135–6
 British 118
 democratic 129
 differentiation by territory 180
 implications of multiculturalism **114 17**
 literature 265–6, 271, 281
 multicultural **117–19,** 127, 269
 multilogical 128
 split-level, democratic 180
 see also multicultural citizenship
'Citizenship and Social Class' (Marshall, 1950) 182–3, 271, 285
Citizenship Surveys (2001–) 50, 52, 255–6

civic culture   266, 268
  comparisons (challenges)   **49–50**
  decline (UK)   **47–55**
  findings   **48–9**
  pattern of change   **50–5**
  social divides   53–4
  Civic Culture (Almond and Verba,
    1963)   44, 51, 53, 55, 250
  Civic Culture Revisited (Almond and
    Verba, 1980)   48–9, 250, 268
civil rights (USA)   92, 113
civil service   277
  decentralization   277
civil society   94, 119, 207, 242, 246
  global   33, 135, 216, 217, 241
Clausewitz, K.M. von   200, 202
climate   38–9, 75, 189, 194, 209,
    211, 227–9, 238, 251
  carbon emissions   143, 222, 232,
    235, 242
  global warming   46, 213, 217–18,
    247
climate security   191, **193**, 200
Climate Security Bill (USA, 2007)
    193
Clinton administration   141, 205
coercion   29, 46
cognitive psychology   61–2
Cohen, G.   164
Cold War   190, 191, 197, 199, 210
  end/aftermath   149, 164, 192–3,
    195, 208, 211, 217, 232, 239,
    247
  analytical failures   198
collateralized debt obligations   136–7
collective action   64, **74–6**, 82, 212
  impact of Internet   76, 271
  individual tipping points
    (Schelling)   77
  starters (critical mass) (Schelling)
    77
collective bargaining   114
Colomer, J.   77, 256
colonialism   110, 236, 237
commodity prices   148, 159
commonality   124–5
communications   217
  global   216
  high speed   45

communitarians/communitarianism
    112, 135–6, 146
Communities and Local Government
    52, 256
community   **175**, 208
community security   207
comparative political sociology   178
comparative politics   136
comparative research   **107**
comparative welfare
  concepts imperfectly
    operationalized   **183**
  reconsideration required   185
complexity   **17–19**, 21, 35, 39, 41–2,
    61, 166, 185, 278
  institutional interdependence
    31–4
  interdependence   25–6
  international security   197, 198
  reserve currency   163
  'synonym of interdependence'   **18**
  US domestic politics   228
complexity of joint action (Pressman
    and Wildavsky)   33
Conceição, P.   268
Congo (Democratic Republic)   232
Congressional Research Service
    192
constitutional change   175, 181, 186,
    251
constitutional courts   126
consumer choice   10–11, 13, 22
consumer demand   153
consumption   16, 225f
context   6, 62, 244, 246, 248
  politics of equality   **90–2**, **98–9**,
    106
contractualism   **233–40**, 242–3,
    246–8
control state   66
Coordinated Market Economies
    155, 156
Copenhagen School   206, **207–8**
corporate governance   221
cosmopolitanism   110, 172, 252
Counter-Terrorism Strategy
  ('CONTEST', UK, 2003–)
    192–3
Cox, M.   196, 256

crèches sauvages 184
credibility 181
credit-rating agencies 30, 159, 280
  conflicts of interest 160
Crenshaw, K. 103, 256
Crick, Sir Bernard (1929–2008) 46,
  256
crime/criminology 6, 197
critical constructivism 201
critical distance 197, 198
critical security studies 197
critical theory **240–3**, 244, 246–8,
  260
Croft, S. **xi, 4–5**, 11, 16
Crotty, W. 67, 267
culture 10, 36, 37, 38, 100, 111,
  113, 234, 253, 268
currencies (weak) 144
currency swap guarantees 142
current account deficits 144
Curtice, J. 180, 257
Curtis, J. 275
Cutler, F. 179–80, 257
cyber [political] parties (Margetts)
  78, 271
cyberchiefs 76
cyberculture 83
cybernetics 32
cynicism 50, 51, 57
'czars' 37

Dahl, R.A. 72, 257
Dahlerup, D. 94, 257
Dalton, R. 67, 72, 257
Darfur 232
Das Kapital (Marx) 165
data
  nation-state basis 177
  qualitative 84, 85
data deficiencies 183, 185–8
de Rynck, S. 186, 257
de Wilde, J. 255
death (premature) 211, 217, 218,
  237
debt 138, 144, 159, 161, 165
debt-servicing 142
decentralisation of penury 185
decentralization 4, 169, 172, 178–9,
  181, 184, 277

decentralizing turn 168, 170–1
decision-making 45, 71, 89, 215
  accountable, effective 229
  bounded rationality **61–2**
  capacity of citizens to influence
    50, 51–2, 55, 57, 59–60, 62
  constraints 59
  domestic (international purchase
    on) 146
  participation of women **94–5**
  political 111
  poor 62
  transnational 146
deep green solutions 39
democracy 1, 19–20, 29, 63, 67, 82,
  126, 168, 188, 226, 228–30
  de-nationalized 177–8
  economic theory 258
  global mechanisms required **241**
  levelling the playing field 64
  'liberal democracy' 3, 73, 81,
    114–15, 145
  literature 257–8, 263, 266, 281
  multi-scalarity 181
  'needs politics' 45–6
  representative 2–3
  sub-state versus state-wide **181**
  territorial differentiation 181
democratic consent 217, **218**
democratic deficits 214
democratic innovations 59, 280
democratic mechanisms, formal and
    informal (central to meaning of
    justice) **240–1**
'democratic peace' 206, 279
democratic statecraft **27–30**
democratization 182, 244, **248**, 260
Democrats (USA) 140
demography 184, 217
Denmark 126
Denver, D. 180, 257, 266
Department for Communities and
    Local Government 50
dependence 5
  versus interdependence 6–7
dependency 29, 165
Der Derian, J. 202
deregulation 29
derivatives 28, 137

Deschouwer, K. 178, 258, 268
desecuritization (Waever) 208
developed countries 132, 157, 217
  industrialized economies 158–9,
    161, 165
  rich countries 133
developing economies 132, 148,
  155, 158, 161, 202, 214, 217,
  219, 222, 226, 228, 238, 285
  debt-afflicted 159
  less-developed economies 157,
    165
development **222**, 238, 244, 268
developmental policies (Peterson)
  184
devolution 4, 21, 170, 172, 180,
  183–4, 257, 262, 265–6, 275,
  285–6
Dezeure, K. 186, 257
diasporas 75, 83
difference 124
difference and equality **112–14**
Digg 70
digital divides **71–2**, 82–3
digital technology 3, 16
digital-era governance (DEG) 80,
  81
Dillon, M. 201
direct democracy 66
disability/disabled people 88–92,
  94, 96–7, 101, 104, 106–7
disaggregation 31
disciplinary boundaries 10
  need to retain 23–4
discourse 92, 122, 123, 191, 201
discrimination 103
  intersectional 98
  see also anti-discrimination law
discursive construction 40
  spatial interdependence **27–30**
distributive justice 111, 112, 145,
  234
distributive policies (Lowi) 184
division of labour *see*
  specialization
Doha Round 157, 161
'doing good by stealth' (Lister, 2001)
  93, 270
domain interdependence 6, **8–11**

domestic violence 246
donations 54, 54–5t
dot.com bubble 153
Dowding, K. 85, 258
Downs, A. 73, 258
Drahos, P. 30, 254
Drew, D. 73–4, 258
dual voting 180
Dumont, P. 257
Dunleavy, P. 36, 37, 258
Dunn, J. 230, 258
Duverger, M. 78, 259
Dworkin, R. 92, 101, 259

e-Bay 83
East Asia 142, 153, 162, 219
  financial crisis (1997–8) 141,
    150, 159, 161, 165
Eastern Europe 106, 144
Easton, D. 32, 259
Ebeid, M. 179, 259
economic development 180, 234,
  238–9
  regional 186
economic discretion **136–42**
economic governance
  effective 151
  global 154
  problems and opportunities
    218–25
economic growth 165
  global (1960–2000) 219
  political gain 140
economic inequalities 232, 242–3
economic interdependence 237
  global (and study of IPE) **163–5**
  global economic crisis (chapter
    seven) **4, 148–66**
economic policy 265
  one size does not fit all 222
economic power (global shift) 161
Economic and Social Research
  Council: Participation
  Programme 49
economic take-off 220
economics 66, 163, 226, 279
  behavioural 164
  neo-classical 164
  versus political science 9

Economist, The 82, 286
economists 43, 86, 197, 198
education 81, 97, 114, 180, 184,
    186, 220, 275
educational attainment 91, 101
effectiveness 5, 16, 33, 151, 215,
    217, 218
egalitarian theorists 92
egalitarianism (social democratic)
    114
Egypt 284–5
Eichengreen, B. 156, 259
elderly people 96
election promises 50, 51
elections 173, 177
    data deficiencies 181–2
    first-order 257
    Japan (2004) 73
    national/state-wide 143, 170,
        178–9, 187
    regional 179, 180
    Scotland and Wales (devolved
        versus UK level) 180
    second-order 179, 180, 277
    sub-state 168, 179–82, 186–7
    territorial differentiation 180–1
    territorial politics **178–82**
    valence evaluations 180
    see also turnout
electoral politics 265, 286
electorate/voters 21–2, 56, 77, 178,
    186, 252
electronic government 67, **71**, 87,
    274
Eleventh of September (2001) 15,
    28, 111, 153, 191–2, 198, 209,
    223, 229
elites 22, 29, 35, 36, 38, 48, 92, 154,
    166, 189, 224
    transnational norm dissemination
    94
emancipation 206, 208
Emergency Economic Stabilization
    Act 2008 (USA) 145
'emergency measures' 207
employment 94, 101, 133, 148–9,
    183, 221
    equal treatment 97
    unskilled 53, 55n

empowerment 47, 101, 110, 115
Enlightenment 36
environment (natural) 1, 4, 10–11,
    13, 16, 22, 190–1, 217, 220–2,
    229, 234–6, 238, 242
    'impending catastrophe' 232
    feminist ethic 244–5
environment (socio-economic) 91
environmental security 207
envy 91
epidemiology 7, 8, 17, 18, 38,
    176–7, 201, 210, 252, 269, 285
equal dignity **113–14**
equal pay 91, 97
equal respect **113–14**
equality 3, 106, 255, 259
    concept 113
    difference and **112–14**
    discourse 92
    distributive **92–3**
    horizontal measures 88
    multi-dimensional 88, 90
    new and old politics 106
    'out of fashion' (Toynbee) 90,
        282
    paradigm shift 91
    redistribution, recognition,
        representation **100–4**
    vertical approach 97
equality bodies **93–7**
    separate 106
    single **104–6**, 107
equality experts 99
Equality and Human Rights
    Commission (EHRC, UK) 106
equality of opportunity 89, 92,
    94–5, 100–2, 106
equality of outcome 89, 91–2,
    101–2, 106
equivalence principle **215**
Escher, T. 271
Esping-Andersen, G. 183
essentially contested concept (Gallie)
    200
ethnic communities 55, 88, 91, 94,
    96, 106, 110
ethnicity 89, 91, 104, 111, 113, 119,
    124, 127, 207, 228, 266
euro zone 143

Europe of regions 187
European Consortium for Political
    Research 182
European Convention on Human
    Rights 99
European Court of Human Rights
    126
European integration 167, 174, 259,
    270
    disorganization of nation-state
        184
European Parliament 179
European Social Survey 70
European Union (EU) 15, 30, 89,
    95–6, 105–6, 131–2, 135, 168,
    175, 185, 227–8, 240, 247
    directives on gender equality 97
    home affairs mandate 208
    literature 252, 281, 283, 286
    market-driven character 99
    new politics of equality **98–9**
    over-representation in IMF 158
    populist anger 144
    reconciliation of work and family
        99, 281
    response to global financial crisis
        (2008–9) **142–4**
    sub-state/state relationships 186
    trade agreement with Mercosur
        158
    transnational governance 142–3,
        146
European Union: Charter of
    Fundamental Rights 99
European Union: Directives
    Employment Equality 97
    Racial Equality (2000) 97, 104
European Union: EU-27 144
Europeanism 110
exchange-rate management 133,
    158–9
exchange-rate risk 141–2
expectations 21, 131, 133, 134, 139,
    144–6, 178
expenditure (luxury items) 226t

Facebook 70, 85
failure of integration 125
family 117, 169

Fannie Mae/Freddie Mac 137,
    140–2, 282
Feddersen, T. 73, 259
Federal Funding Accountability and
    Transparency Act 2008 (USA)
    79
federal systems 168, 180, 183
federalism 172, 276
feedback 61, 81–2, 185
Fein, L.C. 195, 273
feminism 103, 123–4, 231, **243–6**,
    248
    ethic of care 243
    literature 253, 256, 271, 275
    problems of generalization 244
feminists 98–9, 104–5, 108, 116,
    117, 247
Ferrera, D. 170, 184–6, 188, 259
finance 28, 222
financial crisis (global, 2007–)
    130–2
    causes 139–40
    economic interdependence and
        148–66
    EU response **142–4**
    financial crisis current/impact
        148
    literature 265–6, 279, 285
    miscellaneous 1, 4, 9, 15, 19–20,
        30, 34, 40–1, 146, 153
    political emotion unleashed 145
    prediction failure 198
    'something old, something new'
        150–1
    and the state **136–42**
financial institutions 150, 152
    improved regulation 155
    nationalization 137, 149, 154
    poor lending 149
financial market actors 40–1
financial markets 10, 29, 139, 162,
    229
    light-touch regulation 34, 140
    turnover tax 222
financial sector 145
financial services 30
Financial Services Authority 140
Financial Stability Board (2009–)
    162

Financial Stability Forum (1999–) 162, 286
Finland 106
firms 137, 160, 215
  corporations 137
  financial corporations 130
  multinational corporations 153, 239
  rescued by state 130
fiscal balancing 131
fiscal burdens 139, 153
fiscal expropriation 29
fiscal stimulus packages 130, 138, 155, 166
Flora, P. 182–3, 260
food security 207
Forbes, D. 279
foreign direct investment (FDI) 153, 220
foreign exchange 159
  daily turnover (2007) 152
foreign policy 29–30, 83, 128
Foreign Policy (journal) 165, 198
Forst, R. 241, 260
Foucauldian analyses 103
Foucault, M. 201, 208
fragmegration (Rosenau) 31
France 143, 159, 168, 182, 184, 195
  headscarf ban in state schools 126–7
  republican citizenship 118
Frankfurt School 208
Fraser, N. 100, 241, **260**
free-riding 74
freedom 234
  from fear/want 207
Freidenvall, L. 94, 257
Friends of Earth 57, 193
full employment 40
funding councils 12
future generations 229

Gallie, W.B. 200
Garrett, R.K. 69, 261
Gates, W. H., III ('Bill') 214, 272
gender 53–4, 89–91, 94, 100–1, 104, 106–7, 114, 116, 119, 122, 169
  see also feminism

gender mainstreaming 94, **95**, 105
general public 189
generalizability 18
genocide prevention 249
Gerber, M. 259
German Economy Fund 137
Germany
  civic culture 47
  failure of bond auctions (2009) 139
  federal versus Länder elections 182
  literature 265, 269
  miscellaneous 111, 126, 155, 159, 168, 187, 224f
  national security 195
  post-communist eastern 180
  retreat to nation-state (2008) 143
  state-wide government–opposition relations 181
  trade surpluses 162
Giddens, A. 38, 261
Gilpin, R. 202, 261
Glazer, N. 111, 261
Glick Schiller, N. 174, 176, 285
global age
  rethinking politics **229–30**
global audience 231, 249
Global Business Regulation (Braithwaite and Drahos, 2000) 30, 254
global dynamics
  versus local electorates 21–2
global economy 16
  governance 229
  regulation **156–63**
  world economic order 239
  world economy 254
Global Fund 214
global governance 4, 5, 22, 166
  accountability and effectiveness **211–30**
  limits **212–16**
  politics of change **225–9**
  see also governance
global justice 5, 15–16, 22, **231–49**, 260
  economic 238–9
  procedural 241

global justice (*cont.*):
  state-based versus individual
    rights-based   247
  between statism and globalism
    233–40
  theories (two broad trajectories)
    232–3
  theorizing (contested)   231–2
  theorizing (feminist)   246
  theorizing (future)   **246–9**
  theorizing (beyond statism and
    globalism)   **240–6**
  theorizing process   **248**
  theory (construction versus
    discovery)   **249**
  see also   human rights
global order (contested)   248
global web (Braithwaite and Drahos)
  30
global–local connections   12, 16
globalism   42, **233–40**, 241–3, 249
globalization   4, 15, 21–2, 33,
    45–6, 89, 98, 110, 130, 137,
    167, 169, 173–4, 176, 188, 220,
    227, 229
  benefits and costs   194–5
  constraints on policy options of
    state   151, **152–6**
  corporate   65
  current understanding (impact of
    global financial crisis)   151,
    152–6
  deep drivers (Held)   **216–17**
  deep-rooted problems (Held)
    213–15
  definition (Ravenhill)   152
  economic   27–30, 40, 240
  financial   150
  golden age   156
  impact on states   **155–6**
  literature   252, 279, 282, 285
  political backlash   131
  state as agent of political identity
    135–6
  state in international sphere
    134–5
  winners and losers   219
globalization discourse   142
  limitations   146–7

globalization thesis   139, 145
  claims   132–3
  economic discretion of the state
    132–4
  sceptics   133
gold standard   152, 259
Goma, R.   261
goods and services   30, 97, 104, 216
Google   68, 69, 84, 86
Google Trends   70, 84–5
governance   45, 107, 276–8
  changing patterns (new politics of
    equality)   **98–9**
  cosmopolitan   135, 263
  institutional interdependence
    31–4
  networked   34
  'open-book'   83
  post-modernist theorists   41
  supra-state   228
  transnational   132, 135–6, **142–4**,
    146, 147
  see also   global governance
Governance of Britain (Green Paper,
    2007)   58, 265, 276
'governance' school of thought   31
governance theory (antecedents)
    32–3
governing (act)   39
governing crises (1970s)   39
government   36
  electronic processes   85
  front office   81–2
  institutional interdependence
    31–4
  responsibilities   40
government deficits   149
government policy agendas   197
government solutions
  critiques by political scientists   58
government–citizen interactions
    78–80
governmental system
  matter of pride (1959)   52
governmentality school   35
governments   30, 91, 96, 130, 133,
    137–8, 145, 148–9, 154, 159–61,
    163, 166, 181, 185–6, 199, 214,
    216

comparative powerlessness in
foreign exchange markets 152
early responses to global financial
crisis 155
'primary duty' 190
regional [sub-state] 187
social democratic and socialist 93
tyrannical 235
Grande, E. 171, 173, 252
Great Britain *see* United Kingdom
Great Depression (1930s) 148, 153
Greece 100, 127, 202
Greenspan, A. 160, 286
Greer, S. 171, 262
gross domestic product (GDP) 102,
205, 224f
gross national income (GNI)
223–4f, 225n
gross national product (GNP) 102,
224n
group identity 113, 122
group representation **93–7**, 122–3
Group of Seven (G7) 142, 159, 161
Group of Eight (G8) 161
Group of Ten 159
Group of Twenty (G20) 152
central role 161
Finance Ministers 285
London Summit (2009) 154–5,
161–2, 261
groupness **121–4**

habeas corpus 117
Habermas, J. 240, 262
feminist critique 243
hacker charisma 76
Hague, R. 66–7, 262
Hall, S. 123, 262
Handbook of Internet Politics
(Chadwick and Howard, 2009)
67, 255
Handbook of Party Politics (Katz and
Crotty, 2006) 67, 267
Handbook of Public Administration
(Peters and Pierre, 2003) 67,
276
Hansard Society 50, 54–5n, 72, 262
Harlem (NYC) 100
Harrop, M. 66–7, 262

hate speech 128
Hay, C. **xi**, 28, 45, 57, 58, 62–3,
63n, 107, 176, **263**
health 37–8, 101, 180, 207, 214,
218, 220–1, 226t
health care 117, 222
websites 80, 81–2
health and safety 34
Heclo, H. 85, 263
hedge funds 137
Hediar, K. 78, 263
Held, D. **xi**, **5**, 16, 22, 28, 166, 213,
215, 219, 222, 227, **263–4**, 276,
283
model of cosmopolitan democracy
241, 263
platform for action 230
Helsper, E. 259
Hepburn, E. 187, 264
heroic leadership 76
Herz, J. 203, 264
heuristics 199
Hibbing, J. 63, 264
hierarchy 5, 27, 31–3, 243, 245,
248–9
high-mindedness **222**
Hinds, K. 275
Hirst, P. 282
Hispanics 110, 111
history 10, 20, 25, 27, 28, 44, 46,
72, 110, 117–18, 135, 147,
154–5, 167, 174, 176, 182,
191–2, 197, 202, 230, 236,
243–4, 246, 249, 285
nineteenth century 38
twentieth century 280
twenty-first century 128–9, 193,
199, 229
see also time
History of the Peloponnesian War
(Thucydides) 202
Hobbes, T. 202
Holyrood 180, 181, 257, 266
Home Office 50
homosexuality 116–17
Hood, C. 80–1, 265
Hooghe, L. 171, 271
horizontal equality 91
Hough, D. 179, 180, 265

House of Commons 190
  expenses scandal (2009) 44–5,
    47, 51–2, 79, 266
  voting records 79
housing booms 141–2
Howard, P. 67, 255
human capital 222
human condition 2, 20, 25, 279
human development 217, 274
Human Development Report (UNDP)
  102, 207, 225–6n, 250, 283
human life 35, 38
human nature 202, 203
human rights 75, 90, 99, 125–6, 207,
    218, 221–2, 227, 235, 242, 276
  basic 244
  feminist approach 245
  fundamental 237, 280
  global economic justice 238–9
  universal 250
  women 243, 271
Human Rights Act (UK) 106
human rights theory 237–240, 244,
    246–9
  see also Pogge
human security 27, **28**, **206–7**, 226,
    229
'humanitarian intervention' 232,
    247, 249
humanitarianism ('top-down') 244
Hungary 144
Hutchings, K. **xi**, **5**, 22, 249
Hyde-Price, A. 202

IBM 30
Iceland 137, 139, 151
idealist internationalism 264
identity 115, 116, 180, 207, 243
  civic 125
  depoliticized 124
  multiple 123
  political **144–6**, 147
  public–private distinction 114
  territorial 172
  see also national identity
identity groups 88–9, 91, 93–4, 96,
    100, 103, 106
  competition for title of 'most
    oppressed' 104

identity politics 124
  Muslim **119–21**
ideology 57, 121, 180, 193, 196,
    205, 247
  high modernism 36
ILGA-Europe 99
Imai, K. 265
immigration/immigrants 109–11,
    126, 191, 266
  economic 238
  securitized policy 21
  see also migration
imperialism 120, 129, 236, 249
Implementation (Pressman and
    Wildavsky, 1973) 32–3, 276
income distribution 91, 94
India 159, 161, 192, 219, 226, 274
individual rights 118
individualism 102, 114
inequality/inequalities 6, 64
  feminist critiques 244
  global 5, 89, **90–2**, 234, 244, 264,
    276
  global economic 246–7
  income 100, 220, 283
  literature 264, 276, 279, 283
  multiple 103
  non-socio-economic 91–2
  political and cultural focus 96
  social and economic (digital divide)
    82
  socio-economic 100–1, 105
  vertical or unitary approach 94
infant industry protection 222
inflation 150, 151
inflation target 138
inflation targeting 149
information asymmetries 80
information exchange 162
information society (global) 83
information technology (IT) 71, 85,
    216, 271, 278
infrastructure (physical) 222
injustice
  intersections 243
inlinks versus outlinks 86
Institute of Practitioners in
    Advertising 55n
institutional design 82, 156, 164

institutional interdependence **26**, 27, 30
  government, governance, complexity **31–4**
  new world (scepticism) 33–4
  robust evidence 33
institutional investors 150–1
institutional structure **180**
institutions 41, 69, 108, 122, 186, 205–6, 268
  accountable and effective 16
  democratic 1
  design 64
  fairness 218
  formal 241
  global governance 5, 22
  national character 2
  novel 25
  politics of equality **93–7**, **104–6**
  politics of equality (new and old) 106, 107
  private 30
  single equalities bodies **104–6**
  sub-state 180
  transnational 96
instrumental rationality 57
intellectual capital 29
inter-disciplinarity (theme) 5, 6, 12, 45, 60, 197–8
  idea **8**
  interdependence and **8–11**
  research **107**
inter-governmental organizations (IGOs) 156, 213, 214, 227
inter-sub-disciplinarity **14–16**, 24
inter-subject communication versus monological reasoning 246
interculturalism 127
interdependence (theme) 5, **6–8**, 186–7, 218, 231
  careful interrogation 209
  complexity, and possibility of political science **17–19**
  concept **6**, 20
  concept (how it might be made more useful) **41–2**
  concept (limitations) 41
  concept and character **2**, **25–42**

crucial point 7
discursive sense 27, **28–9**
economic 4, 22, 142, 238
global 189
global (three aspects) 232
illusions **83–4**
many faces 39
national security 194
necessary condition 6
new kinds 31
new or newly-acknowledged **19–22**
old and new **25–7**
paths to inter-disciplinarity 10
societies 217
spatial 4, **11–12**
spatial, institutional, policy 83
statecraft and rhetoric **39–42**
sufficient condition 6
three concepts (Moran) **26–7**
types 83
versus 'dependence' 6–7
interdependence theory 205
interdependent security, common ground lacking 209
interdependent world 45–6, 56, 130
  new security challenges **189–210**
  policy-making **25–42**
interest groups 55, 186
  ecology (reconfigured) **74–6**
  organizational costs 74
  transnational 83
  wholly online 75
interest rates 138, 141, 143, 145
interests
  aggregation mechanisms (sub-state) 186
  reconciliation 45–6
intermestic issues (Held) 213
international anarchy 202, 204, 208
International Civil Aviation Organization 212
International Criminal Court (ICC) 227, 239, 245–7
International Criminal Tribunal for former Yugoslavia (ICTY) 245
International Criminal Tribunal for Rwanda (ICTR) 245

international financial institutions
219, 222
international governmental
organizations   214, 247
International Monetary Fund (IMF)
142, 144, 148–50, 152, 212,
214–15, 219, 222, 265–6
country quotas   158, 161
fails to fulfil intended role   158
new role   161
pre-emptive action   161
structural adjustment programmes
98
voting rights   158
International Monetary Fund : Interim
Committee   158–9
international non-governmental
organizations (INGOs)   228,
238–9
International Organization (journal)
201, 267
International Organization of
(national) Securities
Commissions   30
international political economy (IPE)
4, 136, 146, 149, 151–2, 268,
269
critical approaches   163
fragmentation   163
global economic interdependence
and   **163–5**
International Political Science
Association   182
International Political Sociology
(journal)   201
international politics   203
power versus security (Morgenthau
versus Waltz)   204
world politics   208
international relations (IR)   2, 4, 7,
12, 31, 90, 107, 136, 146, 172,
174, 196, 201, 203, 252, 268,
282
realism versus its critics   134
realist approaches   149
role (Rawls)   236
theory   14, 199, 253, 277, 285
US versus European theory   200,
284

international security   189
concepts   209
contested field of study   209
examined in three ways   190
far less novel   209
see also   national security
International Security Studies
Anglophone   195–6, **196–200**
disciplinary lessons   198–9
literature   200
post-Cold War 'salvation' of field
198
subject matter   197
International Studies Association   201
international system   33–4
Internet
effects on politics (further research)
84
filtering   83
lapsed users   82–3
literature   265–6, 274, 282, 284–5
matching capability   75
online petitions   69–70, 75, 77, 85
organizational costs (reduction)
74–5
political science understanding
(current state)   **66–8**
range of activities   66
structure   85
utopian versus dystopian
possibilities   67–8
Internet in political science (chapter
three)   **64–87**
challenges   **65–6, 72**
trends   **68–72**
intersectionality (Crenshaw)   103–6,
108, 256, 283
interviews   49, 50
investment   132–3
ethical   239
see also   institutional investors
investment banks   137, 141, 160
investor panic   150–1, 164
Ipsos/MORI   51, 52, 266
IRA   192–3
Iran   192
demonstrations (2009)   69, 83–4,
87
election (2009)   65

Iraq War (2003–) 15, 65, 189–91, 198, **204–5**, 252
Ireland 137
Islam 124, 226
Italy 47, 159, 168, 224f
ius sanguine 127

Jabri, V. 201
Jacobson, J. 123, 266
Jamaica Meeting (IMF's Interim Committee, 1976) 158–9
Japan 37, 152, 158–9, 224f
  Internet (effect on voter turnout, 2004) 73
Jeffery, C. **xi–xii**, **4**, 15, 20–1, 179–80, 186, 265, **266**
Jenkins, L. 176, 252
Jeong, S.-J. 165, 254
Jews 122
jihad 128
John, P. 49, 61, 63n, 266, 271, 281
Johns, R. 180, 257, 266
Johnson, T.J. 73, 266
Jones, B. 61, 266
Jones, M. 262
Jones, R. 262
Joppke, C. **126–7**, 266
Jordan 284–5
justice/fairness 50, 52, 218, 277, 286
  Janus-faced **233–7**
  principles **240**
  redistributive 134
  universal **237–40**
  'within' versus 'between' political communities **274**
  see also global justice
justification 241

Kabbani, R. 120, 267
Kagan, R. 205, 269
Kantianism 111
Kantola, J. **xii**, **3**, 15, 16, 112–13, 231
Katsumata, H. 195, 267
Katz, R. 67, 267
Katzenstein, P.J. 164, 201, 267
Kavanagh, D. 48–9, 51, 54, 268
Kaya, A. 219, 264, 276, 283

Kaye, B.K. 73, 266
Keating, M. 168–9, 171, 176, 180, **268**, 275
Kennedy, H. 58
Keohane, R.O. 164, 267–8
Keynesian approaches 149, 154, 166, 183, 188
Kindleberger, C. 150, 268
King, A. 33, 268
King, M.L., Jr 113
Kirshner, J. 162, 268
Kiva (online NGO) 75, 83, 85
Klingemann, H. 67, 72, 257
Knight, S. 192, 274
knowledge economy 91
Kollmann, K. 185, 255
Kolodziej, E. 202, 268
Korea: North 71, 192, 274
Korea: South 142, 159
Kosovo 232, 239
Krasner, S.D. 267
Kristol, I. 205, 269
Kristol, W. 205, 269
Kuhnle, S. 182, 269
Kymlicka, W. 231, 269

La Porte, T. 33, 269
labelling 10
labour 29, 40–1, 99, 133, 222, 244
  cheap labour 111
Labour Party 54, 181
  women's section 114
Lake, D.A. 163, 269
Länder elections 182
language 110, 111, 195–6
language of politics 21
Latin America 158, 161, 165, 203
Latin America and Caribbean 219
Latvia 139
law 34, 107, 119
  international 227, 229, 235
  international economic 221
  regional and international 213
  sole author (the state) 134
  transnational 221
Law of Peoples (Rawls, 1999) **233–7**, 238, 277
Lawrence, R. 265
Le Goulven, K. 268

leadership (online)   **76–7**
legislatures   145
legitimacy   5, 51, 95, 105
    representative democracy   2–3
legitimation   29, 41, 146–7, 188,
    193, 233
Lehmbruch, G.   181, 269
Leitkultur   126
Letter to Christendom (Kabbani,
    1989)   120, 267
Leyden, K.   179, 269
liberal institutionalists   164
liberal justice   236
'Liberal Market Economies'   155
liberalism   112, 126, 235, 240, 247
    classical   114
    normative priorities   249
liberalism (security studies)   **205–6**
liberals (USA)   202
Liberia   226
liberty   237
life expectancy   94, 100, 101
lifestyle   209
'light-touch steering'   34
Lipset, S.M.   172, 178, 270
Lisbon Treaty   99
literacy   226t
living standards   144, 237
lobby organizations   56–7
'logic of collective action'   270, 275
    reconfigured   **74–6**
London   140, 151
    bombings (2005)   120, 253
    G20 Summit (2009)   154–5,
        161–2, 261
long boom (1992–2007)   29
long-termism   160
Los Angeles   65
Loubser, M.   86, 87, 270
Loughlin, S.   268
Lowi, T.   184, 270
luck egalitarians   92
Lupia, A.   74, 75–6, 84, 270
Lutheranism   126
Luxembourg   137, 159
Lynch, P.   187, 270

Maastricht Treaty 1992   143
    social chapter   221

Machiavelli, N.   202
MacKinnon, C.A.   243, 271
macroeconomic policy   40, 132, 133,
    138, 163
madman theory   192, 274
Mair, P.   178, 252, 271
malaria   214, 272
Malaysia   125
Maldives   193, 209
male breadwinner model   117
malnutrition   223, 226t
management accounting   36
manufacturing   91, 153
Margetts, H.   **xii, 3**, 16, 37, 67, 76,
    77–8, 81–2, 85, 271
market economy   92
market failure   220
market forces   90, 130, 139
market participation   93
markets
    global   220, 222
    self-regulating   149
    self-regulation capacity (loss in
        faith)   160
    unregulated   154
Marks, G.   168, 171, **271**
Marshall, T.H.   109, 117–18, 182,
    269, 271, 285
Martins, H.   171, 175, 271
Marx, K.H.   275
Marxists   164–5
mass demonstrations   65, 69, 83–4, 87
    online   70
    protest movements   56–7
    riots   139
    student protests (late 1960s)   172
mass politics   64, 188, 260, 278
Massey, A.   277
Mattli, W.   159, 164, 271–2
McCrone, D.   275
McMillan, J.   277
McNeal, R.S.   73, 282
Mearsheimer, J.J.   198, 204
media   45, 57, 59, 68–70, 78, 84,
    119, 196, 199
    'news consumption'   68–9
Meikle, J.   214, 272
Mendoza, R.U.   268
mental health   100

Mercosur 158
methodological cosmopolitanism
(Beck) 174, 175–6, 187, 252
methodological innovation 19
Internet in political science 67
methodological nationalism 20,
167–88, 252
beyond **4**, **173–6**, 255, 285
coined by Martins (1974) 171–2,
271
critiques 186
definition 170
further research 4
modernization and territorial
politics **171–3**
methodology 8, 17, 107, 108
Internet (in political science) 64,
86–7
meaning 176–7
Metropolitan Police 151
Mexico 47, 142, 159
micro-lending 75
migration/migrants 28, 89, 91, 125,
174, 217, 239, 281, 285
see also immigration
military expenditure 222, 224–5f
Millennium Development Goals
(MDGs) 148, 211, 217, 218
mimesis (concept) 195, 267, 273
minimal transnational justice (Forst)
241
minimum capital requirement
exemptions (Switzerland) 138
minimum wage (statutory) 93
minorities within minorities 122–3
minority cultures
national identity and **124–9**
minority nationalism 270
Missouri Accountability Portal 79
Mitchell, H. 170, 172, 273
Mitchell, J. 172, 257, 266, 273
Mizruchi, M.S. 195, 273
modernism 36
modernity 38, 261
modernization 67, 169, **171–3**, 188,
260
Modood, T. **xii**, **3–4**, 11, 15, 20, 93,
100, 104, 112, 117, 121, 124–5,
272, **273**

monetarism 149
monopoly of legitimate use of
physical force (Weber) **27**, 31
Monroe Doctrine 203
Moody's 30
Moran, M. **xii**, **2**, 7, 17, 20–1, 75, 83
Morgenthau, H. 194, 203
mortgage-backed securities 136–7,
140–1, 150
mortgages 138
sub-prime 13, 141, 150, 162, 165
Motion Picture Association of
America 30
Mulhall, S. 231, 274
multi-level governance 15, 174–5,
271
multicultural citizenship
dispersed **118–19**
multilogical **118**
non-transcendent or pluralist **118**
work-in-progress 119
multiculturalism 124, **109–12**
citizenship and national identity
3–4, **109–29**
implications for liberal citizenship
114–17
literature 272–3, 275, 283
miscellaneous 15, 20, 90, 96, 103,
107, 231
part of the solution 129
multiculture 121, 125
multilateral organizations 214–16,
229
multilateralism 227, 228
multilogues 118, 119
multiple discrimination 105, 108
multiple inequalities 107, 283
multiplicity (Sen) 101
Mumbai 192
Muslims 109, **115–17**, 123, 126
'disaffection' 127–8
dual loyalties 121
identity politics **119–21**
mutual conditioning 6, 12, 18
MySociety 79

NAFTA (labour and environment)
221
nation **175–6**

nation-building   172, 176, 182, 185,
    188, 260
    state-building   235
nation-state/s   83, 110, 132, 135–6,
    143–4, 146, 167–70, 184, 213,
    232, 246, 252, 255
    comparative analysis   177
    conceptually elusive   171–2
    construction (function replacing
        geography)   182
    data based on   177
    popular identification   **186**
    satisfaction of justice-claims   231
    territorial differentiation   176, 187
National Audit Office (NAO, UK)
    86, 274
national economies   29, 41, 132, 236
national identity   **109–29**, 146, 228
    and minority cultures   **124–9**
national interest   205, 269
national security   194, 267
    see also   security
National Security Act (USA, 1947)
    195
National Security Strategy (UK,
    2008)   190, 195, 254
'national welfare state' concept   185
nationalism   110, 172, 177, 180, 186,
    275, 280
    ontological   4, 20
    see also   methodological
        nationalism
nationality   111
nationalization [economic]
    banks   137, 139
    financial institutions   137, 149,
        154
nationalization [political]   187, 188
    homogenization of social substance
        within states   185–6
NATO   194
natural resources   234
Natural Resources Defense Council
    (NRDC)   192, 274
Naughton, P.   192, 274
neo-classical economics   164
neo-classical realism   204–5, 279
neo-conservatism   202, **205**, 206,
    269, 277, 285

neo-liberal institutionalists   205–6
neo-liberalism   57–8, 89–90, 106,
    149, 155, 185, 205, 228, 231
    loss of credibility   166
neo-realism   198–9, 202–6
NES data   73
Netherlands   63, 126, 137, 159, 192,
    283
networks   31, 32, 42, 87, 98, 123,
    216
    global   134–5
    international   134–5, 147
    literature   253, 258, 277
    online   85, 258, 263, 277
    private and public–private   156
    self-steering   33
New Deal   142
new ethnicities (Hall)   123, 124, 262
New Labour   93, 140, 93, 270
new left versus new right   92
New Political Economy (journal)
    165
new politics
    of equality (Kantola and Squires)
        3, 15, 16, **88–108**
    of welfare retrenchment   185
New Public Management (NPM,
    1980s–)   36, 37, 80
new regionalism   178
new social risks   169
new territorial politics (Jeffery and
    Wincott)   20–1
new world order   198
New World Order (Slaughter)
    29–30, 280
New York: World Trade Centre   28
NHS Choices (UK)   82
non-discrimination principle   126–7
non-governmental organizations
    (NGOs)   31, 194, 199, 207,
    216, 242, 244
non-state actors   194, 214–16
    security threats   190–1, **192–3**
NOP   128
Nordic countries   224f
normative theory   246, 249
normativity   199
Norris, P.   70, 274
North America   153

Norway 106, 151
novelty, **27–30**, 33, 36, 42, 209–10, 216, 231
Nozick, R. 233, 274
nuclear energy 38, 215, 217
nuclear weapons 190–2, 203, 210–11, 217–18, 253, 274
Nussbaum, M.C. 101, 246, 274

Obama, B.H., Jr 84, 87, 205
President 44, 79, 137–8, 145, 192, 228
Senator 79
OECD 168, 224f, 275
undifferentiated data 183
offensive realism (Mearsheimer) 204
Office of National Statistics (UK) 91, 275
offshore balancing (Walt) 204
oil 159, 162
Okin, S.M. 243, 275
Olson, M. 74, 75, 275
ombudsmen 106
On War (Clausewitz) 200
Ontario 179–80
ontology 4, 8–9, 10, 17, 20, 23–4, 176–7, 252
open economy politics (Lake) 163
opportunity costs 26
oppression 93, 103, 112
optimism 128
'organised social complexity' (La Porte) 33, 269
organizations
contested 212–13
design 61
membership 53t, 53
othering **197–8**, 239
outlaw peoples (Rawls) 235
overlapping consensus 111
overloaded government 33, 39
Oxfam 213, 227
Oxford Handbook of Political Behaviour (Dalton and Klingemann, 2007) 67, 257
Oxford Internet Survey 68, 82–3, 258–9, 275
Oyster card (London) 81
Ozga, J. 186, 275

Pakistan 192, 193, 274
Pakistanis (in UK) 266, 279
Palfrey, T.R. 73, 275
Pallares, F. 180, 275
Pantich, L. 165, 275
Park, A. 275
Parekh, B. 112, 113, 231, 275
Paris School 206, **208**
parliaments (sub-state) **179**
'parsimony' (versus 'complexity') 18–19, 23
Parsonianism 172
Parsons, C. 56, 275
Partin, R. 179, 250
party politics 67, 267
passivity 56–7, 60
paternalism 101, 234–5, 242
path dependency 155, 182, 187
pathologies of command 34
Pattie, C. 49, 52, 53n, 257, 266, 276
peace 200, 218, 222, 235
women's interests 245
peer production (Benkler) **70–1**
penal policy 37–8
People, States and Fear (Buzan, 1983, 1991) **199–200**, 255
perception **25**, 35, 38, 102, 112, 115, 127, 185
performance politics 56
peripheralization hypothesis (Rokkan) 168, 178–9, 278
Peru 158
Pesendorfer, W. 73, 259
Peters, B. 67, 276
Peterson, B. 263
Peterson, P. 184, 276
pharmaceutical industry 220
Phillips, A. 93, 100, 276
Pierre, J. 67, 276
Pogge, T. 218, 219, **237–8**, 239, 244, 260, **276**
dead-end debate with Rawls 242
theory of justice 240
policing (global) 238
policy effectiveness 217, **218**
policy failure 32, 34, 37
policy interdependence (Moran) 21, **26–7**
practical solutions 35

policy interdependence (Moran)
(*cont.*):
  specialization, tacit knowledge,
    catastrophic risk 35, **38–9**
policy networks 31, 258, 277
policy science 35
policy-makers 11, 19, 79, 185, 236
  newly-acknowledged
    interdependence 21–2
policy-making 3, 7, 17, 71, 81, 98,
    166
  constraining versus enabling
    factors 29
  exceptional period 89
  high modernist image 40
  implementation **26**
  in interdependent world (chapter
    one) **2**, **25–42**
  machinery 26
  new technologies 35
  organization 29–30
  sub-contracted 22
  three credible claims to novelty
    27–30
political versus economic 8–9
  analytical versus ontological
    distinction **9**
  boundary 11
  socially-constructed **10–11**
political action 246
  costs and benefits 64
political activism 69–70, 249, 274
  coordination via Internet **76–7**
  disengagement 55
  global 65
political actors 6–7, 248
political agenda
  domestic versus regional [supra-
    national] 15
political analysts 13–14
  search for parsimony 18–19
political association
  faith-based 4, 15, 20
  new modes **3**, **64–87**
political behaviour 67, 72, 257
political charter
  proposed by Russell (2005) 59,
    279
political communication 67, **69**

political culture 47, 48
political disenchantment (chapter
    two) **2–3**, **43–63**, 72
  further research 46, 63
  ideational explanations 56, **57**, 58
  institutional explanations **56–7**,
    58
  physiological explanations 56
  structural explanations **56**, 57–8
political economy 183
  global 163, 242
  inter-disciplinary 8–9
  literature 158
  see also international political
    economy
political equality **82–3**, 100
political forces
  unbundling **215–16**
political identity
  globalization and **135–6**
  state as agent of **135–6**
political institutions 52, 82, 167,
    171, **175**
political knowledge 50–1, 54–5, 68,
    82
  acquisition costs 73
  rationality **72–3**
political lexicon 44
Political Liberalism (Rawls, 1993)
    111, 277
political life
  micro-level 87
  multi-scaled **170**
  systems analysis (Easton) 32, 259
political mobilization 84–5
political participation **69–70**, 87, 94,
    117, 263, 282
  class differences (2007) 54–5,
    55t
  gendered differences (2007) 54,
    54t
political parties
  alignment patterns 178
  concentric circles of solidarity
    (Duverger) 78
  functionally-based competition
    178
  impact of Internet 86
  involvement 82

membership 52, 56–7, 66, **77–8**, 263
miscellaneous 83, 259
nationalist 180
and party systems 186, 255
provincial-level issue-profiles ('valence' judgements) 179–80
websites 73
political science
agenda changed decisively 22
bad at prediction 87
challenge posed by Internet **86–7**
contemporary context 2
defining problem (Stoker) 43–4
design science arm needed 44, 63
failure to supply solutions 58, 59
further research 10, 84
ghettoization 67
global age **229–30**
inherited corpus rejected 174
interdependence, complexity, and possibility of **17–19**
Internet **64–87**
limitations 23, 44
mapping of arguments 56, 275
methodological challenges **84–6**
new approaches/directions 2, 6, 17, 26, 63
normative theory 243
relevance 61
research (quantitative or qualitative) 61
role (Rawls) 236
secularist biases (challenged) 109
sub-state scale 'needs to be taken more seriously' 187
task 248
textbooks 66–7, 262
theoretical preoccupations 1
three tasks (Held) 230
understanding of Internet (current state) **66–8**
political science of design **60–2**, 281
political science profession 43–4
political scientists 46, 239
implicated in rise of anti-politics 58–9
procedural errors 60–2
role **58–9**

political security 207
Political Studies Association (PSA) 22–3, 47, 58, 167, 182, 276
sixtieth anniversary 24
political theorists 108, 231–2, 239, 248, 249
political theory 109, 111–12, 136, 202, 240, 246, 275
application **248**
liberal 249
nature and role (Rawls) **235–6**
normative principles 235–6
task 242
quantitative or qualitative 61
political will 140, 224
politicians
honesty about mistakes 59
politics
defended by Crick 46, 256
domestic 31–2
economic analysis 57
human construction (Stoker) 43
institutional professionalization 58
interdependence (newly-)acknowledged **21–2**
judicialization 107
multi-level 20
near universal contempt 1
needed by democracy 45–6
no neutrals 59
objective laws (Morgenthau) 203
representative 59
state-wide dynamics (danger of misconstruing) 187
unfreezing (Rokkan) 172, 178
Politics Among Nations (Morgenthau, 1948) 194, 203
politics of difference 286
politics of distribution
challenged 93
politics of equality/inequality
concepts **92–3**, **100–4**
context **90–2**, **98–9**
further research 3
institutions **93–7**
interplay of theory and practice **108**
new 88–9, **97–106**, 107

politics of equality/inequality (*cont.*):
  old **88–97**
  paradigm shift **88–90**
  problem-driven research 108
  transnational and international
    levels **107**
politics of presence (Phillips, 1995)
  93, 276
populism 58, 251
  economic 131
positive action 89, 93, 95, 105–6,
  111
positivism 163
post-colonialism 243
post-disciplinarity **8**, 10, 14, 23, 24
post-modernism 36, 41, 201, 243,
  253
post-national trend 125, 281
post-war era (1945–) 109, 110,
  133–4, 136, 149, 162, 167–8,
  176, 178–9, 196, 212, 227, 229,
  260
  multilateral order 222
poverty 89, 91, 105, 148, 199, 207,
  211, 232, 234–5, 237, 240, 248,
  276
  global 239
  no longer the focus 96
  relative versus absolute 100
poverty alleviation 161, 219, 220, 223
poverty lines
  dollar-a-day, two-dollars-a-day
    219
power 46, 131, 147, 204, 243
  economic and political (global
    relations) 248
  interest defined as (Morgenthau)
    203
power competition (vicious circle)
  203
Power Inquiry 58, 251, 276
power relations 103, 189
  gendered 245
prediction failure 198
Pressman, J. 32–3, 276
pressure groups 75–6, 83, 119
principal–agent issues 78, **80**, 160,
  166
printing money 138

Pritchard, J. 258
private corporations 31
private reward versus public risk
  164
processes (transnational) 12–13, 14,
  15
production (global) 148, 153
professionals/managers 53–8, 78,
  80, 98, 184
Progressive British Muslims 120
Progressive Era administration
  (Hood) 80–1
project societies 99
property ownership 30, 244
protectionism 157, 228
psychology 10, 233
public administration 67, 80–1, 85,
  276
public expenditure 26, 35, 133, 145
public goods 74, 220–1
  global 218, 228
public management reform **80–2**
public opinion 1, 217, 228, 241, 260
public policy 166, 167, 169, 171,
  213, 216, 220, 270
public–private distinction 117
Putin, V.V. 191–2, 253

quality of life 101
Quebec 110
quotas **94–5**, 158, 161, 257

race 89, 91, 100, 104–6, 111,
  113–15, 119, 122, 124
racism 92, 103, 110, 113, 125, 256
Rapport, D. 205, 277
rational choice 64, 163, 164
Ravenhill, J. **xiii**, **4**, 9, 16, 19–20,
  28, 34, 158, 272, 277
Rawls, J. 101, 111–12, **233–7**,
  238–40, 243, 277
  dead-end debate with Pogge 242
  liberal international order 236
  selectivity 239
real world/reality 1, 2, 7–8, 12,
  18–19, 23, 32–3, 41, 61, 132,
  134, 170–1, 196, 201–2, 209,
  235–6, 248
  social 28, 40

realism   134, 199, 202, 203, 207
  classical   203, 204
  neo-classical   204–5, 279
  realists (IR)   134, 208
reciprocal causation   12, 18
recognition   **92–3**, 102, 107, 119,
  260, 282
redistribution   100, 101, 107, 134,
  184
  quiet   93
regional authority index (Marks *et al.*)
  168, 271
regional trade agreements   158, 280
regionalism   178, 180, 275
regulation
  failure   162
  financial   34, 154, 156, 259
  further research   166
  global   30, **156–63**, 166, 254, 272
  improved   150, 155
  key question   156
  light-touch   34, 140, 156
  local   52, 54
  miscellaneous   4, 34, 139–40,
    228–9
  national   52
  private actors   166
regulation of regulators   159–60
regulators   137, 164
  national versus international   30
  private actors   160
'regulatory failure' (label)   10
regulatory power   131
Reif, K.   179, 277
Rein, M.   35, 277
Reissfelder, S.   271
religion   15, 96, 97, 106, **111**, 107,
  113, 116, 184, 266
re-politicization   4
representation   59, 100, 107,
  214–15, 257
Representation (journal)   58
Republic.com 2.0   (Sunstein, 2009)
  68, 281
Republican Party (USA)   140, 228
republicanism   127
resource allocation   90, 138, 212
responsibility   27, 213, 214, 215,
  269

political   258
public versus private (shifting
  boundaries)   11
'Responsibility to Protect' (Bellamy,
  2008)   232, 238, 253
responsiveness   50, 52
retribution (against wealthy)   145
*Review of International Political
  Economy*   163–4, 277
rhetoric   **39–42**
Rhodes, R.   31–4, 85, 172, 277
right to life   237
Rio Declaration on Environment
  213
Rischard, J.F.   212, 277
risk   141, 166
  catastrophic   **35–9**
risk society theorists   38, 252
risk theory   38, 261
Rittel, H.   35, 277
Robeyns, I.   101, 277
Rodden, J.   179, 259
Rokkan, S.   168, 172–3
  literature   260, 269, 270, 273, 278,
    283
  macro-historical framework   182
  peripheralization hypothesis   179
Rokkanian approach   178, 180,
  183–4, 185–6, 188
Roma   105
Rosamond, B.   28, 263
Rose, R.   178, 278
Rosenau, J.N.   31, 33, **278**
Rosenthal, H.   73, 275
Roy, D.   192, 274
Rudd, K.   154–5, 279
Rushdie, Sir Salman   120
Russell, M.   58, 59, 279
Russett, B.   206, 279
Russia   159, 209, 226
Russia–Georgia War (2008)   191
Rwanda   198, 202, 232

Saami people   99
Saddam Hussein   191
Sarbanes–Oxley Act (USA, 2002)
  140
Satanic Verses affair   119–20
Save the Children   213

Scandinavia   41, 221, 257
Schakel, A.   271
Schelling, T.   77, 279
Schmitt, H.   179, 277
Scholte, J.A.   28, 40, 279
Schweller, R.   204, 279
science of artificial   43, 44, 63
sciences of artificial things (Simon)
   60–1, 280
Scotland   110, 123, 183, 275, 279,
   286
   election (2003)   180
   election (2007)   180, 257, 266
Scott, J.   36–7, 279
Scottish National Party (SNP)   181
Scully, R.   180, 286
secularism   116–17
securities [financial]   28, 30, 141
'securitization' [defence]   21, 28,
   206, 207–8
security   21, 218, 226, 237, 251
   contemporary concerns   **190–6**
   critical approaches   206, 207
   essentially contested concept
      200–2
   Foucauldian sense   208
   internal and external   208, 253
   meanings   **200–9**
   new challenges in interdependent
      world   **4–5**, 16, **189–210**
   see also   international security
   *Security: New Framework for
      Analysis* (Buzan *et al.*, 1997)
      207, 255
security dilemma (Herz)   203, 264
security studies
   Anglophone (evolution)
      196–200
   foundations (Kolodziej)   202
   rest of Anglophone world (outside
      USA)   **206–9**
   USA   **202–6**
security threats   11
   climate   191, **193**
   far less novel   189
   non-state actors   190–1, **192–3**
   states   190, **191–2**
   weapons   190, 191, **192**
self-determination   234, 239

self-interest   6–7, 51, 57, 59, 165,
   230, 233
self-management   279
self-regulation   216
Sen, A.   101–2, 250, 274, 279–80
services   91, 158
sex   91, 115
sexism   92, 103
sexuality/sexual orientation   89, 92,
   94, 96–7, 99, 104–7, 114–17
Shadlen, K.   158, 280
Shah, A.   225n, 280
short-termism   56, 160
Shue, H.   238, 240, 280
Sierra Leone   226
Sikhs   122
silent majority   62–3
Simeon, R.   175, 251
Simon, H.   **60–1**, 280
Sin, G.   74, 75–6, 84, 270
Sinclair, T.J.   159, 160, 280
Singapore   142, 158
Slaughter, A.-M.   29–30, 280
Smith, Adam   165
Smith, Anthony   174, 280
Smith, G.   59, 266, 280
social capital   100
social citizenship   117, 182–3, 187,
   266, 285
social class   53, 58, 89, 91, 100,
   104–5, 109, 112, 115, 119,
   122–3, 175, 178, 182, 184, 271
   political activism (2007)   54–5,
      55t
social cohesion   121, 125
social democracy   106, 114, 117,
   155, 166, 227, 228, 264
social exclusion/inclusion   72, 88–9,
   93, 95
social information   75
social interaction/interdependence
   7–8, **8–11**
social justice   101, 128, **217–18**,
   221, 226, 229–30, 274
social networking websites   70, 85
social policy   168, 188, 214
   sub-state   185
social protection, long territorial
   parabola (Ferrera)   185

social science/s   25, 45, 46, 63, 66,
   86–7, 173, 201, 285
   biography   269
   'cultural turn'   28
   integrated   24
   integrated (limits)   8
social services   183, 184, 250
social structures   103
social theory   112, 171–2, 271
   inherited corpus rejected   174
social transfers   183, 184
social welfare   89, 90–1
socialism/socialists   115, 123
Socialist Register (journal)   165
societies   177, 229, 233
socio-demographics   184
sociologists   43, 86, 197
sociology   10, 66, 85, 123, 174, 271
   macro-historical (Rokkan)   172,
      176
   Parsonian   172
software   85, 86
solidarity   **217**, 226
South Sea Company   150
South-East Asia   195, 267
sovereign wealth funds   141
sovereignty
   internal versus external   134
   parliamentary   32
   unbundling   **215–16**
   see also   state sovereignty
Soysal, Y.   125, 281
Spain   127, 137, 159, 168, 180, 182,
   258
   nationalism and regionalism   275
   state welfare versus regional
      welfare   261
spatial interdependence   6, **26**, 40, 75
   discursive construction and
      democratic statecraft   **27–30**
   objective evidence   28
   premises   13
   realization   **28**
spatial scale   **12**
Special Drawing Rights (IMF), 161
specialization/division of labour
   35–9
   bureaucratic   31
   corporate giants   30

global   41
global economic   29
   see also   sub-disciplinary
      specialism
Squires, J.   **xiii**, **3**, 15–16, 112–13,
   231
state/s   35, 109–10, 194–5, 203,
   214–15, 232, 274
   agent of political identity   **135–6**,
      144–6
   behaviour (non-structural
      explanations)   204
   bureaucratic, territorial   32
   character   **4**, **130–47**
   conceptual and empirical debates
      132
   demise (premature forecast)   15
   economic agency   137
   economic discretion   **132–4**
   failings (neo-liberal framing)
      57
   further research   147
   future intellectual agendas
      146–7
   globalization   **132–6**
   in international sphere   **134–5**
   just [fair]   247
   legitimacy   4
   liberal   234, 236, 240, 248
   looking inside   **174–5**
   modern   229–30, 263
   not exclusive site for citizenship
      118–19
   only agent capable of preventing
      economic collapse   130
   role   149
   security threats   190, **191–2**
   site of authority and power   147
   territorial agency within   177
   territorially defined   26, 177
   territory, nation and   **175–6**
   Weberian   32
state authority (disaggregated)   34
*State Formation, Nation-Building and
   Mass Politics in Europe*
   (Rokkan, 1999)   188, 278
state regulation   34
state responsibility (core sphere)
   27

state sovereignty   27, 134, 136, 147, 213, 247
    sovereign state   29, 31
    see also sovereignty
state system   31
statecraft   **39–42**
state-formation   172, 176, 182, 185, 188, 260
statism   208, **233–40**, 241–3, 249
'stealth democracy'   264
Stein, R.   179, 281
Steinbrück, P.   143
stereotyping   120, 121, 123
Stockholm International Peace Research Institute   224–5n, 281
Stoker, G.   **xiii**, 1, **2–3**, 7, 19, 22, 42, 44, 46, 49–50, 56, 58–61, 72–3, 266, 281
strategic studies   199–200
Stratigaki, M.   99, 281
structured financial products (IMF)   150
structured investment vehicles   137
sub-disciplinary specialism   11–12, 23, 24
    transcendence (theme)   5
sub-realist formats   202
sub-state level   177, 179
    further research   174–5
    policy entrepreneurs   184
    structures   **175**
    territorial actors   186
Subirats, J.   261
suicide bombers   193
Sunstein, C.   67–8, 72, 281
supranationalism   156
Surridge, P.   275
Sweden   106, 159, 184
Swift, A.   231, 274
Switzerland   138, 159, 168
Swyngedouw, M.   257
Syed, P.   276
systems analysis (Easton)   32, 259
Sznaider, N.   173, 252

tacit knowledge   **35–9**, 40
Taggart, P.   251
Taniguchi, N.   265
tariffs   158, 220

taxation/taxes   91, 133, 149, 153, 222
    authority to levy   143, 144
    corporate   155
Taylor, C.   113, 114, 282
technologies of insecuritization (Paris School)   206
technology/technologies   37, 66
    hard versus soft   36, 38–40
    warfare   28
territorial differentiation
    comparative analysis (challenges)   187
    development of data sources   177
    scholarly neglect   182, 183, 187, 188
territorial politics   **4**, **167–88**
    challenge   **167–70**
    challenge for political practice   **170–1**
    contribution to new direction for political science   **169–70**
    elections   **178–82**
    methodological nationalism, 'modernization' and   **171–3**
    sub-state   167, 186
    within the state   **176–8**
territoriality   183
    'unbundling'   **215–16**
territory   171, 262
    nation and state   **175–6**
terrorism   128, 189–91, 195, 199, 201, 252
    global   197
    international 'blowback'   121
    'new form', 'new response'   193
Theiss-Morse, E.   63, 264
Theory of International Politics (Waltz, 1979)   200, 203–4, 284
Theory of Justice (Rawls, 1971)   111, **233**, 235, 243, 277
Theory of World Politics/Security (Booth, 2007)   208, 253
theory
    challenge of Internet to political science   86–7
    international security   209
    Internet in political science   64, 67
    IR (realism versus its critics)   134

methodological nationalism
170–1
multi-dimensional equality
considerations 107
political science project 230
politics of equality **92–3,
100–4**
politics of equality (new and old)
106–7
politics and IR 45
state, the 132
statehood 147
Thomas, B. 258
Thomas, C. 200, 282
Thompson, H. **xiii, 4,** 9, 11, 15, 28,
34, 149
Thucydides 202
time 28, 61, 86, 131, 142, 177–8,
190, 201, 285
time matters 169, 253
Time–Warner 30
Tolbert, C.J. 73, 282
Tonge, J. 58
trade 149, 150, 220, 222, 227,
229
global 148, 152, 162
international 153
multilateral regime 218
trade agreements 277
bilateral 157–8, 280
mini-lateral 157–8
trade unions 54, 114, 119, 221
trans-state phenomena **174**
transnationalization 89, 98, 106,
132, 135–6, **142–4,** 146–7, 221
transparency 78, **79**
open government 82
transport/transportation 81, 220
Travis, A. 123, 282
Treasury bonds (USA) 141
trigger episodes 106
trust/distrust 1, 6–7, 50–1, 55, 59,
63, 70, 266
truth 201, 247
Turkey 111
turnout/propensity to vote 52–5, 63,
65, 66, **73–4,** 82, 265, 275
see also voting

UCLA 165
unbundling (sovereignty,
territoriality, political forces)
215–16
uncertainty 56
under-development 199, 207
unemployment 6, 53, 153
unilateralism 226
Union of Soviet Socialists Republics
197, 205
collapse/demise 149, 189, 198
see also Cold War
United Kingdom: general 30, 82,
91, 93, 118, 149, 150, 152, 156,
159, 165, 181–4, 224f
banks forced by government to pass
on interest-rate cuts 139
core British values (problem of
definition) 128
decline in civic culture **47–55**
devolution and decentralization
172
expenses scandal (2009) 44–5,
268
health service (information
prescriptions) 80
Internet penetration 66, 68, 72
literature 256–8, 262, 265–6, 268,
270, 271, 275–6, 279, 286
NPM 81
second 'long boom' (1992–2007)
29
sub-state elections 180
sub-state electoral tier (1999–)
168–9
territorially-based differentiation
183
transparency 79
United Kingdom:
territorial/geographical
Britain 48, 49, 52, 54, 58, 71,
110–11, 116, 127–8, 138, 155,
192, 195, 202, 266, 276
England 275
Great Britain 44, 47–50, 52, 256
Northern Ireland 183
Scotland 110, 123, 180, 181, 183,
257, 266, 275, 279, 286
Wales 180, 286

United Kingdom: HM Treasury 139, 265
United Kingdom Financial Investments 139
United Kingdom Government 120, 137, 139, 145
  HM Government 58, 265, 276
United Kingdom Tribunals Service 80
United Nations 194, 212, 227, 238–9, 242, 247
  budget 222–3, 223f, 225f, 283
  data source 223n, 283
  UN Charter 213
  UN Convention on Rights of Persons with Disabilities (2006) 97
  UN Global Compact 221
  UN International Decade for Eradication of Poverty (1997–2007) 91
  UN *Platform for Action* (1995) 94, 95, 98, 283
  UN World Conference on Women (Mexico City, 1975) 96
  UNAIDS 214
  UNDP 207, 225–6n, 283
  UNESCO 212, 213
  UNICEF 213
  UNSCR 1325 (2000) 245, 247
United States of America
  anti-missile technology 191
  civic culture 47
  fiscal stimulus 145
  foreign policy 226, 280
  ideological power 205
  immigration policy (2006) 65
  life expectancy 100
  literature 250, 253–4, 258–60, 266, 269, 271, 280–1, 284
  membership of political parties 78
  miscellaneous 13, 37, 48, 63, 71, 82, 92, 110, 111, 113, 120, 125, 128, 135, 148–50, 155–6, 159, 165, 184, 194–5, 197, 207, 223–7
  power 204, 284
  presidential election (2008) 65, 68, 74

second long boom (1992–2007) 29
security studies **202–6**
state versus federal elections 179, 250, 259, 269, 281
transparency 79
unilateralism 226, 228
US Congress 137, 138, 140, 145, 160, 192
US Department of Homeland Security (DHS) 190, 258
US Department of Justice 84
US dollar 141, 142, 158
US dollar (reserve currency/future role) **162–3**, 268
US Federal Reserve 138, 141–2, 160
US Government 137
US House Oversight Committee 160
US House of Representatives 145
US Senate 193
US Treasury bills 162
Universal Postal Union 212
universal principles/values 212–13, 221, 222, 227
  see also justice
universalism 112, 114, 126–7, 136
Unnecessary War (Mearsheimer and Walt, 2003) 198, 272
Urwin, D. 168, 172, 178, 273, 278, 283
utopianism 243, 274

valence issues/judgments 56, 179–80
value-rational social action (Weber) 76
Van Wessel, M. 63, 283
Verba, S. 44, **47–55**, 72, 250, 268
Verloo, M. 90, 105, 283
Vickers, D. 258
Vietnam 219
Vietnam War 69, 196, 197
violence 46, 121
  feminist interpretation 245
  political 247
von Hippel, E. 81, 283
Voters for Peace 193

voting **73–4**, 78
  multi-level 180
  regional 179, 263
  see also elections

Wade, R. 219, 283
Waever, O. 200, 208, 255, 284
Walker, R.B.J. 201
Walt, S. 198, 204, 284
Waltz, K. 197, 200, 203–4, 284
war 201, 223
War and Change in World Politics
  (Gilpin, 1981) 202, 261
war crimes (sexual violence) 245–6
war and peace 212
war on terror (2001–) 192, 252
Washington Consensus 219–21,
  226, 264
water supply 38, 226t
We Are All Multiculturalists Now
  (Glazer, 1997) 111, 261
wealth gap 211, 232
wealth redistribution 88, 89, 133,
  144, 234, 237–8, 242, 244
weapons 190–3, 195
Weaver, D. 73–4, 258
Web 2.0 66, 70, 81
Webb, P. 251
Webber, M. 35, 277
Weber, M. 27, 31, 32, 76, 80–1, 284
Weber, S. 154, 284
webmetrics 86, 87
websites 71, 83–5, **286–7**
  Cabinet Office (citizenship
    surveys) 255
  Climate Security Now 193
  Communities and Local
    Government (citizenship survey,
    2007) 256
  HM Treasury 265
  http://sasi.group.shef.ac.uk 258
  Ipsos-MORI 266
  NGOs (wholly-online) 75
  NHS Choices 82
  ONS (UK) 275
  political parties (Japan, 2004) 73
  PSA 276
  readthestimulus.org 82, 287
  White House 79

www.iwantgreatcare.com 81, 286
www.patientopinion.org 81, 287
www.theyworkforyou.org 79,
  287
www.writetothem.org 79, 287
welfare 94, 169, 173, 177, 180, 186,
  259
welfare nationalist projects 185
welfare policy 21
  'bottom up' perspectives 185
  types 183–4
welfare regionalism (Ferrera)
  184–5, 261
welfare rescaling **182–6**
welfare state 133, 167–9, 260
  conventional wisdom 188
  retrenchment 139
welfare-to-work programmes 91
well-ordered peoples (Rawls)
  234–6, 248
Welsh language 114
Welsh School 206, **208**
West, the 129, 209, 226
Westphalian state system 20, 27
  disaggregation (Slaughter) **29–30**
  post-Westphalian world order
    241–2, 260
  transformation 31, 278
Wheeler, D. 87, 284–5
White Paper on Defence and National
  Security (France) 195
Whiteley, P. 276
Why Politics Matters (Stoker, 2006)
  56, 58, 59, 281
Why We Hate Politics (Hay, 2007)
  57, 58, 263
wicked problems 35, 38, 40, 277
Wikipedia 65, 68–70, **86**, 270, 286
Wildavsky, A. 32–3, 85, 263, 276
Williams, M.C. 205, 285
will-to-power 230
Wimmer, A. 174, 176, 285
Wincott, D. **xiii**, **4**, 15, 20–1, 182–3,
  285
Wohlforth, W. 204
Wolf, M. 219, 285
women **243–6**; 54, 88, 91, 93, 106,
  114, 116, 122–4, 226t, 245, 271,
  274–5

women (*cont.*):
    black   103, 256
    policy agencies   94, **95–6**
Woods, N.   164, 272
work and family (reconciliation)   99,
    281
working class   53, 54
World Bank   148–9, 161, 212,
    214–15, 219, 222
    change in orientation   161
    data source   223–5n, 285
world government   205
World Health Organization (WHO)
    213, 214
World Meteorological Organization
    212
World Trade Organization (WTO)
    148–9, 156–7, 161, 215, 239,
    242, 285

Dispute Settlement Mechanisms
    (DSMs)   157
GATT/Uruguay Round   157
world wars   196
Worldwatch Institute   224–6n, 286
Wyn Jones, R.   180, 286

xenophobia   110

Young, I.M.   93, 231, 286
young people/youth   54–5, 72, 74,
    122, 228
Youth Citizenship Commission
    58
YouTube   65, 69, 70, 85
Yugoslavia   198

zero-sum game   194
Zimbabwe   207

JOIN THE
POLITICAL STUDIES ASSOCIATION
Setting the agenda for global political science

The Political Studies Association exists to develop and promote the study of politics. We are the leading UK organisation linking academics, theorists, practitioners, policy-makers, journalists, researchers and students in political science and current affairs.

AS A MEMBER YOU WILL RECEIVE:

- *Political Studies* 4 times a year
- *Political Studies Review* 3 times a year
- *POLITICS* 3 times a year
- *BJPIR: The British Journal of Politics and International Relations* 4 times a year
- Newsletter 4 times a year
- Annual Directory – listing all political scientists in the UK and Ireland by university and department
- Members' discounts on conference and workshop fees – you will save more than the cost of your membership when you attend our annual conference
- Exclusive online members-only services at **www.psa.ac.uk**
- Access to a network of 40 specialist research groups
- Opportunities to compete for annual Political Studies Association prizes
- 35% discount on books from Wiley and Polity Press

 **Political Studies** Association

TO FINDOUT MORE, CALL
+44 (0) 191 222 8021

E-MAIL psa@ncl.ac.uk
WEBSITE www.psa.ac.uk

Political Studies Association Specialist Groups

The Political Studies Association supports a diverse range of Specialist Groups covering all major fields of political research. The groups act as networks through which individuals can make contact with colleagues with similar research and teaching interests. Groups disseminate information of interest to their members via newsletters and dedicated websites and hold seminars and conferences to supplement the Annual PSA Conference. They receive financial support for their activities from the Political Studies Association.

To find out more about the Specialist Groups online visit: **www.psa.ac.uk,** click on **'About the PSA'** and then follow the Specialist Groups link.

American Politics

Anarchist Studies

Art and Politics

British and Comparative Territorial Politics

British Idealism

British Liberal Political Studies

Britishness

Caribbean Politics

Citizenship and Democracy

Communist and Post Communist Politics

Comparative European Politics

Conservatives and Conservatism

Development Politics

Disability and Politics

Elections, Public Opinions and Parties

Ethnopolitics

French Politics and Policy

German Politics

Global Justice and Human Rights

Greek Politics

Interpretive Political Science

Irish Politics

Italian Politics

Labour Movements

Local Politics

Marxism

Media and Politics

Pacific Asia

Parliaments and Legislatures

Participatory and Deliberative Democracy

Political Activism

Political Economy

Political Leadership

Political Marketing

Political Thought

Politics of Health

Politics of Property

Politics of South Asia

Public Administration

Scandinavian Politics

Security and Intelligence

Sport and Politics

State Theory

Teaching and Learning

Urban Politics

Women and Politics

www.psa.ac.uk

Political Studies
Association

palgrave
macmillan

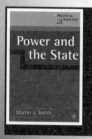

The best texts in political analysis come from Palgrave Macmillan

For more details visit:
www.palgrave.com/politics